ROAMIN' THE RANGE

TOGETHER

ROAMIN' THE RANGE

TOGETHER

PART TWO
GOING DOWN THE BOULEVARD
(1980 – 2005)

PETE ALLEN

A CIP catalogue record for this book is available from the British Library.

ISBN 978-0-9569733-1-3

Book and cover design by Clare Brayshaw

Prepared and printed by:

York Publishing Services Ltd
64 Hallfield Road
Layerthorpe
York YO31 7ZQ
Tel: 01904 431213

Website: www.yps-publishing.co.uk

For Linda my Wife and Vicky my Step-Daughter
&
In Loving Memory of Walter and Abigail Allen

Contents

About the Author

Pete Allen is a retired local government officer who lives in Beverley, East Yorkshire with his wife Linda and step-daughter Vicky. For six years he has produced a weekly Rugby League blog, 'The Dentist's Diary' and this book is the second and final part of an anthology that follows his life and that of his team, Hull FC, between 1950 and 2005. His previous book, 'Roamin' the Range Together; Living in the Shadow of Giants' was published in 2011.

Acknowledgements

To Linda my Wife for her support, advice and unending faith and patience, to Vicky White for all her help and advice with design and marketing and to Kathy Kirk for her hours of proof reading and encouragement.

For all their support, encouragement, advice, and hospitality my heartfelt thanks also go to Ian, Sarah and Adam Desforges and everyone at Hull FC, especially Adam Pearson, Tony Sutton, James Clark, Lee Jenkinson, Kirk and Lisa Yeaman and the staff in the Club's retail stores. To everyone at the Hull History Centre for their patience, with thanks also going to Andrew 'Wolfie' Phalen, Steve Roberts, Richard Kirk, Vince Groak, Brian Chapman, James White, David Burns, Stephen Kirkwood, Barry Edwards, Raymond Fletcher, Andrew Frankish, Ian Puckering and Mike Jacklin. Steve Wray for the rainbow and to the Hull Daily Mail and particularly James Smailes for their invaluable help with the photographs.

Very special thanks also go to 'the people who make dreams come true', Duncan, Clare, Paula and all the crew at York Publishing Services, and to all the loyal and wonderful readers of 'The Dentist's Diary' without whose support and encouragement this book would simply not have become a reality.

Finally the biggest thanks of all to all the wonderful players, officials, local government officers, artistes, friends, adversaries and compatriots who have shared my life and my story and made it such a wonderful journey over these last 60 years.

"It's not much that I leave, but this is the only way I have of taking part in the victory"
Monet

Foreword from Kirk Yeaman

When I originally signed for Hull FC it was one of the proudest moments of my life and now after 12 years of service at the Club I am honoured and humbled to have been granted a Testimonial Year. Over the years I have been involved with the Airlie Birds I've always been conscious of the great passion and love that the fans have for their Club and its players, not only for the current team but also for the long history with which Hull FC is blessed. The fans have stuck with this great Club through some really hard times and always been there when the going got tough. As a fan as well as a player I think that it's important that we always remember this heritage and so I was really pleased when Pete Allen asked me if his second book could be included as part of my year. I hope you find something in here to enjoy and to bring back some memories and thanks for all your support!

'Yeamo'

A donation from every copy of this book sold in the Hull FC retail outlets will go to the Kirk Yeaman Testimonial Fund.

Prologue

When I set out to write this book, the second part of the story of 55 years in the history of a very special Rugby League Club, I considered at length what photograph should adorn the front cover to best depict the essence of the story. I contemplated using a photograph now included inside which features an iconic hero of Hull FC (Peter Sterling), a glittering Trophy (The Yorkshire Cup) and a can of Hansa Lager, because I guess in the end that sums this tale up perfectly.

In the year since the first part of this odyssey was published I've been rummaging about in my jumbled box of beer stained memories, trying to find some semblance of order in the story that is to be found in the years between 1980 and 2005. I certainly hope that the personal stuff from an average sort of life provides something of a passing interest for the reader but what's much more meaningful, I think, are the highs and lows and triumphs and disasters of the back drop to that life, Hull FC my Rugby League Club.

Yes, this is an account of 25 years in the life of a fanatical sports fan, but no-one should ever think of it or its predecessor as an auto-biography, because that makes it sound much more full of itself than it actually is. Again, as I start the second volume in the adventures of an ordinary bloke who is haunted by an almost unhealthy obsession with a Rugby League Team, it's necessary to stress that this is only how I remember it.

I soon realised that there was little point in even attempting to try and tell my life story, because most of it isn't that interesting even to me, and anyway as you grow older they say that when it comes to personal memoirs you only remember the sunny days. In truth, like any fanatical follower of any sports club knows, they are the last thing that spring to mind. In fact too often the memories that are seared on your brain are about winding up orders, treacherous heroes, heavy defeats, bitter disappointments and heart-breaking betrayals.

That said, for me there are still one or two gloriously 'sunny days' that are occasions of such unbridled joy that they make all that has gone before so worthwhile and even necessary. It's always those dire days that make the good times so good! This book is unlikely to be factually correct in every detail, nor indeed meticulously accurate in its content, because it's simply how a series of events have been etched in my psyche.

After writing 'Roamin' the Range Together Part One, Living in the Shadow of Giants', and hearing the views and comments of its readers, I have grown to realise that although there may be other bands of supporters that are considered as great, there is without doubt no greater sporting family than that of Hull FC. Of course, thousands spread across the sporting landscape will disagree with me, because they all have their own Clubs and their own stories to tell. However if writing this has taught me anything, it's that as long term sports enthusiasts we'll forget hundreds of games and hundreds of incidents, before marking out our lives with those that we remember.

Yes, this book is about recording what it was like 'Being there' with the Airlie Birds, but it is also written in the hope that it will encourage others to remember some equally significant milestones in their own lives. 'Going Down the Boulevard....' and the first book were predominantly written to ensure that someone records, for future generations, just what 55 years in the history of Hull FC was all about. I wanted to do it before the era is no more, and the extraordinary happenings and the heroes and villains it produced become nothing more than myth and legend.

All I have tried to do in these two books is encapsulate just what it was like for one fanatical fan 'looking in' at 55 years in the history of one sports Club. It reflects one man's lifelong preoccupation that has over the years, towered above school, work, play and life.

All fans can point to adversity, hardship and disappointment in their sporting lives, but I honestly believe that perhaps at Hull FC we have had to endure more than most. We have certainly had more than our share of problems and complications over the years. We have lived and worked within a kinship that has seen trawling disasters and their subsequent loss of life, the demise of that fishing industry, the decimation of large swathes of the community in the name of 'Slum clearance' and the subsequent scattering of the fan base to the four corners of the City of Hull.

Then there are the rugby related disasters such as the coming of David Lloyd, the untimely deaths of Clive Sullivan and Roy Waudby, the seemingly unending threat of mergers and the sad demise of the Boulevard. Plus, of course, the numerous times over the years that Hull FC have been just hours away from bankruptcy, or from finding the necessary finance to complete our fixtures. These incidents remind us all that despite some well publicised triumphs, our history as both a Club and a community is littered with disenchantment and disappointment.

Sports fans everywhere can list their own tragedies and setbacks, but few can lay claim to occurrences so numerous or indeed boast so many loyal and perhaps even crazy individuals sticking with their team through so many lean times. It's that weight of fanatical support, sustained through adversity over the years, no matter what has been thrown at it, that makes the 'FC Army' truly 'barmy' and truly great.

It is also the legacy of all that which has made periods in our history like the 'Golden Years' of the early '80s, the Brian Smith Era and the 2005 triumph in Cardiff, so memorable and so satisfying.

You see, I believe that in the hierarchy of its peers, the importance and status of a Sports Club is not judged by short term indicators like its current performances, or its players. Instead, I think it's measured by its heritage, its history, the passion of its devotees, the sacrifices they have made and the adversity that those fans have been through together.

Supporters are quintessentially worriers and I am always mindful of the words of the great Australian Coach Wayne Bennett when he stated, "Worry is like a rocking-chair. It gives you something to do, but gets you nowhere". If that's the case, my life as a Rugby League fanatic has seen me (and millions of other sports fans) getting nowhere.

When compared with the first book, this second tome is certainly different. Stuffed with sporting frustrations and whimsical and sometimes poignant episodes from the life of an ordinary northern guy, it's also very much the record of a fan's preoccupation with his dream as it has endured for three very different decades when the culture of the great West Hull community was changing and becoming closer to the way it is today. Unlike 'Living in the Shadow of Giants' this is not so much of a nostalgic journey, but more a revelation of how devotion to a sports team can monopolise your life.... if you aren't careful.

So here it is the second and final part of my personal history and that of a very special Rugby League Club. I write it in the hope that it will strike a chord with anyone who has found themselves at work or at home, drifting off to recall a brilliant try in the corner, a massive tackle on the line or a curving 'flapping' conversion from the touchline that won the game in the last minute. This book is just about being a fan.

If you bought it thank-you, I hope you find it value for money and if you received it as a gift, I hope it's a 'surprise', but not too big a one. Most of all however, I honestly hope you find something in here with which you can associate and something that brings back to you some of your own memories about life in Hull and at Hull FC in the 25 years between 1980 and 2005.

Chapter One

So, where were we?

If you somehow survived the first part of these ramblings then perhaps you will now journey with me through the second and concluding part of the story of an ordinary guy, living in an ordinary northern City, who is part of an amazing family that have just one thing in common, their love of Rugby League in general and Hull FC in particular.

In the last book I progressed from schoolboy to adolescent and from apprentice gardener to the manager of Hull's premier music venue. My parents had guided me, supported me and departed and now in 1980, after a few unsuccessful relationships that invariably failed when it came to 'rugby versus romance', I was pretty much on my own, with just work and my parents' lasting legacy, (an obsession with my Rugby League team), to keep me going.

When the previous book drew to a close the two Rugby League Clubs in Hull had just completed the historic 1979/80 season and I was working for Kingston upon Hull City Council as the Manager of Hull City Hall and living in a flat at the front of the building, overlooking Queen Victoria Square. I was 30 years old and had just lost both my parents to Cancer in particularly heartbreaking circumstances. As an only child with now no family the start of the decade saw me finding the going tough both at work and in my private life and perhaps at that time I was as lonely as I had ever been in my life. It was, looking back, a condition best explained by the fact that the highlight of my week, when there was no work to do and no rugby to watch, was lying in bed on a Saturday morning watching Noel Edmonds' 'Multi Coloured Swap Shop' on the TV.

I had been involved with Hull FC since I was born in a little 'two up two down' in Aylesford Street just opposite the famous Boulevard ground. By now, there was simply no escaping my fascination with that team because despite being beaten at Wembley in the most significant Final the British game had seen and that, by the mortal enemy from across the River, my team was on the up and becoming a force in the game again. Thousands of 'latent' fans, no doubt buoyed by the euphoria, excitement and occasion of 'that Final' the previous May were in August 1980, dusting off their 'bobble' hats, buying their season passes and declaring (as Hull fans always did at euphoric times) that they were at that Huyton match all those years ago in 1976, when in reality just 950 people actually attended.

At work, I was starting to find my way in a completely new career and the going was tough. In addition to the stress that created, I still missed Mum and Dad who had died within three months of each other less than a year previously and I guess, if I'm honest, I was struggling to find a bit of direction. Rugby and its associated drinking, banter, arguing and partying were a welcome escape from the everyday turmoil of life as once again, when I needed them most, Hull FC offered a way out of the daily grind. Rugby was a welcome distraction which certainly helped me through the grieving process.

Not that it was plain sailing at the Boulevard because the 1980/81 season, although at times successful, was still a period of transition and there was still a deal of disappointment involved. This however just went to confirm what I had already discovered over the previous 30 years, in that, although all this 'loyal supporter' stuff is at times gloriously rewarding, the instances when it is are still fleeting moments in the grand scheme of things and in general being a fanatical supporter of any sports team does, for the most part, make you perennially miserable.

Living 'over the shop' at No.1 Queen Victoria Square

With a background predominantly in the City's Parks Department, the change of career which was initially only prompted by the availability of that flat, was certainly 'stretching' me and I often wondered if I had made a big mistake.

The mandate I received when taking over running the City Hall was to develop the business and attract more entertainment for younger people, whose needs, it was felt, the Council had neglected in the past. The music scene at the time was an interesting one. Punk was still popular but still the lowest possible denominator as far as music was concerned, whilst there were the first green shoots of the 80's electro revolution starting to appear and 'middle of the road' artistes like Glen Campbell, Roger Whittaker and Cliff Richard were still selling lots of records and concert tickets. At that time too there was a revival of 'Heavy Metal' music, with bands like Uriah Heap, Deep Purple, and Wishbone Ash reliving those halcyon days of the early 70's, on unending tours of smaller venues around the country. I loved music almost as much as I loved Hull FC and so that part of the job was pretty exciting but the City Hall was not equipped to become a major player in the pop music industry. The ageing staff were great guys but too few in number to cope with the revolution I hoped to instigate, and the venues electrical and staging facilities were totally inadequate and more Black Dyke Mills than Average White Band.

For too long Hull City Hall had been what some would call an 'elitist' venue and home to more traditional musical organisations like the City of Hull Youth Orchestra and the Hull Choral Union, while it also possessed one of the most extensive Concert Organs in the Country. This instrument at least provided me with the unlikely 'Chat up line' of "Come back to my place and I'll show you the biggest organ in the north of England" which although factually correct, would inevitably lead to a unanimous sense of disappointment.

There is of course nothing wrong with a bit of culture, but it wasn't something that the majority of the 'rate payers' of the City wanted. So, whilst most young people in Hull were battling with the intricacies of the Rubik's Cube, the top toy that year, I was on the telephone to the country's premier pop promoters, trying to get them some concerts to watch.

Big stars and small arms

One company from whom I got an immediate reaction was 'The Kruger Organisation' that was based in both New York and London to handle touring American acts. In March I promoted David Soul who half filled two 'houses' and was accompanied by an all British backing band, management and road crew. However on 21st May following hits in the previous decade like 'Who Loves You', 'December 1963' and 'Grease', Frankie Valli and the Four Seasons took in Hull City Hall on their 'Heaven Above Me' tour. It was their first national tour for ten years and this time the act was accompanied by an all American management team and a huge black Tour Manager named Joshua. He hailed from Brooklyn and was a frightening man. Quietly spoken with a lyrical American drawl, he had a demeanour that immediately told you he meant business.

Everywhere he went he was accompanied by two of the biggest 'heavies' you have ever seen. These guys wore suits and ties, sported flattened noses, never said a word, and walked with their hands hanging from their shoulders, like the gangsters I had seen in American 'B' movies. The afternoon before the show I took Joshua, Frankie Valli and these two 'Enforcers' to Radio Humberside for an interview on the Steve Massam Afternoon Show. Then, whilst we were waiting in the Reception I saw it! As one of the two 'Heavies' (Luther) leant forward across the low coffee table to get Joshua an ashtray for his cigar, his jacket fell open to reveal a shoulder holster with a small handgun in it.

As my eyes widened 'Luther' saw me looking and made no attempt to hide his side arm; in fact he just smiled and winked at me. I remember during the second house that evening as the band belted out their hits and 'aging groovers' danced in the aisles, I received a visit from the local constabulary, who always seemed to be missing when there was trouble but would magically appear when there was something they wanted to watch. They asked me if everything was alright and when I replied "Yes" the Sergeant laughingly added, "Still I don't suppose you'll get much trouble with this lot?" I, deciding not to elaborate any further and just nodded and laughed back.

Down at the Boulevard we started our second consecutive season in the First Division as Rugby League was doing its best to brand itself as a family sport and to distance itself from the antics of the so called 'supporters' we had all seen on TV, rioting in Football stadia across the Country. Sadly however this was something that was endemic in youth culture in general and even in our game, where crowds were traditionally 'self policing', hooliganism was starting to raise its ugly head. Youth was having its 'fling' violence wise and it was certainly a worry for me as a fledgling Venue Manager, particularly when at Hull College a concert featuring Adam and the Ants had to be stopped when the place was set on fire!

Rolling and tumbling at Post Office Road

Sunday 17th August 1980   *Hull 12 – Featherstone 16*

Hull FC fans were ready for the new season, although after the Wembley Final, both Clubs aired on the side of caution and abandoned the usual pre season 'Friendly' Derby match. Despite having left a life of living over a pub for one of living over the City Hall, Barry the Landlord of the 'Mermaid' in West Hull and Ian my pal from the West Riding, who both featured in the previous book, still accompanied me to most games home and away. We were also joined by another old school pal John (who was by profession the Transport Manager for a local bakery) and various other characters from the Mermaid like, Trevor 'The Fish' and 'Hard up Harry'. The latter was a skinny 'bean pole' of a man with unmistakably enormous feet. Although Harry was a lovely guy and invariably the life and soul of the party, at away games he always seemed to run out of money shortly after getting off the coach. He was permanently on the

'Dole' which he seemed to view as the working class equivalent of 'a gap year' and I remember around that time he informed us all that he was "Trying for a family", apparently we found out later, with at least three different women.

Trevor 'The Fish' was different again and one of the nicest blokes I have ever met. He worked at a local printers, had jet black wavy hair, a 'Jason King' moustache, an immovable smile and in keeping with his nick name, an incredible capacity for beer.

So it was with this gang that I travelled to Featherstone for a First Round Tie in the Yorkshire Cup. On arrival we made our usual visit to the Featherstone Rovers' Supporters' Club that was situated on the car park, just outside the Stadium. It was a uniquely 'West Riding' venue with small windows and pink walls where you could have a Pint, a pickled egg and the chance to watch a 50 year old tattooed mother of four, remove her clothes on top of a specially boarded over Pool Table, in a manner that managed to be both comical and mildly threatening. The old guy on the door took your fifty pence on the way in, "For the Stripper", probably because he knew you certainly wouldn't be willing to pay on the way out.

That afternoon we were to taste defeat as despite some heroics from Steve Norton, Charlie Stone and Paul Prendiville we went down 16-12 in a game that was best remembered for some half hearted 'violence' breaking out on the terraces, just as the home team crossed the line for the winning try.

Trevor, a can of Kestrel Lager in his hand, was in his usual 'merry' state by this time and was soon waving and shouting to the protagonists, to "Stop being such Ars*holes and behave" after which he toppled over, rolled down the terracing and sprained his ankle. This defused the 'aggro' immediately and prompted a huge explosion of laughter from both sets of fans particularly when he picked himself up at the bottom of the embankment, dusted himself down and bowed ceremoniously to the crowd. Trevor felt no pain...well not until next morning when the alcohol had worn off!! I never actually saw him 'rolling' drunk, but I did catch him a time or two in the toilets trying to dry his hands under the contraceptive machine. It was also a bad day for another set of Hull supporters who left the game to find that their coach had been stolen and after a heart breaking defeat, they had a three hour wait for a replacement to arrive from Hull.

On 19th August, six Hull men (excluding Trevor) were in court, charged with affray at the game, and, as I said earlier, it was becoming increasingly apparent that 'hooliganism', the bane of the round ball game, was spreading into Rugby League.

Following some high profile signings Hull FC were now gaining a reputation for being the big spenders in British Rugby League. We were linked with every player who was available and some that weren't and if Hull FC showed the slightest interest in signing anyone, the price immediately shot up, as Clubs that were suffering financially got the scent of a bit of cash. That August we went after Harry Pinnar the great St Helens' loose forward but he didn't want to move over to Hull.

Of course the whole of the City of Hull was 'Rugby barmy' as over in the east of the City, the Robins were still full of their great victory at Wembley which was something some of their obsessive followers were to never let us forget. That cross City fanaticism was well illustrated around that time when a Hull FC fan called Mervin Wood put up a set of rugby posts (painted in irregular hoops just like those at the Boulevard), on a five and a half acre piece of land on Great Gutter Lane just so that his son Richard could play there with his pals. Those posts, usually leaning to one side, were to remain a well remembered landmark for many years to come.

Pie Herberts, Fazil, Lumb Lane and 'a belta'

Sunday 31st August 1980   *Hull 17 – Leeds 21*

After that first round Yorkshire Cup defeat At Post Office Road, the Division One season began with a 21-17 defeat to Leeds at Headingley. Despite it being a great game, it's a fixture I remember best for what happened afterwards.

Ian who, as I stated earlier, hailed from the West Riding, decided that it was time that John and I sampled the many delights of Yorkshire hospitality and so with a warning that we should have nothing to eat in advance of the trip, we left Hull in John's company car at around 11-00am for our gastronomic adventure in Bradford.

First stop was a cafe called the Saddlery Bar on Carlisle Road, which was known locally as 'Pie Herberts'. It was there that I sampled the best pie and peas I had ever tasted. However our culinary experience had only just begun. After the game in Leeds and the usual few pints in 'The Three Horseshoes' on Otley Road, we travelled back to Bradford where we were to be treated to that most traditional of West Riding cuisine....a Curry. Ian directed John down the back streets of the City until we got to a bleak district of derelict factories and shabby back to back terraced houses.

This was Lumb Lane which looked a lot like Waterhouse Lane in Hull and was frequented on every street corner by the same 'clientele'. We parked on a piece of derelict land next to an establishment with grease 'caked' windows, a hard board covered front door (with a sealed up letter box) and a roughly painted sign written in Urdu. "This", Ian declared, "Is the 'Lahore', the best Curry House in West Yorkshire". As two scruffy looking felines jumped onto the warm car bonnet John looked at the sign and muttered under his breath, "So few cats, so many recipes".

Once inside, for anyone in our inebriated state the place was just amazing, however what our sober, 'designated driver' John made of it all, is anyone's guess. Lit by two plastic chandeliers with half the bulbs missing, the tables were well scrubbed but devoid completely of any cloths or cutlery. The proprietor, wearing a greasy 'pinafore' and a turban, only seemed able to say "Welcome to the Lahore" in English, as he shuffled about and motioned to enquire as to what we wanted to eat. It soon became apparent that there were only two things available as you could have either a 'Balti' or a 'Belta'. Not liking the sound of the latter at all, I settled, along with John, for a Balti whilst Ian, an old hand at this sort of stuff, ordered a 'Belta'.

The owner lifted the phone on the counter and started babbling away in Urdu. "He's probably ordering the Chapatti's" Ian said, and as the place was unlicensed, we amused ourselves until the food arrived by playing the juke box over in the far corner, on which every title was written in strange indecipherable squiggles. Our intoxicated state deemed that we took a liking to 27A, and as we were the only customers in the place, we played it incessantly throughout the evening. When our Curry arrived it looked more like a thin soup with pieces of meat floating in it, it was quickly followed by the Chapatti's, delivered by an Asian lady in slippers and a housecoat, who had obviously made them at her nearby home. As we settled down to our meal we dipped our Chapatti's in the Curry, before slurping it down, as our throats caught fire!

Suddenly, as John and I scrambled for a jug of water, the door burst open and in rushed a rather plump Sergeant and several members of the West Yorkshire Constabulary who, completely ignoring us, marched straight up to the proprietor to demand his name. He replied, "Fazil" to which the Sergeant replied in a broad West Yorkshire accent, "Fazil what". At this point my alcoholic state got the better of me, as I retorted in a loud voice, "Brush?" The 'fat jolly policemen' didn't appreciate my somewhat misguided attempts at humour and ambled over to warn me that "Any more of that and your nicked son".

As the juke box blasted out the umpteenth rendition of 27A the police tried to explain to poor Fazil that they had come to impound his juke box because he didn't have a music licence. Personally I think the implied fact that he didn't understand English too well suited Fazil down to the ground, but in the end after several aborted efforts to explain, "We have come to arrest your juke box" seemed to do the trick. The four Police officers then unplugged the offending piece of equipment and as 27A ground to a scratchy halt, they huffed and puffed as they slowly edged the bulky 'Rockola' the length of the restaurant, to the front door. To our unbridled amusement uniform jackets came off, ties were loosened and brows were mopped and by the time they reached the front door, all four officers had florid, glowing faces. Imagine their dismay when they found that however hard they struggled, the juke box simply wouldn't go through the door. In the end, after watching this drama unfold for around ten minutes and to the raucous laughter of the ten or so people who were now awaiting their 'Belters', Fazil finally offered the advice (in impeccable English), "So sorry gentlemen, but it came in through the back door!"

What a night and what a laugh, although it took weeks for the skin in my mouth to recover and it's a good job I decided against a 'Belta', that night in Lumb Lane.

That adventure wasn't quite finished yet either because three nights later after John had just arrived home from work and was having his tea, there was a knock on the door and yet another member of the West Yorkshire constabulary confronted him on the doorstep. It was soon made apparent to him that whilst we had all been in the 'Lahore' enjoying the drama, the police, cruising the area as part of the Yorkshire Ripper surveillance operation, had taken John's car registration number, parked suspiciously, as it was, in Bradfords 'red light' district. They had traced it back to his employers at the Bakery and so to John. That took some explaining, not so much to the Police, but to John's wife, who he had omitted to inform that our meal the previous Sunday had been in one of the seediest districts of Bradford!

As far as rugby was concerned, the following week we got back to winning ways beating Barrow at home which set us up for an away trip to Leigh, and a difficult looking encounter against a strong Lancastrian team that had yet to register a win that season.

The 'Dark Satanic Mills' of Leigh

Sunday 14th September 1980   *Hull 23 – Leigh 20*

What I remember most of those trips to darkest Lancashire was just how dour a place Leigh was. We arrived as always a little the 'worse for wear' and descended from the coach in that misty, drizzly half light that seemed synonymous with that area of the 'Duchy of Lancashire'. On accessing his premises at 11-00am by the back door, we were pleased that Bill Bentley the Landlord of the 'Our House Inn' had put on some food to sustain us weary travelers. The place was lit by several yellowing plastic lampshades that hung from a green ornately plastered ceiling and of course the curtains were drawn because it was still well before 'opening time'. It was yet another shrine of sticky carpets, cheap beer and nicotine stained old people, who obviously thought that smoking 40 Park Drive a day was a good workout for the lungs. However we were soon tucking into some great cheese and pickle sandwiches and leathery Savaloys, all washed down with frothing pints of Thwaite's 'Best' Bitter. Then at 12-00 noon, the curtains were thrown back, the front doors opened and in walked the regulars, only to find copious amounts of empty plates and us lot, bedecked in black and white, devouring the last vestiges of Bill's buffet and grinning over the top of our half empty pint pots. Their humiliation was not over yet either, because I recall we had some fun taunting them with talk of Hull FC making a bid for John Woods, Leigh's charismatic and much coveted half back.

Looking out of the grimy window and through the now driving rain, you could see the stark outline of a pit head looming out of a misty grey sky and just across the road the Stadium itself, which looked a cold and inhospitable place, with just three cars on the car park and a couple of yellow jacketed stewards huddled in the doorway of a turnstile trying to keep dry. Thankfully by the time that the game kicked off, it had stopped raining and a watery sun was shining through some rather threatening clouds. We stood on the open terrace behind the posts where we were separated from the pitch by a low concrete wall, whilst the brash and loud home support in the Tommy Sale Stand to our left, harangued us about our defeat at Wembley and being the 'Money bags' team of the competition. A ritual we were used to by now, as it happened everywhere we went.

Hilton Park was certainly a dour place, at one end the edifice of the 'Parsonage Pit' and 'The Victoria Mill' loomed through the mist like leviathans from a bygone age, and it's certainly understandable as to why it was a vista that was referred to by Eddie Waring as the "Dark Satanic Mills end of the ground".

However the crowd of 4,500 made for a great atmosphere and as we kicked off, Leigh hit us with some dazzling rugby as Hull's defence gave them far too much freedom. Each time we tried to set up any pressure on the Leigh defence, we were faced with some great field kicking from Alan Fairhurst and Tom Gittens that drove us back time and again. In fact we had two narrow escapes in the first four minutes before a towering kick from John Woods caught in the wind, went straight up in the air, fell into a melee of players and bounced off someone's head straight into the open arms of Gittens, who cantered in under the posts for Fairhurst to goal. This shock turn of events certainly pressed Hull into action but as both Walters and Dennison were guilty of high tackles on Leigh players, Fairhurst landing the penalties and we found ourselves 9-0 down after just 16 minutes. As yet we hadn't even ventured over the opposition's twenty five yard line.

Then in the 25th minute Leigh struck again. As a raking downfield kick found touch, the home team won the scrum against the head and John Woods somehow smuggled the ball out of a tackle near half way and released Bilsbury, who shot down field on a dazzling 40 yard run to the line. As Fairhurst added another goal we trailed 14-0 and were already facing defeat. A good 'lecturing' to our players from Norton and Birdsall behind the posts saw us come back to the half way line with some determination in our stride and as our defence closed ranks, our attack started to fire. Norton was as usual the instigator, having a hand in two great attacking moves in the next three minutes.

On 28 minutes he sent Dennison away for our stand-off to swerve round Donlan and pass onto Wilby. The rangy three quarter ran on through the centre channel before getting Prendiville in at the corner flag. In that last ten minutes of the half Leigh began to 'wobble', as Skerrett, Stone and Birdsall ripped into the home side's forwards and they in turn started to show signs of fatigue. Just before the whistle went, Charlie Birdsall crashed in for Lloyd to goal and at half time we trailed by 6, although it was obvious to me, queuing for a cup of Bovril, that the last twenty minutes of play had left us visiting supporters a lot happier than the now rather 'grumpy' home crowd.

The second half started much as the first finished with Hull pressing and Leigh desperately trying to cover up. Then after seven minutes Norton broke brilliantly from a three man tackle on the left, he fed on to Wilby who ran straight at Hogan, before releasing Prendiville, for the Welsh flyer to cruise in at the corner for his second try. To chants of 'Super Taff, Super Taff', Lloyd landed a brilliant touchline goal and as the rain started to fall again we were just one point behind. Next Pickerill broke from a play the ball and a neat reverse pass sent Skerrett charging in under the posts and another Lloyd goal saw us 19-15 in the lead. The rain was now lashing down but our rampaging style continued, as Robinson joined the line from full back and the supporting Wilby shot down field to touch down. At 23-15 we looked to have it won but in the last ten minutes Leigh bombarded our line. As our early failings crept back into our game, we needlessly conceded an incredible 6 penalties in the last 9 minutes, and Leigh sensed the possibility of a comeback.

It was 'backs to the wall' stuff until with just 3 minutes to go Gittens broke through again and Fairhurst scored. At 23-20 we were struggling to hold on, but Hull's pack brilliantly led by Norton just withstood the home team's onslaught. Prendiville finally relieved the pressure by intercepting a desperate pass on our ten yard line and, kicking ahead, he was just beaten to his hat-trick in the last action of the game, when, as 'Taffy's' hand went down towards the ball, Dave Bullough the Leigh winger stretched to kick it dead. Mr McDonald the referee blew for time and as the hands of all the Hull players shot in the air, the FC Army clambered over the low concrete perimeter wall and onto the pitch to celebrate in the rain and the mud. It was a great victory in which everyone played a part, although looking back it was almost totally dominated by the man through whom everything that day was channelled, the great 'Knocker' Norton.

So what of Leigh now? Well, I went back there a couple of years ago and watched a Championship game at their new ground which is far removed from the Hilton Park of 1980. However the town centre doesn't seem to have changed at all, although I did notice a sign that indicated "Leigh twinned with...." and then nothing, it was as if everyone was waiting for a name to be chalked underneath. Doesn't anyone want to twin with the good people of Leigh?

My theory, for what it's worth, is that they maybe declined to get involved in the twinning stuff and instead entered into a suicide pact with that other most dour of Rugby League destinations, Oldham of which there is plenty later in this tome.

As for John Woods well he had a fantastic game and right on cue the following Wednesday it was announced that we had offered Leigh £100,000 for their 'talismanic' number 6. However despite us being the 'Big spenders' of the competition, Leigh turned us down, and so, unbeknown to us supporters, our Board of Directors turned their attention to another great number 6 who was plying his trade at Wakefield.

At the City Hall business was building nicely, but with an increase of trade came a myriad of problems. The five strong work-force consisted of Foreman Ted Puckering and Chargehand Frank Green, plus three other attendants Frank, Ken and Charlie. Charlie, Ted and Frank were all Hull FC supporters whilst 'Greeeny' didn't go to rugby, but as was the case with many people back then, he decided he would be a Rover's fan, just to be 'controversial'. We had a lot of laughs with Frank! With a combined age of over 290 the staff of five had to often work through the night to prepare for events which involved a tremendous amount of hard labour. However I have to say they were great guys and we had lots of fun. Charlie even bought a season pass for the seats which had been newly installed in the Best Stand at the Boulevard and sat with us all in there that year.

'Trevor the Fish' and the blazing anorak

Sunday 5ᵗʰ October 1980   *Hull 10 – New Zealand 33*

As I stated in the last book, the folks who went on the 'The Mermaid' bus trips to away matches were certainly a crowd of characters, but no one was more colourful or entertaining than 'Trevor the Fish'. A passionate cigar smoker, Trevor, as I said earlier, could drink an amazing amount of beer which seemed to have little effect on him until the game had started, when, without any warning, he would suddenly fall asleep in a coma like state, from which it was hard to rouse him. He almost caused a riot at the match against the New Zealand tourists on 5th October which incidentally we lost 33-10. Trevor was enjoying his usual cigar in the second half when all of a sudden he was 'gone', out like a light and snoring profusely. He slumped forward in his seat as at the same time, the cigar rolled from his lips and into the hood of the anorak worn by the guy sat directly in front of him. Trevor was oblivious to this and Ian, John, Charlie and I, despite witnessing what had happened, were in fits of laughter and could do little to help.

The lad in front had no idea either, although when a thin strand of smoke started to curl up from his hood it was time to take some action. Quick as a flash Charlie threw the remains of his half time 'cuppa' straight at the back of the guy's head at which point he sprung to his feet and went 'ballistic'. It was mayhem! The guy hopped from one foot the other with smoke rising behind his head and although he was still unaware that he was on fire, we couldn't tell him for laughing, or in Trevor's case, snoring. Two weeks later after a victory against Leeds we couldn't rouse Trevor at all and so we left him sat there on his own in his seat after the game had finished. I can still picture the scene as we turned at the top of the South Terracing before descending to the gate. There was this beleaguered figure, sat in the gathering gloom, slumped in his seat in the now deserted Stand. That night though, as was usual at opening time, he walked into the pub whistling away, just as if nothing had happened, he just commented on the win, grinned that infectious grin and ordered a pint.

It was certainly apparent that the visit to Wembley and the Floodlit Trophy victory the previous year plus and a great first season in the First Division, had captured the imagination of the fans and attendances were on the increase. That October the Board at the Club announced a £22,468 profit for the previous season, generated by an extra £86,000 from season ticket sales which had accrued £200,000 in total. Speedway still helped too and the Hull Vikings paid the Club £10,900 which was an increase of £2,000 on the previous twelve months trading.

Ozzie bites the head off a chicken and it's 'Fanx Tara' from Sad Cafe

Back in the day job, it was certainly still difficult getting the major national rock promoters to consider Hull for a date on their tours. However after some 'arm twisting' and offering a lucrative introductory deal, I did manage to get a big concert from top promoters 'Wasted Management' of Birmingham, who in mid November brought 'The Ozzy Osbourne Blizzard of Oz' tour to the City.

With the sweet smell of patchouli everywhere, a sell out crowd of 'ageing rockers' in leather jackets, bandanas and 'Engineer's' boots enjoyed a great concert that finished with covers of Black Sabbath's 'Iron Man', 'Children of the Grave' and the final 'anthemic' encore, 'Paranoid'. At one point the show included Ozzie biting the head off a chicken and throwing the entrails into the crowd. Actually it was a rubber chicken and the entrails were pieces of liver purchased that afternoon by the Tour Manager, who got them from the local butchers. The crowd absolutely loved it, particularly the chicken bit!

This success was followed by our first concert with the agency that handled most of the Manchester Bands back then. Kennedy Street Artistes was headed by the charismatic and flamboyant figure of Danny Betesch who had for many years, before he set up on his own, been personal assistant to the world famous impresario Harvey Goldsmith. This show again sold out and featured current chart band 'Sad Cafe' who included in their set their hits 'Every Day Hurts', 'My Oh My' and 'Strange Little Girl' from their latest album 'Fanx Tara'.

The Colts run riot in the rain

Saturday 29ᵗʰ November 1980   Hull Colts 73 – Widnes Colts 0

Around that time I decided to go and 'run the rule' over the much celebrated crop of youngsters we currently had playing for the Club. It was the general consensus that Coach Dave Elliott was doing a great job developing our highly acclaimed Colts team, who were that year, taking their competition by storm. Before the game I downed a few pints in the Lion in Redbourne Street, a smashing little pub that was on weekday lunchtimes the haunt of many a young seaman doing his 'tickets' at the Nautical College around the corner in the Boulevard. When I got to the Stadium it was pouring with rain and standing on the Threepenny Stand I witnessed a real one sided game on a heavy pitch which had none the less attracted around 1000 other curious onlookers. We won the match against Widnes Colts easily, 73-0. Young Paul Redfearn scored five tries and there were great performances from Keith Foster, Mike Ridsdale and Kenny Jackson but amazingly it was only Wayne Proctor, playing in the second row, who was destined to ultimately make the grade into the first team. Having a great 'A' and Colts team was fine and very commendable, but the fans (and it appeared the Board) were hungry for success and if any position needed strengthening there seemed to be no time for the youngsters to be 'blooded', as invariably we just went out and bought someone, a philosophy that was great for us fans at the time, but one that would lead to problems in the future.

In early December, as work got more and more hectic I had a couple of beers in the Punch Hotel with one of the nicest guys I met during my time at the City Hall. Eminent trombonist and comedian George Chisholm whiled away an hour with me, talking about his appearances on 'The Black and White Minstrel Show' and with 'The Goons'. Then three days later I promoted the first Professional Boxing show that the venue had seen for years. On an exciting night attended by over 1,200 boxing fans local hero Ricky Beaumont lost a Final Championship Eliminator to Dave McCabe, while another local lad Steve Pollard won on points and Bobby Welburn knocked out Glen Rhodes in just 47 seconds! The place was packed and despite the proliferation of 'No Smoking' signs around the venue, by the time the last bout was over, the whole place, toilets, corridors and vestibule included, was enveloped in an atmosphere heavy with a fog of acrid cigarette smoke.

'Mud, Mud Glorious Mud'; enter the Sports Turf Research Centre

Sunday 7th December 1980   *Hull 11 – York 10*

Down at the Boulevard it was John Player Trophy time again although we had certainly experienced little joy in that tournament since our heroics at that 1976 Final against Widnes, when we just failed to lift the Trophy. In the first round we drew York the then leaders of the Second Division and so on 7th December, on a cold and frosty afternoon, almost 11,000 fans turned up to witness Hull FC and the 'The Wasps' being literally buried in the Boulevard mud. The pitch gradually depreciated and as both teams had to change shirts twice, any semblance of open flowing rugby was impossible. Although we just won it was apparent to all of us that Arthur Bunting was producing a rugby team suited to fast, open, exciting play, that was now performing on a pitch better suited to mud wrestling.

The Club called in the Sports Turf Research Centre to ascertain what could be done to improve things and immediately received a stark warning from their Managing Director Mr Eskritt that if they persisted with that pitch, "The Club could be in danger of causing serious injury to their players". This was a real concern and the Club immediately set about trying to rectify the problem. By the next home game against Wakefield three inches of the mud in the centre of the pitch had been scraped away, dumped behind the terracing at the Gordon Street end and replaced with one hundred tons of sharp sand. It wasn't the first time we had used sand in this way, far from it, and in the past it hadn't worked at all, but this time we had at least removed the mud first. These actions however left the whole area between the 25 yard lines resembling a beach.

Dick Gemmell goes scouting for Kiwi's

At a time when the world was mourning the tragic and premature death of John Lennon, we learned that the Club had dispatched Director Dick

Gemmell to France to meet up with the New Zealand touring team in an attempt to sign three of their International players, Fred Ah Koi, Dane O'Hara and James Leuluai. One of the problems he faced was that Hull KR were interested in O'Hara too and had made him an offer, however nothing was signed and Gemmell was apparently still in with a chance of enticing the mercurial winger and his fellow countrymen to the Boulevard. These three had really impressed during the recent Kiwi Tour and although Gemmell still had some work to do, it seemed that the players were interested, although it was to be another 6 months before two of them donned a black and white shirt.

At work life continued with a host of Christmas services, Carol Concerts and Winter Proms but I had at least managed to get some rock music into the venue for the festive season and first up were the Undertones who played to a full house. The Irish pop/punk band were quickly followed two days later by a concert featuring Sheffield heavy metal band Saxon who helped by the use of bass bins on the floor of the Hall to enhance the 'bottom end' of their sound were loud.....really loud. In fact when you opened the doors at the rear of the main hall the thumping of the bass and drums made your chest vibrate and next day the Manager of 'March the Tailors', a shop under the City Hall, complained that on arrival that morning he had found that his ceiling had collapsed. He stormed into my office shouting, "It's showered my best bloody suits with bloody plaster". Still, 'it's an ill wind' and that same day Sydney Scarborough's the record store a few doors down the Street ran out of copies of Saxon's latest CD, 'Strong Arm of the Law', as at least someone in the local economy was benefiting from my attempts to bring the City Hall 'kicking and screaming' into the 80's.

Not a Happy Christmas, if you're a welder!

Sunday 28th December 1980   *Hull 1 – Oldham 2*

Christmas came round at the City Hall and as was to become the norm, I was exhausted after a really busy year. Following the final concert,

'Christmas with the Choral Union' I took all the staff to 'The Punch' where we had a drink to celebrate the end of the busy autumn season and I have to admit that I was just amazed that my ageing 'crew' had made it through at all. It was however a tough festive period for many in the City as over at the soon to be completed Humber Bridge, 400 welders were laid off after completing their work, as they joined the other 24,000 who were out of work in the region that December. When 'Father Christmas' arrived at the City Hall Flat that year he brought a copy of the first ever Rothmans Rugby League Year book, which kept me occupied until 'The Punch' opened at tea time on Christmas Day. As the only customer that night, Mary the Land Lady presented me with a bottle of wine. "Not very original" I thought, "But I gave it a good home!"

254 minutes without a try!

Sunday 5th January 1981   *Hull 10 – Leigh 9*

That festive season Hull FC was struggling. Having beaten York 11-10 at home in the mud and Whitehaven 13-0 away, we lost 5-2 at the Boulevard to Wakefield Trinity and suffered a 2-1 loss at Oldham. What was worse still was the fact that throughout that period we didn't cross the try line once, with all our points coming from penalty or drop goals. This produced an unwanted record of having played 254 minutes without scoring a single try.

It was not until after 68 minutes of the Leigh game at the Boulevard that we finally scored with a try that was superbly engineered and executed. It started when scrum half Clive Pickerill linked with Steve Norton at the base of a scrum 20 yards from the Leigh line. 'Knocker' who had caused the visitors problems all afternoon, suddenly stepped right to carve out a huge opening. He ran on, turned inside and found Gaitley open on his left and he barrelled in next to the right hand upright to the jubilation of his team mates and the fans on the terraces.

You could feel the sense of relief throughout the ground and the spectator's reaction could not have been more vociferous had Gaitley scored the winning try at Wembley. In the late stages of the second half Clive Pickerill got a real slap across the face from a Leigh forward and it looked like he might have sustained a broken nose. After a lengthy spell of treatment on the side line he returned to the game to feed a scrum in front of the 'Threepenny's'. Immediately one of the great orators' in that famous Stand shouted, "Hey, Pickerill, with a nose like that you look like a f*cking parrot, you should be sat on the cross bar". A late try by that man John Woods almost snatched a victory for the visitors, but in the end we held out and won the game 10-9.

There were a host of problems off the field too and although we all look back at those 'good old days' of the early 80's as some of the best times we experienced as a Club, we should never forget with so many big name players in the squad there were a lot of egos in the dressing room too. Thankfully one of Arthur Bunting's strongest qualities was the fact that he was a diplomat, a good talker and a great 'Man Manager' so most of the problems that raised their heads behind the scenes, were kept right there.......behind the scenes.

That was however not the case when on 8th January 1981 the 'backstage' rumblings spilled out into the media and the players threatened to go on strike over the win bonus they had been offered (£300) to play in the upcoming John Player Semi Final against Barrow. Knocker Norton was as usual the spokesman, but Chairman Charlie Watson backed by his deputy Roy Waudby immediately retorted that, "Should the players 'withdraw their labour' the Board and Coach will play the 'A' team in the semi final at Headingley". Within twenty four hours the players backed down and agreed on the original bonus payment offer, which was inconsequential in the end anyway, as Hull lost the game 10-13. As we will see in the coming pages, this was not the last dispute between the players and the Club in that most glorious of eras.

The return of John Newlove, Mick Crane and Lenny the Lion

Across town at the Hull New Theatre the Pantomime featured Lenny the Lion and ventriloquist Terry Hall, who had come out of retirement especially to do the show, and he wasn't the only one returning to 'perform' in Hull either. At the Boulevard our continuing injury crisis in the half backs saw John Newlove, (who had by this time been retired for 5 months), come back to help out. At work I was trying my best to get more and more touring rock shows into the City but whilst the country was celebrating the announcement that Princess Diana and Prince Charles were to marry, we FC fans were more interested in the 'engagement' of Mick Crane, the enigma who had left us to join Leeds and then moved onto the enemy across the River. He had now walked out on the 'Red and Whites', and so for a fee of £15,000, he made a welcome return to the Boulevard.

'Craney' was exactly what we needed, because his off the cuff and unpredictable style would add some unpredictability to our squad. However, it was certainly still not all 'sweetness and light' in the dressing room as a deal of unrest continued. Tim Wilby and Graham Walters were both sanctioned for, "Discussing Club business outside the Club" and the Board put both players straight on the transfer list. The unrest was however tempered somewhat by us signing another new player. Tony Dean, who had been a thorn in our side for years when playing for New Hunslet, signed for £8,000, to offer a more long term solution to our half back problems. Tony was to prove a very astute purchase and his arrival was all the more significant as far as the Hull fans were concerned when Dick Tingle in the Hull Daily Mail revealed that Hull had beaten Hull KR to his signature.

The season continued and wins at home to Bradford, Widnes, Leeds and St Helens saw gates soaring past the 12,000 mark with the Club installing two faster turnstiles to cope with the pre-match demand. Speedway was still helping the finances too but their input, which for so many years had kept Hull FC afloat financially, was now far outstripped by the Club's own income streams. Still, on Wednesday 1st April, in front of 5,430 spectators the Hull Vikings rode their 300th meeting since being formed back in 1971, when they arrived at the Boulevard as part of a desperate attempt to keep Hull FC alive.

Mayhem, carnage and shame....the long Good Friday

Friday 17ᵗʰ April 1981   *Hull 16 – Hull KR 17*

So we come to one of the most significant events in our Club's recent history and to one that is sadly remembered for all the wrong reasons. Those were dire times for the workers of a region when the demise of both the Docks and the Fishing Industry saw the local economy in decline. This situation was well illustrated in early April when local bakers 'Mackmans' went into liquidation shedding 180 jobs over-night. Still the residents of the City seemed able to afford their rugby, as the rivalry between the two Clubs, (fuelled by the goings on at Wembley a year earlier), reached 'fever pitch'. The game that saw this antagonism and pseudo-hatred reach its zenith took place on Good Friday 1981. That Spring afternoon there were 18,500 packed into the Boulevard for a Derby game that saw the old rivals clash in an encounter that created an atmosphere that was, from the moment you entered the Stadium, supercharged with tension, emotion and a deal of menace. I really wanted to omit this game altogether because quite frankly as a Rugby League fan I am still ashamed to talk about it. However perhaps the old adage that "Those who cannot learn from history are doomed to repeat it" is pertinent here and so I include it 'Lest we ever forget'. It was probably one of the blackest days in the history of our great Club. What happened was nothing short of a riot and a disgrace to the game, both Clubs and the City!

On that fateful afternoon I settled in my place, in the 'new seats' at the South end of the Best Stand, to join what was the biggest League attendance the British game had seen since the inception of two Divisions back in 1973. I have already mentioned the bane of football hooliganism and that day it was all around, as the atmosphere in certain factions of the crowd was menacing and uneasy.

The match started well and we witnessed an exciting first quarter. From the kick off Hull KR pressed our line but after 9 minutes it was Hull who took the lead when Tony Dean picked up a loose ball, ran thirty yards and put Graham Walters away. Paul Woods converted and we led 5-0. Back came the opposition with two quick tries from Hogan on 12 minutes and Hartley 3 minutes later. Both conversions were missed and Woods restored our lead and pushed us further ahead with two penalties. Leading 9-6 Hull were starting to get on top when on 22 minutes the unthinkable happened.

In what was dubbed by the National Press "The Long Good Friday" and "The Battle of Bunker's Hill" by the local media, all hell broke loose at the Division Road end of the Ground. All of a sudden the unseasonably blue skies were blacked by a hail of flying debris as thousands of innocent supporters ran for cover. Initially there was no fighting, just a bombardment of bricks, mud, rubble and wood from the 'Building Site' behind the embankment.

It all seemed to start when 30 or so Hull and Rovers supporters who were standing in the middle of the South terrace started throwing missiles at the policemen on the Speedway track below. The regular, 'decent' fans on that part of the terracing soon stopped this happening, but the protagonists then moved around the back of the embankment and started throwing bricks and rubble over the terracing and into the crowd. The Club were undertaking some improvement work to increase the capacity of the Boulevard and the Police had been warned about the debris, but they couldn't stop a handful of 'idiots' leaving the terracing and congregating behind it, to launch the onslaught.

As referee Laughton took the players off the field, the St John Ambulance staff led old people, children, and young women along the touchline in front of us. Many had head wounds streaming with blood whilst others staggered about aimlessly, apparently suffering from shock. On the Gordon Street terrace many fans from both sides who were desperate to escape, swept over the fence and onto the pitch leaving two small factions of 'idiots' battling it out on the steps behind them. Then as we watched from our seats in the Best Stand a Policeman went by on a stretcher, obviously unconscious, and elsewhere mothers shepherded their children away from the melee and out of the ground. We were all just sat there stunned as we witnessed what was later described as Rugby League's 'Blackest Hour.'

In the 14 minutes that the teams were off the field 40 people were reported to be hurt and 13 more arrested as the Boulevard started to resemble a battlefield. Amazingly, slowly but surely the Police got control and shepherded the fans back onto the terraces and the game eventually restarted when the referee led the teams out and ordered a scrum to Rovers on the centre spot.

If we the fans had lost our appetite for the game on the pitch, Hull had, as a team, lost all the momentum we had before the stoppage. We all just looked out at a surreal scene, as the game went on with people still being treated on the grass behind the posts, in front of the Gordon Street terraces. The incidents I describe here were I suppose a shameful blot on a game that, looking back now, had many exciting pieces of action and some nerve tingling moments. Rovers had used the enforced break to collect themselves and tore back at us for the rest of the first half. Within seven minutes evading both Norton and Woods, Hubbard crashed in at the corner and at half time the scores were tied 9-9. Tony Dean almost got over after just two minutes of the second half and then we saw Hull's best move of the game. Dean beat Sanderson to the ball when Rovers had won a scrum and as he was tackled he got up quickly, played the ball to himself and shot in under the posts. Woods converted and we were 14-9 up and in command again. Woods the man who had back at Wembley in 1980, asked the Queen Mother for her autograph, tried to have a laugh with the lads in the Threepenny's as he walked back but everyone was, in general, just too 'shell shocked' to respond!

However Hull KR's International second rower Phil Lowe crashed through two tackles and despite a valiant effort from Mick Crane he scored another try and Hubbard landed his only goal to level things up again. A high tackle by a young Steve Crooks on Hull's Steve Norton saw Woods edge us ahead and with ten minutes to go we looked to be hanging on for a win. Unfortunately with seconds left Lowe broke through again and right in front of us he kicked through and touched down in the corner and Hull KR were victorious 17-16.

If that defeat and those terrible scenes were not enough, imagine the shame we all felt when the 'riot' featured as the headlines on the

BBC's national Nine O'Clock News that night. There we all were, as the shameful scenes of a few hours earlier were laid bare 'in all their glory' for the whole country to see. Next day the headlines in the Hull Daily Mail read "Hull's Revulsion in Wake of Riot" and there followed a catalogue of local politicians, Churchmen and MP's all decrying the actions of those few idiots that had brought our City into disrepute. Much retribution and condemnation of the goings on that Good Friday followed, as did a RL hearing, but for me it's a memory that is perhaps best forgotten however I feature it here for future generations of sports fans as a warning about what can happen when banter and rivalry cross that thin line and turn to hatred!!!

So much coverage was given to the 'Riot' that most of us FC fans missed completely a piece in the local paper that indicated that over in New Zealand, Fred Ah Kuoi, had decided to turn down Hull's offer of a contract and had instead joined South Sydney. That fateful day was also significant for something that was actually only revealed as part of a TV interview two decades later. Ray French, BBC TV's Rugby League match commentator, then revealed that on that occasion he had been match summariser with the legendary Eddie Waring. That terrible day the pair climbed down the ladder from the rickety scaffolding gantry, accompanied by the usual hoots of derision and goading from the Threepenny Stand below. Once back on 'terra firma' Waring turned to French and said, "Well that's the last time, you'll get me up there Ray" and sure enough the Challenge Cup Final a few weeks later was Eddie's last game for the BBC. He had one of the greatest voices the game has ever heard and it was then that he passed into folk-lore. Eddie was a character that was loved by some and hated by others, although he certainly possessed some memorable defining characteristics. He will always be remembered for his occupancy at the Queen's Hotel, his appetite for copious amounts of grapes to keep the vocal chords clear, that famous trilby hat (an impersonators dream), his numerous catch phrases, that camel coat and his constant and proud grooming of a full head of wavy hair.

'Toppo' arrives as Charlie Watson departs

Saturday 16th May 1981   *Hull 7 – Hull Kingston Rovers 11*

The rest of that season was pretty nondescript really, we had promised much but in the end it all fizzled out, although we did get into the Premiership play-offs at the end of the season. Hull KR actually reached Wembley, something most of us in the West of the City purposely ignored, but as a member of the 'Mermaid Wembley Weekend Club', I'd paid my £2-00 every week and so I went down to London as usual, wearing my black and white scarf and hat and of course supporting Widnes. I always think that those people that say you have to support Rovers because they're a Hull team really don't get it at all!

As if to steal a bit of our rivals thunder on the eve of the final Hull announced that they had engaged Wakefield stand-off David Topliss. 'Toppo' was signed for a fee of £15,000, which was a small outlay for the contribution he was to make to my Club in the forthcoming seasons. Our Premiership campaign was a pretty successful one and although Toppo was 'Cup Tied' we played and beat Warrington at Wildespool and Castleford at Wheldon Road in a fantastic game in which Steve Norton starred and where after trailing 10-0 at half time we eventually came back to win 11-10. So the stage was set for a Final against Hull KR which we lost 11-7 at Headingley. It was not a great game and I don't intend going into the details of it here, but sufficient to say that the winners went to a Council Reception while the rest of us went looking for counselling. However two interesting things surrounded that last match of the 1980/81 season.

Firstly, 3 days before the final there was more trouble about bonus payments, which led to Clive Pickerill asking for a transfer. He was promptly dropped from the starting 17, and he and Graham Walters were soon on their way to Wakefield. It was also the game that was to see the end of the tenure of Chairman, Charlie Watson, who decided to stand down after the defeat. Some said that he was under pressure from his deputy Roy Waudby, whilst others pointed to the trauma and disappointment he faced after the events surrounding that Good Friday debacle. However I think that having brought Hull FC from the Second Division to a Wembley appearance and a Premiership Final, he had decided he had 'done his bit'. It is said Charlie cried that day, but it's unclear as to whether it was because of a defeat to the old enemy or the fact that he was leaving the Chairmanship of the Club he loved, or even because at the Final he actually lost his wallet. Perhaps it was a bit of all three.

Roy Waudby takes the Chair

Within days Roy Waudby, whose business acumen and financial clout had been behind much of our revival and who was gaining celebrity status with the faithful fans, was named the new Chairman. Roy immediately announced a plan to spend £1.4m to revamp and improve the Boulevard Stadium. This controversially included the proposed demolition of the Threepenny Stand at the end of the next season. However the Threepennies had survived bigger threats than that, including one posed by the constant visits of Mr Hitler's Heinkels in 1940/41 and needless to say, it was to survive again, for the time being at least.

Around that time I got myself one of those 'new fangled' video recorders and having wrestled with the instructions, one of the first programmes I recorded was a documentary shown on Yorkshire TV called 'Another Bloody Sunday'. It was a fabulous insight into the game in the lower divisions and featured Doncaster, a Club whose run of defeats the previous season had got them into the Guinness Book of Records. The hour long feature followed the 'Dons' fortunes on and off the field and those of their colourful and at times controversial prop forward, ex Hull FC player Tony Banham, who features in the previous volume of this tale.

Wrestling with the Cultural Services Committee

While the City Hall was quiet during the summer I was having a real battle with the Council's Cultural Services Committee which was responsible for the running of the venue. Some of the more, shall we say traditional members, including Alice Tulley the Chairman, (who was a kind and gentle lady), were up in arms about what I wanted to promote there. What was it that had them so outraged? Was it Strippers or indoor hare coursing? Well in fairness it was nothing so controversial and more to do with an approach I had received from Jackie Pallo the famous TV wrestler who wanted to bring his touring show to the venue. The debate in the Guildhall that Tuesday afternoon in June went on for about an hour and had the Hull Daily Mail's Committee correspondent scribbling away until his pencil was blunt. Concerns expressed included, "What will happen if we get blood on the walls?" to "Men in leotards in the City Hall, it's immoral and hardly conceivable". Still in the end it was agreed that it could go ahead for a trial period, even though a couple of councillors had at one point threatened to resign over the issue.

The thing was of course, wrestling was an absolute 'picnic' compared with that 'Damned' concert, (which turned out to be the 'Night of the fire Extinguishers'), that I described in the last book and then there was Ozzie Osborne's gastronomic antics with that chicken! It was certainly a good job, I thought, that the worthy members of the Cultural Services Committee were not in the habit of attending anything but Orchestral Concerts at the City Hall.

The Kiwi's are coming as Dick Gemmell gets his men!

On 6th June we all discovered from the Hull Daily Mail that Director Dick Gemmell was in New Zealand. The interview, conducted by Dick Tingle over the telephone and reported in a special late edition of the broadsheet, was exciting news indeed. The lead article told how Gemmell had gone to the Southern Hemisphere to finalise the contracts of both Dane O'Hara and James Leuluai who Hull FC had now been pursuing for six months. On arrival Dick found the players were not at home in Auckland, but actually at New Zealand's International Training Camp some 60 miles away. Dick travelled there to see them and was told that although both players wanted to join Hull they also wanted to first speak to North Sydney for whom Fred Ah Kuoi had signed, just in case they were wanted there.

It was Wednesday and Dick, having travelled half way round the world in good faith, gave the ultimatum, "Sign before Friday or its all off!" Within an hour of him arriving back at his hotel, he received a phone call to say, "Bring us the forms and we'll sign right now". Back he went by train to the Training Camp and at last secured the signatures the fans had craved for so long. Within ten days Garry Kemble, the New Zealander's full back had also signed and it was the start of a golden era at Hull FC when these three antipodeans and the recently acquired David Topliss, would etch their names into the history of the Club forever.

The news had economic repercussions in West Hull too and in the first week of going on sale, Hull FC sold £35,000 worth of season tickets, which was, by any standard, a phenomenal achievement. In addition the Club, despite their high hopes and plans of earlier that year, reviewed their finances and decided to abandon the idea of building a 'new' Threepenny Stand'. That decision was something that we the fans applauded, but one that in future years and in the wake of the Bradford City disaster, the Board of Hull FC were to bitterly regret.

The opening of 'The bridge to nowhere'

During that summer the Council took the opportunity to have the City Hall redecorated and we followed that refurbishment with another professional boxing promotion at which, in front of 1000 partisan fans, Steve Pollard got a fine points victory in a North of England Eliminator bout.

Then the region made history! After eight years in the building at 12-04pm on 24th June 1981, the Lord Mayor of Kingston upon Hull, Councillor Alex Clarke drove his battered Triumph Herald Estate across the Humber Bridge to open the longest single span suspension bridge in the World. We all crowded round the windows on the top floor of the Council's Leisure Services Offices in Ferensway to see if we could see the first lorry go across, and although it was just a dot in the distance, we actually saw it and accompanied the sighting with an impromptu round of applause, for which we were all immediately embarrassed. On a more sober note, three days later at an independent tribunal at Rugby League Head Quarters, Hull FC were fined £1,000 for their part in that Good Friday riot and the whole affair was thankfully finally confined to the history books.

Rugby League, it's all anxiety during the season and boredom during the summer!

By the middle of August and after a relaxing 14 days in Tenerife, I was starting to get a bit impatient for the start of the new season. I resolved to continue sitting in the new seats in the Best Stand and was joined as usual by Charlie from the City Hall, Barry from the Mermaid, Trevor the Fish and a few other pals. Charlie, the City Hall Attendant who was now a close friend was stocky, with a jolly florid face, a shock of white hair who always had a permanent smile, whatever the circumstances.

His most memorable feature was the fact that long before the writers of Coronation Street had even thought about introducing Fred the Butcher, Charlie used to say "I say" before repeating most of his statements. So there we all were on 12th July lining up to buy our season tickets, about a dozen places from the front of the queue as the window opened and sales began. That queuing for season tickets on the first day stuff is strange indeed, but I still do it to this day. I suppose in the twisted mind of the average sports fanatic it's just another means of animating how committed you are to the team you love, and one thing's for sure, after all these years, I'll never change now!

Pomp, Circumstance and conflicting National Anthems! Who'd be a politician?

I had been working at the City Hall for two years and business had improved so much so that the Council had invested in a brand new 'Three Phase' electrical system which meant that we could now start to compete with the bigger venues on the rock music circuit. In fact the Authority had in general been very kind in supporting me in my efforts to rebuild the business, although for someone who was in the end just an ordinary gardener they did cause me a deal of amusement and indeed confusion at times.

Take Orchestral Concerts for instance. This type of entertainment had always been a tradition at the City Hall and the venue had over the years played host to most of the World's top Orchestras, particularly those hailing from the then Soviet Block. I certainly won't be mentioning much at all about local politics, but it is fair to say that the majority of the ruling Labour Group were moderate, hard working public servants who put party politics and ideologies aside to concentrate on the greater good of the people. For most Politicians, politics was left for the Council Chamber, although one or two were slaves to their 'beliefs' and their support for other more radical administrations around the world. You know the type, I called them 'Marxists of the Groucho variety' and it was not unusual to see one or two of them at these orchestral concerts standing for the Russian National Anthem and sitting for the British one!

In fact after the Moscow State Symphony Orchestra had, as a mark of respect to the country they were visiting, included Pomp and Circumstance March No. 2 'Land of Hope and Glory' (and by co-incidence the 'theme tune' of the Conservative Party') as an encore, I was confronted by one Councillor claiming that she had just seen a vision of 'Thatcherite Britain marching through the City Hall' She obviously missed the point completely. About that time the Council even thought about barring Punch and Judy Shows because of, as one Councillor said in a meeting, the "Feckless and Violent" always won the day. At least that idea never came to fruition and they were probably right to allow the traditional entertainment as it's unlikely that many Hull children grew up to be crocodile worrying murderers because of it.

Dave Topliss shines as the Kiwi's fly in

Sunday 27ᵗʰ September 1981   *Hull 42 – Castleford 24*

As things were quiet at the City Hall during the summer I was asked to do a bit of work in the Entertainments Tent at the Hull Show in East Park, where I had started my career with the Council 26 years earlier. It was mostly a day long programme of kids' participation stuff, (which included endless renditions of, 'The Birdie Song') and the Miss Hull Show contest. I will leave you to guess which I found the most entertaining!

Then at last the new rugby season kicked off with the Eva Hardaker Memorial Trophy game played at Castleford. The decision to stop playing Hull KR in this fixture was something that perhaps, after the happenings the previous Easter had been, with hindsight, a fortuitous decision. We all went to Wheldon Road to watch Hull field a makeshift team with second rower Sammy Lloyd at centre, winger Paul Prendiville at stand-off and try scoring debutant Barry Edwards on the wing as we won an entertaining encounter 24-23. A second friendly was hastily arranged against Featherstone, again away, and again we won. This match also saw the long awaited debut of Dave Topliss in the number 6 shirt however the next week we were dumped out of the Yorkshire Cup at the first round stage by Leeds at the Boulevard.

Two days later the first of our three Kiwi signings flew in, as Gary Kemble arrived in the Country. He made his debut in an 'A' team game (which I missed) at Featherstone and was reported to have been the 'Man of the Match' in his first outing, during which, because of our mounting injuries, 'A' team player/coach Clive Sullivan was forced out of retirement.

Val Doonican goes off his rocker! While there's an eventful debut for Dane O'Hara

Sunday 24th September 1981   Hull 42 – Castleford 24

The new season at The City Hall was booking up well as we started off with a great gig by the Scottish rock band Nazareth. They were touring a live album they had recorded the previous year call 'Snaz' and despite a terrible day when the groups equipment was brought into the Hall in pouring rain, and the lift broke down three times, almost 900 people attended the concert. We also had a bit of an 'incident' at the Val Doonican Show three days later when the cardigan wearing Irish singer famed for his singing from a 'Rocking Chair', refused to go on stage. Apparently he was less than impressed when my pal Charlie, who was working back stage, said to him, "If you've got any old 'Cardi's' to give away I'll have them, I say, I'll have them". Obviously the laid back Irishman had no sense of humour and I had to go and intervene and calm the rather irate troubadour so that he, and his rocking chair, eventually went onto the stage. There was however no cardigan for Charlie!

The Hull FC 'publicity machine' had certainly learned their lessons from the almost stealth like arrival of Gary Kemble and heralded with much ceremony the arrival of both Dane O'Hara and James Leuluai on 24th September 1981. It is said that Kemble had written to the two newcomers before they arrived to tell them what it was like in Hull. He is reported to have said, of Mick Crane, "We have a player who stubs out his cigarette in the tunnel before he runs out onto the pitch". It was an interesting day on other fronts for FC fans as well, because it was also announced that afternoon that we had put in an unsuccessful £80,000 bid for Featherstone second rower Pete Smith and that Paul Woods, 'Psycho' to the adoring 'Black and Whites' fans, who had recently left for the new Cardiff Club, had been sent off in his second game in Wales and was banned for a record 13 matches. With Gary Kemble already making the Hull FC No.1 shirt vacated by Woods his own, the scene was now set for the other two Kiwis to make their home debuts against Castleford at the Boulevard the following Sunday.

We won the game easily by 42-24, but disaster was to strike for Dane O'Hara in his first match. Following several good breaks that had us all applauding, the left winger was tackled on halfway and failed to get to his feet. He lay on the ground in front of the Threepenny Stand completely motionless for several minutes whilst the medical staff and St John Ambulance boys swarmed around him. 'Dane O' had sustained a punctured lung, which was to see him sidelined for the next 6 weeks. All three newcomers had played their part in a good victory but the loss of O'Hara so early in his Hull career, took the shine off the afternoon.

A new Music Venue arrives down the road

Since the 'Adam and the Ants' 'inferno' at the Queen's Gardens Technical College there were, with the exception of The Lawns in Cottingham and the University Student's Union, few venues in Hull besides the City Hall willing to host rock music. However in October that year everything changed as the derelict Tower Cinema was bought by local entrepreneur Wally Mays and reopened as a venue catering for 1,000 people and ideally suited to standing rock concerts. I had met and advised Wally's son Robert about setting up the place as a venue, because I thought that with its size it would compliment rather than conflict with the City Hall and thus improve the local music scene. Which I think in hindsight it did.

Jon Clarke a post graduate who was working with me organizing all the 'humpers' that we employed at the City Hall (to man handle the equipment for concerts in and out of the venue), worked with a gang of lads on a voluntary basis refurbishing the old Picture House. The Tower then opened to much publicity with concerts by 'Starfighter' and punk outfits 'Theatre of Hate' and 'Tenpole Tudor'. At the City Hall we countered with a concert by the Shadows on 7th October which had sold out in a single day. That night was a great success and Charlie, Frank and the rest of the ageing City Hall staff were falling over their feet as they attempted to do the Shadows' distinctive stage 'walk' along to the music. The band were certainly nice people to work with and at the end of the Concert Hank Marvin and Bruce Welch came down to the staff 'Mess Room' and gave copies of their new album, 'Change of Address' to each of the lads.

As Speedway 'hits the boards' there's a first win at Wigan for 59 years!

Sunday 25th October 1981   *Hull 18 – Wigan 5*

Hull FC was having a really good season and the crowds were packing the Boulevard for every home game. This success was probably behind a controversial move by the Club when, on 12th October, directly after the last meeting of the Speedway season, they rescinded the lease to the Hull Vikings, claiming that the Speedway promoters had breached the terms of their contract. At the time, as rugby fans, we were all sick and fed up of the mess that the motor sport left around the place and the thin film of red grit that it deposited everywhere. In fact the boggy state of our pitch was often blamed on the Speedway shale blocking the land drains under the playing surface. Although popular with their own fans there were, I think, few Hull FC supporters who mourned the passing of Speedway in the City.

That was strangely ironic really, because it was only through the income gained from Hull Speedway that the Club had managed to keep going at all in the 70's, but things were progressing at Hull FC and Speedway had to go. Their promoter Ian Thomas threatened Court action and with claims and counterclaims being exchanged in the local media, it all got very messy. However at Hull FC we were all engrossed in a superb run in the John Player Trophy which was good considering we had been decimated by injuries but at least Dane O'Hara had recovered after that serious injury sustained on his debut and was back in full training.

Dane had his comeback game at Wigan on 25th October when we won at Central Park for the first time in 59 years. That day the Hull fans were still singing on the terraces long after all the home fans had left the ground, for it was a memorable victory. After 30 consecutive defeats over there in darkest Lancashire the famous old ground rocked to the sound of 'Old Faithful', being sung after the game by 1000 Hull fans who simply wouldn't go home. Instead we remained and sang "Hello, Hello, FC are back, FC are back" till we were hoarse and the stewards threw us out.

Up to the final ten minutes, when we only led by 5 points, we were all convinced that Wigan would come back to snatch a victory from 'the jaws of defeat'. However then everything clicked into place and Leuluai, playing out of position at stand-off half dominated the final action. Firstly he scored a fabulous try after bursting clear and rounding the Wigan full back Birts with ease and then he put O'Hara in for his first try for the Club, after Paul Prendiville had run 50 yards downfield with the Wigan chasers in his wake. In the end we won 18-5, and everyone in Rugby League started to sit up and take notice.

Judas Priest hit town with a 'Hog' up the City Hall stairs

I hardly had time to celebrate after that great win before I was thrown straight back into work. Although we still saw artistes like Max Jaffa and Billie Joe Spears visiting the City Hall technical improvements had certainly made the big Rock Promoters of the Country start to consider us. We staged our biggest concert so far on 6th November when heavy metal giants 'Judas Priest' took the stage. They were real 'Rock Stars' and all arrived in separate black limos which were parked in a row on the pavement outside the venue in Paragon Street; much to the consternation of the local traffic wardens. Their dressing room 'rider' included, "12 dustbins filled with ice, with ten bottles of 'Moet and Chandon' in each". The event was promoted by local Grimsby Promoter Steven Stanley's Solid Entertainments agency and the stuff he was asked to supply for the band was quite unbelievable and included Venison, Quail, boxes of Turkish Delight with the icing sugar removed and 10lbs of grapes 'stripped from their stalks'. Afterwards in the dressing rooms, most of this was left untouched.

It was the first date on the tour and the stage show itself was spectacular to say the least, with dry ice (delivered from A. J. K. Cold Stores on Hessle Road by men in protective suits, who looked like they would be better placed at Cape Canaveral), and seven smoke machines. In the song 'Killing Machine' the band actually shot real machine guns (loaded with blanks) into the air and in 'Hell Bent on Leather' lead vocalist Rob Halford rode a Harley Davidson onto the Stage. Getting that into the building was challenging to say the least, it wouldn't fit in the lift and so we ended up allowing one of the 'Roadies' to ride it up the red carpeted foyer stairs into the Hall. That was certainly a sight I will never forget.

It was great night of Rock 'opera' but sadly the public didn't share my enthusiasm and only 1,200 people attended leaving Steven Stanley, who as local promoter was certainly at the end of the financial 'food chain', severely out of pocket. The drama didn't end there either, because during the concert, several people walking past outside the Hall thought the place was on fire because of the amount of 'stage' smoke coming out of the windows. They rang the fire brigade who arrived ten minutes later......in six fire engines with sirens wailing! The show was just too big for the stage and directly afterwards the group's management made the decision to scrap a lot of the lighting rig and effects for the rest of the tour. Two days later we promoted the greatest Jazz violinist there ever was when 74 years old Stephan Grappelli took to the stage. I don't remember his Dressing Room rider but it probably included Sanatogen, haemorrhoid cream, and a bath with a door in it.

A naked lady doesn't hit the headlines

Later that month, still on the Heavy Metal theme, we hosted the last night of the 'Gillan' tour which featured the ex lead singer of Deep Purple on his third solo outing around the World. He demanded an equally extensive and bizarre 'Rider' which included Jacob's Cream Crackers and "Three tins of Carnation Milk", as well as the mandatory, crates and crates of beer. The last night of most tours is always a nightmare for venue managers. The crew are tired, bits of the kit are starting to fail and the whole proceedings are notorious for the staging of pranks and jokes both on and off stage.

That evening however it appeared that we had got away without anything untoward happening. In fact the only mishap that had occurred was when the drummer Mike Underwood first struck his drums to be confronted by clouds of talcum powder which had been placed on the skins by the road crew. However I had heard that there was to be a surprise during the band's final encore (a rendition of Deep Purple's famous anthem 'Smoke on the Water') and so, in an attempt at self preservation, as the iconic opening riff rang out from the stage, I escorted the Hull Daily Mail's reporter, and then 'Mail Beat' columnist, David Blows to the bar. Seconds later a beautiful young lady wearing only high heeled shoes and a smile walked onto the stage. Those were more conservative times but thankfully for me, such was the draw of a free beer to the local 'Journo' he never got wind of what had happened, the appearance didn't make the front page next day and the venue and the Authority again got away with its reputation intact.

At the Boulevard the Board was as always on the lookout for new players and despite being in the middle of a 9 game winning run, we signed centre Terry Day from Wakefield and scrum half Kevin Harkin from York. These announcements and our recent results, meant that our administration were certainly popular with the fans and that led to me attending my shortest ever Shareholder's Meeting, when the whole proceedings at the Royal Station Hotel, lasted just 29 minutes. After much success on the field the Club announced increased profits of £60,000 but this was tempered by Roy Waudby who also announced a new share issue to assist, he said "With the further development of the Club".

I was certainly perturbed to hear in his closing remarks that at the end of the season the Club were reviving their plan to pull down my old spiritual home the Threepenny Stand. Still the sweet smell of success was in the air that night and this, as with everything else discussed, went by unchallenged from the 'floor' of the meeting.

The road to revenge

The John Player Trophy had, as a competition, certainly gained a lot more popularity since our last appearance in the Final back in 1976 when David Doyle-Davidson's 'raggle taggle' heroes ran the cup kings of Widnes, so close. The competition was now receiving good coverage from the BBC on Grandstand and although the luck of the draw (as far as home games were concerned), seemed to have deserted us that year, it was inconsequential really as we beat Halifax and Castleford away but then just when we needed a home draw in the quarter finals we were drawn away at Barrow. So it was on Saturday 14th November at 7-00am that bleary eyed and still half asleep', the 'Mermaid' coach left Boothferry Estate and headed off towards North West Lancashire and the Rugby League outpost of Barrow.

Barrow had been the 'surprise package' of the tournament thus far and really fancied their chances at home in front of a partisan crowd who always made it a hard place for other teams to visit. We arrived in Barrow-in-Furness at around 11-00am and went straight to the British Legion Club with whom Landlord Barry had made one of his 'prior arrangements'. I remember little of the drinking or eating that day but 'Hard Up Harry' actually took some money for a change and even won the Club's raffle which was a £20 meat voucher for the local butchers. He promptly sold it to a barmaid for £10 and so with a little arm twisting actually bought the one and only round of drinks I ever remember him purchasing!

The game itself was to be a tense bruising encounter which certainly had the whole of the crowd of over 9,000 on their toes throughout. From the start Barrow poured towards our line and in the first five minutes their prop Herbert twice shot through our defence, scattering tacklers as he went. Onward poured Barrow and from a tap penalty Mason broke free of a tackle by Tindall and Crane and dived over under the sticks as with just five minutes gone the home side took a deserved 5-0 lead.

Things looked ominous too as from the re-start the Hull defence had to race back to tackle Hadley who had been put through a big gap by scrum half Cairns, who was controlling things for the home team. Then at last we started to find some space and after some enterprising play from centre's Leuluai and Harrison, Barrow were penalised and young Lee Crooks landed a good straight penalty to reduce the arrears to 3 points.

Hull then started to turn the screw and with 25 minutes gone their pressure finally paid off when Duke shovelled the ball from the scrum, Norton took it forward to the line but lost it backwards in the tackle, Day had the presence of mind to pick it up and dive over under the posts and a Crooks conversion saw us leading 7-5.

The second half started with Barrow pressing again but with 9 minutes gone Norton spotted an opening and shot through it. We all thought that the break was in vain because no one appeared to be backing up, but as 'Knocker' hung a high looping pass in the air for what seemed like an age, from nowhere Terry Day snatched the hanging ball and beating the cover, touched down near the corner flag. Crooks missed the chance to improve the try but at 10-5, we all started to breathe a little more easily.

However our relief was short lived as Tindall was penalised by referee Mr Fox for stealing the ball and Tickle reduced the deficit to just one try with a 'steepling' penalty kick from 35 yards. A great break by the home sides centre McConnell had try 'written all over it' but somehow with no one anywhere near him he dropped the ball and Charlie Stone picked it up to defuse the situation, but we were struggling to keep Barrow at bay.

At the back Barrow's Tickle seemed to be able to field everything we hoisted towards him and so Norton decided to run the ball at the end of a 'set' on the 63rd minute. He drew the defence and sent Crane running towards the Barrow winger who had dropped back anticipating the usual kick. As the defender approached, Mick passed back inside to Norton who sent Leuluai racing away to score in the corner and with seventeen minutes to go we led 13-7 but again Crooks failed to improve the score. That was the signal for Barrow, roared on by a partisan home crowd, to make one last desperate effort. 'Barrowvians', with a fierce sense of community fostered by their isolation, are proud people and as the gloom gathered they certainly let us know that they were there doing their bit for their heroes.

We had to defend three sets of six before a Kemble break relieved the pressure and Mick Crane dropped a goal to stretch our lead to 14-7. With 6 minutes to go and both our substitutes, Lloyd and Banks on the field, the game took another twist when Barrow's Lupton made a break and was just held by Stone before Tickle almost got in but was tackled by Duke at the foot of the post. From the play the ball Cairns shot through and following an easy conversion, there were just two points in it.

In what must have been an exciting encounter for the television audience, on the terraces as the rain started, we were all now very nervous with many unable to watch at all as a perfectly good shoulder charge by Mick Crane on Szymala saw Referee Fox award the home side a penalty to the left of the posts 35 yards out from the line. After taking an age to prepare the kick, up stepped Tickle to stroke the ball inches past the left upright, and we all breathed again. In the final minute we faced another Barrow onslaught after Harkin was penalised on half way for feeding the scrum, but we survived and hung on for a great if not fortuitous win.

A drinking town with a fishing problem

That night in a depressed City where the fishing industry and its ancillary trades had all but disappeared, folks were out of work and times were hard, the whole of West Hull, who hadn't travelled to Barrow, used the televised victory as an excuse to celebrate. We arrived back at around 10-00pm and had a few beers in the 'Mermaid' where everyone was merry, singing and falling around after watching the game in the bar that afternoon.

It's funny what you remember and that night I was disappointed that we had missed 'Cockle' Humphrey, who used to come into the pub at around 9-30pm on weekend nights selling shellfish. He was a real character dressed in a long white smock coat, and carrying a big wicker basket stuffed with polystyrene trays of shrimps, whelks, mussels and of course Cockles. These were covered in cling film and 'spiced up' somewhat by the condiments served from a large vinegar bottle and salt pot that he carried in his large patch pockets. After a few pints there was nothing I liked more than a bit of sea food, so after that mammoth journey home, I was sorry I'd missed him!

The Cup draw took place that Monday evening on BBC Look North when we were pitted against Oldham thus avoiding Hull KR and setting up a possible 'return' final at Headingley. The formalities of an easy win over the Lancastrian side were played out at Headingley on Saturday 28th November, when we were victorious 22-8. Rovers got through too and so the stage was set for a 'revenge mission'. That Final was to be against the team we all 'loved to hate' and the one that had broken our hearts at Wembley just a year and a half previously. Retribution was in the air and the City of Kingston upon Hull was 'bouncing'.

Chapter Two

Slade 'Bring the House Down' and Charlie gets a fine!

Perhaps in starting this the second chapter of the story of one ordinary guy's fanatical obsession for his Rugby League team, I should apologise, because so far, it's been all working, drinking and supporting Hull FC. However the day job back then was taking up around 60 hours a week, I just had to be there when the 'Airlie Birds' played and the lure of a great little pub like the Punch Hotel just across the road was really all there was time for. In between I tried to look after myself as best I could and I was probably the best customer for those sloppy Fray Bentos tinned meat pies in the whole of the City. Back then mine was a pretty singular existence.

The City Hall programme was a relentless procession of Carol Services and Christmas Parties but, on 8th December 1981 another sell out rock concert saw Slade continue their triumphant 'Lock up your Daughters' tour, with their first gig in Hull for many years. Their new found popularity, after several years in the doldrums, came about after they had been the surprise success of that summer's Reading Festival, when the band took over from the withdrawn Ozzie Osbourne.

Most members of Slade had by this time, 'seen it all' and certainly quietened down from their hell raising days of the early 70's, most that is with the exception of 'Super Yob' Dave Hill. He turned up for the sound-check that afternoon in an outrageous outfit that included a voluminous purple silk blouse, a bandana tied round his shaven head and the tightest leather jeans and highest stacked heeled boots I had ever seen. As he tottered in at the back of the hall, and to screams of laughter from the sound crew and the rest of the band, Noddy Holder shouted from the stage, "Look out lads here comes Lady John Silver",

The concert was as usual just one big party which started with a thunder flash and Noddy screaming out the first line of 'Get Down and Get with It' from the depths of a darkened stage. That night Slade included all their hits and some of their more recent material like 'Wheels ain't Coming Down' and 'We'll Bring the House down'. They used copious amounts of smoke and dry ice and also featured their 'low tech' but long established tradition of throwing toilet rolls from the stage into the crowd, (something that always pleased the cleaners next morning). The whole evening finished as it always did, (be it a Summer Festival or Christmas concert) with Noddy dressed in a Father Christmas outfit, belting out 'Merry Xmas Everyone' as the crowd all sang along. What a night and what a mess to clear up next morning! Still, I wouldn't have minded so much had I not discovered that the toilet rolls they threw had actually been 'nicked' from the back stage toilets before the show. 'Rock and Roll eh?'

Although a totally different type of entertainment, two days later I enjoyed going to the Boulevard and watching a game of rugby lacking the stress and tension that I usually experienced when watching Hull FC. The occasion was an International between England and France which the 'Brits' won 37-0. The game was almost called off because of a heavy overnight frost but despite the cold, 13,000 attended and enjoyed a great encounter featuring some superb tries and our own Steve Norton being named 'Man of the Match'.

That winter weather meant it was the only game we saw that month. In fact we didn't see a home game between the 22nd November when we lost to Bradford Northern, and the 3rd January 1982 when we defeated Hull KR.

The problems I discussed earlier concerning egos and discipline within the Hull FC squad were still apparent. Next to be in trouble was likeable second row forward Charlie Stone who missed training and thus selection for the next game, claiming that he had contracted the flu, only for him to appear the same night at Keith Tindall's Testimonial Dinner at the Willerby Manor Hotel. That got Charlie a two game ban and no doubt a loss of wages.

'Cold as Christmas' but a Derby victory always warmed us up!

Sunday 3rd January 1982   *Hull 11 – Hull KR 1*

While the bad weather curtailed most live sport across the country everyone in West Hull was looking forward, with retribution in mind, to another final appearance at Headingley, when Hull would meet the 'old enemy' in the John Player Final. Quite amazingly the two Clubs had joined forces and asked the Rugby League to put the prices up so that they could make a bit more money out of the showpiece game. They asked for ground admissions to go up by 50p and for seating prices to increase by £1-50 a request that was turned down by the governing body on 23rd December.

After the frost and snow had subsided the first game played after the long lay-off was the traditional New Year fixture against the same Hull KR at the Boulevard. The Boxing Day game at home to York had been cancelled as snow fell on the pitch and as Eddie Waring was no doubt celebrating his OBE in the New Year's Honours List, Arthur Bunting brought the players in for extra training on New Year's Day.

The Boulevard was finally declared playable by referee Billy Thompson on the eve of the Derby and so at last we had some rugby to watch as 17,229 people packed the Boulevard to see Hull victorious by 11-1. After that confidence boosting win all the talk was of securing tickets, arranging transport and where the 'Mermaid' coach would stop for 'pre drinks', before the big Final on the 23rd.

However another row broke out between the two local Clubs and the Rugby League, this time about the allocation of tickets for the game.

It appeared that all the best seats had gone to the governing body and Peter Darley, Hull FC's Secretary, ironically said, "True fans are being asked to pay too much for poor seats". Not bad, we thought, from a Club who four weeks earlier had requested that the prices go up anyway!

Stuck in a lift with a Haystack!

Since that afternoon of the big debate in the Guildhall about staging Wrestling in the City Hall, the promotions by Jackie Pallo and his associates had been going reasonably well. However I was then approached by Relwyskow and Green the famous West Yorkshire Promoters (who had traditionally staged their shows at Madeley Street Baths on Hessle Road) with a view to them also using the Hall. Their first show was staged on Tuesday 19th January and featured some well known 'TV' wrestlers including, Adrian Street, 'Kojak' Kirk, Johnny Saint, Jim Breaks and a top of the bill pairing between Wild Angus and the legendary wild man of Wrestling 'Giant Haystacks'. 'Stacks' was a 'private' character who didn't like to be seen until he arrived in the ring. Most wrestlers didn't really care much and walked through the Main Hall around tea time with a cheery smile, and a duffle bag slung over their shoulders, but Giant Haystacks thought he was too big a star for that.

So that day I waited for him at the stage door to bring him up the backstage lift to the dressing rooms. At 5-00pm a battered white transit van with the front number plate hanging on by a single screw, pulled up and out of a specially adapted rear compartment complete with 'throne like' chair, struggled the man himself, all 33 stone of him. He was huge and obviously had difficulty getting clothes to fit him as the ones he wore looked like they had been 'adapted' with a pair of scissors. His hair was thick and greasy, although he wasn't the sort of guy that you would ask when he'd last washed it! I guided him to the lift which was pretty small and showed him the controls. He looked at me, then at the buttons, then back at me and grunted; obviously I had to take him up!

I shut the doors and closed the sliding gates. At first the lift started to rise, then gave a judder and stopped altogether between floors. 'Mr

Haystack' just parted his hair looked at me and said "Stuck!". "Wow" I thought, "He's bright for a Wrestler!" After a few minutes of me shouting and him grunting and sweating profusely, it was all starting to get a bit smelly.

Finally we were discovered but it was an hour before the lift engineer arrived to 'hand crank' us back down again, and in that time we didn't exchange a single word. Still the lift technician was brave indeed, because I remember as we finally got down again, he said to the Wrestler, "You're a bit too fat for that lift mate". I just looked at my shoes whilst 'Stacks' snarled at him and grunted again. That was the last time I ever went in that back stage lift at the City Hall with anyone.

Talking of lifts, later that year a temporary member of staff who was covering for Charlie, managed to get the whole of the Vienna Boys Choir stuck in the lift at the front of the building. I told him to "Bring the choir up in the Lift" but apparently omitted to say "but not all at once!" On that occasion the lift again stopped this time with just a foot gap at the top of the lift cage and it must have been an unforgettable experience for those 25 cherubic Austrian choir boys, as Frank and I dragged them through the gap, one by one, by their arm pits.

Big trouble at Boothferry Park

Sport in Hull, and more particularly its supporters, was starting to suffer somewhat at the hands of the media. The memory of that Good Friday riot at the Boulevard was re-kindled when after a Third Round Cup Replay against Chelsea at Boothferry Park, some idiotic City fans 'bricked' the Chelsea team coach and then threw bottles at the players as they tried to get off it. One missile hit goal keeper Steve Francis in the eye and he had two stitches inserted into a broken eye socket. The national papers loved this sort of thing and were full of it next day. However despite what was fast becoming a real concern for the Police, the sports clubs and the citizens of Hull, the Black and White supporters had just one thing on their minds; Cup revenge against Hull KR.

Revenge is a dish best served ... by Ronnie Wileman!

Saturday 23rd January 1982   Hull 12 – Hull Kingston Rovers 4

The much awaited John Player Cup Final was played at Headingley on a freezing cold Saturday afternoon. This venue was always chosen for these mid winter games because it still had under soil heating, to keep the surface temperature just above freezing. We had several players out injured and on the terraces we fretted and worried about the possibility of a repeat of what happened the last time the two rivals met in a Final, in 1980. There was a lot at stake because as always with local Derbys you couldn't lose. Losing to Rovers in a final is worse than death, because at least with death you don't have to go to work next morning.

We needn't have been concerned however because the game turned out to be both memorable and rewarding, featuring as it did two players being sent off, an amazing 50 yard try by our hooker and several Hull KR players refusing to go up for their loser's medals at the end! That final act of petulance didn't surprise us FC fans at all, but was, in hindsight, probably instigated after our Captain Charlie Stone went up to receive the Trophy, despite being sent off with 'Rovers' player Holdstock towards the end of the match. Charlie was never far from controversy and probably gained a deal of notoriety with the games historians that day. Afterwards he was hailed as the only skipper to have ever raised a trophy after being dismissed during a game.

The Final itself was a dour affair played out on glue pot pitch with plenty of aggression between the games two greatest rivals. The Wileman try was the only one scored and many of the national papers next day commented that unlike the Wembley Final, on this occasion it was Hull KR who appeared to be the 'bad guys' resorting to cynical and often 'rough house' tactics, whilst Hull FC concentrated on playing rugby, tactics that in the end proved to be a winning formula.

After the final whistle had sounded and as the strains of 'Old Faithful' echoed around the ground, the 'sweet smell of revenge' was everywhere, as we sang and sang well after the players had left the field. That day it was the turn of the Hull KR fans to trudge off home shaking their heads and rueing several missed chances that could have swung the game their way.

However, if I have just one lasting recollection of that match it has to be that Ronnie Wileman touch-down. That try was so special and will live in the memory of those that attended the game forever, because it was scored by a small, nuggety, 'Pocket battleship' of a player who, as well as being a wonderful hooker, was a real character. A tough Featherstone lad, Ron was an uncompromising competitor and a real 'mud ball' of a hooker.

On the day of the final, he seemed unlikely to play at all having aggravated an old injury at training that morning. However injuries never seemed to stop Ronnie and by 2-30pm he was out there battling his way through the game in his usual manner. In the 27th minute when we held a slender 2-0 lead, Mick Crane was tackled just inside our half in front of the North Stand. Ronnie stepped forward, scooped up the ball from acting halfback and from 50 yards out, started to lope down 'the blind-side'. Further and further he progressed with the Rovers' cover, led by George Fairburn, gaining by the second and just as they caught him, he dived over in the corner for the most memorable of scores. It is still debatable to this day as to whether he put the ball down properly, but who cares!

Everyone who saw him play will have a Ronnie story but his career was probably capped by that fantastic run away try, it was simply magnificent. After the game it is said that when the lads came back on the coach to Hull for a night out on the town Ronnie, who had been celebrating hard all the way home, hung the trophy out of the coach's rear emergency exit window and was seen to be swinging it around as they drove along Ferensway.

Wileman signed for Hull FC from York, he was a miner and had a reputation as a youngster for coming straight off shift and onto the rugby field. He was certainly talented and a great passer of the ball, although in the days when you had to win the ball from the scrums, he was also a tough individual who was never adverse to an exchange of punches if the opportunity presented itself. The bigger the forward the more Ronnie liked it.

That great day when he scored THAT try after being so near to missing out on playing altogether, Hull coach, Arthur Bunting said, "You can't stop Ronnie when he wants to play" and so it was! A hero was crowned. Wileman only played 87 first team games for Hull but he scored 23 tries, many of which unlike the try in that final, were brave, scrambling efforts from close to the line.

I can still picture that tousle haired muddy little character, throwing himself into tackle after tackle and often scaring forwards twice his size to death! He could measure a pass to perfection and on the heavy pitches he was a tenacious tackler. He never looked 'smart', even when dressed in his Wembley suite, because Ronnie always appeared more comfortable caked in mud sliding through the scrum to reach the ball, or sitting in some local hostelry after the game amusing the rest of the team with his best pal Tony Dean as they did their infamous Cannon and Ball impersonations. Our Ronnie was quite a guy!

The Mermaid gang's tribute to Ronnie!

For me, with Wileman, it's not just the player himself that features in my memories but also the ritual that evolved for the members of those 'Mermaid' coach trips. As the Coach had broken down several times on journeys to Lancashire in the past, the bus containing Garry, Trevor the Fish, Charlie and all the usual suspects would set off from the pub on Boothferry Estate, much earlier than was needed. Invariably, we would get to a predetermined 'watering hole' with time to spare and at about half past eleven you could often see 40 or more Hull FC supporters kicking their heels in the deserted car park of a public house in some far away destination in Cheshire, Lancashire or even Cumbria. Sometimes the back door of the hostelry would swing open and a hand would beckon us all in but often we just stood there staring at the sky...'thirstily', waiting for 12 noon.

Then the shout would go up 'Let's do a Ronnie!' and with great enthusiasm grown men, some in their seventies, would shed their coats and jackets and 'set up' to recreate that piece of action at Headingley. Every week, until in the end it had no comedic value at all, 'Zorro' Mortenson (don't ask me about the name, I have no idea), who was 30 stone and well over 60 would say, "I'll be Fairburn (Hull KR's full back), I've got his pace", and so the drama unfolded using a duffle bag, full no doubt with someone's sandwiches, for a ball.

Anyone passing on those Sunday mornings, in say Leigh, Whitehaven or Widnes, would no doubt rub their eyes as they witnessed 20 or so men running up and down a pub car park shouting 'Run Ronnie Run!!!' and that, long before Winston Groom had even written 'Forrest Gump'. In the early 80's one thing was for sure, everyone in West Hull loved Ronnie Wileman.

Another signing that makes the rest of the League take notice

After that great final victory Chairman Roy Waudby treated the whole squad and coaching staff to a short break in Spain but by the time they returned, the rumours were circulating that the Club had been lining up two big signings. Roy himself confirmed that this was true but declined to 'name names' until the deals were done. We didn't have to wait long and on 4th February Hull revealed the signing of 24 year old International Stand-Off Half Steve Evans from Featherstone for a fee in the region of £70,000. Evans was probably the best young half back in the Country and only a week after he signed he was named as Captain of the Great Britain Under 24's to play Australia. Evans achieved a unique feat by this move too because he was the only player to have ever played for a team knocked out of one Cup competition and then to win it with another. We signed him just 4 days before the Challenge Cup registration dead-line but he had played for Featherstone the previous week against Hull KR. However, Steve then went on to play in every round, the final and final replay, for Hull FC.

The Club were certainly ambitious and were still pressing ahead with their plans for a new Threepenny Stand and in the match day

programme they were advertising the price of the seats in there, for the following season.

Alf on 'the Oche'

Sunday 14th March 1982   *Hull 16 – Halifax 10*

On 5th March I went to the Westfield Club in Cottingham with Trevor, Barry and Garry to watch the finals of the 'Humber Bridge Match Play Darts Competition' and despite a bit of a scare in the final we were all delighted to see 'Super' Alf Macklin, the FC hero of the 70's, win the Trophy. Jim Bowen of TV's 'Bullseye' fame told a few jokes and made the presentation of an imposing Cup and a cheque for £200. Macklin was a fine darts player and would go on to win more trophies and become a well known personality on the local Darts scene. There was a scare on Sunday 14th March down at the Boulevard too, as Hull FC almost got dumped out of the Challenge Cup at the quarter final stage by a feisty Halifax side. On a rain soaked 'mud bath' of a pitch, we came close to defeat when with the scores locked at 10-10 Gary Kemble pulled off a couple of try and indeed game saving tackles. Then as the crowd of over 16,000 held their breath, Topliss dropped a goal and finally in the last few minutes we stretched our lead to a match winning seven points when Charlie Stone put Paul Prendiville in at the corner and with Sammy Lloyd landing a magnificent conversion from the touch line, we were through to the semi-finals again.

Despite one or two players being full time, many back then had other jobs and Paul Prendiville the hero in that quarter final was, I remember, getting quite an interesting reputation as a bricklayer. Although these days he is a builder of much repute, back then one of his first jobs was at the home of ex-player Barry Edwards. Barry tells a great story about the 60 foot wall at the front of his house on Hessle High Road that 'Taffy' first built back in 1982. According to Barry the job took three days. Prendiville built 30 foot on the first day, another 30 foot on the second and on the third day, according to Barry....it fell down!!!! Great winger but back then, a questionable bricklayer!

Back in the 60's and 70's, as I recorded in my first book, Hull City were certainly top dogs as far as sport in the City was concerned. However now they were 'hitting the buffers' in a big way. That April in fact, City fans had to endure the spectacle of the famous old North Stand (or the 'The Clock End'), at Boothferry Park being bulldozed to make way for a Supermarket and worse was to follow as Hull FC's Chairman Roy Waudby and City's Chief Christopher Needler started informal talks about the two Clubs getting together, redeveloping the Boulevard and sharing our Stadium in future seasons. However Needler then appeared to run out of patience (and money) and put the Club up for sale, whilst at the same time calling in the Official Receivers.

Judy Tzuke

Music wise, as I said previously, things at Hull City Hall were always quiet at the start of the year, however no doubt starved of live entertainment the public of Hull turned out in force on 18th March when Judy Tzuke appeared as part of her 'Shoot the Moon' tour. She has always been an amazing performer and her rendition of 'Stay with me till Dawn' that night is still one of the most atmospheric and touching live performances I have ever seen. The concert was staged by promoter Phil McIntyre who was just starting out on his way to becoming one of the Country's top musical entrepreneurs.

Phil later moved on to manage many of the top British comedians and is now often identified as the producer of some of the top comedy programmes on British TV. Back then he was a keen young businessman and dressed in overalls and looking more like a painter than an impresario, he was to bring several big acts to the City Hall in the future months.

We're back at Wembley again....just!

Saturday 27th March 1982   *Hull 15 – Castleford 11*

After battling our way through the early rounds, Hull FC arrived at another Challenge Cup semi final which was a listless, close, affair that in the end we just won 15-11. It was a torrid match which prompted ex Castleford player Steve Norton to ironically comment as he left the field at the end, covered in blood and bandages, "I'm just glad I was playing against my old pals!" Castleford were intent on scrapping their way to Wembley and the Headingley crowd of just over 20,000 looked on as Norton and O'Hara scored early tries for Hull. A late Prendiville touchdown put paid to a strong Castleford come back and once again the fans were back queuing in Airlie Street for tickets with all the camaraderie and humour that involved. I honestly believe that probably honed by years of wartime rationing, the British 'queuing gene' ensures that we are often at our happiest in that state of united anticipation. We were off to Wembley again this time to face the much acclaimed 'Cup Kings' of Widnes.

The 'Falklands Conflict' which in essence started in a dispute between Great Britain and Argentina over the sovereignty of two pieces of British rock in the Southern Atlantic Ocean, was to reach boiling point that Spring as Margaret Thatcher put on her breastplate, the talking stopped and we went to war. A massive flotilla of ships of all shapes and sizes headed by HMS Hermes and HMS Invincible set sail for the little islands and on 21st April the Passenger Ferry the 'Norland', left Hull after being hastily converted into a troop carrier. Captain Ellerby and his crew bade farewell to the folks on the quayside in King George Dock and set off to war wondering, I guess, whether they would be coming back again in one piece. It was a surreal feeling for everyone and of course a tough time for the loved ones left behind. It was also moving to see so many folks on the dockside in their Hull and Hull KR shirts and scarves as they waved goodbye to the lads on board and many tears were shed that day.

Kensington, Harrods and the Prince of Wales in Drewery Lane....'Wembley Weekends' with the Mermaid

It was a long way to the Falklands and a strange calm descended across the nation as the 'Task Force' made its way across the equator and into the South Atlantic, whilst back in Hull everyone tried to get on with life as usual. Nothing was usual for us lot though and despite these national distractions most of West Hull was gripped with Cup Final fever. It was, along with the imminent conflict, the only topic of conversation there was and once again the queues for tickets stretched down Airlie Street and onto the Boulevard, as day after day the fans lined up to get their 'passport' to watching their team walk out on the hallowed turf of the National Stadium. Personally I didn't have to do any of the queuing stuff because since the 1980 season I had been a member of first the Half Way Hotel's 'Wembley Weekend Club' and then, when Landlord and Landlady Barry and Joan Nicholson moved onto the Mermaid Hotel, I joined their annual outing.

There was a great tradition of these trips to the Challenge Cup Final being organised by the pubs and clubs of the area and it was estimated that back then around 100 of them, of varying sizes, were organised each year in the region. Of course when you started to pay your weekly subscription in June, you had no idea whatsoever who would be playing but in the six years that I went, I was really lucky because on four occasions, it was my team Hull FC that featured.

However these trips were not always enjoyable for everyone and every year you would hear or read of some unfortunate band of fans left waiting outside their pub or on Paragon Station for their transport and tickets which never materialised. Usually, the person organising the outing had absconded with the members' subscriptions or more likely spent them throughout the year as they collected them.

Our trip, which included a three night stay in the Capital, was popular and attracted around 75 members. Each Sunday Joan and Barry would sit at a table in the pub collecting our £2's which were recorded on our payment cards and in a large leather bound ledger. The trip was certainly good value for money because for your £100 you received train travel to and from London, good tickets for the game and three night's accommodation in a 4 or 5 star hotel. The local travel agents in the City had identified these trips as a good source of business and so Thomas Cook and Matador Travel to name but two had staff specifically dedicated to dealing with the needs of these 'Wembley Clubs'

We always stayed in a top hotel, and the fact that we never ever seemed to go to the same one twice probably indicated the proprietor's dislike for some of the antics the 'Mermaid' gang got up to. That year we stayed in the International Hotel in Knightsbridge, which was an imposing building with a giant rotating globe on the forecourt. The look on the faces of the Bell boys, Reception Staff and Porters as we arrived, some with leather luggage, others with plastic carrier bags, probably indicated that this would be our last visit to 'The International' too.

After seeing the team off from the Boulevard on the Wednesday, the whole adventure started on Thursday 29th April as our party congregated on Paragon Station ready to board 'Wembley Special No.4' that departed at 9-30 from the Excursion Platform adjacent to Anlaby Road. The bank rate had been kind to us that year and as was the custom any surplus finance from interest gained on the account was spent on cans of beer and bottles of wine for the train. That day we had six porter's barrows full of the stuff and a jolly and entertaining journey was assured. Travelling with us that year were Hard up Harry, Trevor the Fish and Garry. Trevor was his usual self, drinking copious amounts of beer and then having his customary snooze. However when we arrived at King's Cross some four hours later he was first out of his seat and sporting the usual cigar he got to the carriage door and jumped onto the platform to start his assault on the alcohol reserves of the Capital.

However as he landed on the platform his foot was instantly crushed by the metal wheel of a porters four wheel cart that was passing stacked high with cases (and plastic carrier bags). Trevor was obviously in pain but fortified by a couple of swigs from a can a passing 'well wisher' offered, he hobbled off down the platform singing, with the throng "We're the Famous Hull FC and were off to Wembley.....Wembley.... WEMBLEY" as the 'FC Army' began their quest to take over London. What a great feeling that was as we marched up the platform, banners unfurled and flags waiving. Trevor was obviously in some discomfort throughout the weekend but never missed a session or the game, although when we returned to Hull on the Sunday he went straight to Hull Royal Infirmary and was diagnosed with a broken ankle. If ever there was a better testament to the anaesthetic power of large doses of alcohol, I have yet to find it!

That afternoon, once we had checked into our rooms and marvelled at our tiled bathrooms, where Garry didn't quite get the bidet until Trevor quickly explained, "It's French for Bum Flusher", we all walked down the street to Harrods. There we whiled away the hours until opening time, marvelling at the 'knobs' doing their shopping. We all bought a sausage roll each, at some ridiculous price, just to obtain the Harrods bag that we insisted it came in. After tea at the Aberdeen Steak House, everyone crammed into taxis' and went to what was to be our second home whilst we were in the Capital 'The Prince of Wales' in Drewery Lane.

Those readers who have endured the first volume of this rambling journal will remember that I first visited that establishment when I travelled to London with some pals from St Matthew's Youth Club, to watch the a Great Britain v Australia International at Wembley. I then suggested in 1980, on the occasion of the Hull v Hull KR final, that it was a hostelry worthy of a visit and it was now our accepted 'London' base. Two years previously there had been a brilliant blind piano player to entertain us. Vernon could literally play anything although on the occasion of that previous visit I think by the time we left to make our way back 'Up North', he was sick and fed up of playing 'When the Red, Red Robin' and 'Old Faithful'. Still that Thursday as we opened the door and made our entrance, there he sat at the upright piano and as he thumped out the first bars of our spiritual anthem, we knew we were 'home'! Meanwhile, as we drank the hours away towards the Final the Hull team made their own preparations, well out of the way, at the Runnymede Hotel in Windsor.

No one knew quite what to do, the strangest Final ever!

Saturday 1st May 1982   *Hull 14 – Widnes 14*

The final itself was one of the strangest games I think I have ever attended although the imminent conflict in the Falklands made the pre-match singing of 'Abide with Me' led by Ken Dodd very moving, particularly as some people attending no doubt had friends and family out there in the South Atlantic on the Norland. In fact people who watched the game at home told me that the broadcast even experienced an unprecedented interrupted for a News Flash by Jan Leeming, about the 'Falklands Conflict' while the BBC even did a special relay to the Norland for the exiled FC fans sailing into the theatre of War.

There was also the first appearance of a short lived hero back then, a guy dressed in a gorilla suit and Hull FC scarf who joined in the half time marching display with the Coldstream Guards. However the fact that the game ended in a draw left me and everyone else there, whoever they supported, at a loss for what to do next! On the field the players were confused too and wandered about shaking hands whilst the officials clarified the situation and the announcement was made that there was to be a replay at a 'date and venue to be confirmed'.

In fairness when Wright intercepted a Hull pass on his own line and ran the length of the field to touch down and make the score 14-6 to Widnes, a draw seemed highly unlikely. We looked doomed until a Steve Norton 'Special' saw him scythe through the defence to touch down for a converted try and with the scores at 14-11 the Hull 'Faithful' found a new voice and roared on the team to a great finale. With time running out a break by Lee Crooks put Dane O'Hara away and he scored in the corner with some ease, only for Sammy Lloyd's conversion to drift, according to the Touch Judges, past the upright. To this day, Sammy will tell you that he believed it was so high the two officials got it wrong and the ball actually went over. Shortly after that action the game finished and a strange uneasy calm descended on the National Stadium. Next day, after a heavy night of revelry in the Prince of Wales, we arrived back at Paragon Station at noon and it was straight back to work, whilst Trevor went straight to the Casualty department at Hull Royal Infirmary. There is little doubt that what the Government today brand as Binge Drinking' was, back then in the early 80's, simply referred to as a 'Wembley Weekend'.

Fancy Dress at the Premiership Final

Saturday 15th May 1982   *Hull 8-Widnes 23*

The Challenge Cup Replay was scheduled for eighteen days later at Elland Road. That delay was down mainly to the extended season and the Premiership Trophy games that had to be accommodated in between. The players like the fans seemed to have that replay on their minds and as a team, although we beat St. Helens 23-8 and Warrington 27-7 in quick succession we were outplayed by Widnes in the Final on the Saturday before the replay, 23-8. However the fans decided that game was to be a fun event and part of the build up to the 'Big One' at Elland Road as hundreds turned out in fancy dress that day.

After that defeat the national and local media made the opposition big favourites for the 'Final Replay' the following Wednesday and I guess Widnes were pretty confident too as they were seen out Bowling in Leeds on the Monday and at Pontefract Races the day prior to the game, whilst at the Boulevard Arthur Bunting had everyone in the first team squad training every day, for the last and most important game of the season.

Panic, apprehension and a forty mile traffic jam

That famous Wednesday night in May 1982 I was (like thousands and thousands of the Black and White Army) to experience one of the longest traffic jams the M62 Motorway had ever seen. It was caused by 25,000 people all trying to get to Leeds at the same time. Most had just left work and were desperately trying to make the kick-off. The whole motorway was gridlocked with one of the worst jams that Humberside Police had ever experienced, stretching as it did from South Cave to the Leeds turn-off, a distance of around 40 miles!

I thought that we would be OK, as Barry, Ian, Trevor, Harry and I crammed into my lime green Opel Ascona to make what we thought would be the relatively short journey to the game. We started well, but hit heavy traffic at about 4-30pm on the A63 at South Cave. We made slow progress to the North Cave turn-off, a distance of 3 miles that took around 35 minutes and from a position where I thought we had loads of time, I was starting to panic. I would have no doubt consulted the others had they been awake, but as they had been drinking all afternoon they weren't, and so I took the decision to leave the Motorway and go down the old A63 through Newport and Howden, and over the toll bridge at Selby.

Several others had decided on the same course of action, but at least we kept moving as finally we arrived at the Outer Ring Road in Leeds. We worked our way around it until we got parked in Pleasant Street about a mile to the north of the ground and continued from there on foot to Elland Road, where we arrived at the turnstiles at about 7-15pm. The detour had certainly proved to be a good move as afterwards there were many stories about fans not getting to the game until after half-time.

Touching the Dream; A glorious night, a wonderful occasion, and a famous victory

Wednesday 19ᵗʰ May 1982   *Hull 18-Widnes 9*

After drawing at Wembley in such dramatic fashion and then getting drubbed by Widnes the previous weekend in the Premiership Final we were quite understandably a bit apprehensive as to the outcome of the replay. That was stress enough without being stuck in traffic for hours before we even got there! We had a few injuries from that Premiership Final too and Ronnie Wileman, the hero of our last Cup success in January, was replaced at hooker by veteran Tony Duke. However the biggest surprise was on the wing where Clive Sullivan, now 'A' team Player/Coach and another at the veteran stage of his career, replaced the injured Dane O'Hara. In addition to these enforced changes we found that Coach, Arthur Bunting had made a couple of tactical moves too. Terry Day was dropped to the bench and in came Tony Dean, for Kevin Harkin at scrum half, whilst Lee Crooks and another veteran Keith Tindall, started in place of Sammy Lloyd and Mick Crane.

The match kicked off with hundreds of people still arriving and numerous announcements being made for people to move to the front of the 'Kop' end. This action caused the crowd to spill onto the pitch on several occasions during the first half. Widnes kept faith with their full Wembley line up and were visibly surprised by the tenacity and spirit the patched up FC side displayed in the first few minutes of the game. On 20 minutes Widnes took the lead. Mick Burke kicked an audacious penalty goal from well inside his own half and as the ball flew through the posts the crowd, craning their necks to see the outcome, again tumbled onto the field behind the dead ball line.

As the half wore on and the crowd settled down, we started to exert some pressure which culminated in Hull producing two tries that will be seared into the memory of everyone who was there. They were actually that good that they will stay forever in this fans top ten 'Desert Island' tries of all time. Seven minutes from the break we were awarded a scrum inside the Widnes 25. This broke up and our adversaries were penalised. Dean took a quick tap behind the collapsed scrum and passed the ball to Norton. 'Knocker' quickly linked with Dave Topliss who found Gary Kemble on a superb inside run and he touched down before the Widnes' forwards could free themselves from the remnants of the scrum.

The next try came just on half time and featured that famous, 'Wrap round move' that was, back then, a trademark of Dave Topliss. Dean snatched the ball from a scrum and fed Leuluai, he passed to Topliss and then ran round him and gathered a return pass. This 'switch' move completely 'wrong footed' the Widnes defence and finished with Topliss touching down without a hand being placed on him. I can still see it now and will no doubt be able to until the day I die. Young Lee Crooks converted the first try but hit the post with his second attempt as, to the surprise of every one, we went in 8-2 up at half time.

The second half started with the expected Widnes' pressure which led to a successful penalty by Burke and when Wright overlapped on the wing they scored a try wide out although this time it was Burke's turn to hit the post and forfeit the two points. We looked down and out and as fans we feared the worst, however a pulsating chorus of "Come on You

Hulllaaarrr" circled the ground and the team responded brilliantly as great hands and a dummy from Norton sent 'Toppo' in from 15 yards out for another try. The capacity 41,711 crowd were then treated to some thrilling rugby as both sides tried to settle the game in their favour. In the end it was down to 18 year old Lee Crooks to fain a drop goal attempt and then dart over under the posts. The crowd behind him in the Kop went 'bonkers' and once again spilled over the fences and onto the pitch. Hull had won the Challenge Cup in one of the most exciting games I have ever seen.

For me the original game at Wembley was an anti climax, that I rarely re watch but over the years I have viewed that game at Elland Road over and over again and I still do, particularly when I feel a bit down in the dumps. Despite traffic jams, a weakened team and chaos on the terraces we had witnessed one of Hull FC's finest hours!

As Dave Topliss raised the Trophy aloft, the first Hull Captain to do it since the 1913/14 season, I was in pieces. It was then that I experienced that strange sensation of laughing whilst crying that only the sports fan (who thinks he has seen everything there is to see in his sport and who has so often been abused, goaded, broken hearted and disillusioned) really understands. It was a magical moment in a lifetime of following my Club, when just for a few hours I felt as though I was actually 'touching the dream'. In the dressing room afterwards a BBC TV audience of around 5 million saw Tony Duke respond to the question, "How did it feel as the final whistle went", by replying in his distinct Hull accent, "I bust out Roooring". Didn't we all Tony!

It was a great season....probably the best ever!

That 1981/82 campaign had been one of the most successful that our illustrious Club had ever experienced and I was honoured and a little humbled to be there at Elland Road that night to experience its amazing climax. The players were on a bonus of £1,200 a man to win the final, whilst a draw would bring them £500. In the end because of the replay, they got both payments; they all had a few beers and the Club made a fortune.

With all those spectators packed into Elland Road it was amazing when after the match West Yorkshire Police stated that despite all the traffic problems and congestion in the ground there was just one arrest that night and that for drunkenness well away from the ground. Broadcaster Simon Kelner probably witnessed this arrest as in his great book about Rugby League, 'To Jerusalem and back' he states that the only incident he saw, was a minor fracas in the Town Centre before the game when, "A Hull supporter dressed in a homemade black and white cape and a striped top hat tried to push into a taxi queue, claiming he was the Minister for Sport"

We all went to the Guildhall a couple of days later and watched as our heroes, many of whom had obviously 'had a few', raised the Cup in turn, under the watchful eye of Lord Mayor Councillor Phyllis Clarke. I then went round to the 'Watchman's Entrance', bluffed my way into the Reception and ducking a few flying bread cakes coming from the direction of Sammy Lloyd and Steve Norton, managed to get a souvenir menu card signed by all the players. Then it was time to reflect on an excellent season. Barry, Trevor, Garry, and a few of the other guys came back to the City Hall Flat were we watched the game again, raised a glass in celebration and savoured a moment that some fans never ever experience in a lifetime of supporting the team they love.

There was so much to celebrate as Hull FC had won two of the three principal trophies in the British game. On Friday 21st May we all went to the Boulevard for a Friendly game against Carlisle, which was Keith Tindall's Testimonial game. It was memorable because of a final appearance by that 'Gorilla' who had marched with the Coldstream Guards at Wembley and because 'joker' Tony Dean took over from the referee for a while.

Steve Norton was voted 'Truemann's First Division Player of the Season' and reached his 100th career try, while Arthur Bunting won 'Coach of the Season'. The average home gate was 13,190 and a new aggregate attendance record for the Boulevard of 197,844 was attained. We played 45 matches and lost just 7 and the Colts won all three of their trophies at junior level. What a year to be an FC fan, particularly if you had endured those barren and bleak 60's and 70's. Of course in the end it was those bad times that made that magnificent campaign, so, so sweet.

As a foot note, winning all those trophies did cause a few problems for the Club because when Hull FC had those Cups in Hull, the security at the Boulevard was so bad that the Police advised them to make 'alternative overnight arrangements' for their storage. Ivy and Ernie Mason those great stalwarts of the Club who lived just across Airlie Street in Graham Terrace, came to the rescue and ended up sleeping on numerous occasions with the Trophies 'under the bed'.

Adventures with Bucks Fizz and Worzel Gummidge

That summer the City Hall was reasonably quiet, but on the 22nd July there was a concert promoted by local radio presenters Tim Jibson and Steve Massam that featured kid's favourites of the time Bucks Fizz. Although there seemed to be children everywhere and the show was brilliant, sadly only 1300 tickets were sold and the lads lost a deal of cash that night. Still I managed to get sat next to female singer Jay Aston in the tour catering area and that made it a memorable night for me! Mind you, all she did was complain, about the hotel, her uncomfortable shoes and the quality of the cup of 'Council' tea she was drinking. She was certainly a bit 'pop starish' and even asked me what I knew about her and her career, I replied, "Not a lot but I do know that your middle name is Hilda", I don't know where I dragged that up from, but it certainly shut her up!

That year at Hull Show, I was again drafted into East Park this time to run the Entertainment Tent. As a new departure and to try and arrest flagging attendances, the Council decided to feature a 'celebrity' and settled for kids favourite and popular TV personality Worzel Gummidge played by Jon Pertwee. Charging the princely sum of £1,800, he arrived with a massive entourage of minders, managers and assistants and took two hours to get made up. However he walked around the showground frightening the children and amusing most of the adults and at 2-00 pm appeared in the Entertainment Tent which was packed with kids, prams and Mums and Dads.

I was backstage and as the compere Councillor Brian Petch, (a kid's entertainer himself) announced, "Here's Worzel Gummidge" and the place went wild. Pertwee however seemed reluctant to go on the stage and when I asked, "Are you OK" he turned to me and through a face full of straw and makeup said, "Ok?....OK?? I would be if it wasn't for all those f*cking kids"

This attitude extended onto the stage too and as the kids persisted in chanting, "Where's Aunt Sally?" (His girlfriend from the TV show) in exasperation he shouted, "The Council couldn't afford her!" Still, his presence at the show had the desired effect and attendances increased with over 35,000 people attending East Park over the two days.

Hull's 'White Star' is destined not to be in the ascendancy

Around the same time at Hull FC, we appointed our first full time Club Secretary and General Manager, Mike Dooley, who took over from new Vice Chairman Peter Darley. A tireless worker for the Club, Peter is probably best remembered by most Hull FC fans for an incident when the admissions from one match were stolen from the boot of his car while it was parked on his drive! Dooley however came from Leeds United and brought a lot of new commercial ideas with him. He subsequently announced that the Club was thinking of launching a new team in the Second Division called Hull White Star (our Club's original name) in which all our Colts and 'A' team players would feature. The Rugby League however took a dim view of this idea and blaming the possible implications of players being registered for two Clubs at the same time ensured that the idea never got off the ground.

August saw us play the newly formed Cardiff City in Clive Sullivan's Benefit Match at Boothferry Park while on the 23rd (on our way to play a game at Barrow and to solve our current 'hooking' problems) we signed Barry Bridges in the public bar of the Trafalgar Hotel in Blackburn.

We also had an interesting night at the Boulevard when there was an evening in aid of the 'Stadium Development Fund'. Organised by new Secretary Dooley, it was a floodlit Cricket Challenge between a Freddy Trueman XI and a Brian Close XI and included several big name players like Clive Lloyd, Colin Croft and Desmond Haynes. Two windows were smashed in houses in Carrington Street, behind the Best Stand, as Clive Lloyd cut loose and 6000 turned up for what was an enjoyable, if somewhat bizarre night; for me cricket and the Boulevard just didn't seem to go together at all.

The Yorkshire Cup Final and its Bradford Again

Saturday 7ᵗʰ October 1982   *Hull 18 – Bradford Northern 7*

The 1982/83 season threw up some interesting statistics none more so than the fact that we met Bradford Northern a total of five times, twice in the League, twice in the Cup (including a replay) and once in the Yorkshire Cup Final. We might have been going well but after we had fought our way through to the Yorkshire Cup Final at Headingley we met a Bradford team who were going through tough times. We in fact stood third in the First Division table whilst Northern were second from bottom.

For my part I travelled to the game on the 'Mermaid' coach that as usual visited 'The Three Horse Shoes' on Otley Road in Leeds before the game. We were really confident that day and with about 8000 FC fans making the trip out of a record Yorkshire Cup final attendance of over 11,000, no one gave Bradford a hope. However nobody told their players that!

Although we had a couple of withdrawals before the game, Bradford had real problems. Despite their first choice scrum half Alan Redfearn being withdrawn with a broken rib Bradford did have one secret weapon, their Coach, the wily and controversial Peter Fox. He was certainly a character, who when he came to the Boulevard with the Northern 'A' team would often exchanged insults with the regulars in the 'Threepenny Stand', expletives and all! That day 'Foxy' put together an excellent game plan that was almost Hull's undoing.

From the start it was apparent that the Bradford lads had decided that they would, by fair means or foul, stop everything or anybody that handled the ball. Their rugged defence led by full-back Keith Mumby had to be seen to be believed and despite an excellent Paul Rose try, another by Paul Prendiville and a drop goal from Crooks we only led 7-6 at half time. I remember the shock of that half time score sobered me up no end! The second half started with both teams exchanging drop goals and then Arthur Bunting brought Steve Norton on from the bench and the rest as they say is history!

'Knocker' immediately drew the defence to the right before firing out an immaculate inside pass for Rose to crash in for his second try, "There's only one Knocker Norton" resonated around the South Stand and we were on our way to winning another Cup Final. Crooks converted and added a penalty before Evans completed the scoring in the last minute and we lifted the Trophy!! We had really had a scare and as supporters we were drained by the end, but as always the celebrations were long and very loud and the feeling fantastic.

Sleeping rough in Leeds!

What a party we had afterwards as the team joined us in the bar under the Main Stand where Paul Prendiville led the 'choir' in several renditions of 'Old Faithful'. We filled the cup with Tetley's Bitter and were all still singing at 8-00pm. It was then, through an alcoholic haze, that the terrible truth struck me; I had forgotten to re join our coach at 6-00pm as arranged and so, with the lads from the 'Mermaid' now back in Hull, I'd been left behind.

Abandoned by my mates, 'alcoholic logic' pointed me towards a night out in Leeds and having been told by a couple of 'sage like' Leeds supporters who were obviously 'Only there for the beer', that the last train home was at 11-00pm, I accompanied these 'new found friends' around the City Centre pubs. We had a great night and I arrived back at Leeds City Station with five minutes to spare before my train left. However when I enquired of the chap at the barrier which train went to

Hull he said, "There's an 11-00 o'clock train every weekday night but the last one on a Saturday goes at 10-22!" I was stranded. Meandering down the platform in an alcoholic daze, I suddenly felt tired and, drained by all the emotion of the day, I staggered into a darkened railway carriage and slumping on the first seat I could find, I was asleep in seconds.

Perhaps it was just luck, or more likely the fact that it was Sunday next day, but when I awoke, the train and I were still in Leeds Station, although it was 7-30am on a chilly, bleak morning. I got off the train, (which I noticed had started its engine and had 'Skipton' displayed on the front destination board), and got home by a scheduled service to Hull. Everyone was enthralled as I reached the Mermaid (to pay my Wembley money) that lunchtime and commenced to relate the details of my adventure in Leeds. In the end, I finally arrived home at about 4-30pm, almost 24 hours after the final whistle had sounded at Headingley.

In the entertainment world, things were decidedly slow at the Hall but even worse over at the Hull New Theatre and I witnessed a long and vociferous debate in a Cultural Services Committee meeting at the Guildhall, when it was announced that 'Jesus Christ Superstar' had lost a staggering £30,000 on a three week run at the Theatre. One Councillor named Richard Barry, shook his head in disgust and under his breath muttered, "I reckon that we could have just about afforded JC in person, for that!"

Welcome to the Home of the Tubigrip Bandage
(When you see the sign for Oldham you know it's going to rain, if you can't see it..... it's already started)

Sunday 7ᵗʰ November 1982   *Hull 5-Oldham 2*

You'll remember no doubt my earlier reminiscences about those dreary trips to Leigh? Well now it's time to talk about another dank and dreary place and the highest ground in the Rugby League, 'the Watersheddings' in Oldham.

Games in the 80's were never entertaining affairs over there as the quality of rugby seemed to match the gloomy surroundings. I remember a game in late 1980 when we had all travelled to Oldham to witness a dire 2-1 defeat and we all knew that we could expect little different when we visited that November. We travelled over the Pennines as part of the usual away day outing, sipping our tinned Hansa Lager and peered through the steamy windows of the coach at the pouring rain outside. As we drove beneath the railway bridge that announced, 'Welcome to Oldham, home of the Tubigrip Bandage' we reflected on the fact that things must be pretty grim, if a bandage was the mill town's only real claim to fame.

If the place itself was dour, then the ground was even more stoic. Devoid of any signs of modernisation and precious little running water, it had a grimness of aspect that made Thrum Hall at Halifax look like 'Old Trafford'. The last improvements had been made twenty years previously, when apparently a new score board was erected, but otherwise 'The Watersheddings' was a memorial to the austere post war era of flat caps and whippets with which our great game had invariably been associated. It was always freezing cold too. Sometimes when you left the M62 you could see pedestrians in their shirt sleeves but by you reached the stadium everything was shrouded in mist.

I suppose it probably had a lot of character, with one stand, although long since renamed, keeping its post war knick-name of 'The Penny Rush'. That afternoon we all had a few beers in 'The Standard' pub before taking our places in the ancient Herbert Street Stand which leaked like a sieve and always seemed to face the rain and sleet. That day by the kick-off the rain had abated, but a dank 'Baskervillian' mist had descended over the ground and although you could see all four corners of the pitch, the tops of the goal posts had disappeared altogether. Hull FC arrived in Oldham gracing the top of the League, having won fourteen games and lost just three. Oldham were in fourth spot and as with most Clubs back then, they saw this game as a chance to shine against the 'Big Spenders' from Humberside. They boasted some good players too, and it was with a deal of trepidation that we huddled together, sang 'Old Faithful' and waited for the kick off.

Oldham started in a lively fashion and it was obvious that they intended to frustrate us and knock us out of our stride. Our defence had to be at its best too as Props, Goodway and Hogan and Second Rower Worrall, ploughed into our line. Garry Kemble was I remember outstanding at Full-Back that day, stopping everything that came towards him.

Then Mick Parrish put the home side in the lead with a penalty awarded for off-side after just 6 minutes. Shortly afterwards however Hull's Dave Topliss looked certain to score until Referee Mr. McDonald brought him back for a forward pass, something the official repeated with Dane O'Hara just five minutes later. It looked like it was not going to be our day, when just before half time Oldham got some possession and all McCurrie had to do was fall over the line to score under the post, but he dropped the ball. As the rain started to fall again, the teams tramped off for the break with the 'Rough'yeds' of Oldham in the lead 2-0.

The second half started with the home forwards battering our pack again, then, in an attempt to suddenly open the play out, Platt threw out a long pass in the direction of Vigo. Had it landed in his hands the winger would have gone the distance and scored against us, but from nowhere up popped Dave Topliss, hands at full stretch over his head, to intercept.

So intent on pressing home any advantage were the whole of the Oldham team, that Full-Back Taylor was up in the line and so when 'Toppo' sidestepped his marker and hit open ground there was no-one in front of him. It was then down to one of those spectacular 'sprints' where everything for the watching fan goes into slow motion. With our off-half haring down field and wingers Vigo and McEwen flying across the ground to try and cut him off, we all held our breathe. However Topliss just got to the try line first and planted the ball between the posts, before both the chasers hit him and forced him to the ground over the dead ball line. It was another one of those memorable tries that stays with you forever. Crooks made no mistake with the 'extras' and we led 5-2.

Then it was 'backs to the wall' as wave upon wave of Oldham attacks 'floundered on the rocks' of our brilliant defence and we were still protecting that flimsy lead as the game ended in torrential rain which was now driving under the front of the Herbert Street Stand and into our faces. Still, before a handful of beleaguered stewards could do anything about it we were over the fences, onto the field and slipping and sliding on the greasy turf to congratulate the lads. I was drenched that day and developed a heavy cold the following week which all the regulars in the 'Mermaid' christened "Oldham Flu", but it was all worthwhile after having experienced such a hard fought win.

Garry anoints the crowd in the Threepenny's

Wednesday 10th November 1982   *Hull 24 – Featherstone 15*

After that trip to Oldham we were back at the Boulevard for a mid week game against Featherstone Rovers. It was a memorable encounter on two counts, firstly it was the first match at which the Club banned alcohol on the terraces and secondly, it was one of those games that you expect to win easily before, that is, fate takes a hand in the proceedings.

The alcohol ban followed some well publicised 'happenings' in the crowd at a couple of games which led to the RL deciding that the bringing of alcohol into the Boulevard should be banned. This was not met with much enthusiasm by the regulars on the 'Threepennies' who enjoyed the odd 'tinny' during a game and so we all put our minds to ways of getting round the new regulations. That night fans were searched on their arrival at the Division Road turnstiles and any beverages were duly confiscated by the stewards (who could later be found drinking them, behind the Stand, as the game progressed).

Of course Garry, John, Ian and I laid our plans and decided to solve the problem 'scientifically'. Garry, who was always the most inebriated after our pre game sessions, was sent down the little Avenue of houses in Division Road that backed onto the pathway behind the Threepenny Stand. There he stood, in the dark, with a carrier bag full of Kestrel Lager whilst the rest of us paid our admission, and then, when level with the Avenue, we shouted to Garry to throw the cans over the wall.

As the curtains twitched in the houses down the Avenue, it became apparent that all that pre match Bitter on an empty stomach had affected our ability to time our 'catches' properly and although we caught most of the cans of Beer, we dropped a couple too. Those, we decided, should be Garry's cans. Once he had paid and joined us on the Stand, (which was absolutely packed), we presented him with his cans of beer. You can imagine the consternation that ensued when Garry tore the ring pull off his first can, only to soak everyone with his 'Shaken up' beer. Punches were thrown and curses exchanged and we all had to move, only for Garry to then repeat the episode with his second can, another ten yards down the Stand!

The match against Featherstone, who had won just three of their 12 games (whilst we were unbeaten at home in over a year), was seen by many as just a formality. Featherstone's fixture the previous weekend had been postponed because the pitch at Post Office Road was waterlogged and so, having had a weekend off, they started the sharper and brighter of the two sides. That tough match at Oldham the previous Sunday's had certainly taken its toll on our forwards but I remember they kept plugging away and in the end we came out winners on a very heavy pitch, 24-15, but it was very close. Keith Bridges had a brilliant second half at hooker and Mick Crane set up all five of our tries. A standout moment was when the doctor went on the field and heralded by two loud screams, pulled two of Tony Dukes dislocated fingers back out again, right infront of us lot in the Threepenny Stand. As for the 'Mermaid' contingent, well we were thankful to get a result, but freezing cold and of course, thanks to Garry, soaked to the skin in beer. Sporting our 'beer shampoos' and sticky clothing, we went back to the pub for a 'Night cap' where Garry said, "In the future, if it was all the same to you lot, I'll manage without a beer at the game"

15 unlikely heroes......the Aussies get a scare

Tuesday 16ᵗʰ November 1982   *Hull 8 – Australia 13*

Big games were coming thick and fast and just a week later the Australian Tourists came to town. The touring 'Kangaroos' of 1982 were all conquering, as they literally steamrollered teams into submission. This style of 'total' rugby meant that they arrived at the Boulevard having played 11 games on the tour without coming close to a defeat. We were top of the League and had ourselves won 14 of our last 15 games, and although the Second Test was only 4 days away, the Aussies paid Hull the ultimate compliment by fielding their full Test team. There had been a big controversy in the City too, as forged tickets were circulating everywhere and extra checks were carried out at the turnstiles by Police and stewards. This caused a delay that saw queues stretching right down Airlie Street to the Boulevard. I'd bought my ticket from the recognised outlet in 'Ewebanks' the furniture store in the City Centre, so I was confident it was alright, but several dozen people were turned away or 'detained for questioning' by the bobbies.

I remember on that night having a feeling of foreboding as I hurried down Airlie Street through the 16,000 other supporters trudging to the game. A tough match against Carlisle had robbed us of half our team through injury and missing were heroes like Charlie Stone, Trevor Skerrett, Knocker Norton, Ronnie Wileman and Sammy Lloyd. That meant we brought in veterans Mick Harrison, Mick Crane and Keith Bridges and youngsters Lee Crooks and Wayne Proctor. In fact hooker Bridges was the only player in our forwards that night who wasn't born in Hull. It hardly helped that this Australian team had just beaten Great Britain 40-4 in the First Test Match either. After leaving work late, a capacity crowd meant I had to give up my usual spot in the 'Threepenny's' and I ended up standing, at times on tiptoes, on the terrace at the Gordon Street end.

The game started ferociously with Crooks seeking out the tourist's notorious hard man Les Boyd, Lee just walked straight up to him, said something and followed through with a perfect left jab! Both teams joined in a spectacular brawl that was so heated Referee John Holdsworth had difficulty keeping order and it was five minutes before he was able to restart the game. I vividly remember just how inspirational Dave Topliss was that night as he completely outplayed their star player Brett Kenny. 'Toppo' scored a great first half try from a little kick through and the dominance of the Tourists was clearly illustrated when you consider that it made Dave one of only seven British players to score against them on that whole 15 match tour. Man of the Match Mick Crane was also prominent that night, producing one of those heroic displays that completely belied his off-field reputation and lifestyle. We were really put to the sword late in the first half, but hung on and following some brilliant tackling we went in 7-0 up!

Within five minutes of the restart the Aussies were back. The mercurial Peter Sterling sent Kerry Boustead in at the corner and then Mal Menninga put Grothe in on the other side. As the crowd tried to rally the home side with rounds of 'Old Faithful' there followed a hotly disputed, disallowed 'try' by Dane O'Hara, which many, including me, believe to this day should have won us the game. After a broken jaw for James Leuluai, Grothe scored his second touch-down to give the Tourists some 'breathing space' and although we pressed and pressed, after one of the best 80 minutes of tenacious rugby I have ever seen, it was all over and we had lost 13-7.

We hadn't tasted victory over the Aussies as a Club side since 1908 but that night we took them to the very edge of defeat. Our 'make shift' pack was awesome, meeting the touring six head on and never giving an inch throughout. The Australian's went on to win all their matches on that Tour, with that game at that Boulevard giving them their only close call.

'The Two Degrees' visit 'The Punch'

That month the City Hall paid host to the 'Most Successful Female Group in the World'. The band that warranted that title at the time was 'The Three Degrees' and they arrived on the last night of a 25 date British Tour that had sold out in advance everywhere.

The show itself was a big American production akin to those Krugar Organisation events in 1980 and at 6-30 just an hour and a half before the concert was due to start, I was summoned to the Dressing Room by the Tour Manager Zak Wadlinski. When I opened the door I was confronted by three of the most beautiful women in the World. "Hey Fella", said Zak, "The girls are finishing their tour tonight but there is one thing they haven't done here in England and you can help!!", "What's that" I said clearing my throat and wondering what was coming next. "Well" said Zak "They haven't been in a real British pub". So, although Sheila Ferguson declined the invitation, preferring to stay gargling in the Dressing Room, some ten minutes later as the queue waited patiently at the front gates of the City Hall, I sat with two of the Three Degrees in the bar of the Punch Hotel.

Mary the landlady said behind her hand, "Who are them two?" gesturing towards the two beautiful women in full length fur coats sitting at a chipped formica topped table in the corner. "It's the Three Degrees" I said, to which Mary replied "Nahhhhh.... can't be, there's only two of em!" Zak indicated that they would both have a Martini Rossi, and Mary disappeared to the depths of the cellar to see if she had any. Then it all got even more bizarre as Valerie Holliday took some darts from the bar and had a few throws at the dartboard. This scene was witnessed by just four other people that night, Harry the shoplifter ("If you want it I'll nick it") and three of his pals. They all just looked round to the dart board, rolled their eyes and turned back to the bar to finish their pints. What a memory. The concert was a great success and enjoyed by everyone who attended, but few people ever knew what had happened beforehand.

Cliff Richard rides in and 'Rolls' out!

There was another 'historic' promotion at the City Hall that December when we staged the biggest concert the venue had seen in years. For about a year I had been working with the local chairman of the Hull Branch of 'Tear Fund' to bring a big fund raising event to the venue. 'Tear Fund' is still active to this day as a leading relief and development charity, working in partnership with Christian agencies and churches worldwide, to tackle the causes and effects of poverty (well that's what Wikipedia says anyway).

These concerts had started back in 1971 at the Royal Albert Hall when their senior patron Cliff Richard performed to raise cash for projects in Africa. Since then he had done a mini tour each year but in much larger venues than the City Hall. However we had hatched a plan to have a concert with two 'Houses' that would mean 3,600 people could attend. Although it was a Gospel Concert as opposed to a pop event, it still sold out in 6 hours, as the punters queued all night long outside Gough and Davy in Savile Street to get one of the cherished tickets.

Cliff arrived that afternoon by train at Paragon Station and the crew were superb and a pleasure to work with, particularly when compared with the normal touring companies I had experienced. However the logistics of getting all those fans in and out of the Hall with just a half hour between shows was a nightmare. We had as many 'Bouncers' on duty as there were at the Judas Priest concert the previous year, but this time they were in suits and acting as stewards, litter pickers, and catering staff. Still everything went well, although the Police did stop all the traffic around the Hall between shows as hundreds of people spilled out onto the streets.

As for the concert itself, Cliff sang his gospel songs, including his Christmas hit of that year, a reworking of 'Oh Little Town of Bethlehem' but the crowd went wild when he ended both shows by performing his big hit and Number One from 1979, 'We Don't Talk Anymore' followed by an unaccompanied rendition of 'Silent Night'. Cliff came and thanked me in the City Hall Office before leaving by the side door, only to find 200 fans crowded round his next mode of transport, a Rolls Royce Silver Shadow. He did however manage to keep his 'overnight hideaway' under wraps but the patrons at the regular Wednesday night dinner dance at Willerby Manor will have no doubt looked twice when they saw who was checking in at the Hotel Reception that night.

Soaked again at the Boulevard and a "Ho Ho Ho" of a Christmas!

Sunday 19th December 1982   Hull 2 – Oldham 8

At the Boulevard despite the continuing efforts of the ground staff, there was little change in the condition of the pitch and in pouring rain and a game that resembled a mud bath, we were defeated 8-2 by a poor Oldham side in front of an atrocious gate of 5,300. It was a shocking day and despite watching from the Threepenny Stand, I was so wet when I got back home to the City Hall, it soon became apparent that I had managed to wash my underwear without taking it off.

That Christmas was also a bit of a bleak affair too. Willis Ludlow's, the department store across the road from the City Hall flat left it's laughing Father Christmas Window display switched on right through the holidays and after 60 hours of it incessantly declaring "Ho Ho Ho, Welcome to Willis Ludlows" by Boxing Day I'd had enough of Christmas spirit as had Mary and Albert across the road at the Punch. The other reason for my seasonal melancholy was that both the rugby fixtures over the holidays, away at Leeds on Boxing Day and at home to Wigan on New Year's Eve had been postponed because both the opposing teams were to feature in the John Player Trophy Semi Finals the following weekend. To amuse myself over the holidays I read the then cult novel, 'The Secret Diary of Adrian Mole aged 13 and three quarters', which I had bought myself for Christmas. All across the country this book was inspiring people to keep journals, although I dare not admit to the fact that I had actually been maintaining a diary for years, for fear of someone asking to see it and discovering that they were all full of nothing but rugby!

On 1st January, following its success in Australia, the 'sin bin' was introduced to British Rugby League and the first Hull player to go in there, in a game that we won against Halifax at the Boulevard on 16th January, was unsurprisingly, Lee Crooks.

It's always a GOOD Friday when you beat the Robins!

Friday 8th April 1983   *Hull 21 – Hull KR 3*

The first part of 1983 passed pretty uneventfully and after two periods of unusually heavy snow, it was just starting to look a bit like spring as our traditional Good Friday Derby game arrived and I walked down Anlaby Road to the Boulevard a bit later in the day than usual. The new idea of playing the seasonal local Derby that evening certainly seemed to have worked because by the time I got to the Stadium the queues at the Division Road turnstiles came snaking across the little car park and out into the street. Once inside, the ground was already buzzing with anticipation.

The Division Road terraces had been taken over by a sea of Red and White as the other side of the City had their annual 'day out' and as the Threepennies were already overflowing, I made my way through the Well of the Best Stand and took up a position on Bunker's Hill at the Airlie Street end of the ground. The pre match atmosphere was fantastic as to great adulation several red and white scarves were burned in the Threepenny Stand and there was an even bigger response when the Rovers' fans tried to do the same with a black and white one on the open terracing and almost set fire to the crowd!! By the time the teams ran out an amazing 20,569 fans were packed into the Stadium, to register the biggest home gate of that memorable decade. Before the game started the tense and intimidating mood was lightened somewhat when a Hull KR fan ran onto the bare and muddy centre of the pitch carrying a plastic carrier bag. To emphasise the poor condition of the playing surface, he then commenced skipping around the half way line scattering grass seed he took from out of the carrier. The Police escorted him off the playing area, but not before he had received a big cheer from both sets of supporters.

The 'Robins' arrived on a five match winning streak and the game looked to be evenly poised as we had ourselves only ended a nine game unbeaten sequence four days earlier with a narrow defeat at Castleford.

With just four games of the season to go Hull KR were still 5 points behind us in the League whilst we sat at the top, level with Wigan.

As Lee Crooks was missing that night 'the Sidewinder' Barry Banks, who had been playing 'A' team rugby of late, was brought onto the bench. Billy Thompson must have felt the tension as he ran out to a chorus of "Oh, Oh, Oh, Oh what a referee" (complete with the usual final flourish containing a string of expletives) as he called both Captains to the centre spot, to give them a lecture before we had even started. Kevin Harkin kicked off and after an early scare when Terry Day dropped a ball near the corner flag, the game settled down with Hull KR camped in our half and pressing our line.

Then we got the ball and Bridges drew a perfectly positioned Rover's line before passing to Norton. The visitors defence was arranged 'man on man' but they had forgotten to cover Garry Kemble who stormed up from Full-Back onto a beautiful Norton pass to score wide out. In an atmosphere akin to a 'Pressure Cooker' Prendiville, who had been handed Lee Crooks' kicking duties, missed with the conversion but we were in the lead.

Then on the 29th minute we saw a dazzling try. Back on our own 40 yard line Dave Topliss got through the first two defenders with ease and as the cover came across he passed to a rampaging Paul Rose. The ex-Robin swatted a couple of tackles away before moving the ball to Harkin who immediately sent Leuluai galloping downfield. The centre drew the defence, before passing onto the unmarked Prendiville who squeezed in at the corner and then brilliantly converted his own try. The rest of the half was typical cut and thrust Derby fare and as the whistle went for half-time a brawl broke out as Hogan and Hull's Charlie Stone 'exchanged compliments' .

This was Mick Cranes type of game because the unlikely hero, who loved fish and chips and a smoke and hated training, revelled on 'the big stage' of such occasions. The second half was only three minutes old when 'Craney' ran into acting half as Bridges was tackled fifteen yards out from the try line. Immediately he dummied to the blind side and ambled through the defence to touch down in his typical matter of fact

The Battle of Bunker's Hill, Good Friday 17th April 1981; a black day in the history of a proud City as a section of the crowd riots, causing the local Derby to be stopped.

The Yorkshire Cup Final 1981, at Headingley as Tony Dean breaks away from a collapsed scrum and Steve Norton prepares to switch play to the left. (*Courtesy of Hull Daily Mail*)

9th April 1982, 'Dane O'Hara runs faster than the Argentine
Army'; the FC Army arrives at Kings Cross Station London for the
Challenge Cup Final against Widnes.

1st May 1982, Hull 14 Widnes 14. Kevin Harkin bursts through a Widnes tackle with Mick Crane in support during the Challenge Cup Final at Wembley Stadium. *(Courtesy of Hull Daily Mail)*

"What was all that about then", seems to be what a bemused Charlie Stone is saying to Mick Crane in the dressing rooms, after the 1982 drawn Final. *(Courtesy of Hull Daily Mail)*

Fans queue patiently across the car park at the Boulevard for tickets for the 1982 Challenge Cup Final replay at Elland Road.

Knocker Norton leads the way as the team take a training run out over the Hessle Road Flyover. *(Courtesy of Hull Daily Mail)*

19th May 1982, the Challenge Cup Replay, Hull 18 Widnes 9.
The author's all time favourite (and now rather battered) picture.
(Courtesy of Hull Daily Mail)

Parading the Trophy at Elland Road 1982
Day, Topliss, Bunting, Sullivan, Stone, Tindall and Lloyd parade the
Challenge Cup for the fans after a famous victory.

'Knocker Norton sells more dummies than Mothercare'.
The scene from my flat window in the City Hall, as the Hull team
triumphantly returned with the Challenge Cup in 1982.

The 1983 Hull FC team photograph

Back row. (l to r): Skerrett, Day, Edmonds, Crooks, Wilby, Norton.

Middle Row: Rose, O'Hara, Banks, Bridges, Evans, Kemble, Proctor, Crane.

Front Row: Duke, Dean, Harkin, Topliss, Stone, Prendiville, Leuluai. *(Picture: Mike Jacklin)* style. Then it was Bridges and Crane again, as this time the pair linked superbly for Harkin to finish off with a magnificent long pass that put Dane O'Hara in at the corner.

Although 'Taffy' Prendiville missed both goals he made the next try for James Leuluai. That score was perhaps the only one of the night which had an element of luck in it as Prendiville came inside looking for the ball and got a short pass from Steve Norton. He looked up and seeing four Rovers defenders bearing down on him kicked a mighty 'up and under' that caught in the wind and rebounded off the upright straight into Leuluai's hands. Hull KR looked a dejected team as they awaited the conversion and argued amongst themselves behind the try line. With just 4 minutes to go Hall got a consolation try for the Robins but then Referee Thompson blew for the final time to herald a great victory over the old enemy which left us on the threshold of the title.

What stays in my memory from that win was the all round strength of the Hull side. The Man of the Match award went to Norton and Rose jointly, but for me that night it should have gone to Kevin Harkin, who had probably his best ever game for Hull FC.

Afterwards the Club announced that they had signed Patrick Solal, a winger from the French Club Toinneins and as Wigan lost to St Helens, a win at Leeds on 13th April all but guaranteed us the title, but just to make absolutely sure that a monumental points difference could not be over turned, we needed to win our final game at the Boulevard against Barrow on Sunday 17th April. As he couldn't speak a single word of English when he signed, Club jesters Tony Dean and Ronnie Wileman offered to teach Patrick, the rudiments of 'Queen's English'. Apparently they soon had him communicating in his rich deep French brogue, with a strong West Riding accent! There was certainly a really good team spirit in the camp at that time and those two weren't the only two jokers in the squad, as was perfectly illustrated when Trevor Skerrett, recognising that Dave Topliss was a bit depressed after being out injured for two months, had a T shirt produced that stated" I've seen Dave Topliss Play" on the front and "Once" on the back!

We ARE the Champions!

Hull 31 – Barrow 13

That afternoon Barrow desperately needed to win because defeat would see them relegated to the Second Division. There was however no sign of any sympathy, as Hull FC set about the visitors from the off. Barrow started well despite us taking a lead in the second minute from a Lee Crooks penalty but they actually played some neat rugby as Hull struggled to get their hands on the ball in the first ten minutes. Soon however that clinical, slick rugby that had bemused and bewildered much greater opposition over the season, started to come to the fore again.

Trevor Skerrett opened the scoring for Hull with what was the prop's first try of the season. Then almost straight from the re-start Crooks and Evans created an opening for Crane and Leuluai to engineer an overlap which saw Prendiville scoot in at the corner untouched. Five minutes later Les Wall the Barrow centre ran 35 yards to touch down for a score that momentarily delay the inevitable.

Harkin fed Topliss who then produced that wonderful, trademark 'run around' move with Evans and 'Toppo' took the return to score again. After the restart, and before Barrow had time to 'catch their breath', we won a scrum against the head and Crane took the ball and in his usual carefree manner, dummied twice and sauntered in to score. Crooks added all the conversions and Hull were 'out of sight' whilst we the fans spent half time dancing on the terraces.

More drama followed as the second half started, as referee Peter Massey tumbled over and collapsed in a heap clutching his leg. He had pulled a muscle and had to be replaced for the rest of the game by touch judge Henry Mason. The stand in official was soon being berated by the Threepennies with shouts of 'Get back on the Touchline' as he awarded two quick penalties to Barrow and the visitors reduced the arrears when Wall scored his second try.

Tickle added the goal but then came the best try of the game. Crane broke and linked with Rose and as so often happened back then from nowhere steaming through a gap from Full-Back came Kemble. He ran towards Tickle, swerved round him and on to the try line without changing pace. Leuluai then scored and despite another try for Barrow by David Cairns, the demolition of the now relegated opposition was completed when Crane again supplied a peach of a short pass to Banks who characteristically ran across the field before putting O'Hara in at the corner. A brief skirmish between Charlie Stone and McConnell was the final act of the game, as the relieved stand-in referee blew the whistle and the party started.

The Trophy was presented amid frantic appeals for the fans to "Get off the pitch" and after some semblance of order was restored, the players paraded the Cup around the Stadium. There was singing, chanting, cheers and tears. I was doing well until Kemble and Stone came past, but then my eyes filled up and my emotions took over, as they so often have at moments like that one! Laughing and crying again; what a great feeling that is and what a great season we had experienced!!

We'd finished top of the League for the first time since 1935/36, I watched as Hull's New Zealanders led the 'Haka' and the rest of the team followed suit or at least tried too. In the middle of the semi circle was coach Arthur Bunting, cigar in mouth, doing it with the best of 'em! Those who attended will have cherished what was one of our Club's greatest ever moments and will have told their sons and daughters, (as Max Boyce who was a popular Welsh comedian back then always said) "I know 'cos I was there!"

Eddie Kidd 'defies death' at the Boulevard whilst I get promoted!

After they had announced Gary Kemble as 'Player of the Year' the Board of Directors of Hull FC, always resourceful, hosted another fund raising event at the Boulevard on 23rd April when 3000 attended the Eddie Kidd Daredevil Show in which the world famous motor cyclist/stuntman performed motorcycle leaps and firewall crashes, drove cars on two wheels and produced dozens of 'wheelies' in what was an exciting night; or so I am told. I'd had enough excitement on the rugby field and didn't go! However three days later with my current boss the City Entertainments Officer having left the Authority to take up a position in Whitby, I was promoted into his job and although still in overall charge at the City Hall, I was at least able to bring in a Manager to help with what was becoming a time consuming job.

There was a historical re-enactment event in the City Centre that weekend too, which featured the English Civil War Society and a huge fabricated mock up of the old gates of Hull was constructed in Whitefriargate. It was staged to depict what is generally accepted as the first act of the English Civil War when after 'having a few' pints in the 'Olde White Hart' the elders of the City refused to admit the King's General the Earl of Newcastle. This after the King, in order to secure his 'Royal Town' and arsenal, had sent him to take possession of it. I walked down to Market Place to witness a 'skirmish' that was staged outside Holy Trinity Church. I remember thinking at the time that there is something rather surreal about watching 'the Royalist foot soldiers' in full armour, fighting the Parliamentarians with pike staffs, swords and knives, whilst sporting Leeds United tattoo's, driving gloves and Rolex watches.

Wembley III; The nightmare returns!

Saturday 7th May 1983   *Hull 12 – Featherstone 14*

No sooner had we won the League title and it was Wembley again and another weekend of drinking and debauchery with the 'Mermaid Wembley Beano'. If the experience of the Widnes 'drawn' Final the year before had been surreal then this game was just plain excruciating, because Hull have suffered many heartbreaks and disappointments over the years in Cup Finals, but there was never anything to match the depths of despair that we all felt that day. I particularly pitied those who had made a big financial effort to attend. One gang of lads I knew travelled down in a beat up Vauxhall Viva and slept in it on the car park outside the Stadium, just to be there.

Hull were newly crowned Champions, whilst Featherstone had just managed to avoid relegation after finishing 12th of 16 Clubs in the First Division. Many of the players admitted in later years that all their partying on the week leading up to the game was certainly 'inappropriate' and the lime green suits, white shoes and yellow ties that the team wore for the walk round before the game, should have forewarned as to what was about to unfold.

The result was the biggest shock at Wembley for 50 years, and caused a real stir, but that was absolutely no consolation to the Hull fans who were gutted. In a game where Hull's Paul Rose was the first player ever to be 'sin binned' at Wembley, both teams scored two tries a piece and Featherstone snatched a 14-12 victory with a penalty goal by Quinn just 3 minutes from time, which sent the fans of the unlikely victors into 'Dreamland'. We were without doubt the architects of our own demise because with 20 minutes to go Hull lead 12-5 but then with Terry Hudson in the sin bin, instead of us taking the initiative, we threw it away. A try by Hobbs and a conversion and penalty by Quinn saw the little West Riding team home for what was for everyone in the game besides us, a great victory for the underdog and 'The Game'. In a game that was full of records, Hobbs became the first forward to score more than one try in a Wembley Final while 40,000 Hull FC fans stood there that day at 4-47pm in total and absolute disbelief. Charlie from the City Hall who had sat next to me throughout the game, said in his own inimitable fashion, "Well, that's the last time, I say, the last time, I'll see Hull in a Challenge Cup Final" Of course we all shouted him down, and said, "We'll be back next year" but Charlie's sage like statement was unfortunately to be proved sadly and chillingly correct.

One lasting memory? Well I vividly recall getting absolutely 'blathered' that night and ending up in "The Sherlock Holmes" in Baker Street. There I met a lad of about 45 who had supported the Featherstone Club all his life and who just sat at a table by himself and cried. We tried to console him, but it was no good because he could just not believe what he had witnessed that afternoon. It was his nirvana and all we could get out of him was, "That has to be it, I won't be wasting my money and going to Post Office Road again, it can't ever be any better than this". Poor 'bugger'; I wonder where he is today?

The following Monday the team attended another Civic Reception at the Guildhall, which as I was now a 'senior' Council Officer I managed to get admitted to, although it was certainly a very low-key affair. The players seemed to know that they had let the fans, the Club and most of all themselves down and looked as if they would have rather have been anywhere else that night. The team appeared on the Balcony to a mixed welcome from a crowd of about 4000 diehard fans stood in the drizzle, but everyone was disappointed. Mick Crane always the comedian lightened the mood temporarily when he whipped the Lord Mayor's ceremonial three cornered hat off the head of Councillor Harry Woodford and declared to the masses below, "I'm gonna slash the tax on beer and cigs", which got a big laugh, but in general it was an altogether forgettable occasion, which got too much for Coach Arthur Bunting's wife who took one look at the crowd assembled below the balcony and burst into tears. I often tell younger supporters about what happened there on the terraces of Wembley that day in May 1983 because grown men cried, not one or a few, but hundreds.

That defeat and a further reversal against Widnes in the Premiership final seven days later at Headingley, totally took 'the shine' off the season for most FC fans, particularly those who expected to win everything and had jumped on board the 'success train' a couple of seasons earlier.

The 'Sing when you're winning' fans and Iron Maiden, 'Run for the Hills'

Of course those 'casual' fans had every right to be fed up because they had invested their passion and 'hard earned cash' following their chosen Club around the country. We full time obsessives have always done the same of course but we're different, we're incurable and in it for the long haul, we're the fanatics (or idiots) we had no choice and unlike that lad from Featherstone, we'll probably never get to where he had and so have no option but to blindly continue on. We also knew that despite the abject disappointment we all felt, it was certainly still 100 times better than those dark days of the mid 70's when we almost folded. Still, we had won the Yorkshire Cup and been crowned Champions of the Rugby League. The latter accolade being probably the hardest to earn and the most cherished to hold.

However as sports fans we're never really satisfied with what we've got and we invariably look for more. There were recriminations and a deal of "I'm not going to watch that again" however we still had two Trophies from a season that had started so well and that saw us play an amazing 49 games.

Of course life went on, although it took weeks to get over the disappointment of that Final. In fact I was ready for a period away from the game that had once again managed to find a way, in the midst of adulation and celebration, to thrust me back down into the depths of despair. At least we had a big concert on at the Hall to give me something else to worry about. It was a 'Warm up Gig' for Iron Maiden at the start of their 'World Piece' Tour. The top Heavy Metal band of the time sold 1800 tickets in just 4 hours, five weeks in advance, for what was a really prestigious concert for the venue. All the rest of the arenas they played on that tour had 3000 plus capacities but they always liked to do a 'warm up' where they could 'snag' everything and thanks to Phil McKintyre having such a good night the previous year promoting Judy Tzuke, he offered us the chance to do the concert.

The band was based at the City Hall for two days, one for technical rigging and the second for rehearsals. The actual concert was the public culmination of this period of preparation and was a brilliant night. It was a polished performance and when the band played their new single, 'Run for the Hills' it literally brought the house down, as amidst the mayhem a rotating gel-wheel dance floor light, fell from the balcony and crashed to the floor narrowly missing a section of the crowd. We had them all chained up after that (the lights that is not the crowd!)

'Ada the asthmatic' makes an entrance at the cinema and the 'Boss' changes my life forever!

At Hull FC the season finished with the Seven Seas 'Sevens' competition at the Boulevard. We didn't win or even get in the final. However there was some worrying news when the annual accounts were released by the Club, because despite a very successful year our average home attendance fell to 11,525 and we showed an operating loss of £49,276. It was, for Hull FC, the beginning of a slide into debt which was to be ignored by many at first, as we were all still blinded by the great time we were having supporting our team.

On 25th May 1983, and as part of my 'closed season rehabilitation', I queued for three hours to see the first showing of 'Star Wars; Revenge of the Jedi' at the ABC Regal in Ferensway. I was a big fan of the original trilogy of films but mention this here because of one particular incident that I'll remember forever. There we were, sat in a packed cinema, as the cabin doors slid open on the Shuttle Craft and that tell tale heavy breathing that heralded the arrival of the Chief henchman of the Empire, hissed out through the stereo speakers around the walls. It was a moment of high drama as totally captivated the little lad in front of me remained stock still in his seat with his eyes glued to the screen. Without turning his head and with one of those loud 'stage whispers' that echoed round the place, he said to his Mother, "Mum, Mum, is that Daft Ada!"

On 7th July, as Boris Becker was winning Wimbledon, it was still the closed season and I was as usual pretty bored. So, with nothing better to do, I drove over to Roundhay Park Leeds and using a ticket 'scrounged' from Phil McKintyre I came face to face with what was to prove a life changing musical experience.

That afternoon I found myself just 10 rows from the front at my first Bruce Springsteen Concert. On stage for four and a half hours, that day Bruce changed my view of music forever and as he sang Rosalita (Come out tonight) it was a seminal moment in my life. The City Hall this was not!

As the sun beat down and hundreds of lads draped in the Stars and Stripes danced around me, Clarence Clemons stood on top of a grand piano blowing sax, the security staff threw half naked women back off the stage, bare breasted girls rode on the shoulders of their boyfriends and the Hells Angels in front of the stage 'necked' Jack Daniels and threw buckets of water over the crowd. It was the best bit of live 'rock theatre' I have ever seen. After family and loved ones, that experience decreed that music and rugby would remain my only two real passions, for the rest of my life.

Chapter 3

Probably the best concert I've ever been paid to attend

After three and a half years of living and working at the Hull City Hall, I was starting to get a lot more blasé about rock concerts but just occasionally you came across something that was so good, you stopped being the Manager of the venue and became just another fan. That was the case on 24th July 1983 when Hull played host to the 'The Crossing' tour featuring Scottish rockers Big Country.

What a night that was, their first album, after which the tour was named, had been out just 3 weeks and they played every track in the order they appeared on the disc. The high spots were invariably the big single release 'Fields on Fire' that had been a hit earlier that year and 'In a Big Country' that was at number 8 in the music charts that week.

I remember the encore at the end of the show which featured an amazing cover of Smokey Robinson's, 'Tracks of my Tears' and then because they were short of material the band repeated 'Fields of Fire'. They finished the number by first the drummer walking off and whilst the music continued he was followed by the Rhythm Guitarist and then by Tony Butler the Bassist. This just left lead singer and guitarist Stuart Adamson on stage lit by a single spotlight and still playing. When he stopped and walked off it brought the house down. It was certainly really effective, so much so that ex local boxer Jackie Turner and ex Hull FC forward Alan Wardell, who worked as security staff that night commented that it was the best end to a show they had seen.

Barbara Woodhouse! Siiiiiiiiiiit!!!!

Now that I was City Entertainments Officer, things had certainly changed since the days of pruning roses and chasing girls in the Parks, because I was now managing the Hall and the whole City wide entertainments programme, which included the ubiquitous Hull Show. That year, after the success of Wurzel Gummidge at the previous year's Show, we persisted with 'a personality' by securing the services of Barbara Woodhouse the eccentric TV dog trainer. Eccentric she certainly was, something that was never more evident than when within five minutes of arriving she smashed the window of a Ford Cortina because she said that the dog inside was likely to suffocate. She did that despite it being a grey, cool morning and the cars sunroof being left open. Still the local kids seemed to enjoy themselves scaring her witless as they jumped out from behind marquees, shouting her trade mark catch phrase of "Siiiiiiiiiiiiiiiit!!"

Despite Ms Woodhouse, the dry weather and Harvey Smith, Show Jumping in the Main Arena, attendances were down by 600 to 31,158.

Rule changes at the Boulevard, anarchy at Boothferry Park and a sad farewell to Dukesy

Sunday 21ˢᵗ August 1983   *Hull 22 – Warrington 22*

The start of the 1983/84 season was fast approaching and as usual I got my season pass, deciding this time to watch my rugby with Barry, Charlie, Trevor 'the fish', 'Hard up Harry' and (Beer Shampoo) Garry in the 'New' seats in the Best Stand. It was then announced that Tony Duke our 'hooker in waiting' for so many years was to retire, although we would never forget the part he played in that wonderful night when we won the Challenge Cup at Elland Road. Off the field Tony was a real gentleman, while on it he was a dumpy, hard, nuggety Hooker who was brilliant at winning the ball in the scrums and 'mixing it' with the best players around.

Hull FC Head Coach Arthur Bunting said, "Tony had over the years every reason to complain, as players like Ronnie Wileman and Barry

Bridges have been brought in over him, but he just went about his business played hard and well in the 'A' Team and waited his chance". Another surprise was the naming of young Lee Crooks as Club Captain; a decision that we fans thought was probably more to do with the responsibility keeping him out of mischief, rather than his ability to lead the team.

I have already reported on the sporadic trouble we had at the Boulevard with so called 'football hooligans' but at Boothferry Park it was ten times worse as the scourge of the 'Beautiful Game' continued to manifest itself in Hull. The Tigers had a 'Friendly' pre season game which erupted into hand to hand fighting between the two sets of fans on the pitch at half time. In the end 140 Middlesbrough supporters had to 'sleep rough' in Hull overnight, when three coach drivers who had seen their vehicles ransacked on the journey down from Teeside, refused to take them home.

It was around that time too, that the Rugby League decided to change several of the rules of the game which that year included the introduction of 4 points for a try. In addition the number of scrums in a game was drastically reduced as they introduced the rule by which at the end of 6 tackles, you had to hand the ball over to the opposition.

The 83/84 season at the Boulevard kicked off on a boiling hot Sunday afternoon against a feisty, tough Warrington team. In the end we were fortunate to get any sort of result really as with a minute to go and the scores tied Stone fouled Hesford in front of the posts. It looked as if we were destined to lose but there followed a memorable example of the real power of that most influential of viewing galleries, the Threepenny Stand.

As Hesford walked up to take the kick the crowd fell quiet, no doubt in preparation for the inevitable chorus of 'boo's' that was always forthcoming as the goal kicker ran up to address the ball. In that 'silent moment' as Hesford meticulously constructed a small pyramid of sand on which to place the ball a lone rasping voice rang out from the Threepenny Stand, shouting, "You might be here kicking a goal Hesford, but do you f****** know what your wife's doing?" What effect that lone voice had, we will never know, but as the ball sailed wide of the left upright, from a simple straight kick, the Warrington Player glared across at the Threepennies where they were all dancing as if we had won. It was certainly a very unlikely draw in which, completely unannounced, Hull FC gave a debut to a young West Riding lad called Gary Schofield. He was 'welcomed' to first team rugby by Warrington centre Ronnie Duane who gave the youngster a really hard time. Afterwards Garry said that he would remember his debut forever. Not because of the occasion, or the game but more for the bruises he carried for the next six weeks.

John Woods, "Six points away, 'in off' the wall"

Sunday 11th September 1983   *Hull 20 – Leigh 12*

I have already covered all the 'dark satanic mills' stuff regarding our trips to Leigh and Oldham and that year's visit to Hilton Park was little different to those that had gone before, however it did contain one particular incident that sets it out from every other game I have seen.

It was early September and the country was experiencing what the weathermen were calling an 'Indian Summer' with everywhere bathed in warm, unseasonal sunshine. Everywhere that is except Leigh. It was never anything but dull there, but after we had walked from the 'Our House' pub to the ground in our shorts and Hull FC T shirts and taken our places on the South terracing, at least the sun was straining to get through the leaden sky, as the fair skinned, drizzle loving locals were goading us from the safety of the Tommy Sale Stand.

Despite Leigh being at the top of the table in those early stages of the season just 5000 were in attendance, of which at least 2000 were from Hull. Deep in the second half we were dominating a tough forward battle and leading 10-4. We would have benefited from an even bigger margin but for the fact that Paul Prendiville was struggling with his goal kicking, however we still looked pretty certain to get a win. Well, we did until the 67th Minute.

It was then that Leighs John Woods hoisted a high 'bomb' but the trajectory was angled much too far towards our line. The ball hit the hard ground on the try line and Trevor Skerrett, Paul Prendiville and several other Hull players watched as it bounced harmlessly over the dead ball line and were none too worried when it hit the old concrete perimeter wall and Woods, following up, dived half heartedly on it to touch down. To the players and everyone in the ground's disbelief, referee Mean immediately pointed to the ground to indicate that John Woods had scored a try. The fans protested at what was an incredible blunder, but the referee who was 20 yards away when the incident occurred, refused to consult his linesman and just looked away and awarded the try. "Mean, you're like our lass... bloody useless" came a shout from a guy behind me as 3 minutes later Woods stroked over a penalty and we were trailing 12-10 in a game we had never looked like losing.

Many teams would have folded at that point particularly after such a devastating turn of events, but not Hull FC. Leigh were relying on Woods and his high kicks to keep us pinned in our own half but after 78 minutes, with time fast running out, he hoisted another 'steepling' kick which Harkin took on the run on his own 25 yard line. He swept back up field, fed Leuluai who drew the cover and sent French winger Patrick Solal off on a 55 yard sprint to the corner. He was just caught by Des Drummond who made the tackle of the game to save a certain try. Playing the ball quickly, we moved it right across the line and Barry Banks fed Dane O'Hara who slid in at the other corner for us to regain the lead. Hull hadn't finished either because, accompanied by the chants of "You're not singing anymore" from the now jubilant Hull fans, in the 80th minute we scored again when Mick Crane and Dave Topliss put Wayne Proctor over.

There was no time to restart the game and as the final whistle went we had 'snatched victory from the jaws of defeat', and won 20-12. However that 'in off the wall' incident will live in my memory forever.

Tragedy strikes as Charlie bows out doing what he loved!

Sunday 18ᵗʰ September 1983   *Hull 24 – Wigan 8*

When you talk to the real fans of any sport about death, there is little doubt that most would want to be around the people and the Club they love when the grim reaper 'comes a calling' and that fact is something that always reminds me of a game that year against Wigan. That day we watched the match with Charlie's daughter and son in law. Charlie, my pal and trusted work mate was in really good form but as the game was about twenty minutes old he tried to get up from his seat, slumped back again and had what I can only describe as a massive seizure. Ashen faced he stumbled to his feet again, collapsed and fell between the rows of seats.

We struggled to carry him out through dozens of strangers who all paid concerned but ultimately detached attention, before the St John lads took over and we got my workmate and dear old pal into a waiting ambulance. He looked very grey and lay silent, and we feared the worst as the doors slammed shut and they raced him, with bells ringing, to Hull Royal Infirmary. The fact that we won that day was pretty incidental really because our thoughts were with Charlie and his daughter and son-in-law who had accompanied him to hospital. We left before the end of the match and went straight to Hospital, only to meet them both coming out with all Charlie's possessions and clothes in a plastic bag, and that was it, Charlie was gone.

One minute he was watching his beloved Hull FC beating Wigan, the next he was not around anymore. It was a stark reminder of the futility of life and how you can be taken at any time, even when you're watching your favourite team. We would all miss Charlie!

That incident left me with a lasting legacy and to this day I suppose dying like that would be the ideal way to do it, if it were not for the distress it would cause those loved ones and pals at the game with you. Of course, when you do die, your team, its fans and their aspirations just continue as usual, you might have moved out of the 'cheap seats' but the 'circus' rolls on. Perhaps, if there is a lesson to be learned from what happened to Charlie it has to be that its best not to look to closely at that 'Glorious' next season. Charlie knew four months earlier that he would not see another Wembley, he told us so that day as Featherstone paraded the Cup and if he were here now, he would probably tell us all to, "Enjoy it, I say, enjoy it, while you can"

'Sterlo' almost arrives and the Numan family visit the City Hall

On 21ˢᵗ September I opened the evening paper as amazing news was breaking for all Hull FC fans. The headlines on the back page stated that the Club had signed the best scrum-half in the world, Peter Sterling. The plan was for Sterling to come to England and play 16 games in what was the Australian closed season. It was certainly an exciting time for us supporters because in addition to this amazing news, the Club's long awaited 'Mystery' signing from New Zealand, turned out to be none other than International half- back Fred Ah Kuoi, who we had failed to sign a year previously. Fred flew into Heathrow to join Hull FC, accompanied by Hull KR's new signing Mark Broadhurst.

Hull's Chairman Roy Waudby was certainly pleased to have captured two iconic players but he had other things on his mind that September as after numerous letters to the local paper and calls to Radio Humberside, he met the Police and residents of the area around the Boulevard, to discuss the chaos that parked cars were causing around the Stadium on match days. However, as often happens in sport just as you are on a high, the fans hopes were dashed, when we found out that because of a foot injury and a serious chest infection Sterling was advised not to come after all.

At the City Hall, although there was little in the way of concerts going on, we did promote a well attended meeting of Dockers where they finally voted to end their longest ever dispute with the National Dock Labour Board. The strike action and work to rule had gone on for seven months and I well remember that after the event, despite the 'No Smoking' signs around the walls, the air in the Main Hall was, as usual, blue with the smoke that had been produced by hundreds of 'contraband' 'roll up' cigarettes.

The first big concert of the season featured Gary Numan's Tubeway Army and despite his rather outrageous stage persona he proved to be a decent 'down to earth' lad. This was the first concert that Charlie was missing from his usual back stage role and it was a really sad occasion for us all. Numan's 'Dressing Room Rider' was certainly 'austere' for a 'Rock Star' and he was particularly well behaved and certainly quiet, probably because of the Aspergers syndrome that was to blight his later life. This behaviour was, I guess, not too unexpected either as his Dad Tony was his Road Manager, his Mum Beryl was there as his Fan Club Secretary and his brother John played sax and keyboards in the Band. The Stage Set was however spectacular. It took all day to erect and featured the side of a half demolished four storey building set against a skyline of Sky Scrapers. The wall at the first floor level appeared to have collapsed and that is where Numan performed whilst the rest of the band appeared at large windows in other parts and levels of the building. The concert was staged as part of the 'Warriors' Tour and although Gary seemed to struggle at times reaching the high notes, it was an inspired event and everyone in the 1400 audience, many of whom sported jet black dyed hair and white powdered faces, went home happy.

Back in the Yorkshire Cup Final against Malcolm Reilly on one leg!

Saturday 15th October 1983   *Hull 13 – Castleford 2*

That October we were back at Headingley for another Yorkshire Cup Final this time against Castleford. Like all Hull supporters perhaps I was taking another final appearance a little for granted because back then if we didn't get to a Final, we were disappointed. However commonplace it was becoming it was always great to be there in the midst of that throng of humanity that was the 'Black and White Army' but I often think that as far as Finals are concerned, it's the odd one in the middle of a barren period of form, that is invariably the sweetest. As holders of the Trophy we went into the game as favourites and this time the match would highlight the amazing skills of that most unlikely of heroes, the legendary Mick Crane. We had a great day out with the Mermaid crowd, who I joined again on the bus mainly because it gave me the chance to steady my nerves at the 'Three Horse Shoes' on Otley Road. We all raised a glass to Charlie, had a few beers and after a buffet of chips and savaloy sausages we were ready for the fray.

Leeds was notorious for its football hooligans with Elland Road often featuring on the national news. This led the Police to treat rugby games as they did football matches and so that afternoon they closed all the pubs in a three mile radius of Headingley. When we arrived 'The Horseshoes' was closed with all the curtains drawn, but we trooped round the back and joined another 100 or so Hull FC fans in a room illuminated by the mandatory plastic chandeliers. By the time we left it was raining and it steadily became torrential as we made our way to the ground.

Once there the crowd of 14,049 witnessed Hull seeing little of the ball in the first quarter, although after 18 minutes Kemble charged through and put O'Hara in at the corner. There were no more scores in the first half but with the second half just 7 minutes old Mick Crane took control of the game. In the first half he had seen colleagues squander his defence splitting passes and so this time he decided to 'do it himself'. Castleford were left reeling as Mick produced a little dummy and a big hand off to Timpson that saw him over the line in an instant for a superb try. 'Craney' featured in Hull's last try too, as he put Proctor in with a superb inside pass, and three minutes from the end a low dipping drop goal from Mick just crept over the cross bar, to seal a match winning, 'Man of the Match' performance for our unlikely hero. We had won the Yorkshire Cup for the second year running, by 13-2. 18 year old Garry Schofield and 19 year old Lee Crooks both had brilliant games and Tony Dean also had a 'stormer'. Even an appearance of veteran Castleford prop forward Malcolm Reilly, who at 35 risked aggravating a serious knee injury to lead his home town Club, couldn't stop Hull grinding out a great victory in a game which we never looked like losing.

After our Black and White heroes had retired out of the rain and into the dressing room the 'gentlemen of the press' were treated to seeing Mick Crane with his Man of the Match trophy sitting on a bench puffing away on the mandatory cigarette. When asked about his smoking, he simply replied, "I smoke 30 a day and feel as fit as ever, I think I am playing better now than I have done for ages". We all agreed with that statement as we made our way back in a convoy along the M62 on route for a few beers and choruses of 'Old Faithful' back at the Mermaid. We had won a Trophy again and the bitter recollections of that disappointing end to the previous season were fast evaporating.

At the City Hall we promoted a prestigious international event as the National Conference of the Mothers' Union came to town. Their 'Madam' President met me at the Station Hotel to discuss the arrangements and we walked down to the Hall for a look around. She was just as I expected really, tall, immaculately made up, dressed in a tweed suit and sporting a pair of glasses on a gold chain around her neck. During the two hour meeting she constantly mentioned the need for there to be a "Modesty curtain" available at all times. I just nodded in agreement and noted this on my clipboard, although I didn't have the slightest idea what she was talking about.

Later I mentioned it to Frank, (who was now the Foreman) and he enlightened me by saying, "Oh she means that she wants a long tablecloth on the top table on the stage, so that no one sat on the main floor can see her knickers".

The Magnificent Eleven

Sunday 6ᵗʰ November 1983   *Hull 8 – Castleford 4*

There are in the life time of a sports' fan those moments and matches that you remember forever, and a game in November 1983 is one such instance for me. It was a match that the national Newspapers next day hailed as "Simply fantastic", with the Daily Mirror stating that, "It could have been from a comic book, but this was real life and possibly one of the 'great' displays of all time, in any sport!" Big words indeed, but it was all that and more, particularly if you were a Hull fan at 5-00-pm on Sunday 6th November 1983.

It was Coach Arthur Bunting's 'way', back then when the team were playing in the West Riding, to take them for a light training session at Rothwell and an even lighter lunch in the local pub. Although Arthur was actually ill and this was to be the first of 6 games for which Assistant Coach Kenny Foulkes would take temporary charge, the same procedure was followed that day. That was however where the trouble started, as our charismatic loose forward, Steve 'Knocker' Norton pulled up injured (on the training pitch, not in the pub) and was a late withdrawal from the starting line up. This left Foulkes with little option but to ask current hero and local character, Mick Crane, to captain the team and it turned out to be an inspired choice.

By 3-30pm Wheldon Road was packed with the 'FC Army' as it made up around two thirds of an 8,000 gate. So full was the West Stand, that I watched a game that is burned on my memory forever, stood with my pals on the South Terrace adjacent to the railway embankment.

It was fast and furious from the off and if the first 31 minutes were exciting, the last 49 had to be seen to be believed. As coal trains rumbled by behind us, the first half hour was tight. Both sides were cancelling each other out and although Schofield made one 70 yard break only to be caught by Marchant, both teams kept the lid on things. After Fred Ah Kuoi was floored by a kick from Gary Connell, the Castleford player should have been sent off, but all he received was a lecture from the Referee Billy Thompson however at least the ensuing penalty from Lee Crookes put us into the lead. It was then cancelled out by a Castleford penalty just four minutes later. Then in the 28th minute Paul Rose was subject to a brutal stiff arm tackle from Hyde, which saw a skirmish break out between both sets of forwards and it was obvious what was to happen next. Wileman got a blow to the head in the melee and came away rubbing it furiously and pointing at a Castleford player.

As the home team moved the ball along their line, Ronnie Wileman stepped out of ours and 'flattened' Horton off the ball. The Castleford player lay on the ground and although Referee Thompson let play go on for almost a minute, he whistled when Castleford had got into our twenty five yard area and promptly sent Wileman off. It has to be said Ronnie deserved it but then, five minutes later, prop forward Trevor Skerrett followed him down the tunnel, as the referee lost control.

This was a completely uncalled for dismissal as Trevor lined up one of his famous big, but legal, hits on winger Steve Gill. He seemed to have timed it perfectly taking the Castleford player squarely across the shoulders but the referee immediately dismissed him for a high tackle. After the game Skerrett protested that he "Took him by the shoulders", something that was borne out by the fact that Gill was later admitted to hospital with a dislocated collar bone.

So Hull FC were down to 11 men against a team that was known as 'Classy Cas' because of their reputation for throwing the ball around and playing fast expansive rugby. Once the commotion had died down Beardmore coolly stroked over the penalty and we trailed 4-2. But Hull's 'Magnificent 11' was not going to give in. As the adrenalin pumped and the self belief grew, they played like a team possessed and tackled everything as they formed an impenetrable line across the field. The Hull fans around us and across the other side of the ground were probably as loud that day as I have ever heard them and the lads responded brilliantly.

As we tackled and tackled, half time and a rest grew nearer and nearer. However we could not have had a better boost when three minutes into added time, another big break by Schofield from 60 yards out, saw him tackled 30 yards from the Castleford line. At the play the ball Steve Evans rushed in, pushing Harkin away and scooped the ball up. He then chased his own kick and touched down wide out just before the ball rolled dead. Crooks missed the conversion but we still amazingly led 6-4 at half time. The break was a blessed relief for all the Hull fans, whilst the Castleford supporters smugly sipped their Bovril and looked forward to a landslide of points in the second half.

Hull came out after the break determined to hold onto that lead and give nothing away. At the scrums we just packed down four players, although in fairness there were no forwards or back's just 11 determined heroes. On numerous occasions close to our 'in goal' area, backs O'Hara, Leuluai and Ah Kuoi took on the role of driving forwards, to clear our lines. Castleford started to get frustrated and just as Hull looked to be buckling, Hardy was dispatched to the sin bin for a blatant trip that was a far worse offence than the one Skerrett had been sent off for earlier. Coolly Crooks got us another two points and the lead was stretched to 8-4. From then on, it was all Castleford attacking, all Hull defending and all the 'FC Army' singing, as the place shook to 'Come on you Hull" and we repelled attack after attack from Castleford.

Props Crooks and Rose battled and tackled themselves to a near standstill with Crooks despite carrying a first half leg injury, never shirking a collision. In that last quarter Schofield pulled off 4 tackles that were top draw, whilst Kemble dealt with three towering 'Up and Under's' from the boot of Bob Beardmore, and drove the ball back up field like an additional forward. At the helm of this terrific effort was Mick Crane who tackled, ran and 'generalled' the play as if his life depended on it. He was 'Captain Fantastic' as time after time he drove the ball at the home defence always making ground. These tactics led to a lot of the game being played in the host's half and despite a big scare in the last minute when Hyde scythed through only for Proctor, Harkin and Kemble to hold him up over the line and push him back out to safety, our line held and we were home. When Ronnie Campbell finally blew the whistle Castleford probably heard the biggest cheer it had ever experienced from any group of visiting supporters, as our players fell to their knees and the FC fans went berserk, dancing, singing and cheering from the terraces.

The Castleford players were clearly upset about their performance and Hull's victory and many refused to shake hands with our players. In fact after the game, in the tunnel, Connell was sent off for swearing at the Referee. Even after a great journey home and a few pints back in the Mermaid there was a last surprise to come from the weekend's heroics, because next day the media carried a story about how a disillusioned and injured Steve Norton, had announced his retirement (a decision he would thankfully reverse later that season).

Some great news was soon to follow however as on 24th November the Hull Daily Mail announced that after his doctor's previous instructions and out of the blue, Peter Sterling had contacted the Club and offered to come to England for a ten match spell. He had recovered from his foot injury and bronchial problems and was soon on his way to the Boulevard. Finance was an issue but it was said that Sterling was not asking a lot of money and with the help of sponsors North Country Breweries, he flew into the Country at the same time as Wally Lewis, another iconic Aussie half back, who was joining Wakefield.

As so often happens in sport, serendipity then took a hand in the proceedings and the debuts of these two icons of the Australian game coincided with both their new Clubs meeting at Belle Vue Wakefield in a League fixture on 4th December 1983. The marketing men couldn't have written the script any better had they tried.

Enter a legend and a Wally!

Sunday 4th December 1983   Hull 32 – Wakefield Trinity 16

There are times in the course of being a life-long follower of one Club when you remember that on a particularly significant occasion, "You were there". There when it happened, there when history was made and there when you simply couldn't imagine being anywhere else in the world. Often it's Cup Finals and critical, last gasp wins in successful seasons that offer these fleeting glimpses of perfection, but sometimes it's just about a monumental episode in the history of your Club. That day at Belle Vue was for me at least, one such occasion. There we were stood amongst around 4,000 Hull fans on the open Western Terrace frantic with expectation, as out ran Hull FC and Peter Sterling, his long blonde hair blowing in the wind. Of course all the talk in the West Riding City was about Wally Lewis making his debut for Trinity but in the end it was Hull FC that spoilt the party, as led by Sterling we took the home team apart.

After just a couple of days in the Country and at just 22, Sterling produced a magnificent debut to lead us to victory. Our team that day was a mix of young and old, as the continuing injury crisis at the Club bit into our reserves of playing strength. Without six regular first teamers and several players that were on International duty, Hull knitted together surprisingly well and Keith Tindall, at 36, and returning after 15 months absence, was a revelation.

However it was Sterling that ran the show and despite a bright opening from an obviously inspired Wakefield side, he took all the plaudits at the end of the day. Indeed we even had a Trialist winger playing on the right who popped up to score a try. Lewis was outstanding in the first quarter particularly when executing some brilliant cut out passes to set up attacks and we soon trailed 8-0 before Edmonds scored a try off a brilliant 'scissors' pass from Sterling. Then Mick Crane opened Wakefield up and sent Evans in for a try, but a Geary try right on half time saw the scores tied at 16-16 at the break.

The second half was all Hull as Dannett, Evans and Banks scored tries, each of which was engineered by Sterling. Lewis retired after 70 minutes, but 'Sterlo' played out the whole game, as we ran out winners 32-16. It was a moment to savour as our new hero came over to the 'Kop' to receive the adulation of us fans and I can still see him now waving to us all, before taking the bindings off his hands and throwing them into the crowd. Despite only playing 8 games in that spell at the Club and a further 28 the following season, you'll hear a lot more about Peter Sterling in here.

The early part of 1984 saw him leading Hull to success on the field as we went on a seven match unbeaten run. Sterling was an instant hero with all the fans and quickly became a local personality, being followed everywhere (even on his regular visits to the local casino) by an entourage of autograph hunters and ladies. He was a real hero who I always wanted to meet and I had my wish granted one night in the Casino when after numerous pints I came face to face with him and said, "Your Peter Sterling" to which he replied, "I know" and that was it really.

'Bunting's Babes'

Sunday 8th January 1984   Hull 16 – Bradford Northern 8

That January on a cold and windy night Barry, Garry and I, went to the Boulevard to watch the Hull Colts team who were undoubtedly still the best young team in the country. They played New Zealand Universities and won 13-10 and over 4,000 people turned out that night to witness the visitor's only defeat of the tour. Try scorer Phil Windley dropped the vital goal and Carl Newlove was, I remember, Man of the Match.

A slump for the First Team coincided with a host of injuries, the most serious of which saw Trevor Skerrett admitted to Nuffield Hospital to have an operation to repair snapped ligaments. So, as a few injuries became a 'crisis', we brought in the youngsters.

It was around that time, after we had beaten the then all conquering Bradford team at the Boulevard, that the media coined the phrase 'Bunting's Babes'. The FC players led by Peter Sterling in imperious form, wrestled the initiative away from a Northern team that was on a 6 game unbeaten run and despite featuring youngsters Gary Divorty, Shaun Patrick and teenage second rower Wayne Proctor on the wing, victory was secured when Leuluai stormed in off a perfect 'Sterlo' pass to the unbridalled joy of a big crowd. That day the team included three teenagers, two twenty year olds and a twenty one year old and it was a famous victory.

Dance, in the old fashioned way?

At work despite still being the licensee, a new Manager at the City Hall meant I was able to concentrate a little more on the duties involved in my new role as City Entertainments Officer. There had been a big resurgence in the interest in Ballroom Dancing fuelled by a new craze called 'Sequence Dancing' which took the long held wedding reception tradition of 'doing the slosh' (a sort of line dance for inebriated female attendees) a stage further and within a few weeks hundreds of new 'formation' dances were introduced. These included such exotic titles as 'The Emmerdale Waltz' and the 'Mayfair Quickstep' and saw the over 50's streaming back to the Dance Schools and Dance Halls of the nation.

We had tried a couple of Saturday Night Dances featuring the Frank Cleveland Band and the records of John Riley, but having seen the popularity of 'Tea Dances' at some of the country's more salubrious venues, such as the Pump Room in Bath and the Ritz and Savoy Hotels in London, we decided, to try a couple of Tuesday afternoon Tea Dances at the Hall.

The first of these events took place on Tuesday 17th January and even before we had opened the doors the queues were stretching around the front of the Building as that afternoon we were just short of our dancing capacity of 650. Tea and biscuits were available, but few partook of more than a couple of gulps before they were on 'the dance floor' and 'twirling' the afternoon away to a mixture of 'Old Time' and 'Sequence' dances. The whole idea was hailed as a great success and fuelled by the enthusiasm of everyone that attended and a full page article in the Hull Daily Mail the following night, entitled 'Dance in the Old Fashioned way' we decided to make these 'journeys back in time' a regular fortnightly occurrence.

The siege of Victoria Square!

Our success got regional coverage on the TV and other local authorities around the North of England were soon on the telephone keen to find out more. Little did we know what would happen next! We scheduled the next Tea Dance for Tuesday 31st January and seeing the success of the initial event, decided that we would not advertise this one, but instead rely on word of mouth in the now burgeoning local dancing community. Despite the doors not opening until 1-30, by 11-00am the queues were starting to form outside the Hall. We opened early and two of our usual 'bouncing' staff were employed (we thought) to tear tickets at the door. Ticket sales reached the legal dancing capacity of 625 by 1.50pm and still there seemed to be hundreds in the queue. I announced that we were full and put up the 'House Full' signs as a near riot broke out in the foyer and spread quickly down the queue outside.

The more vociferous shouted 'We pay our Rates' and 'I pay your wages', whilst several ladies in their 70's tried to conduct a sit in and collapsing to the marbled floor of the vestibule, refusing to move until they were admitted. Eventually we got everyone back outside and pulled the big metal hinged gates across the entrance. By now things were turning ugly, as dozens of 'Grannies' chanting 'Let us in, Let us in' were banged on the gates with their umbrellas and shoe bags, whilst several 'Grandads' shook their fists at the attendants and particularly me, as we peered out at them through the gates.

Two resourceful gentlemen, who claimed that they had travelled from Rotherham on the train especially for the dance, thought they had beaten the system by climbing into the Hall through an open window in Paragon Street. Sadly as the Main Hall is on the first floor their plans were thwarted when they realised that they were actually in the stock room of Gordon Clarkes the School outfitters. What's more, the window was too high from the inside for them to get back out again. It was absolute mayhem and when eventually the police had dispersed the crowd who departed no doubt to write their letters to the local newspaper and ring Robin Pulford on Radio Humberside, one Police Sergeant commented, "Give me the South Stand at Boothferry Park anytime!" "You don't", he continued, "Quite know what to do with three hundred irate pensioners wearing anoraks and long party dresses, swinging cloth bags with high heel shoes in them"

On talking to some of the fortunate dancers inside the Hall it was apparent that people had travelled from as far afield as Sheffield, Scarborough, York and Wakefield to attend what had been hailed in many regional newspapers around the north of England as "A new dance craze for the over 50's". In future, on Police advice, we sold tickets in advance for these events, which continued at the Hall for the next ten years. However, there is little doubt that few will ever see anything in the future like 'The Siege of Victoria Square'!

That week the great news for all Hull FC fans was, that after a brilliant few weeks at the Club and on the day before he was due to return to Australia, Peter Sterling signed a contract to return to Hull for the whole of the 1984/85 season. Our Club Chairman Roy Waudby was pictured in the Hull Daily Mail smiling victoriously as 'Sterlo' signed and everyone, (particularly the local casino operators and bookmakers), was pleased that the new hero at the Boulevard was to return to lead the team again next season.

More riots, this time right outside my front door

It was certainly un-nerving that February, when I was awoken at 1.00am on a Sunday morning by the sound of shouting, chanting and breaking glass. I knew that the City Hall itself was secure because there had been no events that weekend but I certainly wasn't going downstairs to find out what was happening! In those early hours of Sunday 19th February store windows in Carr Lane and Paragon Street were smashed as the hooliganism that we had seen at Boothferry Park and at times at the Boulevard spilled out onto the streets, as drunken 'skinheads' ran amok around Victoria Square.

In total eight store windows were smashed and as the burglar alarms whined and the police sirens echoed around the deserted streets, 19 arrests were made and three policemen injured. Being in the middle of it all was pretty scary and I decided there and then that perhaps it was time to look for somewhere else to live.

I move out and Hull FC finish second

After almost 4 years of living 'over the shop' those riots in the City Centre made me realise that I certainly needed to get out of the City Hall. I looked around and settled for a house in the east of the City in Lime Tree Avenue on Garden Village, while Nigel the Hall Manager moved into the flat so there was still someone 'living over the shop'. My final weeks living at the Hall had seen sporadic outbreaks of violence and vandalism and just as things were quietening down a headline in the Hull Daily Mail of 'We'll Stop the Riots' saw it all break out again. Perhaps that's what's mean by a campaigning newspaper?

The City Centre was certainly changing as Whitefriargate, once the main retail focus of the City, was dealt a massive blow when, at the end of March, Woolworths closed its doors for the last time. However it was good to welcome the first commercial radio station to the region when on Monday 16th April the dulcet tones of Dave Fewster heralded the advent of Viking Radio. The Station soon got involved in joint promotions at the City Hall, their first being another ill fated visit of Bucks Fizz in May which saw just 600 people attending and the promoter Steven Stanley from Grimsby, losing a lot of money; so much, we thought, for the power of radio.

The rest of the rugby season saw some great performances and, after a run of 10 victories in the last 11 games and a great win over Rovers at Craven Park, we finish just behind the old enemy as Hull KR were crowned Champions. Even so it had been a great year, although slowly but surely finance wise at least, the alarm bells were starting to ring. Despite all the great performances and a squad of players that were the envy of every other Club, average gates fell by over 1,500 to 10,679.

However rugby wise it had been a great season when we'd introduced several young players and set a new First Division record by scoring 147 tries and racked up 831 points. It was for me, the consummate fanatic, my second 'watched every game' season, (after the great undefeated one of 1978/79) so at least I'd done my bit. I'd also seen every one of young Garry Schofield's record 37 tries in what was a year of changes, as Kevin Harkin had retired and Terry Day, Paul Prendiville, Charlie Stone, Ronnie Wileman, Garry Peacham, Mick Sutton and Steve Portz all left the Club. In a campaign when we recorded 30 wins in 42 games, we at least managed to lift one Trophy as we retained the Yorkshire Cup. As fans we had just wanted more, but with finance becoming a problem across the competition perhaps we failed to grasp completely too, the fact that compared with the followers of struggling Clubs like York, Doncaster or Oldham, at Hull FC we 'didn't know we were born!'

Strikes, injured stunt men and torrential rain: Hull Show goes out with a whimper!

Summer that year came and went, with the Hull fans captivated by some 'creative' advertising on Viking Radio featuring Peter Sterling who encouraged us to buy our passes and of course we all queued, as usual, on the first day they were issued.

At the City Hall we staged a sensational sell out show by Van Morrison, who is I'm told a nice bloke. I say I'm told because that night he refused to speak to anyone, including the audience. However despite the good weather that summer seemed to never end. There were the usual rugby rumours circulating and we went close to signing Kerry Boustead the Australian International winger, but his business interests finally precluded that deal. Then we went after his fellow countryman Les Boyd and got him signed before the Rugby League refused his registration because of a 12 months suspension he'd received in his home country. It seemed to us fans in Hull that the Rugby League were perhaps not happy with the two Hull Clubs monopolising the competition and soon afterwards Hull KR missed out on another big signing when Noel Cleal had put pen to paper, only for the Adelaide giant's registration to be refused because, over in Australia, he was declared bankrupt.

At work it was once again Hull Show time and I had a major problem to solve. A strike of Council staff was called after two gardeners were suspended for refusing to take out the new 'ride-on' multi mower grass cutting machines, because, they said, "The blades threw dog dirt at the driver". On the Monday and Tuesday of the week preceding the Show, there were pickets at the gates of East Park, with staff 'blacking' any work on the event and joining the strike. Things got a bit heated when, whilst I was in the Offices negotiating with shop stewards, another manager's van entering the park, refused to stop and hit one of the placard waiving strikers, catapulting him into a rose bed; perhaps that's what is meant by a flying picket! The whole unfortunate affair was over by Wednesday when the Council agreed to re-instate the staff and run tests on the mower and then it took a massive effort (and plenty of additional overtime), to ensure the show went ahead that Friday.

That incident set the tone for the week as the event was fraught with problems. The Police Dog Display Team had to cry off because they were deployed on the picket lines of the Miner's Strike, and the 'Dive of Death' was cancelled when stuntman 'Mr Incredible' put his back out getting out of his van. Then, whilst all over the media there were images of the hot summer days and shirt sleeve crowds at the Los Angeles Olympics, on the Friday night the heavens opened over East Park, so much so that some areas were under two inches of water. Of course, attendances were well down, which cast a major doubt over the future tenure of the event. Still the region was pretty upbeat as Walkington's Sue Hearnshaw won bronze in Los Angeles in the Long Jump, while down the road from the City Hall, the Tower had finally abandoned its short but 'interesting' role as a Rock Venue to concentrate on promoting 'popularist' entertainment, like drag artiste Kandy Le Barry and a rather voluminous lady called 'Busty' Johnson.

Fans are simply never satisfied

Sunday 2ⁿᵈ September 1984   *Hull 46 – Workington 2*

Despite the imminent arrival of Peter Sterling and his brother-in-law John Muggleton from Australia, the interest of the fans was certainly waning as season ticket sales dropped again. It was a situation that was possibly down to the fact that some supporters, almost drunk with our previous success, had become pretty disenchanted with finishing behind Hull KR in the previous campaign. Our opening league game against Workington saw us wearing new shirts sponsored by ABI Caravans, but the team was welcomed onto the field by a crowd of just 9,200.

That campaign began badly as Coach Arthur Bunting suspended four players after they turned up for training 'allegedly' drunk. Paul

Prendiville, Knocker Norton, Lee Crooks and Gary Kemble, expecting the scheduled video and tactical meeting at the Club that night, decided to go out for a few beers in the afternoon. Perhaps they went down to the Minerva where their old pal Sammy Lloyd had just taken over as Landlord and was brewing the new 'signature' ale 'Pilot's Pride'. Of course for our four heroes one beer, led to 'a bucket full' and on arriving at the Boulevard they discovered that Arthur Bunting had now scheduled a full training session. From the start it was apparent they were all struggling and when Paul Prendiville started being a bit 'too loud' Bunting lost patience and the four were sent home and dropped into the 'A' team the following weekend.

As the City's Entertainments Officer, my new duties included overseeing the operation of Hull Fair. The traditional ringing of the Hull Fair Bell by the Lord Mayor of Kingston upon Hull was that year conducted on the 'running board' of a brand new Superbob/ Matterhorn ride. This was preceded by a speech by Councillor (Mrs) Bell the Chairman of the Leisure Services Committee, which included in it an assurance to the Showmen that the Fair would, "Always remain on Walton Street", a reference to a recent Hull Daily Mail article that suggested that it was the proposed site for a new housing development. Some things never change and the use of the Fairground for various alternative projects has over the years been a regular talking point in the local media!

The running of the event was a massive responsibility with around 1,000,000 people attending that year, but despite working 18 hour days for over a week my thoughts were never far away from the growing excitement that surrounded the imminent arrival of Sterling and Muggleton from Australia. On the same day that we signed Welsh Rugby Union winger Kevin James, the two antipodeans flew into Heathrow after staying on in the Southern Hemisphere an extra week to attend team mate Brett Kenny's wedding in Sydney. They also arrived despite not having been granted work permits. However back then these were easily secured and the pair made their season debuts in a 33-30 defeat at Leigh.

A 'gnome' game at Boothferry Park

After beating Halifax, York and Leeds in the various rounds of the Yorkshire Cup, Hull again made the Final for the third year running and it was to be played out this time against the old enemy from across the River. There was still a tremendous rivalry between the fans, players and officials of the two Hull Clubs and all parties quickly agreed to the Rugby League's suggestion of playing the game at Boothferry Park. Hull KR, the Champions, were top of the League again whilst our slow and inconsistent start had left us languishing fourth from the bottom in the table! Although the game was not initially 'all ticket', they still sold quickly because the fans were worried they might not get in and caught up in this 'panic' I queued for about 2 hours for mine. In the end over 25,000 were in attendance for what was to be a truly extraordinary game.

There was certainly no end to the inventiveness and humour of the fans back in 1984 and both sets of supporters would constantly exchange insults and jibes whenever they were in each other's company. On the morning of the Final the Boothferry Park ground staff arriving to prepare for the game certainly got a surprise from a stunt that actually made the national newspapers. Overnight someone had climbed into the ground and left 13 perfectly painted garden gnomes resplendent in their Hull FC kits and pointed irregular hooped hats on the centre spot. These had been perfectly arranged in a circle around one Hull KR gnome, who was broken in half.

Hull KR fans; not very good at losing!

Saturday 29th October 1984   Hull 29 – Hull Kingston Rovers 12

Although we had 'held' the Yorkshire Cup for two years, few pundits believed that we could beat the table topping 'Robins' this time but as I took up my place in the South Stand, (with no segregation), I ended up next to the most obnoxious Hull KR supporter you could imagine. He was a short, stout individual, with a florid face, a big mouth, an enormous belly and several double chins which gave him the appearance of 'peering over a pile of pancakes'. He started as soon as we arrived with his "Scummy Dullers" remarks. You know the type, for whoever you support you have met them often enough on the terraces. Never looking at you, they don't direct their remarks at you personally, but at the team, the coach, the fans in the other stand etc. etc. but they do it right next to your ear! It was packed where we were stood and we had a great view and as Trevor said at the time, "There's no show without Punch, why the hell should we move".

The game kicked off and within 20 minutes we were in big trouble. Having conceded three early tries, the opposition's overwhelming supremacy was only disguised by the fact that George Fairburn their goal kicking Full-Back had missed all three conversions. You can just imagine how 'Motor mouth' Cyril (as we later found out he was called) was behaving by this time. He ragged us relentlessly as most of the 'friends' that were with him soon melted away into the crowd, while one or two of the less long suffering lads around us had to be restrained from 'poking' him there and then!

Although our defence was being swamped, a rare sortie down field saw Garry Schofield get us on the scoreboard with a penalty and then after Crooks had managed to somehow crash over the try line from close range, he converted that try to make it 12-8 at the break. However despite that try we all realised that we had never really looked like winning! Fat 'Cyril' even refused the chance to go for a 'cuppa' at half time, announcing that he would rather stay and "Take the p*ss out of these losers".

If we were to have any chance of winning at all, we needed to wrestle the initiative from the Red and Whites early in that second half. We pressed their line and forced a drop out and what happened next will certainly be a lasting memory for all FC fans that were there that day. The kick was fielded by Full-Back Gary Kemble right on the centre spot from where he started out on a fantastic arcing run beating first one player, then the next until he ran out of opposition tacklers and touched down in the corner. Schofield converted; the crowd erupted, while Cyril just grunted!! That was also his response when Schofield dropped a goal to make it 15-12 to Hull FC.

Our resurgence in the second half was all down to the magic of Peter Sterling. Cyril had commented on a few occasions in the first half, that Paul Harkin the Hull KR scrum half, had "Got Sterling in his Pocket" and few would disagree. But 'Sterlo' came out a different player and was soon completely eclipsing his opposite number.

I remember well not wanting to say too much to our fat friend because things were still in the balance, but after Norton and Kemble had scored two more tries, I could resist it no longer. After another Schofield conversion, I turned to him, to triumphantly give him 'both barrels', and of course, you guessed it, with still 15 minutes to go, Cyril had gone, slopping off towards the exits, with hundreds of other Hull KR fans!

The best was yet to come though, as Steve Evans intercepted a Hall pass near our line and shot off down the field for a 90 yard try, the crowd went mad and a few over excited FC Fans clambered over the fence and ran onto the field to mob the scorer. After what resembled 'The Retreat from Moscow' there were few Rovers fans left to witness ex Rovers player Paul Rose come on and last just a minute, before being sent off for "illegal use of the elbow".

As the final hooter went and with Dave Topliss the Club Captain an unused substitute, 21 year old Lee Crooks went up to receive the trophy and in so doing became one of the youngest Captains to have done it. I have not seen our 'fat friend' since, but over the years I have experienced countless dozens of his ilk across the Rugby League grounds of this country; they're just an accepted irritation when you're a fanatic!

Dietary tips from 'The Big Yin'

On Monday 26th November the City Hall staged one of its biggest shows to date when Billy Connolly played to a full house of adoring fans. At the peak of his popularity and notorious for the risqué nature of his act, the Scottish comedian was a cult figure and famed for his regular and often outrageous appearances on the Michael Parkinson Show on BBC TV. I was therefore a bit in awe of him, when I first met him. I was to accompany him to the Waterfront Hotel, where he was to make a cheque presentation to the Operation Raleigh 'outward bound' fund that was based in the City at that time. I first encountered Billy sat in the Main Hall stretched out over two chairs plucking at a banjo with his eyes closed. Immediately he struck me as just an ordinary if not a little hypersensitive guy and very much a person who displayed no malice, no hatred and little cynicism. I also soon discovered very quickly that he possessed an abrasive and wicked sense of humour, both on and off the stage and every sentence and statement he made seemed to end with a 'punch line'.

As we walked across Victoria Square and people did a 'double take' at this tousled haired 'beanpole' of a man dressed in purple pants and a vivid orange shirt, he talked as if we had been friends for years. I remember under his breath he asked me, "Why does every 'wee' lass in Hull look like those Cabbage Patch Kids?" (The toy of the moment back then) but he waved, smiled and occasionally did a little dance for the passing folks who recognised him. A sense of humour and natural timing radiated from everything he said and did and as I made 'conversation' about the much publicised birth of his first child Daley, he said, "Ohhhhh Yes! It was great; I was there when it happened. She came out one leg at a time, like a 'Can Can' dancer!" In an effort to keep the conversation going I mentioned the fact that despite most things he spoke about relating to food, he was still amazingly skinny. His response to my observation was to brush back his long hair from his face, laugh and say, "Accch, whilst I'm on the road I stick to a strict diet. I have a big plate of All Bran three times a day and drink around ten pints of 'Heavy' (beer) a night; I call it 'The Shit yourself thin' diet". I liked Billy!

That Boxing Day we went to Featherstone for a League match where despite the reversal at Wembley, we had always had a strong sense of camaraderie with those West Yorkshire fans. I well remember all 3,000 of the FC fans in attendance there subscribing to a half time bucket collection and reverently singing "Feed the Miners" to the Band Aid tune, as they did it. The miner's strike was hitting Featherstone hard and there were several young kids outside the ground selling homemade Marmalade and Jam just to try and earn a bit of cash. On that occasion we lost 20-4, but revenge was sweet as we beat the Colliers at the Boulevard, 4 days later.

The Road Back to Wembley

Saturday 9th March 1985   *Hull 6 – Widnes 6*

That was to be the season when, led by the mercurial Peter Sterling, we would return to Wembley for what is still generally accepted to be the best Final of all time. We had also reached the climax of the John Player Trophy, but this time our near neighbours took great delight in exacting revenge and we were beaten 12-0 at a snow covered Boothferry Park on Saturday 25th January. Our indifferent start to the campaign had rendered the League title out of our reach and so 'Sterlo' and the boys were intent on victory at Wembley to right the wrongs of our previous three visits to the Capital.

Our progress through the early rounds of the competition was clinical. We beat a poor Carlisle side 52-2, and then went to Halifax to win 22-6, on a day when the 'Mermaid' coach again broke down on the journey home, this time near Bradford, where we sat drinking cans of 'Super strength' Lager for two hours in the cold until the replacement bus arrived. Garry said that he thought drinking in such low temperatures had given him hypothermia and his ability to actually pronounce that disease correctly certainly indicated it had given him something! It was then that I decided that, for the sake of my sanity and the survival of my liver, in future I would drive to away games.

When 'the balls came out of the bag' for the next round we came out first, and were drawn at home to 'Cup Kings' Widnes. We immediately fancied our chances of progressing, but so did 'The Chemics'. Almost 12,000 crammed into the Boulevard for a televised game we simply had to win and in what was a tight, 'cagey' encounter, both teams felt one slip up could lead to defeat. With 'Sterlo' injured and sat with Arthur Bunting on the bench, defences were very much on top and so it was no surprise when at half time neither team had scored a point. We were all entertained throughout by a lady stood near us, who was hysterically shouting at Lee Crooks and who eventually turned out to be his girlfriend Janet.

Then, on the 57th minute, Norton finally broke away and passed on to Topliss who, using Muggleton as a foil on one side, found Divorty on the other and the youngster went crashing in to score and a Crooks conversion made it 6-0. However, just three minutes had passed before Lydon broke our defensive line wide out. He fed Currier who flew in for Burke to convert and make the scores level again. Despite Crooks shaving the outside of the post with a penalty attempt in the 72nd minute, that was how it stayed and the game ended tied at 6-6. So, having looked to have missed our chance, we faced the daunting prospect of a replay at Naughton Park in Cheshire the following Wednesday, where the home side had not lost a cup match for three years.

It's not often a Yorkshireman has a good night out in Widnes!

Wednesday 13th March 1985   *Hull 19 – Widnes 12*

Widnes were a tough proposition at home and so it was with some trepidation that I drove to the game that Wednesday night having feigned sickness to avoid working at an Orchestral Concert at the City Hall. Naughton Park (on the site where the current Widnes home now stands) was a funny old Stadium. Trevor the Fish who travelled over with me that night commented that it was like, "The Land that Time Forgot" which was an apt and accurate description. I had queued on the Tuesday to get one of a limited number of seat tickets that were on sale at the Boulevard, but the facilities were 'Spartan' when we finally found our seats in the 'Popular Side'. The gap between the rows was so narrow and I seemed to spend the whole game with my knees under my chin.

Once you were in, there was simply no chance of ever getting out again, and I was glad that I hadn't risked the 'Mermaid's' coach and had the mandatory few pints before the game, because if I had, I would almost certainly have been searching for a bottle!

About half the crowd of 10,000 had travelled from Hull, but the feeling of the locals was that we'd had our chance the previous weekend and that the 'Cup Kings' would 'blow us away' that night. It was a damp misty evening and the visibility was not improved by the home team's sparse flickering floodlights. We were playing the 'Cup holders' in their own 'backyard', although as usual, the 'FC Army' had little difficulty in 'out singing' the home fans.

Things were tough from the off, a couple of players were suffering from knocks and such was the state of the injured list that we drafted James Leuluai into the team despite him being sidelined with a broken hand. The physio just bandaged it up and sent him on. Lee Crooks commented years later that everyone was nervous that night and no doubt a few had a swig from the sherry bottle that Arthur Bunting used to leave in the dressing room to calm anyone who was suffering from pre game nerves!!

Widnes kicked off and tackled and harried us back into our own 25. Once they got the ball the home team looked sharp and confident and we all feared the worst when after just four minutes Widnes scored. Kurt Sorenson returned a long Schofield kick and broke our line to pass to Kevin Tamati. He brilliantly cut inside to pass back to the 'unmarked' Joe Lydon who shot in to score a great try which Mick Burke converted. Behind the sticks as our players awaiting the conversion, 'Knocker' Norton gave the lads a real 'finger wagging' but things looked bleak as we returned to the centre spot to kick off again.

We battled on and our hopes were raised and then dashed as Steve Evans narrowly missed an interception from a long Lydon pass and Kevin James was stopped in full flight by John Basnett. After half an hour some superb Hull handling by Muggleton, Leuluai and Norton created a half chance for Evans who shot between O'Loughlin and Currier to spin out of another tackle and fall backwards over the line to score. Schofield converted and we were level. Back came the Cup holders and a succession of errors saw us pushed back before Myler suddenly found a huge gap inside our 25 yard area and laid on a simple try for Keiron O'Loughlin which Burke converted.

Down 12-6 at half time, the scramble to get out of the seats and to the toilets was farcical, but no sooner had we got back, then Hull got a penalty which took us deep into the Widnes twenty five. Instead of going straight for the 'killer play', and thus risking losing possession, Hull meticulously went about slowly 'turning the screw' to prize open the home team's defence. After 9 minutes of constant pressure Norton dummied left and then passed right to the on rushing Kemble who was just held inches short by Mick Burke. Then came a defining moment in that season! Norton again broke the line and linked with Evans who passed onto half time substitute, youngster Andy Dannett. Big Andy strode forward, passed to O'Hara, and the winger with three players on his back squeezed in at the corner. Dane had no room to work in at all, but somehow got over the whitewash and we were just two points behind. Crooks however watched despairingly as his conversion headed straight for the centre of the goal posts, before being blown off course by a sudden freak gust of wind.

Then the 'Magician' Peter Sterling, who looked handicapped by that knee injury and had blood streaming from a cut on his forehead, took charge of the proceedings. He received the ball just ten yards from his own line and planted a massive kick down field that amazingly found touch just ten yards from the opposition's corner flag. Widnes won the ensuing scrum but Burke failed to play the ball properly and Schofield kicked the penalty to level the scores. As the crowd roared on the Airlie Birds, Widnes started to look vulnerable.

Frustrated by the superb tackling of Muggleton, Patrick, Skerrett and Dannett that pinned them near their own line, they started to kick desperately down field. From one such panic move the ball was fielded by Kevin James, who superbly kept it in play and then cut inside to beat the covering Basnett. He drew the rest of the cover as he flew towards the line before releasing Schofield who stepped out of two desperate last ditch tackles to touch down. Taking massive gulps of air to get his breathe back, Schofield then brilliantly converted his own try from out on the touch line.

You could feel the tension amongst the travelling supporters as the clock ticked down but in the end a superb drop goal by 'Knocker' Norton from 30 yards out sealed a 19-12 win. This match defining score was brilliantly set up by Sterling and as the ball sailed between the posts the FC fans went wild! Referee Holdsworth had a quiet night really, but had to split up Fieldhouse and Crooks on the hooter as fuelled by Widnes's frustrations a fight broke out. With the home supporters streaming away like water down a drain, the FC fans 'milked' every ounce out of the celebrations and as so often happens on these occasions, we simply didn't want to go home! We sang and danced on the terraces long after the last remaining Widnes supporter had shuffled away and the teams were long gone to the dressing rooms.

Hull had done it; we had beaten the odds (and the bookies) and got ourselves a semi-final tie at Headingley against Castleford. After the game the Club attributed the victory to their Physiotherapist Ray Norrie, who, they said, had worked miracles on a hamstring injury that had threatened to put Peter Sterling out of the game. Resembling a latter day Long John Silver, 'Sterlo', finishing limping heavily, with a bandage round his head, and his long hair caked in blood. Afterwards there was also an insight into how good the team spirit was, when it was revealed that winger Paul Prendiville had, after being dropped in favour of James after the drawn game at the Boulevard, tipped his replacement off about opposing winger John Basnett's tackling style, advice which James admitted later, "Helped me break their line to set up the winning try".

As the excitement was building towards Wembley, Club Captain Dave Topliss the architect of so many great victories, sadly left for Oldham and 'Sidewinder' Barry Banks moved on to Hunslet. Our 'A' Team Coach Clive Sullivan had also departed to take over as first team coach at Doncaster, whilst Lee Crooks was, at 21, voted Rugby League's 'Young Player of the Year'.

However, all us fans could think about was another Semi-Final and the chance of a return to Wembley where we all hoped we would see Lee Crooks crowned as the youngest ever Captain to raise the Challenge Cup. First though there was the little matter of getting past Castleford at Headingley.

Instant replay!! A brutal battle and Wembley again!

Wednesday 10th April 1985   *Hull 22 – Castleford 16*

On Saturday 6th April we played Castleford full of expectation, believing that it was a formality with Sterling at the helm and that later that afternoon we would all be preparing for another trip to Wembley. However no one told Castleford all this and in a dour encounter we ended up drawing the game 10-10, with Peter Sterling who was truly outstanding for us at scrum half, scoring a brilliant late try. Two Cup Final appearances that season were starting to take their toll and we were in the middle of a really tough fixture 'pile up', and so we had to play Barrow in between the two semi finals where, despite sending a full 'A' team, we still managed to draw 12-12.

So, the 'Mermaid' bus was back on the road again the following Wednesday and I was back on it, having decided because of the abject fear and concern I had for the outcome, to break from my now customary car travel and partake of 'pre drinks'. By 4.00pm we were back in the 'Three Horseshoes' on Otley Road, before taking our places on the East Terracing at Headingley in a crowd of over 20,000. There must have been at least 12,000 spectators from Hull, most of whom had learned their lessons from the traffic chaos before the Elland Road Final replay a couple of years previously and set off early. It was certainly turning out to be a season of replays after our heroics against Widnes in the previous round. Castleford had obviously noted the important role that the wonderful Peter Stirling played in the first game and targeted him from the off.

However it was Ian Orum, the Cas' scrum half, and recent convert from Rugby Union, that literally drew the first blood. Whilst we had started slowly, Castleford had scored an early try, but then Orum took Gary Kemble really late with 'a coat hanger' of a 'stiff arm' tackle which left the New Zealand International Full-Back severally concussed. The game was stopped for about 4 minutes whilst Gary was carried from the pitch to play no further part in the proceedings, or the next four games. With the referee taking no action, from the terraces we were 'baying for blood' and were not disappointed as, in the very next play, John Muggleton laid out their centre Hyde. It was then the Castleford fans' turn to go ballistic!

Then began to unfold one of the most intense and brutal halves of rugby I have ever seen. The Hull players were clearly enraged by the earlier foul by Orum (for which he got four games when it was reviewed by the Rugby League afterwards) and tore into Castleford. Sterling started to dictate the play as Lee Crooks broke their line and passed to Dane O'Hara who raced in just below us for Crooks to convert from the touchline. Four minutes later, with Castleford concentrating on retribution; we were ahead from a great Peter Sterling try. This prompted Castleford to bring on their secret weapon, Mal Reilly, their veteran Player/Coach. This was only his second game of the season and although he could hardly raise a trot, at the very next scrum he 'stiff armed' 'Sterlo' as he broke away; the hit was of such force that you could clearly hear the impact echo around the Stadium. The Aussie's feet left the ground and he was out cold on his back. Smelling salts brought him round before Timpson repeated the treatment a minute later and Sterling was carried off in a daze.

Back roared Castleford to equalize through David Rookley who shot through from Full Back to plant the ball between the posts. The conversion was successful and the game was 'all square'. Miraculously Sterling returned to the fray ten minutes later as Crooks broke through and sent Muggleton away, he passed to Kevin James who scorched into the corner to score. Next, 'Man of the Match' Crooks broke again this time sending Leuluei through, to 'shimmy' round the full back and in for another great try, which increased our lead to 22-12.

It was almost half time, but the 'action' wasn't over yet because after the hooter had sounded the linesman down on the touchline near us spotted a Castleford infringement and walked out with his flag held high. Hull took the penalty which Crooks dispatched into touch. He fell onto the ball after he tapped the restart and was immediately penalised for the very rare offence of a 'voluntary tackle' and all hell broke loose. Reilly hoisted a 'bomb' which Sterling caught behind the posts and six Castleford players piled in. There followed a ferocious fight behind the Hull try line which lasted well over two minutes and involved everyone, with the majority of the players openly brawling. Gary Schofield was pinned against the perimeter wall as two Castleford players pummelled him, whilst young Lee Crooks picked on probably the hardest man on the field Malcolm Reilly. The referee stood his ground to separate the teams and was just happy to get the players off the pitch.

In comparison the second half was a 'tepid' affair as Hull's fine defence restricted Castleford to a couple of breakaways and it ended as the first had begun with a solitary Castleford try leaving the final score 22-16. So, singing "We're the famous Hull FC and were off to Wembley, Wembleeeeeey Wemberleeeeeey " at the top of our voices, we all tramped back to the buses, having witnessed one of the most brutal games most of us had ever attended but looking forward to Wembley and Wigan. It had been a dour but sweet victory with a fracas the scale of which made for a lasting memory.

Rick Wakeman 'drains' the Punch Hotel

On the 2nd May the Hall hosted a sell out concert by Rick Wakemen who was to perform excerpts from his 'Rock operas', 'The Six Wives of Henry the Eighth', 'King Arthur and the Knights of the Round Table' and 'Journey to the Centre of the Earth'. It was a real 'boys night' audience made up of 'Ageing hippies' and long haired 'Musoes'. Rick himself walked on stage at the start to say, "Ok, Ok, quieten down guys, tonight I have a special treat for you all as the support act is none other than Top of the Pops dancers 'Flick Colby's Ruby Flipper'. They're good dancers and pretty raunchy too and the louder you scream the more the girls' take off. (Loud cheers) I've arranged that treat for you because myself and the Hall Manager Mr Allen are off to the pub to get pissed". AND we did!!!

I have never ever drunk so much beer in half an hour in the whole of my life, but Rick was superb company and bought everyone in the bar a drink. Mary the Landlady thought he was "A lot better than those Two Degrees women!" whilst Rick went back to the Hall and played a superb set, which I watched before going home to bed with headache. There was no way I was going to the after show party that night. I'd have probably drowned!!!

The greatest Challenge Cup Final of all time? But scant consolation when you lose

Saturday 4ᵗʰ May 1985   *Hull 24 – Wigan 28*

So we were at Wembley again for a showdown with the mighty Wigan, but few would have thought that the Hull FC team could have been anything but exhausted. The game followed another amazing 'fixture pile up' that had seen us play 10 games in 18 days, including three on consecutive days in a period of 5 matches in 7 days. The week before the final we had played Wigan at Central Park in a Premiership play-off semi final game and not surprisingly lost 46-12, in fact previously in that amazing month as the fixtures piled up, we had lost to them again, this time by 40-4 and therefore few outside West Hull gave us a 'prayer' of winning the Final.

All around the City shop windows were decorated and the Hull players were becoming real celebrities, opening events and 'kissing babies'. When the big day came I travelled down by train just as I had with Mum for my first Final, all those years before in 1960. For the first year in six, I hadn't paid into the 'Mermaid Wembley Trip' as it seemed at 35 I was starting to grow out of the boozy entrapments that went with those great years of watching the team I loved. I expect I had a few cans on the train, but remember thinking that the final was possibly the longest I had ever seen, no doubt down to the fact that I was reasonably sober when I watched it.

The old Stadium looked wonderful graced as it was by an amazing 99,801 fans, as the capacity was increased and the segregation abandoned following an unprecedented demand for tickets. The Final also featured, a then record, 10 foreign players with six starting for Hull FC. All the match reports after the game praised both teams and billed the game "The Best Cup Final Ever Seen". It might have been, and I am sure many pundits who were around back then will tell me that it was, but there is simply nothing to compensate for getting beaten at Wembley, and a few statistics are not going to change the fact that for me and thousands of other Hull FC fans it was an unmitigated disaster. There is no greater day in the Rugby League calendar than the Challenge Cup Final at our National Stadium, unless of course you lose.....again! The history, the occasion, the pomp and the circumstance, the colour and the noise were all there in abundance at that 50th final at Wembley, but it was still nothing if you hadn't won.

It was absolutely packed in the North East Corner of the ground where, Barry, Hard up Harry and Trevor the Fish joined me having travelled by taxi from the usual Knightsbridge Hotel (that no doubt the 'Mermaid lads' were 'terrorising'). Our team included Garry Kemble back for the first time since his injury in the Semi Final but he was strangely quiet that afternoon and looked to still not be fully fit. We pinned a lot of our hopes that day on Peter Sterling and John Muggleton who had both been in scintillating form of late, and the "Sterling Silver" and "Arthur Bunting's Black and White Army" banners were all around Wembley that day.

We started so well too. Despite our previous five Finals being hampered by slow starts we were straight out of the blocks, taking play immediately into the Wigan half. Crooks stroked over a 2nd minute penalty and then after 9 minutes we went further ahead. Sterling handled the ball twice in a flowing move before Kemble's deft inside pass found Kevin James who triumphantly planted the ball down near the corner flag, but as we sang "We're the Barmy FC Army" Crooks was wide with the conversion. Back came Wigan who started to make an impression on our defence and soon they were level with a try by Ferguson, who had been flown back from Australia by the Lancashire Club, for the game. He skipped round O'Hara to touch down, for Henderson Gill to convert.

The opposition were now starting to dominate and after 27 minutes Kenny just seemed to be cantering as Mick Ford put him away near half way. He then accelerated past Kemble, to give Wigan a lead they were destined not to lose. By Half Time it was 16-8 after a brilliant try by Henderson Gill had the Wigan fans dancing on their seats and us the 'FC Faithful' crying in our beer.

Half time was a sombre affair, and unlike many times in the past I was even finding it hard to find any solace in the bottom of a plastic pint glass. Subdued and depressed I stood with the other Hull fans around me and faced some considerable taunting from the 'Pies' supporters who were already celebrating. I had in my mind that first Cup Final defeat against Wigan, the one I watched with Mum in the little front room at 23 Aylesford Street all those years previously when we had been thrashed 30-13. Three minutes into the second half and things got worse. Brett Kenny twisted his way round Sterling and released Shaun Edwards who had a clear 25 yard run to the posts and at 22-8 the game certainly looked be up for Hull FC. Then straight from the restart Sterling broke free and went on a dodging run downfield which saw him get within ten yards of the line, as the cover came in he sent out a looping pass to Steve Evans who crossed the whitewash in the corner but Crooks missed again with the conversion.

Back came Wigan as Ferguson broke away from a tackle by Divorty and Schofield and careered downfield for a spectacular 60 yard touch-down. Then, the impossible happened; well at least it almost happened. On the 51 minute mark with Wigan leading 28-12, we produced three great sets of attacking rugby as James Leuluai started what was to be an historic fight-back. A big thrust into the line by Paul Rose saw our second rower release a great short ball which Leuluai grabbed out of the air to score an unlikely try but Crooks missed again. Next up it was the turn of Sterling as ten minutes later he fed a superb delayed short pass to Divorty who scored again, but despite it being nearer the posts, this time Schofield missed the conversion. Then two minutes later as the flagging Wigan defence gave James Leuluai too much room in the centre of the field, he skipped through a gap, ghosted past two players and ran off to score one of the tries of the season to put us within 4 points of the opposition but again Schofield missed the goal. The hooter went and all the Wigan fans who had been dancing at half time breathed a massive sigh of relief as dejectedly we sunk to our knees.

We had come so close to the greatest come back the game had ever seen and had we kicked our goals we would forever have been known as the 'Comeback Kids'. Sadly it was not to be and I travelled home on the train in a deep depression with my only consolation being the thought of the lads from the 'Mermaid Wembley Weekend' trying to dodge the Wigan fans and make the best of the rest of the stay in the Capital. At least on the long journey home I was able to do what I have always done best in those situations and grieve on my own. It's somehow so much easier to take when you don't have to listen to other like minded passionate souls trying to explain it all away and make you feel better.

I wondered if I would ever get over it but at least I wasn't Lee Crooks the local lad who I had seen at the end of the game in amazing isolation sat crying inconsolably on the pitch. He said years later in his excellent autobiography 'From Hull to Hell and Back' "I was the Captain and I was on goal kicking duties. I missed four goals and yet if I had kicked three of them we would have won. Blaming myself for my team losing a Cup Final is the hardest thing I had ever had to deal with". The man destined to never be the youngest captain ever to lift the Challenge Cup was castigating himself, he was distraught, desolate and crestfallen and that afternoon around 45,000 Hull FC supporters knew exactly how he felt. It was going to take a long time for Lee Crooks and I to get over it! Wembley eh? It's a wonderful place to play and support your team, but a shocking, shocking place when you lose.

Chapter 4

Sad times, as Charlie Watson bows out and 'Sully' is taken ill

That summer was a busy one with a full outdoor entertainments programme in the parks and on Queens Gardens but tragedy struck for all Rugby League fans in Hull with the news on 6th July that a collision between a car and an articulated lorry on the M62, led to the untimely demise of Hull FC's revered ex Chairman, Charlie Watson. He was rushed to hospital with his wife, but died shortly afterwards. Charlie had figured in our Board Room in one capacity or another since the early 70's and of course lead the team out as Chairman in the famous 1980 all Hull Final. It was the tragic end to a life dedicated to Hull FC, which I hope I did justice to in the previous book.

As the rest of the world was enjoying the excitement and razzamatazz of 'Live Aid' and Bob Geldof was demanding "Give us your 'Fuckin' Money" on live TV, in Hull the City Council was trying to save some money and we were working on a replacement for the now outmoded Hull Show entitled the 'Hull Summer Spectacular'. This new event, still held in East Park, saw the outlay by the Council cut by half and featured a host of stunt teams, bands, dancers, entertainments, dog display teams, fairgrounds and even a Rugby League Sevens Competition. 23,000 attended over the two days which was still 5,000 short of the figure that was needed to break even, but it was generally hailed as a success. To cut costs, a lot of the old Hull Show's competitive sections that were previously staged under canvas, were transferred to another new event the Autumn Craft Fair at the City Hall. There was bad news circulating amongst the rugby fans of Hull too, with rumours rife that Clive Sullivan was in hospital in Leeds having tests for a serious illness. Everyone thought he would be fine, he was a model athlete with a statuesque sporting physique and anyway he was only 42!!! Nothing could ever happen to Clive, could it?

So what of the season ahead? Well, when the news broke that 'Sterlo' was not to return it certainly didn't do anything to engender confidence. Still, Arthur Bunting and Roy Waudby had flown off to Australia to try and sign a couple of players with, it was rumoured, Scott Gale and Geoff Gerard on their 'shopping list'. The latter was subsequently to sign on a two year deal, whilst the former decided to go back to college, for now!

You can't close the Threepenny Stand!

Sunday 1st September 1985   *Hull 10 – Widnes 33*

In the first part of this chronicle I described in detail the first ever Shareholder's Meeting I attended at the Library Theatre in 1973. Since that day, when Dad got the old tin box from under the bed and handed over the envelope that contained his share certificate, I hadn't missed a meeting. However the one that took place at The Station Hotel that year, was the strangest I have ever attended. As I arrived at 6.45 on Friday 26th July, it was as if no one cared about the balance sheet or the Chairman's Reports because everyone seemed preoccupied with one burning issue. Just six hours before the meeting was due to start, it was announced by Chairman Roy Waudby that following the Bradford City fire disaster and the creation of the Safety of Sports Ground Act, the Threepenny Stand had, because of its wooden construction, been condemned, and from the start of the season it was to be closed.

Everyone at the meeting was stunned by this news! Not one question was asked on the accounts (which showed a massive deficit of £191,000) as the shareholders sat in disbelief. Was the timing of the announcement a tactical ploy? Well we'll never know but if it was it worked, because all the talk was about the demise of the old edifice that was central to our history, while no one seemed to care about the fact that we were in financial meltdown. There was even talk from the floor of the meeting of starting a 'Threepenny Stand Rescue Fund'. In addition to this announcement, once the meeting had finished, Roy Waudby informed those present that Clive Sullivan was seriously ill and that he had liver cancer which was "Causing a great deal of concern".

For the first game of the new season against Widnes which we lost 10-33, the old Stand was indeed shut; the atmosphere within the Boulevard was best described as 'Flat' and the gate of just 7,027, the lowest for five years. The following week we travelled to York and beat them, but the only point of note from that game is that on a thundery night we finished with the Wiggington Road Stadium, which had no floodlights, in almost complete darkness.

A hundred wins against the 'Dobbins'

Sunday 6ᵗʰ October 1985   *Hull 28 – Hull KR 6*

That season I just turned up every week at the Boulevard but it was obvious that a lot of the 'new comer' supporters that had now gone missing had detected that perhaps as a Club we were slipping backwards. Finance was obviously a problem at Board level, as players who retired or left the Club were not replaced. Our form was certainly a bit 'inconsistent' however on 6ᵗʰ October we witnessed a real 'red letter' day for Hull FC, and indeed for Rugby League in the City of Kingston upon Hull. That day we played the 'old enemy' at the Boulevard and in doing so recorded our 100ᵗʰ victory over Hull KR. However it was not just that 'milestone' that made the game so memorable because Hull KR stood undefeated so far that season. For once we beat them comprehensively and in so doing we knocked our arch rivals off the top spot in the League. The wind howled across the pitch and right into our faces as we stood in the only place to be on such occasions, the slightly improved and now newly re-opened Threepenny Stand. It might have been deemed a lot safer having just received a few crush barriers and a new fire certificate, but that didn't stop two fans from being ejected for burning a Rovers scarf in the rafters.

From the moment Garry Schofield scored his first 'Derby try' the result was never in doubt and it was one of those rare encounters when after about half an hour you could enjoy the occasion, because there was no way that the opposition were going to get back into the game.

In the 15th minute Paul Eastwood picked up a bouncing Fred Ah Kuoi pass and took it headlong into a three man tackle before popping out a great one handed pass for Schofield to fly in and score. Seven minutes later Lee Crooks set up Schofield for his second, both of which were converted by Crooks from the touchline. Rovers then started to visibly wilt and from that point onwards the score was never in doubt, but it took us until the 65th minute to score again.

Steve Norton picked up a loose ball, strode into 'the Robin's' defensive line and released a pass to Schofield. He passed on to O'Hara who shot down the wing brilliantly wrong footing Andy Kelly and crossed the line without a hand being placed on him. By now the whole re-populated Threepenny Stand was in full song, demanding 'their father's gun' in that popular chant that, to this day, still graces these occasions. It was also the first time that I can remember our 'Friends' from across the River being referred to as the 'Dobbins'.

The Hull pack were terrorising the Rover's six and the great Gavin Miller had to be substituted after one mighty crash tackle from Gerard and Skerrett. Five minutes later we were again deep in the Rover's half and Gerard put Ah Kuoi through a big gap in the floundering Rover's defence, before he passed onto Gascoigne to touch down to the right of the posts. This was followed by a rare Rovers attack in which Chris Burton the Hull KR second rower squeezed a ball out to Robinson close to our line and the centre scored in the corner.

However, it was Hull FC's afternoon as Garry Kemble came into the line and onto a Divorty pass, before switching play back inside to Stuart

Vass, (a substitute who had only been on the pitch for thirty seconds) who scored under the posts to leave Schofield another easy conversion. As referee Allett blew the final whistle the crowd clambered over the fences and onto the pitch to celebrate a great afternoon's work, as we saw off our deadliest rivals in fine style.

"One of the greatest men I have known"

There are occasionally times in the life of a sports fanatic when that daily 'pain' of expectancy, joy, worry and anxiety is eclipsed by events away from the sporting arena and your beloved team. Times, when you are made to realise that winning that next game and getting one over your rivals isn't everything. Back in the late 70's I had experienced that feeling when Mum and Dad died and that October I was to feel it again when we lost someone who had been an institution in our game, our City and our community. Clive Sullivan was an iconic character, who had been seriously ill with Liver Cancer for a couple of months and although he had fought hard and valiantly, on 8th October it was announced that he had died leaving the rugby communities from both sides of the City united in their grief.

The Sullivan family wanted a quiet funeral and their wish was of course respected, but the people of the City needed a Memorial Service to say a final farewell to one of the greatest and most honest sportsmen Kingston upon Hull had ever seen. In addition to that, with the new south orbital road across the western dockland almost complete, there was a gathering opinion that it should be named after Clive.

As the local newspaper led with the headline, "The Man who united the City", the two Club Chaplains, Allen Bagshawe and John Leeman, were working with Gerald Bridgeman the Vicar of Holy Trinity on a Memorial Service that was to touch the whole City as it celebrated the life of a legend and a giant in local sport.

We all met in the Market Place to ensure that we got to Holy Trinity Church early on that darkest of Fridays, 18th October, and although there was an hour to go to the start of proceedings, the famous 'Mother

Church' was already three-quarters full with the great and the good from both sporting and civic communities. The Lord Mayor of Kingston upon Hull Jim Paton, (a great Hull FC fan who usually stood on the terracing at the Division Road end of the Boulevard), had worked hard for days with the Council Planning Department to get that new road named after Clive.

That day Jim took his place in the front pew flanked by the Directors of the two Hull teams, (for both of whom, Clive had scored over one hundred tries). Roz, Clive's wife was there too, whilst I sat with Frank and Bill from work and 'Hard up Harry' and Garry from the Boulevard. Both sets of supporters were bedecked in their famous colours and there was even a banner outside the Church which simply read, "Night Night Clive: We'll never forget you". Many in that congregation shed a tear and like me became enthralled in the celebration of the life of a great man, whilst at the same time, despairing at the futility of his untimely demise.

The service which was relayed outside into the Market Place for the thousand or more fans who couldn't get into the church, was as much a celebration as a Requiem, and a high point was reached when the Reverend Bridgeman announced, to a deal of spontaneous applause, that the new south orbital road would, as we had all hoped, be named 'Clive Sullivan Way'.

There were several speeches and memorials and Hull Chairman Roy Waudby read the lesson from 'Corinthians', which included the line, "Every-one who competes in the games goes into strict training. They do it to get a crown that will not last; but we do it to get a crown that will last forever"; at which point you could have heard a pin drop. Ex Player, Coach and Broadcaster, David Doyle-Davidson also delivered a passionate address which had the whole congregation spellbound.

He concluded with the words, "He was one of the greatest people I have ever known" and the famous old church fell silent. The Great Britain team named their new mascot 'Sully' in Clive's memory, as at just 42 years of age, the game of Rugby League in this Country lost its first black National Captain and the last British RL player to this day to lift the World Cup. That was the day that the City of Hull and every supporter in it lost a role model, a gentleman and a legend.

Africa (and Hull City Hall) in Crisis

In that month of October the 'Live Aid' effect finally reached the City of Kingston upon Hull. The Country was totally captivated with Bob Geldoff's effort and this euphoria prompted the City Council's Cultural Services Committee to attempt to 'do their bit' for the starving millions in Africa as it was decided that we would stage a concert at the City Hall to raise funds to help the cause. Alice Tulley the Committee Chairman was a revered member of the Quaker Community so there was none of that "Give us your F*ckin Money" stuff, but it was down to me and local promoter Anne Spellman to make the necessary arrangements for what was to be Hull's own 'Live Aid' event. Anne, who was a larger than life 'showbiz type', threw herself into the production and had soon contracted 24 acts to perform at the concert; there was no going back now!!

The people of Hull responded really well and on Monday 28th October 1985, 1300 people sat down in Hull City Hall to enjoy an eclectic mix of music, comedy and dance. Appearing, most bizarrely, in a Frogman suite, Local MP John Prescott hosted the event, accompanied by that ageing stalwart of TV's 'Junior Showtime' back in the early 70's, Bobby Bennett. He wasn't greatly appreciated by the typical Hull crowd most of who asked the question, "Where the hell have you dug him up from". In my youth when he was popular I could understand kids' shows like 'Joe 90', 'Thunderbirds' and even 'Trumpton', but Junior Showtime always had me hiding behind the settee. Quite how Bobby got on the bill that night, heaven knows, but we sat through 'turns' by several local pop groups, a singing Rabbi, (singing 'If I were a Rich Man') several dance troupes and many, many aspiring singers.

One 13 year old girl that appeared quite early in the show that night and did a very polished impersonation of Margaret Thatcher, was in fact Debora Stephenson, who went on to win Independent TV's talent show Opportunity Knocks and subsequently starred in 'Coronation Street' as

Frankie Baldwin. I guess in some small way the staff and I gave Debbie a helping hand, because we first spotted her earlier that year when she got up on the Summer Entertainments stage on Queen's Gardens and did a few impromptu impressions. It was that appearance and her obvious talent that prompted us to offer her a spot on the show that night.

As for 'Africa in Crisis', well looking back the show itself was a bit of a shambles, mostly due to there being far too many acts to cram onto the stage and in the end it over ran by two and a quarter hours. When it finally finished at 12-15am, with the full cast singing the American 'Band Aid' single 'We are the World', there were more people on stage than were left in the Hall. Still they received a standing ovation from Councillor Tulley, Jim Payton the Lord Mayor and the 30 strong audience that were left in the auditorium. A 'pledge line' (Crisis 25252) set up that day by Hull Telephones and staffed by local dignitaries, including the Bishop of Hull and Jim the Mayor, raised £11,000 and when this was added to the takings of the concert, it made for a very worthy donation of £15,000 to the 'Live Aid' funds.

It had certainly been a long day for the Lord Mayor and he commented as he left the Hall, "If Africa's in Crisis, then after sitting there for over 5 hours on those City Hall seats, I think we have a few issues of our own here in Hull, Peter. I'm away to my bed" As for me, well I went home, had a glass of wine and mused on the fact that after co-ordinating that lot, reducing some performances and dealing with irate 'artistes' and in some cases their even more irate parents; at Wembley, Bob Geldoff had it easy.

'Kershaw's Law'

Sunday 17th November 1985   *Hull 10 – New Zealand 33*

As a sports fan, occasionally you remember a game for no other reason than the abject inability of the officials. A match that animates that perfectly was one of the most infamous and controversial matches that the Boulevard ever saw. It was played on a cold and blustery afternoon

Parading the Championship Trophy around a packed Boulevard, as League Champions 1983.

Savouring the moment; the victorious squad that won the Championship in 1983.

The ladies of Glenrose Fishfoods get into the Wembley spirit before the 1983 Challenge Cup Final. *(Courtesy of Hull Daily Mail)*

Saturday 7th May 1983. Fans prepare to depart from Paragon Station en route for Wembley again, where they were to witness Hull's most disappointing Final. *(Courtesy of Hull Daily Mail)*

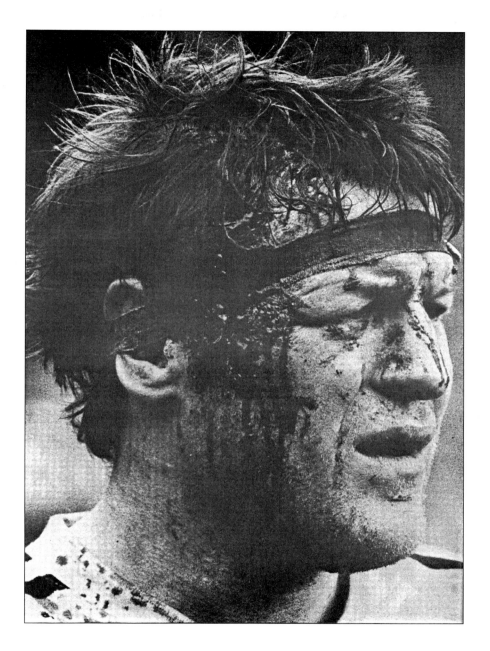

The picture says it all, as battered and blooded Charlie Stone
has to accept the humiliating defeat at Wembley against
Featherstone in 1983.

Back in the Yorkshire Cup final again in 1984 as the great Peter
Sterling weaves his magic at Boothferry Park against Hull KR
(Courtesy of Mike Jacklin)

The victorious Hull team show off the Yorkshire Cup after defeating
Hull KR 29-12 at Boothferry Park on 27th October 1984
(Courtesy of Mike Jacklin)

After the victory and three things that the Hull fans loved;
Peter Sterling, a trophy and a can of lager!
(Courtesy of Hull Daily Mail)

Mark Chalton (left) and the other ball boys sit in the dugout at the
Boulevard during the 1984/85 season.

(Courtesy of Mark Charlton)

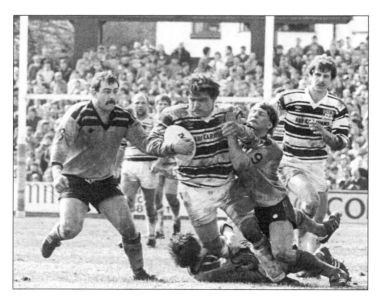

Trevor Skerrett takes on the Castleford defence in the Challenge
Cup semi-final at Headingley on Saturday 6th April 1985.

(Courtesy of Hull Daily Mail)

A concussed Peter Sterling with Dane O'Hara, Kevin James and
James Leuluai in the Headingley Dressing Rooms after the 1985
Challenge Cup semi-final replay win against Castleford.
(Courtesy of Hull Daily Mail)

Almost 99,000 watch probably the greatest Challenge Cup Final
ever, as Sterling breaks from the scrum against Wigan at Wembley
on 4th May 1985.

Consoled by a fan who is about to be escorted from the field, Paul Rose and Gary Divorty leave the pitch at Wembley after the 1985 Final against Wigan.

Paul Prendiville in full flight towards the line against Salford at the Boulevard on 1st December 1985.

and completed the New Zealand tourists 1985 Tour. In an astonishing first half when Easingwold referee Gerry Kershaw completely lost control, five players were sent off and Hull's teenage sensation Garry Schofield left the field on a stretcher. Four of the players that were dismissed went off in pairs. Firstly, Lee Crooks exchanged punches with Clayton Friend and they were both sent off in the 11th minute, to be followed by the two hookers Shaun Patrick and Howie Tomati who emerged from a scrum a little later exchanging blows like two demented boxers. Then in injury time the Kiwi half back Olsen Filipaina was dismissed for dangerous kicking; as he stood on Gascoigne's head.

We led 10-6 at half time but the 10 man Kiwi side stormed back to win with an amazing 33-10 score-line. Our first half try was scored by Garry Schofield, whilst the Kiwi's scored 6 tries in that second half. Both coaches complained about the refereeing after the game and said that Mr Kershaw had been "Overzealous" and a hastily arranged Disciplinary Panel after the match made up of English League chairman Joe Seddon and New Zealand Tour Manager Jim Campbell confirmed that opinion. They found all five players guilty, but ruled that in each case their sending off had been sufficient punishment.

When challenged about his display, after the game by the Press, Referee Kershaw said, "I had to do it, if I hadn't, then the game would have been a farce, it was 'Kershaw's Law' that won the day in the second half, quite simply it was up to me to guarantee the game did not become a succession of brawls and fist fights". At least he explained his actions, back in the days when referees were allowed to answer back and not 'gagged' after games as they are today.

Too many balls spoil the draw; it's another Rugby League embarrassment

Wednesday 11th December 1985   *Hull 14 – St Helens 57*

Having been knocked out of the Yorkshire Cup in the semi final by Hull KR, our bad luck continued that December without a ball being kicked in anger. Despite some patchy form in the League campaign, having beaten Swinton and Salford at the Boulevard in the first two rounds, we had reached the last eight of the John Player Trophy, and so, we eagerly awaited the draw for the quarter finals.

On Monday 2nd December, the day that local poet Phillip Larkin died, I got up early to watch the draw being made in front of a massive TV audience on the new and ground breaking BBC Breakfast Show. In those days each Club in the competition was, before the first round draw, allocated a number in line with their position in the alphabet. They kept that number throughout and it was included in the bag for each draw, until they were knocked out.

We should all have realised that something was wrong when the first ball out of the bag that morning was number 1, which was Barrow, who had been knocked out the day before. However despite this, the draw continued and we were allocated a home match against York, whilst Hull KR were drawn away at Warrington. There was however one too many balls in the bag, which was certainly apparent when David Oxley the Chairman of the Rugby League, (a man nick-named by the Threepenny Stand 'The Cheshire Cat' because he could smile through anything) got to the end of the proceedings with a ball still remaining.

40 minutes later, amidst much confusion, the draw was retaken 'off camera' with, this time, the right eight balls in contention and Hull FC were drawn away at Saints whilst Rovers ended up with another away tie, but this time at lowly York. There were complaints a plenty, but the second draw was endorsed by the Governing Council of the Rugby Football League, and so we made our plans to travel to Knowesley Road, St. Helens the following weekend.

Then the frost descended in Lancashire and the game was postponed 18 hours before it was due to be played. It was rescheduled for the following Wednesday when after I had taken a day off work to travel over to Lancashire, we were 'demolished' 57-14. It was our biggest defeat ever and followed a shambolic performance which epitomised our plight that season. We struggled to contain a rampant Saints attack, dropped lots of ball in our own half and had nothing left energy wise with which to counter attack. I guess, once again at a time of utter disappointment, and a new, unwanted record, I could say "I was there", but there was little doubt that the magic of the last 5 years was fading fast, and the reality was that after a good start to the season my team was falling apart.

The end of the 'Golden Era' as Bunting bows out

Sunday 22ⁿᵈ December 1985   *Hull 8 – Swinton 16*

There were plenty of protagonists and 'doom and gloom merchants' around back then and everywhere you went fans were full of their own theories about what was happening at the Club. The Board, the Players, referees and even the Rugby League were blamed for our demise but most folks who had a theory placed the responsibility squarely, but perhaps unfairly, at Arthur Bunting's door. That's what usually happens with fans when the chips are down, everything has been tried and you're still struggling. Despite his past exploits, it has to be the Coach's fault. On the Sunday before Christmas I drove over to Manchester for the Swinton game in my Opel Ascona, with Harry, Garry and a friend of mine from Garden Village called Andy.

Station Road was a once great Stadium which had fallen from grace and several sections of terrace were closed altogether. The weather was dire too and as, in a biting wind, the rain poured down from a leaden sky, we stood for 80 minutes with water running out of our shoes and lost to a poor but physical Swinton side 8-16. At the end a disheartened chorus of "Bunting Out" rang out from some of the 600 or so diehard fans that had made the trip over the Pennines, but of course I didn't join in, although as we all got back to the car and wrung out our Hull Shirts and 'bobble hats', we could probably see their point.

It was already a well known fact that the Board of Directors had scheduled a special meeting to discuss the Club's plight with Arthur and his Assistant Kenny Foulkes for that Monday and it was there, to herald the end of a 'Golden Era', that Arthur Bunting resigned as Head Coach.

His Assistant Kenny Foulkes was asked to take over and although rumours were rife around the City about Arthur's replacement, Club Chairman Roy Waudby made it clear that Kenny was there until the end of the current campaign. Fast diminishing financial resources, falling gates, ageing players and struggles in the Boardroom, meant that the coaching role was a 'poison chalice' although at least Foulkes still had a job and stated afterwards, "I arrived at the meeting expecting to be sacked and walked out as Head Coach". Fred Ah Kuoi became his Assistant and although in hindsight perhaps Arthur Bunting's tenure at the Club had run its course, it was sad when he left and to this day he is still acknowledged as a Legend and an all time great of Hull FC.

In the New Year things went from bad to worse and the anticipated 'new coach effect' that the Board had pinned their hopes on, was certainly not materialising. Injuries continued to plague the team, whilst there was now an obvious aversion by the Board to spend any money, which indicated things were getting tough off the field. We were knocked out of the Cup in the early rounds by Hull KR, this time by 22-6 and a three week period of inactivity due to some heavy frosts and snow did nothing to help the Club's finances either.

As an aside from the rugby there was sad occurrence on 22nd February 1986 when local Cottingham Cartoonist Ern Shaw died at Hull Royal infirmary. Ern had produced several cartoon strips in the morning papers including the award winning Dingbats and also illustrated a famous set of playing cards featuring Disney characters. Of course for all FC fans he is best remembered for those pen and ink sketched cover illustrations that adorned the Hull FC match day programmes in the 50's. When photography was expensive his caricatures of the Hull team were a regular feature of the 40's and 50's and his passing was marked by the City and the Club.

As the end of the season approached we were beaten away from home 57-14 by Saints, 44-6 by Wigan and 43-16 by Warrington and despite Kenny Foulkes' best efforts, things continued to decline. Home gates were still dropping and it was as if some fans had just had too much success. Although they still 'supported' the Club they certainly didn't do it with their feet or their cash, as average attendances at the Boulevard went down to 6,245 and by April 1986 we were mid table, a situation that we weren't used to at all. Things were not helped by the fact that Rovers had just beaten Leeds in an energy sapping semi-final which saw our mortal enemy progress to Wembley, where thankfully and to the relief of everyone in West Hull, they were beaten by Castleford.

Lee Crook's attempts at marketing go a little wrong!

Sunday 19th March 1986   *Hull 16 – Warrington 43*

There was a good story doing the rounds back then about that defeat at Warrington on 19th March when, at the end, a small group of fans protested at pitch side and Lee Crooks went across to talk to them. He said how sorry he was about the performance and stated he would clear it with the Board so that if they said at the turnstiles at the Boulevard the following week, "We were at Warrington", they would get in free. Lee then added "But don't tell anyone else" Of course word spread like wild fire amongst the Hull fans and the Directors were not happy when they were told after the Salford game that dozens had been admitted without paying after using the 'secret password'. A larger than usual gate of near 5000 for that game, which we won 34-16, certainly added some credence to the story and I bet Lee was popular in the boardroom that day!

Tough times, but we always beat Leeds

Sunday 6th April 1986   *Hull 35 – Leeds 18*

By April my support away from home was on 'auto pilot' I just went, not expecting anything and I was usually not disappointed. On a breezy spring Sunday I went along to Headingley for an encounter against the 'Loiners' which took place the weekend after those cup semi finals. I drove over to Leeds having just changed my car and bought myself an

Opel Manta which I found could really motor. In those days Leeds were not particularly well supported and 500 or so FC fans made up a gate of just 5,829. It was a windy afternoon and the assembled 'FC Army' took up position in the South Stand where despite our demise, the rafters rang to the strains of 'Old Faithful'. The fact that we were all pretty disgruntled didn't matter because when you're away from home, you always sing no matter how you feel. In the end we came out unlikely winners that day. Savoy Tyres, who back then sponsored the Hull FC Man of the Match, gave the award to Lee Crooks who was superb all afternoon in a game in which referee Mr Kershaw of Easingwold had little to do.

It was a tremendous win, but although we were to beat Leeds again at home the following week, the rest of the season was poor fare which saw us lose to Widnes, Warrington, Oldham and Halifax however we beat Hull KR 28 -2 at Craven Park in the penultimate game and as always that made up for a lot.

If easily offended......don't accept tickets as presents!

As summer approached business remained brisk at the City Hall. A few months previously I had received a call from George Foster the Manager of the infamous Roy 'Chubby' Brown, a comedian who had built up quite a reputation in 'Clubland' for being the lewdest around. He was, it was reported, even giving Bernard Manning a run for his money. George suggested that he hire the Hall for Roy's first 'auditorium performance' in the region, and so, against my better judgement, I agreed providing that there was sufficient warning as to the content of the evening's 'entertainment'. We agreed on the abrupt, pointed and rather succinct phrase on the posters of, "If easily offended please stay away". It was a scary proposition for a Council promoted event, made all the more worrying after a conversation I had with George Foster just after he had signed the contract. I asked how Chubby was going down with audiences and he said his reception had been mixed. One gig at a Roman Catholic Club he said ended after it had only just begun, when he was booed from the stage. Apparently the Club had just been burgled and Chubby walked on stage looked up at the 'occupied' Crucifix hanging above it and said, "I see you got the bloke who pinched the telly". Chubby was, there is little doubt, a pretty controversial character.

On the night of the event Monday 12th May, I was surprised to note that although it was a predominantly male audience there were several large parties of women, obviously intent on having a good night out. When you got over the 'language', from the moment he walked on stage and said, "I like Hull it's so well laid out its hard to tell how long it's been dead" Chubby was very funny. However before the show started I became concerned when a couple in their sixties ascending the stairs to take their seats in the balcony area directly opposite the stage; he was dressed in tweeds and she wore a long evening dress and short fur stole. "Very strange customers for this event" I thought, as I began to worry a little. I don't think that 'The Watch Committee' existed then, but had it done so, then they were both prime candidates to be members.

Ten minutes after the show had started they were back descending the stairs and making a swift exit. Fearing some adverse publicity in the Hull Daily Mail the next day, I shouted after them, "Didn't you like it then", to which the lady blushed and replied, "Not quite what we expected, I'm afraid". The man strode over to me and looked from side to side, in lowered tones said, "It's our bloody son, he thinks it's funny I suppose, sending us two tickets for tonight for our Wedding Anniversary and telling us Chubby Brown was an American Jazz Trumpeter" I produced a relieved laugh, they smiled back and left by the side door never to be seen again.

I actually remember the same thing happening about six months later when a couple somehow got into the Hall for a Wrestling promotion when they had tickets for the Opera which was on the same evening at the New Theatre. Not much difference there then!! However I still wonder to this day why it was well into the second bout before they eventually left and went across to the Theatre!

As a foot note, I had obviously had a few problems justifying the booking of Chubby Brown to certain of the more straight laced

Councillors in the first place, but one prominent 'elected member' really liked Chubby and would ride around his Ward on a bicycle listening to Mr Brown's tapes on his headphones and laughing in a demented fashion. He (to save embarrassment we'll call him Larry) felt that it would not be good politics to attend, but asked me to get him a signed poster and to hang it, as a joke next day, in the 'Member's Room' in the Guildhall, which, as a 'good officer', of course I did. Apparently it didn't stay up on the wall long! It was swiftly removed when some of the other councillors saw it hung there portraying a grinning Chubby in his patchwork jacket, flying helmet and shin length trousers and signed across the bottom in felt tip pen, "Bollocks Larry, Regards Chubby" That incident could have got me in big trouble, but the Councillor concerned, and in fairness several other members of Hull City Council, thought it was hilarious.

That event was quickly followed by Jim Payton the Lord Mayor opening the new bar at the City Hall as two years of 'working' on the local licensing magistrates finally came to fruition and Cameron's the Brewers constructed the first purpose built bar at the venue and I was the first ever Licensee. As Mary across the road in the Punch commented "Talk about a poacher turned gamekeeper!"

'Home Thoughts from Abroad' as Kenny Foulkes is shown the door!

Despite scant resources Kenny Foulkes our Head Coach had done his best since Christmas but the Board of Hull FC decided, in the words of Chairman Roy Waudby, that "A complete change was needed". That was the signal for Kenny to leave the Club he had been associated with since the 1960's as we the fans, awaited developments. We didn't have to wait long either because the next day, (no doubt in another cost cutting exercise) the Club withdrew their contract offer to James Leuluai and said that they were open to offers for International centre Steve Evans. One by one the great team was being taken apart simply because they were now unaffordable. Whilst all this was going on, Lee Crooks was over in Australia playing Club rugby and writing a weekly column in the Hull Daily Mail, in which he was advising the Club about everything from who they should sign, to who should be in charge in place of Kenny, which no doubt went down well.

We were pretty underwhelmed when a week later the Board announced that our new Head Coach was to be the unproven ex FC and Rovers stalwart Len Casey. Lee said in his column, "Len will take us back to the top" and although a great player, 'Crooksey' was about to be proved a poor judge of Coaches.

Around that time I appointed a new City Hall Manager when after several interviews I finally settled for Tony Ridley who had little experience in the entertainments industry but was certainly keen and had, I thought, the precise temperament needed for that often crazy environment. His background was in the building industry and I was soon to realise just how useful a Manager who could do a bit of plumbing would be.

County Cricket returns to the Circle and we all get drunk

It was an important day for local sport when on 27th July One Day County Cricket was staged at the Cricket Circle for the first time since 1978. I went with Trevor and we started drinking at noon and finished at around 6-00pm, well I think that was the time anyway. I went along purely to experience that sense of suspended animation Cricket always brings upon me, aided as it always has been with a dozen or so pints of warm lager. The thing was my old mates from the Hull Cheese who featured in the first book, were running the Beer Tent that day and so it was free samples all afternoon. As the sun beat down before the game (quite an uncharacteristic occurrence for Cricket in Hull), the 5000 folks in attendance observed an immaculate minute's silence for the 10 people who had died in a train crash at Lockington on the Hull to Bridlington line just the day before.

We sat on the grass just over the boundary rope enjoying our beer and trying to appreciate the cricket which understandably got more difficult to follow as the afternoon wore on. It was a great performance by Yorkshire who scored an impressive 255 for 6, with Jim Love top scorer with an unbeaten 104. In their innings Nottinghamshire were bowled out for 153 (Score courtesy of the Hull Daily Mail next day, because I fell asleep) and I was awoken by great scenes of jubilation at the end, before settling back down on the grass to finish my beer. I was shaken awake an hour later by a 'litter picking' steward and told to leave! Still I do remember that the old Pavilion looked superb that day packed with spectators and sporting a new coat of paint, whilst all round the Boundary ropes the kids played their own games of cricket as their Mums and Dads got steadily drunk. It was a great day, followed predictably by a throbbing headache next morning.

'Casey says Relax'

We started the season at the Boulevard lacking in depth on the playing roster with a few injuries pre season adding further to our woes. The great team of the early 80's had all but broken up and although 'The 1985 Society' had run a pre season Sevens competition at the Boulevard to raise some much needed cash, we were in trouble. Skerrett and Gascoigne were staying away from training and while Lee Crooks had returned home from Australia, Garry Schofield was held up over there, playing in the play-off series for Canterbury-Bankestown. Steve Evans then left for Wakefield for £28,000, although we did sign 24 year old Australian sensation Brett Clarke, a brilliant young Scrum Half who then four weeks later changed his mind, tore up his contract and signed for Western Suburbs.

After wins were gained against Bramley, Wakey and Batley at the Boulevard without really playing well, we then lost to Halifax and Castleford away and little seemed to have changed really. Len Casey, who took on ex-player Keith Hepworth as his Assistant Coach, announced in the Green Sports Mail, "Relax, by Christmas we will be firing on all cylinders" but none of us really believed him. However we were pleased and surprised when Aussie International Prop David Brown signed on, as did Steve Crooks a second rower from Hull KR, but by then many of the fans had already decided they'd had enough.

The problem was a lack of half backs, and creative players, something that seems to have haunted our great Club for decades. Then, unexpectedly the Board went out and bought three players in two days, and on Sunday 21ˢᵗ September, Hull paraded them all in a game against Leigh at the Boulevard. We first signed Mick Gibbons on loan, but the big news was that we had captured wily scrum half Kevin Dick from Leeds, and former Welsh RU international stand-off Gary Pearce, a rather dumpy looking kicker and play maker from Welsh Club Llanelli. The Dick deal saw Andy Gascoigne and Trevor Skerrett move in the other direction to Leeds and as our new acquisitions were hailed in the local media as heralding 'A new Dawn', we all went to see if it was just that, as an improved gate of over 5,700 populated the sunny terraces that afternoon.

Gary Pearce and Kevin Dick take a bow!

Sunday 26ᵗʰ September 1986   *Hull 31 – Leigh 26*

With plenty of early season injuries, and despite the debutants, the team we fielded that Sunday was still a 'scratch' one, but it was not long before Pearce had opened his account for the Club with a 6ᵗʰ minute penalty. After 12 minutes Pearce, who was showing no signs of only being a professional 'League' player for two days, dummied to the right and ran off to the left to release Dane O'Hara on the wing. He shot in near the corner flag to score a great try. Pearce converted from the touchline before a mistake by debutant Dick at the back of a scrum saw Leigh number 7 Davis snap the ball up and feed Prop Cotterell who made the line with Peppi Brand and McCoid on his back. Johnson goaled and a confident start began to look a bit suspect.

Dick though then showed what was to come in the next two seasons as he 'cheekily' stole the ball from the rampaging Schubert and fed Brand who went on a typical surge to the line. Peppi was an exciting player to watch, as he evaded one tackler and pushed another into touch, before diving over in the corner. Pearce's conversion attempt just failed, and the Lancastrians got two points back after Steve Crooks had punched Gelling, before we witnessed a vintage Mick Crane try that brought the house down.

In typical fashion the evergreen loose forward found a bit of space around the play the ball. He chipped ahead, the ball bounced perfectly, and he 'barreled' in to score a converted try. However it was not long before a Henderson effort made it 18-14, but thankfully winger McCoid scored after Lee Crooks's 'Bomb' bounced off full back Collier's shoulder and straight into his arms and we went in at half time leading 22-14.

The second half was hard going and both Dick and Mallinson featured in skirmishes with the Leigh forwards. Lee Crooks settled things down with a drop goal, but that was to signal a fight back by the visitors. By the 64th minute both Gelling and Fox had scored converted tries and from a healthy situation we were trailing 26-23. It looked like the 'new dawn' was about to turn into another nightmare.

'Loanee' Gibbins was trying 'everything he could', within and outside the rule book, tactics that were upsetting both the Leigh forwards and Mr. Holdsworth the referee. It was however a surprising, but inspired, substitution that was to make the difference, when young Jon Sharp took to the field and came close to stealing the show from the other more illustrious debutants. With four minutes to go he shot out a long pass to Paul Eastwood who blazed in at the corner. Then in the fourth minute of injury time and direct from acting half, Sharp himself galloped in from 25 yards and despite the previously dependable Pearce missing both conversions, we had won by a score of 31-26. It had been a close call but in what was a largely forgettable season, in Kevin Dick and Gary Pearce we had at least found a partnership that looked as if it could organize the team out on the field.

The 'new' City Hall Manager is 'baptized' in three inches of water

Tony the new Manager finally took up his position at the Hall and his first weekend was a busy one. On the Friday there was a concert that featured heavy metal act Saxon who played to 800 people but caused Tony a lot of problems when they staged a food fight in the tour catering area in the Victoria Galleries, which culminated in the paintings on the walls, soft furnishings and even the catering staff caked in Chilli and trifle.

The visit the Hague Philharmonic Orchestra on the Saturday promised to be a more sedate affair although it wasn't without its problems as some of the second violins got stuck in that back stage lift......... again and the concert had to be delayed by 15 minutes while Tony and the 'Lift man' came to their rescue. Then on Sunday the group that caused me so many problems back in 1980, 'The Damned', returned to the venue and although everything on stage and in the audience went well this time around, the fans, true to their 'retro punk' roots took all the ball cocks off the toilet cisterns in the Gents and with three inches of water covering the floor, Tony had to use all his plumbing expertise to stem the tide and avert a disaster. Quite what his wife made of him arriving home from his new 'executive position' with his shoes ruined and his suit trousers soaked to the knees, is anyone's guess.

Three weeks later we staged a triumphant home coming for local heroes the Housemartins who had taken the Single and Album charts by storm, with their debut album 'London 0 Hull 4' and it was a truly memorable night. Sold out weeks in advance, and interestingly supported by the then largely unknown Scottish folk rock duo 'The Proclaimers', the Housemartins treated the crowd to their full repertoire of songs in an atmosphere that was electric. The final encore saw the four lads stood at the front of the stage, lit by a single spotlight, as they brilliantly sang an 'Acapella' version of the Isley Brothers hit, 'Caravan of Love'. That was the first time anyone in the audience had heard what was destined to be that year's Christmas Number One.

Len Casey's finest hour (and there weren't that many!)

Saturday 20th December 1986   *Hull 11 – Wigan 12*

There were, for us intrepid fans attending the Boulevard and tramping around the north of England every week, few games that could be called memorable in that period. However we had done really well in the John Player Trophy that year, having managed to reach the televised semi final at Headingley on the last Saturday before Christmas. It was again that strange format for the competition, in which we had to play all the rounds back to back from 30th November and we reached the semi final by beating Salford at the Willows, Blackpool at Home and Bradford Northern at Odsal. This had been an impressive run indeed, coming as it did after 4 straight defeats in which we conceded 170 points, including a 48-0 defeat by the Australian tourists at the Boulevard and a 50-10 drubbing away at the hands of St. Helens.

The Cup run had certainly captured the imagination of the West Hull public and after we had taken around 5,000 fans to the quarter final at Odsal the previous week and despite it being the last weekend for shopping before Christmas, we all hit the road again this time to Headingley, to face Wigan. Casey made just one change to the line up that had done so well at Odsal the previous week, resting Jon Sharp who had concussion and drafting in Steve 'Knocker' Norton, whose Testimonial Brochure was due out the following Monday. I went with Andy and met Harry, Barry and Trevor in the South Stand.

Gary Pearce got the game underway as Hull came forward strongly and only a desperate last gasp tackle from Wigan's Hampson saved a try. We continued to work the ball forward and a brilliant dummy and pass by Pearce found Crooks in space and from 20 yards Lee dropped a goal to give us a slender lead. Then a good Pearce kick pinned Wigan back and a scrum was formed just 5 yards out from their line. Straight from this Windley spotted a hole on the blind side and shot over but Pearce missed the conversion, and with just minutes to go to half time it was all Wigan. Great tackles from Lee Crooks on Ellery Hanley and Garry Kemble on Russell, kept our line intact and we went in 5-0 up.

It looked like there was to be a sensational start to the second half as Lee Crooks took Hanley's kick off and fed a great short ball to Garry Schofield who shot through the line and headed off on a 60 yard run to touch down. However Referee Holdsworth called the play back for a forward pass which was loudly contested by the Hull fans standing in the cold and gloom of the South Stand. Slowly but surely Hanley and Edwards were wrestling the advantage away from Hull, as Wigan continued to press forward and the Referee appeared to allow some dubious tactics to go unpunished. Twice Garry Pearce stopped Hanley in full flight with brilliant tackles before the Wigan outfit finally went ahead in controversial circumstances. Ellery Hanley shot in next to the posts, but could clearly be seen to drop the ball from his hand as he went over. However the try stood and with Stephenson's conversion, Wigan took the lead for the first time before revitalised by Puckering and Norton coming off the bench, Hull found 'another gear'.

We'd not been in the Wigan 25 yard area for almost 15 minutes, when Lazenby broke and passed onto Crane. Our veteran loose forward, belying his years, showed a touch of that old magic and transferring the ball from one hand to the other, he put Pearce through a huge gap to score and as Gary converted his own try we were back in front, 11-6. It was however to be a short lived lead as Edwards found us out again with a brilliant piece of play. He hung a ball in the air for Hanley, who this time grounding the ball correctly and scored wide out. As Gill curled in the conversion we trailed again 12-11.

Ah Kuoi grabbed a loose ball on the Wigan 25 and Puckering made a great break for the Airlie Birds but tragedy struck when the usually dependable Pearce dropped the ball in his effort to release it to the waiting O'Hara and the chance was lost. The Black and Whites made a tremendous last ditch effort to grab a win and as the crowd roared them on Schofield created a lot of space for himself and passed to O'Hara, who only had to put the ball down next to the flag, but a tremendous effort by two Wigan tacklers, saw him just fail to score. We continued to press as referee Holdsworth missed a glaringly obvious Wigan knock on from a booming Hull up and under, but tragically as the final hooter went, we had lost by one point, and the dream of a Final which had been within touching distance, was gone.

That was Len Casey's one great moment as Coach and one that maybe ensured he kept his job into the following season. It was a defeat that certainly took the shine off Christmas which was a time when once again relationships were fraught at home, as I battled to balance love of Hull FC with other things! However a good victory over Featherstone on Boxing Day at the Boulevard put most of that right and certainly lifted the gloom a little.

The Searchers' Christmas disaster!

Two days before Christmas as parents were scouring the shops for Panini Football stickers for the kids, at the City Hall we promoted the first of what was to become an annual Festive institution, the Searchers' Christmas Concert. Completely sold out, the show also featured Gerry and the Pacemakers and the Tremeloes. Promoter Tim Jibson wanting a big finale hired confetti cannon to shower the crowd with ticker tape at the end of the evening. It didn't seem to bother Tim that the cannon was actually 'For outdoor use only' and he assured us that "It just says that......it'll be fine" This final effect was to coincide with the City Hall staff releasing hundreds of balloons from a net suspended in the roof high above the audience. All went well until the final chords of the last song by the full cast, 'Santa Claus is coming to Town' was starting to fade.

As the customers gave a standing ovation, the Confetti Cannon gave out a massive bang which had people holding their ears as it rattled the very fabric of the building, sending years of gathered dust from inside the Hall's Organ, showering out over the crowd. In the mean time the string that was to release the balloons from the net became taffled and after a couple of strong yanks from the City Hall staff up in the roof it tore the whole net from the ceiling and it fell onto the crowd ensnaring several hundred of the audience like wild beasts captured somewhere in the jungles of Africa. It all seems very funny now, but with patrons in their 'Sunday Best' covered in dust and frantically struggling to get out from under the net, there was certainly not a lot of Festive spirit about and in the following days, we received more complaints than Christmas Cards.

It was just after Christmas, and as rugby got in the way of another relationship, that I left the house in Garden Village and in desperation decided to move back into the City Hall Flat. It was certainly good to see Mary and Albert again across at the Punch as we renewed our nightly 'get-togethers' in the Public Bar. That was a cold January and I recall trudging through the snow covered City Centre streets to the Lockwood Arms to attend a Country Music night hosted by local radio personality Tex Milne that was staged in aid of 'Knocker' Norton's Testimonial Fund.

As I passed the New Theatre it was certainly a festive scene as the snow fell thick and fast on the families slipping and sliding their way into the venue to watch 'Little and Large' in the Pantomime. By the time I got to the pub the place was packed and I pitched into the collection and bought a few raffle tickets. The band 'The Wild East' were OK, but there is only so much 'Crystal Chandelier', 'From a Jack to a King' 'Rhinestone Cowboy' and 'Folsom Prison Blues' you can take. I said "Hello" to Gary Kemble, Jimmy Leuluai and Steve Evans who had come along to support 'Knocker', wrapped myself up in my coat and my Hull scarf and set out back through the snow to the Punch.

It's all part of being a fan, that feeling of needing to be there at any event that has to do with your Club, and although I didn't like country music or trudging through the snow, in the end I felt I'd done my bit for Knocker! The day job was going well too with 450 different events taking place at the City Hall that year. I was back on my own in the flat, it was all work, beer and Hull FC and that I decided, was how I liked it!

After Christmas the fans of Hull FC were certainly hoping that our luck would change and that perhaps we could get a decent run in the Challenge Cup. The draw was made in Huddersfield and we were given an away game in Derbyshire against First Division Club, the Mansfield Marksmen. The team, another fated expansionist experiment, had played at Field Mill Mansfield in their first two seasons however they sustained massive losses and could simply not afford the rent anymore. Their final game there was on 2 February 1986 before they moved on to another football stadium, a few miles down the road in Alfreton. The first game at that venue was on 23 March, and almost a year later we were the opposition in the Challenge Cup.

Alfreton Town, the 'Mansfield Marksmen', 'Nosey' Parker and Alvin Stardust

Sunday 15th February 1987   *Hull 38 – Mansfield Marksmen 7*

So it was that on a cold, drizzly February day we all made our way to the home of Alfreton Town to play our Club's only ever game in Derbyshire. Mansfield Breweries were attempting to secure a footing in Yorkshire and Lancashire and sponsored the team (Marksman Bitter was one of their branded beers) but what a place North Street was! As probably the worst ground at which I've watched professional Rugby League (and I've been to Alt Park, Huyton) the 'Stadium' had three sides surrounded by grassed muddy hills, whilst we crammed into the one solitary stand.

About 1000 of the 1,800 gate (the biggest they were to get as a professional Rugby League team) were from Hull and their then Chairman Dave Parker ('Nosey' of more recent journalistic fame) stood behind the three dilapidated turnstiles, seemingly 'Counting us in'. I didn't see their Honorary President Alvin Stardust (who hailed from Mansfield) but by then he had probably become disenchanted with a Club that was obviously not meeting the expectations of the good folks of the Derbyshire town. Most of us were still rubbing our eyes in disbelief at the surroundings, as the teams ran out.

The stoic Stadium was a stark contrast for the Hull FC players, who had just returned from some 'Warm weather training' in Majorca. The game is still memorable for me, probably because the opposition only looked like scoring once in the very last minute and that was because our defence, despite poor opposition, was simply magnificent throughout.

We kicked off up the 'slope' on a pitch that was like a quagmire, having hosted a football match the day before. The early exchanges were only memorable for a crunching tackle by Tomlinson and Lazenby on Mansfield centre Fletcher, who crashed over the touchline and hit his head on the bottom of a concrete perimeter fence post. The game was stopped for seven minutes whilst he came round and he actually soldiered on with a bloodied bandage round his head, before retiring from the game ten minutes later.

Then we opened the scoring. Windley was tackled and from the play the ball Pearce took the whole defence across the field before feeding Schofield, who stepped inside and shot off for the line. Following the conversion from Pearce, Mansfield huffed and puffed but simply couldn't break our line. Then when Patrick fed a short ball to Tomlinson, our prop crashed in to make it 10-0, and when Pearce converted again it was effectively all over.

Mansfield's full back Edgington was their star, pulling off tackle after tackle as O'Hara, Eastwood and Schofield threatened the home side's line, but Mansfield were getting frustrated and so in desperation stand-off Willis dropped a goal. Then with three minutes to go to the break Ah Kuoi and Windley moved the ball swiftly from a scrum and Eastwood galloped in at the corner. As the hooter went and we went in search of a Bovril to warm us up, it was 16-1 to Hull.

The second half continued the 'procession' as Pearce scored a try he converted himself. Ten minutes later Tomlinson knocked both Stevens and Hough off in a tackle before feeding Wayne Proctor who touched down for Pearce to convert again. Schofield got the next with a 30 yard run and then it was the turn of Eastwood again as Mansfield couldn't cope with our consistent pressure.

With just a minute to go a Lee Crooks' pass looked to have put Eastwood in again when Mansfield winger Courtney Thompson flashed onto the sloppy pass, intercepted and ran 75 yards for a try. This saw those of the home crowd that were left in the ground, cheering as if it was the winner. The game finished with the rickety score board showing a score of 38-7 which saw us through to the next round. However, as I look back on a day out at North Street Alfreton, it will be the shocking condition of the Stadium that will be remembered by those who attended.

Definitely no wet kisses!!

Sunday 29th March 1987   *Hull 12 – Warrington 46*

The talk of the media that spring was the scourge of AIDS that was not only sweeping Africa but gathering pace here in Great Britain, with the

TV full of 'shroud waving' advertisements for 'safe sex' and condoms. It was a terrible, terrible fate to befall anyone but the myths and misinformation of just how you could catch it were spreading much more quickly than the true facts about it. You could apparently contract Aids from toilet seats, coffee cups and according to the Sun newspaper using someone else's underwear. However quite what the circumstances were in which you would be sharing underwear, was never fully explained.

The Hull Daily Mail covered a few tragic local cases on their front page but always kept names and circumstances secret, so for the man in the street it was generally a case of what you don't know, make up! The Rugby and Football League's were however really worried about the 'known fact' that you could be infected with AIDS from other people's blood.

Both organisations looked at the principle of a 'Blood Bin' and both came out with 'a charter'. The Rugby League's included such actions as banning communal baths and not allowing the sharing of drinks bottles or razors. Football also included in their charter, "No kissing in goal celebrations". You can imagine the laugh we all had in the Punch the night after the Secretary of the Football League was asked to explain this clause and said, "The thing is there is no evidence that AIDS can be contracted by kissing but I would say it was dangerous, particularly if it were a wet kiss"

The rest of that season was disappointing, with us winning only five of the last 14 games. Many fans thought that it was only that narrow and unlucky defeat by Wigan in the John Player Trophy semi final that saved Len Casey's job but we were all pretty fed up with Len and the allegations of his 'unconventional' motivational methods in the dressing room and on the training field. One Rugby League paper flippantly described his tenure, as a 'Reign of Terror' although most of us fans weren't laughing! The low point was a terrible 46-12 defeat by Warrington in March, which was one of the only games that I ever contemplated leaving early. I watched from the Airlie Street end of the ground where with 15 minutes to go, with the exception of some chip papers blowing 'tumble weed like' across the steps, the place was deserted. I stuck it out until the final whistle and left for home wondering what could happen to make things any worse. Not surprisingly I didn't have long to wait for the answer.

A hero exits, who is "A Friend to whom I owe so much!"

Wednesday 22nd April 1987   *Hull 21 – Widnes 4*

Ironically we ended that abysmal season with a resounding victory but the significance of a game against Widnes which really held little importance for either team, was the fact that on 69 minutes Len Casey made a substitution that was to see the end of an era, if not the end of an enigma. It was then that Steve Norton left the Boulevard pitch for the last time during a senior game.

A few days later 'Knocker' announced his retirement, as one of the greatest ever players to grace the famous irregular hoops was consigned to the memory of everyone who watched him play. Steve was a fantastic Rugby League player and it was a privilege to see him play. That last season saw him gain a well deserved Testimonial which raised an amazing £41,000, a then record for the Club. It is simply impossible for me to describe in words just how good he was; you had to see it, to believe it. Knocker was one of those rare, beautiful, talents that fans only come across once or twice in a lifetime. Star quality, generosity, crowd pleasing, magical, match winner, loveable rogue, leader...the pundits just ran out of superlatives when describing Norton. He was 'Man of the Match' that day and deserved it too, but that accolade was nothing new for him. In his Testimonial Brochure Sammy Lloyd his Club mate and life-long pal described him as, "A friend to whom I owe so much" and believe me, if you had watched Hull FC throughout the great years that he was at the Club, we all owed 'Knocker' a lot too. Norton wasn't just a great player, or even an inspirational Captain, he was a phenomenon who will be remembered by those who saw him play until the day they die. You probably only really experience one 'Knocker' Norton in a lifetime and the day he left the Club, he took the hopes and aspirations of me and hundreds of other fans with him.

Disaster strikes: Crooks leaves, 'kicking and screaming' for Leeds!

The news 'leaking' out of the Club was all about our perilous financial position and with plummeting attendances, poor results and little progress in Cup competitions, it was hardly unexpected. However on 1st June 1987 Dick Tingle the Hull FC correspondent at the Hull Daily Mail weighed in with the exclusive headline of "Hull May Face Double Sale" and it was followed with the by-line of "Debts of more than £500,000!" The two departures that Dick alluded to were in fact our two most prized possessions Lee Crooks and Gary Schofield.

The fans were in uproar and our new Chairman John Rawlings was certainly feeling the heat. Lee Crooks was already in the news because although he was playing at Balmain in Australia during the summer break, the Mail revealed that he was wanted in Castleford on a charge of dangerous driving and next day the same newspaper dropped the bombshell with the front page banner headline of, "Crooks moves for £150,000". Lee was summoned back from Australia to sign for Leeds in a deal that Rawlings described as, "The only way we can save the Club from extinction".

Crooksey, who was 'Black and White' through and through, was mortified and in the same paper said, "I never ever thought that would happen, I've been forced to leave the Club I love". Next day the nightmare continued as the headlines read "Schofield asks for a Move" and there followed an article which hinted that Gary was leaving because we were no longer "a good Club" for him to play at. The FC 'Faithful' went berserk!!! There were letters to the local paper, personal threats to the Directors and a spate of vandalism at the Boulevard ground. Not only had we seen the Board sell a player we loved and who obviously didn't want to leave, we had now another young International demanding a move, because he "Didn't want to play for us anymore". It was a disaster!

Another AGM as the Press are locked out and I fall at the feet of the 'Windsors'

Money was the big problem as player's contracts had to be slashed and although Dane O'Hara decided to stay at Hull on a reduced salary, Garry Kemble appeared to had enough and packed his bags and returned home to New Zealand. We all looked forward to a stormy AGM, which was that year held in the Directors' Suite at the Boulevard. It was certainly a confrontational affair as the Board banned the Press from attending, explaining before the meeting that, "Len will want to talk about players and we don't want the Press there". As it transpired Casey didn't talk much at all and anyway at the end the shareholders left and went straight to see The Hull Daily Mail's Dick Tingle, who was waiting outside on the Car Park.

The disasters continued as sadly a few days later we lost another great FC fan when local Councillor and Head of Industrial Development in the City, Louis Pearlman, died in a road crash on a Freeway in Fort Lauderdale, Florida. It was a major accident and his wife Rita was seriously injured but thankfully survived. In early July I was introduced to the Queen and Prince Philip in the Ferens Art Gallery when, at a stage managed reception, I was put in a 'meet and greet' group with some Doctors, a couple of ladies from the Townswomen's Guild and three University Lecturers. They could certainly talk so 'Their Highnesses' didn't have time to say much to me except "Hello". I was, it has to be said, a bit over-come by the whole thing and as Prince Philip extended his hand I didn't quite know whether to bow or curtsey, so I did a bit of both and fell over! As he laughed out loud it was no doubt a memorable encounter for both of us, but for contrasting reasons.

At work that summer we staged the City's first Busker's Competition around the City Centre, and Hugh Whittaker from 'local band made good' The Housemartins was one of the judges. Hull wasn't that well blessed with buskers back then something that was reflected in the entries which included Brian Banana and the Busking Blueberry's, Alma King a guitar playing granny, the Blue Moon Band and a fire eater to name but a few. In the end it was won by a brilliant four piece swing guitar group called Ain't Misbehavin'. The main thing that I remember however surrounded the Fire Eater, who everyone was talking about before he arrived. Some of the folks who knew a lot about the guy said "You'll love Nuclear Nigel, he's great" and "Watch Nuclear Nigel singe his eyebrows" and so by the time he arrived I was really looking forward to seeing his performance.

I was a little surprised at the expression on his face when I announced from the stage, "So Ladies and Gentleman let's all marvel to the pyrotechnic exploits of Nuclear Nigel". Afterward, I found out that he was actually called Nigel Johnson, but as he was a big 'Ban the Bomb' activist, everyone gave him the nick name (behind his back) of 'Nuclear'. It wasn't his stage name at all and he wasn't too impressed when I used it and didn't turn up for his second spot!

County Cricket again; £4 to watch it rain!

On August 9th with several of the lads from the Punch Hotel, I again attended the Cricket Circle on Anlaby Road for another day of 'googlies', 'boundaries' and beers. I queued at the gate in West Park, paid my £4 and went straight to the Beer Tent as it started to rain. By 2-00pm Dickie Bird the umpire was out in the middle with his umbrella up and by 3-30, Geoff Boycott was packing his cricket bag and heading home. We had another pint and headed off to get our money back, when we were informed by a cardboard notice on the gate that "If the game is rained off, once in the ground, there will be no refunds". "It's funny how we never saw those notices when we came in" seemed to be the general consensus amongst the disgruntled patrons and just as the complaints about the Board at Hull FC had abated somewhat in the 'Sportsman Say' column of the Daily Mail, more letters were flooding in about the Cricket, or in this case the lack of it.

As Gary Schofield played in Australia for Balmain, Hull were reported to be turning down bids for him from Leeds. As fans we had mixed feelings because although we had all idolised one of the best youngsters to come through the Club, he now wanted to leave us. In any case it transpired that the Club were just holding out for more money and he was soon destined to depart amidst a hail of abuse and acrimony from the aggrieved Hull fans. It was a furore that was to follow him forever!! Garry made it blatantly obvious that he couldn't wait to get away and rumours abounded about how much he had received from Leeds to sign and the underhand way that he had gone about things deemed that it wouldn't be long before the title of 'Judas' was bestowed on him. One rumour I particularly remember claimed that when he returned his 'Club Car' to Hull FC the petrol tank was full of water, as was the car itself. I don't know if it was true, but it was typical of the stories that spread through West Hull like wild fire. Few of us were therefore surprised when Garry became established as the Threepenny Stands, 'Public Enemy Number One', for at least the next decade!

Although it was scant consolation, we signed Hussein M'Baki, a Moroccan winger who actually hailed from Hull, whilst James Leuluai returned from a season long loan at Leigh to reclaim his place in the centre. We also signed a young Full-Back Paul Fletcher from Salford for £30,000 and John Carroll from Batley. Not surprisingly, the numbers of Season Ticket holders was down again, but of course I bought one, because at times like that, I just have to! Sadly only 2,314 turned up for Steve Norton's Testimonial game against Castleford and so after receiving a record breaking benefit cheque, 'Knocker' departed, leaving nothing but an uncertain future for us fans.

Scott Gale breezes in......and out again!

Sunday 4th October 1987   *Hull 22 – Leigh 21*

The 1987/88 season, the second of the 'Reign of Terror' of Len Casey saw the Club's Board of Directors helping our beleaguered Coach by bringing one of Australia's best young players to the Club. You'll remember we had been interested in Scott a couple of years earlier, when Roy Waudby and Arthur Bunting had travelled 'Down Under' scouting for players to bolster the squad. They brought Geoff Gerard back on that occasion, but Gale had decided that he would be better off staying to finish his studies.

Scott arrived in October, a week before his fellow countrymen Dave Brooks and Terry Regan and made his debut against Leigh at the Boulevard on Sunday 4th October 1987. The 22 year old from the Balmain Club slotted straight into the stand-off berth that day beside regular scrum half Phil Windley with our usual number 6, Gary Pearce, moving to centre.

The weather was breezy and sunny as we kicked off towards the Gordon Street end of the ground and I watched proceedings from the relative 'comfort' of the Threepenny Stand. A crowd of 5,051 looked on as Gale started his Hull FC career perfectly when after just three minutes a fine move started by Nicky Elgar and Paul Fletcher saw the young Aussie send out a perfectly flighted pass to Paul Eastwood, who stormed in at the corner.

Twenty minutes later after a period of Leigh pressure Gale was involved again. This time he made a break leaving the Leigh Centre Henderson grasping thin air. He fed onto Divorty who sent out another magnificent pass between two advancing defenders, to put Gary Pearce in for a try. Pearce failed to convert both scores but was successful with a penalty and after 23 minutes we led 10-0. Cottrell scored for Leigh before we lost the ball and Ian Jeffries waltzed his way round Fletcher, Eastwood and O'Hara to round off a brilliant 60 yard run to the line, which levelled the scores. The conversion gave the visitors a 12-10 lead at half time.

Leigh were on top but at the start of the second half a break out of defence by Scott Gale, gave us a rare foothold in the visitor's half. Divorty ran a beautiful scissors move with Phil Windley which had us all wondering where the ball was and he passed onto Pearce who was, by now, having a brilliant game. He stepped one way then the other drew the Leigh winger and released Eastwood on a free run to the line. A brilliant Pearce conversion put us back in front 16-12.

Back came Leigh with a well worked Henderson try which Johnson failed to convert and thankfully their full back went on to miss two penalties after that and as the Threepenny Standers 'got on his back' it became apparent that he was losing his confidence.

However the visitors were level and in fact went into the lead when Johnson dropped a goal from 30 yards out. The young Hull forwards battled on and eventually got their reward as a brilliant solo effort by Gale (which saw him cut inside and beat three players with one step), followed by a conversion from the touchline from Pearce, took us into a 22-17 lead and all we had to do now was hang on. However in the dying minutes Kerr got free for Leigh and released Ford, who 'danced' his way over just 15 yards to the right of the posts. All Johnson had to do was convert the try for the visitors to win but, his confidence shattered and to a chorus of boos from the crowd, he sliced the kick well wide, and we held on to record a great, if somewhat fortuitous victory. Scott Gale sadly only lasted another game before being seriously injured and returning home, to be replaced by Paul McAffrey.

Rather like Rugby League, Wrestling was certainly experiencing a difficult time attracting audiences something that was apparent at the bouts we promoted at the City Hall. Earlier that year Big Daddy had tragically killed 'King Kong' Kirk with his famous 'Splashdown' move (Kirk was later found to have been carrying a serious heart condition and Big Daddy was duly exonerated of any blame) which didn't help the 'sport' at all. Still ever resourceful the promoters Relwyskow and Green resorted to a new gimmick, and on 27th November we experienced a completely new concept when Klondike Kate fought Rusty Blair in the first female contest to be staged in the City. Once again some of the worthy Members of the Cultural Services Committee were not too impressed especially as I didn't tell them about it until after the contracts were signed.

Tim Wilby's (second) debut lasts just 4 minutes!

Sunday 13th December 1987   *Hull 20 – Halifax 16*

I remember well a game at Halifax that year, when about 1000 made the trip over from Hull, most I guess like us, travelling more in hope than expectation.

After 4 years away from the Club at Leeds we had re-signed Tim Wilby and he made his return to the first team that afternoon on the substitute's bench. However his 'debut' was to be a short one. We started badly that day as Andy Dannett lost the ball in a suspiciously high tackle by the 'Fax' second rower Paul Dixon and although Referee Mr. Hague waved play on, Andy was carried from the field of play and took no further part in proceedings that afternoon. Four minutes later the hosts opened the scoring with a well taken try by centre Wilkinson which Whitfield goaled, but our break came when Divorty sent out a long pass to Pearce. He stepped his way to a half break before passing to Regan who flipped the ball out of the tackle and Fletcher's superb 'show and go' saw him crash in wide out. A Whitfield penalty five minutes later after O'Hara had tripped Taylor saw the home team go in at half time leading 8-4.

Amazingly within 15 minutes of the restart we were 8 points ahead. Firstly on 51 minutes McCaffrey found Pearce who stood in a two man tackle before releasing a great inside pass for Shaun Patrick to dive in and score. Then a superb piece of inter-passing between Puckering and Divorty sent Stuart Vass hurtling down the wing before he released winger Paul Eastwood who crossed the line near the corner flag and we led by 8 points. Halifax's Dixon then wrestled his way to the whitewash with three Hull defenders on his back for what was a fine try, that cut our lead again.

Six minutes later and just three minutes after Wilby had come onto the pitch for the injured Welham, MacCallion broke our line. As Paul Dixon stormed through, he passed onto Robinson who was immediately elbowed in the face by Wilby and after just 4 minutes he was sent off reducing Hull to twelve men. We conceded again on the 64th minute when Taylor got an unconverted try and with the scored tied 16-16, I feared the worst.

Neutrals present that day were certainly being treated to a great end to end game, but that was little consolation to us lot shivering and fretting on the terraces. On 71 minutes some great work by Divorty and Puckering set up Pearce for the drop goal. Out of the Halifax defensive line charged both Neller and Pendlebury to try and stifle the kick but Pearce dummied, stepped to the left and wriggled through two tackles to release O'Hara who shot in at the corner to re-instate a 4 point lead. Although Pendelbury went close in the last minute, a brilliant last ditch tackle by our full back Fletcher saved the line, and as the ball was spilled the hooter went and we had won. As we drove home down a now snowy M62 we were happy after a great team performance which we had fought out in the last 20 minutes, with just twelve men.

Armoured Heart catch fire!

There was an interesting event at the City Hall just after Christmas when local rock band 'Armoured Heart' did what they described before hand as a 'do it yourself' concert. They had little money but raised the cash to hire the Hall from two gigs out on the estates and for their big night at the Hall they sold around 800 tickets. The band who styled themselves on American rock outfit W.A.S.P. put on a good show, but we began to worry when they started fire eating and 'fire blowing' on the stage. When one of the security staff realised they were using paraffin for this, we had to stop it before the masses of greasy haired rockers crowding the front of the stage were set alight. Still everyone had a great time and the band loved it. Incidentally their support that night was the then obscure Scarborough band 'Little Angels', who eventually made it much bigger than 'Armoured Heart' ever did.

At the Boulevard things were still tough, but the New Year's fixture against the Old enemy from across the river was an ideal opportunity to put things right. However we lost again and after the match in his press interviews Casey, who was never slow to apportion blame said, "The players let me down today, Pearce and Divorty failed to perform or produce the goods". Rumours soon spread of a post match fracas in the dressing room which ended with promising young loose forward Jon Sharp asking for a transfer.

It was a sad time for the community of West Hull as the last side winder Trawler to operate from the Port, the 'Arctic Corsair', landed its last catch. Gates at the Boulevard also dropped to around 5000 and in an unexpected move the Club called an extraordinary general meeting with the view to trying to increase the maximum shares any one person could hold from £20,000 to £50,000. This took place in March and I attended as usual. The motion was passed unopposed, although it didn't really affect my meagre shareholding of just £100.

Len's 'unconventional methods' finally see him walk

Wednesday 17ᵗʰ February 1988   *Hull 2 – St Helens 64*

'Cast Iron' Casey, seemed to be managing the way that he had played, with brute force and not a small amount of ignorance. I guess you would say that Len's 'forthright nature' was also a problem, as he was never short of an opinion, particularly when openly blaming certain players when games were lost! In February 1988 though, that inclination to blame everyone else besides himself, was to be his downfall. We went to Saints (for a game which I have to admit I luckily missed), and were beaten 64-2. So incensed was Casey by this performance that in the post match Press Conference he went through the entire team, player by player publicly 'assassinating' them, starting with the full back, Fletcher who he observed, "Couldn't tackle his own Granny".

Things couldn't continue in this vein for long and it was reported that a deputation of players went to see the Board to demand the Coach be sacked! After more placing of blame on everyone he could think of, (besides himself) Len stood down on 11ᵗʰ March 1988 and so another chapter in the history of the Club came to a close.

However it wouldn't have been Len to go quietly as he said of his demise, "I have been badly let down by the Board of Hull FC; it has been a constant daily battle for me to continue". In fact in an unprecedented move he even gave his letter of resignation to the Hull Daily Mail, who gleefully printed it on the back page of the paper. One well known player at the time said to me afterwards, "Good old Len, blaming everyone else to the very last" which I guess just about summed it up really! The job of rescuing us from a perilous position just three off the bottom of the League table was handed to Len's assistants Tony Dean and Keith Hepworth, as we all awaited our fate.

Chapter 5

'Mr Magico' gets us banned!

In early 1988 I was suffering from more 'changes' in my life and with that scenario you tend to find that it's usually accompanied by the arrival of a new circle of friends. It was around that time that I started knocking about with Howard. He was another regular in the Punch, a tall angular guy, with a permanently happy disposition, who was by profession, a Custom's Officer. Also around was long standing buddy Andy, a pal of many years who worked on the oil rigs and spent much of his time on shore in the pub too. Andy's 'Party Piece' was usually to promise his wife that he would "Collect something from Monument Fisheries for tea". After several pints of an afternoon he would invariably arrive home with whatever the Fish Monger had persuaded him was, "Just Like Haddock". Andy got into all sorts of trouble when, anticipating a nice piece of Lemon Sole or some Salmon for tea, his long suffering 'Mrs' was confronted by a swaying husband brandishing a parcel containing some Shark steaks or on one occasion a whole Squid; with "Not much breast but a lot of legs", the apparent rationale for Andy's purchase.

However now I'll introduce you to a real 'character'. For reasons that will soon become apparent, he was known by everyone in the Punch and indeed at Hull FC as 'Billy the Wizz'. He was skinny, tall and sported a shock of ginger hair, he always wore leather trousers and was a keen and quite accomplished, amateur magician. Billy did all that 'coins disappearing between your fingers, to be produced behind your ear carry on' and stuff with bits of rope and small metal rings that he would produce from his pockets in the pub, in the queue for the cinema and once at the check outs in Jacksons. These impromptu shows were tolerated by Mary and Albert at The Punch because there was little doubt that our crowd were instrumental in ensuring that they secured their retirement cottage. However once they had moved on and a new Landlord arrived he was not so impressed. On his first weekend in charge the new incumbent of the hostelry banned these impromptu shows and us lot too, when as the locals applauded one of Billy's balancing tricks which featured a pint of beer perched on top of a beer bottle, balanced on top of an upturned bar stool supported precariously on one leg of an upturned table, the whole 'structure' collapsed. This caused a mighty crash as it showered several people in the Lounge with beer and sent broken glass cascading across the floor. 'Mine Host' ran into the room and taking one look at the carnage shouted, "Hey 'Mr Magico' your 'spragged', GET OUT and take your mates with you".

So it was that we were all barred for a week and no doubt Monument Fisheries found themselves left with all manner of strange fish at close of business on the next few days! Billy apologised and paid for the damages and we all started using the Pub again, but any sort of illusionary mysticism was now permanently off the agenda.

Probably the greatest end to a game that the Boulevard has ever witnessed!

Sunday 20th March 1988   *Hull 18 – Wigan 12*

In those days every morning I was woken to the sound of pile drivers and hammering as outside the windows of the City Hall Flat the first concrete supports of the Princes Quay Shopping Centre were rising from the muddy depths of Princes Dock. Meanwhile at the Boulevard 'caretaker' Coaches Tony Dean and Keith Hepworth were doing their best to stave off relegation.

Despite their efforts in mid March we were just two points clear of bottom team Leigh, although we had been really lucky in the Challenge Cup draw with games against some of the 'easier' Clubs seeing us amazingly facing a Cup Semi Final against Halifax at Headingley. Before that game however we had to face table topping Wigan at the Boulevard. The previous week, in our new coaching partnerships first home game we had managed to scrape a win against Halifax but as we trudged down to the Boulevard a victory over the high flying Lancastrians seemed almost too impossible to even contemplate.

So it was that the league leaders, who were chasing a league and cup double, came to town and I watched the game from the terracing at the Airlie Street end. Billy's 'party piece' that week was if, I remember rightly, a trick with a matchbox where the matches disappeared when you opened one end and more often than not (after falling out all over the floor) did the same at the other end! This was to be the game during which I was to discover the infamous 'Lucky Step' where I would religiously watch games until the Boulevard finally closed in 2002. Wigan was always a good draw and that coupled with the victory the previous week and the end of Len Casey saw a very encouraging gate of 6,371 attending that afternoon. With 'Popeye' Andy Gregory, Nicky Kiss, The Iro Brothers, Joe Lydon, Henderson Gill and Andy Goodway in their ranks, the trade mark of the Wigan side was fast open rugby and only the previous week they had scored over 50 points in West Yorkshire against a more than capable Castleford outfit.

The game kicked off and immediately Referee Haigh had to separate Regan and Wigan prop Adrian Shelford as they traded punches. Regan as usual got in the last 'slap' which infuriated Shelford who in the very next play pole-axed our forward with a 'copy book' stiff arm tackle that saw Regan stretchered from the pitch. As the 'Faithful' bayed for a red card the Wigan forward was sin binned, while Regan sat on the grass over the touchline, counting his teeth. On twelve minutes Wigan opened the scoring. Gregory had pushed play wide and Byrne, un-marked on the wing, shot in at the corner, although thankfully Lydon, (who was to have an uncharacteristically poor afternoon with the boot) saw his conversion go well wide, bouncing as it did so, into the terracing just in front of us.

Ellery Hanley, who was showing why he was hailed as the best player in the British game, took a pass from Hampson in the 33rd minute to go in at the corner and Lydon missed again. It was exhilarating stuff if you supported Wigan, but tough for us as Hull just managed to stay in touch. When the hooter went for half time we were relieved to see that the score was still only 8-0, because we had been totally out played. As the Wigan supporters chanted "Champions, Champions" and we replied like a peel of bells, "Same old Wigan, always cheating" the two teams trooped off for half time.

Playing towards the Airlie Street end it was Gary Pearce who led Hull's revival. We pressed the visitor's line and Tomlinson threaded an inch perfect kick through to the corner where veteran James Leuluai pounced to score. Then in a 'watch and learn' moment, Pearce showed Lydon just how to do it, as he slotted the conversion over from a position right on the touchline.

Nine minutes later in total disbelief, the crowd went absolutely wild as after a spell of Wigan pressure Hull took the lead. Prop John Carroll who was probably the pick of a hard working Hull pack, slipped the ball out of a three man tackle and Kevin Dick took it on. He shot through the scattered defence, drew full back Hampson and sent Divorty in under the posts. Another Pearce conversion gave us a four point lead and we all started to believe that the unthinkable could be a possibility.

Referee Haigh then awarded Wigan seven consecutive penalties and eventually their pressure told as Henderson Gill shot in at the corner. It was the sort of bad luck you get when you're struggling, because not only was Gregory's pass forward but all the fans in that corner of the ground believed that Eastwood had Gill tackled into touch well before he got the ball down. However the try stood and as Lydon missed the conversion yet again, the scores were locked at 12-12. In the dying minutes Gill raced back to fly hack a ball into the Best Stand as Fletcher homed in on it, but that seemed to be the final act, however the stage was set for the best end to a game that I have ever seen in 60 years of supporting the Club.

A passage of play in slow motion

I make no excuses for this narrative going into 'slow motion' now, as the next few seconds were breathtaking and perhaps beyond imagination. Frankly it is just impossible to do the whole thing justice, but this is how I remember it.............

With the hooter about to sound for full time, Terry Regan, who had come round from his concussed state and heroically rejoined the fray, shoulder charged Andy Goodway and the 'whistle happy' referee called foul. We all felt aggrieved, but being just in the Wigan half we felt reasonably confident that nothing would come of the penalty. However with time up, from 55 yards out from the posts, Lydon decided to go for goal. Our hearts sank, surely he would not miss another one and surely a great draw and a precious point wasn't to be snatched from us at this late stage? It was a straight kick and as the boo's mounted from around the ground Lydon hit the ball hard, straight and true, but, as was his luck that afternoon, it fell just 5 yards short, right under the cross bar.

At this point, Dick Tingle of the Hull Daily Mail, who was in the Press box, will tell you the two time keepers next to him said, "Next tackle and we blow for time". This play would be the last of the game and with finger on the 'claxon' button, they all watched as the drama unfolded.

The ball was taken under the posts by Pearce who began to run it out. Gary was not the fastest of players, and, as if in submission, he ran straight at Wigan prop Adrian Shelford who was, with the rest of the Wigan team, chasing after the aborted conversion to try and get a hand on the ball. With his last ounce of energy Pearce produced a massive and audacious side step, went past the grasping arms of Shelford and found himself behind the advancing Wigan line. He ran on for about 50 yards, slowing as he went, probably little knowing that just one tackle would see the game end. He started to visibly flag as the chasing cover got closer and closer and just as he was being caught by Hanley and West, out of the blue and on his shoulder appeared veteran scrum half Kevin Dick to take the ball on. How Pearce got that far and Dick managed to keep up with him are to this day, two of the great unsolved mysteries of the Boulevard.

Visibly gasping for air the veteran number 7 drew full back Hampson and passed hopefully to the outside where substitute McCaffrey, (who had only been on 5 minutes) grabbed the ball and had the legs to outpace the defence. As he ran towards us those final twenty yards to the line seemed to have gone into 'slow motion'. McCaffrey, at last, placed the ball over the whitewash and we all went wild as at the same moment the hooter sounded and we had won!!! The Wigan players to a man fell to their knees in anguish and Pearce had to wait while the pitch was cleared of rejoicing Hull fans to tag on the two points, but who cared, certainly not the lads round me, who danced and sang like we had won the League. No video replays, no television recordings, no evidence, all we can now trust to is our mind's eye and the memory. It was simply fantastic and one thing's for sure and that's that anyone from the 6,371 who still survives, will like me, never forget the greatest finish the Boulevard probably ever saw in its long and distinguished history.

Cup-tie Fever Returns to West Hull!

That great win saw a wave of expectation and excitement sweep West Hull as the Cup Semi Final the following weekend at Headingley approached. After the draw was made on Regional TV the Bookmakers immediately posted a 20 point start for Hull over the Cup favorites Halifax. Wins over lowly opposition at Doncaster, Sheffield and Hunslet had got us to that Semi Final as the Club enjoyed a little bit of good luck in an otherwise depressing season.

For a set of fans who had fond memories of the Twin Towers of Wembley and who had struggled so much that year, this was the sort of daydream situation you never believed you would see again. We were on the threshold of an unlikely Final appearance and everyone was going to Leeds for that game.

David Brookes our Australian centre who should have been back home by that time, was granted an extension to his stay to play in the game, whilst a long telephone call 'Down Under' by Director David Kirkwood ensured that Scott Gale was flown back to Hull from Australia for the match. The scene was set for one of those legendary days at Headingley which we all still remembered with so much fondness.

At last a Semi Final, but once again we miss our chance

Saturday 26th March 1988   *Hull 0 – Halifax 0*

We all travelled to the game with much excitement and a deal of trepidation and even though we no doubt felt at home as the 'FC Army' took over the South Stand, it was certainly a big 'ask' to expect us to beat a Halifax side packed with exciting, international players. It was a sunny day and it felt as if this might just be our chance of a little bit of glory, after several depressing seasons. That ethos had certainly captured the public's imagination as we attended in great numbers, making up at least two thirds of a 20,000 plus crowd.

The game kicked off in an almost deafening maelstrom of noise and from the first tackle it was obvious that this was to be an epic duel. Carroll and Regan in our second row were crashed to the turf in quick succession and both were left shaking their heads and needing attention after tackles from Holliday, Pendlebury and Neller in the Halifax pack. Twice Dane O'Hara broke away down the wing in front of us, only to be dragged back in desperate tackles by Eadie and Anderson and then we witnessed a great break by Kevin Dick, which saw an easy pass to Pearce go to ground with the line open. After a tense and close first half, the scores were locked at 0-0 at the break.

The second half saw Halifax probably win most of the exchanges, as with a massive amount of possession they started to press our line. However not to be denied we still had our chances, most of which came from the impressive Divorty who broke away on three separate occasions. 'Man of the Match' Terry Regan was always in the middle of the cut and thrust of a half that had us all on our toes one minute and biting our finger nails the next. He made one superb break down the left, but lacked any support and that was it, as both the defences were at their best and cancelled each other out.

Once or twice Pearce considered a possible drop goal but decided instead to turn the ball back inside and the chance was lost. As the final hooter went it was the Hull side that was celebrating a 0-0 draw, while Halifax coach Chris Anderson 'locked' the favorites in the dressing rooms and gave them a real 'bollocking'. On the journey home I remember musing on the fact that, for the average fanatical fan like me, success always seems to exist just to be tantalizingly out of reach, as the stage was set for a replay the following Wednesday at Elland Road.

Another Replay at Elland Road and our luck runs out!

Wednesday 30th March 1988   *Hull 3 – Halifax 4*

One of my strongest memories of the replay was, once again, the difficulty we all had getting there. Few lessons had been learnt from the mayhem that prevailed when the battalions of 'Black and White' fans had descended on the North Leeds ground for that Challenge Cup final replay against Widnes years earlier and our experience that March evening six years later was little different. 25,000 people attended that night, of which around 18,000 were from Hull. We travelled by car, with Billy driving and Andy and I drinking, and we just got into the ground as Gary Pearce kicked off. Many others not so fortunate missed half an hour of the game because although they managed to get to the ground, the queues were horrendous as the limited number of turnstiles that were open, simply couldn't cope. The problems had started with long tail-backs on the M62, but at the Ground a third of the 75 turnstiles were closed despite Hull FC making a much publicised offer the previous Monday to provide 12 extra turnstile operators to ensure they were all open. With 20 minutes to kick-off there were only around 5,000 inside with 10,000 stuck in traffic, and another 10,000, who had actually got there, queuing to get in.

The game finally kicked off at 8-10pm with hundreds still outside, and although some areas in the Stands were full, folks were still being directed into them. Women complained afterwards that children had to be lifted over fences to prevent them being crushed, as once again Elland Road was in a state of chaos.

At last however the Replay started and for the first 26 minutes it was just as if the previous Saturday's game had never finished, as both sets of forwards tore into each other and there were few running chances for the backs. In fact 104 minutes of the semi final had passed before drives by John Carroll, Terry Regan and Alan Tomlinson saw the ball finally flipped back to Gary Pearce. He effortlessly slotted over the sweetest of drop goals and at last, as we all sang "He's fat he's round he's worth a million pounds Gary Pearce....Gary Pearce," the deadlock was broken. Another 26 minutes of 'biff and bash' ensued and half time had passed before Halifax's Bob Grogan ran in front of his own player (Whitefield) and referee John McDonald immediately indicated an obstruction. From the resultant penalty Pearce slotted over the goal and at 3-0 our Wembley dream was alive.

Halifax looked to be wilting, but then what was initially a bit of bad luck, ended in disaster. Two penalties took the West Riding outfit 60 yards down field, but we tackled heroically until they ran out of plays and it was the end of the set. Confusion reigned in the opposition's ranks as prop forward Nellar found himself with the ball. Panicking he sliced a typical 'Props kick' off the side of his boot. The ball skewed up into the air, came down again, bounced around a bit, and FC Forward David Brooks, who was having a 'barnstorming' game, dived for it. Sadly though he was just not near enough to reach it properly, and as it trickled away from him and over the line and full back Paul Fletcher moved in to kick it dead, from nowhere up popped Halifax centre Anderson to get the lightest of fingertip touches on the ball. The referee immediately awarded the try.

Suddenly from looking a beaten side Halifax grew in confidence, whilst Hull were visibly shaken, and it took us a full ten minutes to slowly scrap our way back into the game. Dane O'Hara got a great ball from Patrick but having stepped out of two tackles he was just grabbed by the collar by Wilkinson, as substitute McCaffrey took it on and passed to Divorty. Tragically his last pass to Kevin Dick was too low and our

Scrum Half dropped it! We were now into the final 60 seconds as we all remembered that great last minute win against Wigan the previous week ......and prayed.

Pearce suddenly found himself in front of the sticks with space and time for the drop goal which would have forced extra time. As we all bayed for one point, he feigned to kick, but then inexplicably passed the ball to Scott Gale. Scott dummied and passed onto Eastwood, who was tackled inches short of the whitewash and the glory! All it still needed was a drop goal and we were set for it, as Pearce went into the 'pocket' behind the attacking line. As the 25,000 crowd held its breath, and before Eastwood had time to play the ball, the hooter went and it was over. For Hull FC, the tears flowed both on and off the field because but for one wretched moment of bad luck, we would have been at Wembley. I sank onto the terracing, too sick to stay on my feet any longer, whilst behind me a pair of teenage girls sobbed inconsolably. I was just dizzy with anger, pain and self pity. I hated times like that and the burden that loving a Club brought but once again there was absolutely nothing that I could do about it.

Poor old 'Brooksey' he was gutted

Friday 1ˢᵗ April 1988   *Hull 21 – Hull KR 14*

David Brooks, was a typical tough Aussie who had come to this country having always dreamed of playing at Wembley and in his last ever season, that game was his last 'throw of the dice'. That night he had found himself just minutes away from 'Living that Dream', but in the end he fell tantalisingly and dramatically short. After the game, in floods of tears, he showed his true emotions. In Dick Tingle's book, "Beards, Buttons and Blue Movies" he tells of his conversation with David after the game, when he said, "I don't believe it Dick, it is over, my chance of playing at Wembley is gone. I know I will never ever get another chance, I have never ever felt so low in my life. It is so unfair, I know someone had to lose, but why oh why couldn't it be them".

Before the game Brooks had said, "If only we can win this one I can retire a happy man, I don't think I have ever wanted anything so much in my life, not even when I was a kid and it was Christmas". His last words to Dick before he got on the plane to Australia are reported to have been, "I don't think I can ever watch another Challenge Cup Final because I will just keep thinking of what might have been!" That, as most of us fanatics know, is exactly how it gets you!!!

The journey home from Leeds was all hold ups and traffic jams and was, in our car at least, conducted in absolute silence. There was a feeling of total and utter dejection and even Billy couldn't 'magic' up a laugh or two. It was a gloom that was to grip the West of the City for several days, however for the players there was no rest and two days later it was Good Friday, and we were playing at Craven Park. There, despite the disappointment and six team changes, to the credit of the whole team, we raised our game again and beat Hull KR 21-14 to ensure Hull FC stayed in the First Division. I don't know whether the buses were on strike that day but I do know that Billy and I walked all the way back to the Punch from Craven Park. Triumphantly, after helping to carry Coach Tony Dean shoulder high around the pitch at the end of the game, we marched home through East Hull, singing 'Old Faithful' at the top of our voices. It was a massive win for the Club and as so often happens in sport, just two days after being totally deflated, circumstances had transpired to drive the disappointment of that 'freak' try at Headingley out of all our systems, to replace it with the warm glow that comes with beating relegation and defeating the 'Old Enemy' on their own patch.

Happy days are here again; enter Brian Smith

Although the season had finished and we had survived in the top Division, as is always the case with sports fans, we were not satisfied with that at all and the customers in the nightly 'debating Club' that was the Public Bar of the Punch Hotel were soon grappling with the interesting subject of who would be our next Coach. Of course we wanted the best there was in the World, you always do, and even back then that usually meant an Australian, but the Club were keeping tight lipped on what was happening. Unbeknown to the fans however, Director Mike Stanley was heading to Australia to interview a young Coach, who was currently doing well at the Illawara Steelers.

All the while the Club said that they were looking at British candidates including Tony Dean who had shared the job quite successfully at the end of the season. On 4th May it was announced that there was a short list of two; Dean and that Australian, who was revealed to be Brian Smith. A day later Smith was named as the new Coach of Hull FC and so began a new era at the Club that was to thrill and delight us diehard fans and see the "Where were you when we were crap" crowd flocking back in their thousands. Having noticed his potential a couple of years earlier when Smith managed a touring Australian School side, Mike Stanley paid Smith's air fare over here and was very much the 'mastermind' behind his arriving.

'Smithy' at a very young (for a Coach at least) 32, arrived in July and immediately started to change things. On 7th August we went along to the Boulevard to watch the first ever Hull FC 'Open Trial', as players from across the country came along to try and impress our new Coach. There were a couple of Welsh Rugby Union players, (no doubt called Di and Taffy 'Other'), several lads from West Riding Amateur League teams and a lot of local amateur players, making up a total of 48 hopefuls. To help in his quest to find new talent Brian enlisted the support of Hull legend Johnny Whiteley and the two ran the rule over the candidates. Whether we found anyone is unknown, although the rumour at the time was that Ian Marlow (a player Smith was to sign from Beverley Rugby Union twelve months later) took part.

Smith also signed four overseas players, Craig Colman, David Moon, David Boyle and Neil Henry, the latter being taken on as his Assistant. It was certainly an exciting time for the fans and also for those of us who liked a beer or two, when on 1st September the Government finally relaxed the drinking laws, to at last introduce 12 hour licensing.

The Punch Hotel was still home from home, particularly on a lunch time when the regulars included retired seamen, shop lifters (who could nick you anything to order), reformed and retired 'Ladies of the night' and a great Juke Box that included an eclectic mix of classics from the past like, Queen's 'Seven Seas of Rye' and 'Killer Queen', Lindisfarne's, 'Meet Me on the Corner' and Dean Martin's 'Little Old Wine Drinker Me'.

One particular shop lifter who used to drink at the end of the bar was well known by everyone including the local constabulary. 'Any Size' Eddie used to steal to order, and would often be asked by someone to 'supply' a shirt of a certain size or a pair of trousers with a specific inside leg measurement. He would drink his pint, wipe his mouth with the back of his sleeve and head off across the road to Willis Ludlow, one of the City's major Department Stores. Five or so minutes later he would be seen returning across the 'zebra crossing' with said shirt or pair of trousers carried at arm's length on a hanger taken straight from the rack. From time to time Eddie 'went missing' for a while and the usual explanation was that he was 'On a training course' which was code for a short stay at 'Her Majesty's pleasure'. However it never stopped Eddie 'taking orders' the minute he was back.

At least the new drinking laws meant no more 'poking' pints down before 3-00pm on a Saturday afternoon or racing from the Punch, to the Club House at the Boulevard on a Sunday, as at last the calming hand of sensibility descended on the Drinks Trade and although we still got drunk, at least now we did it at a respectable pace.

Despite these changes the pubs still closed at 11-00pm, so there was no alteration to our late night eating habits as we continued to frequent The Khyber Restaurant on Lowgate on Saturdays after closing time. It was then that I discovered something very important about Curry in general and the Khyber's Dopiaza in particular, in that, next morning, you realized that it wasn't just your mouth it burned.

At work it was getting busy again, with Hull Fair just around the corner and the Autumn Concert Season starting to take off. On 13th September, Tony and I promoted a concert by 'Goth rockers' (the Hull Daily Mail's description not mine) The Fields of Nephilim who were a strange crowd indeed. Their main claim to fame was that they were still wearing the same clothes they wore three years previously, on their first tour. The thing I remember most though was the fact that before they went on stage to perform their own unique brand of 'slash your wrists' depression music, they covered each other with flour.... bags and bags of it! I didn't ask whether it was Self Raising or Plain but this was supposed to give a gothic 'cobwebby' sort of feel to the act. When I looked round the audience that night they were all covered in flour too!!! It took days to clear the place up but they all seemed to enjoy it!

On 4th October Gary Numan was back at the Hall still touring despite having almost totally disappeared from the mainstream pop music scene and hardly selling any records. His Mum and Dad were still in the entourage for the 'Metal Rhyme Tour' but the crowd, of 'Newmo's', still full of ageing weirdo's with jet black hair, white faces and long trench coats, was dwindling fast. If Gary Newman had his problems then at the Boulevard everything was not going too well for 'Smithy', either because after all the pre-season hype, his Australian imports were arriving later than expected and we lost the first four League games of the 1988/89 season. After the third a 10-16 defeat at the Boulevard to Wakefield, our Coach said, "The fans must hold their nerve, as must the players, I am confident things are improving".

He then proceeded to drop Gary Pearce, Wayne Proctor and Alan Tomlinson into the 'A' team, which certainly seemed to concentrate their efforts and so it was that after another close defeat away at Warrington, we recorded our first win of the season at home to Leeds by 14-12. It had to be Leeds didn't it; however badly we were playing we could always overturn them. At last 'Smithy' started getting some cohesion into our play as slowly but surely, the results started to come. A close defeat at Bradford was followed by an amazing win at Saints after which, full of new heart, we all set off for a game at Halifax. Still smarting from that Cup Semi Final defeat the previous year, it was a game where a win would see us out of the bottom three of the First Division for the first time that season.

Phil Windley steals the show!

Sunday 6ᵗʰ November 1988   *Hull 14 – Halifax 6*

The ground at Thrum Hall had a massive slope that usually worked to Halifax's advantage, it was on an incline tapered towards one corner and it was said the home Club trained at least one night a week on it, practicing their kicking both up and down that 'hill'. That day we all stood at the Hanson Road end of the ground just next to the score board. It was as I said earlier in this tome, a fine old stadium constructed of dour, craggy local stone, which often mirrored the tactics of a Halifax pack that was always tough and uncompromising.

Buoyed by what had happened the previous week at Knowesley Road, I drove over with Andy passing as we went, cars and buses full of the 'Faithful' who made up around a third of the gate that day. I remember Brian Smith supervising an on pitch warm up, which back then was certainly not normal procedure. As the teams ran out our Coach was at the end of the tunnel encouraging each player as they ran by.

The first few exchanges were fast and furious as the two packs ripped into each other. Andy Dannett had a real go at Pendlebury and following this bout of 'slapping' we went ahead with an Eastwood penalty. Then Eastwood scored our first try, as Craig Colman released him and he scampered in and round behind the posts and after just 9 minutes we led 8-0.

The whole crowd was silenced when Hull full back Paul Fletcher was knocked out as his head collided with the knees of winger Mike Taylor as he moved in to smother the ball and there was an eight minute delay while the medical staff of both Clubs attended to him. Paul was finally carried from the field with a suspected broken neck. That injury saw young Phil Windley take the field. He was usually a half back but had to go straight to full back, a position in which he had never played before. Immediately Halifax's Staines ran straight at him, but somehow Phil clung on until Dannett arrived to floor the big forward.

Then, as Halifax tried to use the wind, Windley could only stand under the crossbar and watch as a Pendlebury bomb hit first the upright, then the bar and then the other upright, before finally going dead. Hull hung on although Whitfield kicked two penalties, for the score to be 8-4 at half time. Halifax were famous back then for a novel if not uncompromising defensive pattern which today would probably be known as a 'sliding defence' but back then it was just seen as a 'gang' of players running across the field and tackling everything in its path. The second half began with Halifax using this to great effect to stifle our playmakers but it was then that 'Super Sub' Windley took a hand in things.

As the game wore on Phil started to gain in confidence before Paul Dixon sent the 'Aussie Flyer' Bob Grogen haring down the wing for what looked a certain try. However, Windley just managed to push him towards the touchline and away from his supporting centre before somehow getting to him and with one last ounce of effort, forcing the Australian flyer into touch. Two minutes later, in almost the same position at the other side of the field, Windley repeated his heroics on Scott Wilson. Those two tackles had the Hull fans in raptures and were the turning point of an uncompromising encounter. A penalty by Whitfield reduced the arrears to just 2 points and despite a 12-2 advantage in the scrums and Hull surrendering the ball seven times, somehow we held out.

In the 'Casey years' those errors and the Halifax pressure would have seen us capitulate, but with Smithy (until warned by the referee) running up and down the touch line barking encouragement, we held out. For me the best memory was saved for the last second of the game as Divorty drove the ball into a ruck of Halifax forwards. As the hooter went several of the home team's players started to walk, heads bowed, towards the changing rooms. Quick as a flash Divorty handed the ball out of the tackle and some neat passing from Moon, O'Hara and Boyle saw Price cross the line and Eastwood add the conversion, by which time half the Halifax players were probably in the bath.

It was a great victory and before Eastwood could take that final conversion we poured onto the pitch to congratulate our players, First on the field was of course Brian Smith, who shook everyone's hand and saluted the supporters before the players left the field. It was the start of a great sequence of results, however with Windley's heroics, that surreal ending, and that awful injury to Fletcher, it was a game that holds lasting memories for me. As for Brian Smith it heralded the start of a great three years at Hull FC.

You've got to keep going to the end!!!

Sunday 27th November 1988   *Hull 12 – St Helens 16*

By late November we had just climbed into the top half of the League table although we had already experienced a few of 'Smithies' 'never say die' last gasp wins and were all starting to believe that our new Coach had the makings of a real hero. However, not many neutrals held out much hope for us as we went back to Saints in the Second Round of the John Player Trophy.

Despite some heartening displays, we travelled over the Pennines more in hope than expectation and although we lost, it was one of those rare occasions when despite a defeat the 'FC Faithful' stayed behind and sang 'Old Faithful' long after most of the 5000 Saints' fans had gone home. Disaster struck in the fourth minute, as an ordinary looking St Helens move between Bloor and Dwyer saw Holding easily break the line as Wilby and Sharp missed a tackle and a pass to John Fieldhouse sent Les Quirk speeding in at the corner.

It looked like it could be a landslide win for the hosts, but for the rest of the game Hull stuck to Brian Smith's game plan and kept the Saints at bay. Eastwood landed a penalty after 12 minutes and Laughlin replied with another for Saints three minutes later. The referee Mr. Volante went 'whistle mad' in that half awarding a penalty every two minutes (of which 16 went to the Saints), while the Hull pack brilliantly led by Dannett, Boyle and Jackson, tore into the home side completely knocking them out of their stride.

Although we missed the 'in form' Gary Divorty, whose wife went into labour four hours before the game, his deputy Jon Sharp was everywhere, and behind the pack Craig Colman organized and encouraged the play brilliantly. On the 20 minute mark we scored. Lee Jackson fed Coleman, who dummied twice before sending a superb long range pass to Sharp who turned it back inside for Welham to force his way over the try line. Eastwood missed the conversion wide out and a Loughlin penalty ten minutes later saw the scores tied at 8-8, before Eastwood re-established our lead as he converted the game's 20th penalty, after Haggerty had almost pulled centre Moon's head off on the stroke of half time.

In the second half the referee only awarding 5 penalties in the whole 40 minutes, although 4 of them still went to Saints. After 61 minutes we broke out in our own half and Pearce dummied his way through the line to free Wilby who galloped 30 yards before turning the ball back inside to put Sharp in under the posts. Somehow, as we celebrated, Mr. Volante decided there had been a forward pass and the score was ruled out. As the game wore on 'Porky' Pearce (as Brian Smith had inadvertently christened him in a radio interview the previous week) dropped a great goal, while Eastwood got another penalty and Laughlin grabbed two back for the Saints. So we went into the last five minutes one point in front at 13-12.

Then fate took a hand! Finishing the stronger we had the home side on the rack as we laid siege to their line. However Sharp failed to take a Dannett pass that would have seen him score, the ball went to ground, and Fieldhouse pounced. Quick as a flash he fed Bloor who rifled the ball wide where, despite a valiant chase from four Hull players, O'Connor outpaced everyone to score a heartbreaking try in the corner.

With just 4 minutes to go we just couldn't get back at the Saints and in the end we lost a titanic battle 16-13. I remember well the way that Alex Murphy the Saints Coach, so obviously relieved at the outcome, ran on the field at the end whilst we sang and sang and were surrounded by police who, used to football crowds, didn't understand that from a defeated set of fans at all.

Pies, Orwell, Fictitious Pubs and Wallace and Grommit

Just after Christmas that year we again took the long trip over the Pennines in cold windy weather to attend Central Park Wigan, a place where we had experienced little joy over the years. The Cherry and Whites were riding high at the top of the League and I went in the car with Garry and Billy. For most of the journey we were all debating exactly how we could keep the score down, because although we had done well under 'Smithy' since that shaky start, we still knew that trips to that part of Lancashire rarely reaped any rewards. That night we parked in our usual place in a side street behind some back to back houses about four hundred yards from Central Park.

Wigan's second greatest civic hero was author and raconteur, George Orwell who entitled one of his pieces of literary brilliance; 'The Road to Wigan Pier'. This was, of course, a real conundrum in itself, the irony being that there was no pier at Wigan. Of course the accolade of greatest civic hero of the Lancashire mill town is held jointly by Wallace and Grommit who actually live there, in another fictitious location, 62 West Wallaby Street, which I always felt when I watched the animated TV shows, resembled closely the street where we had parked for all those years.

Occasionally on our visits to Central Park, (although not this time), we had called in at the famous premises of 'Poole's Pies' after which it is generally believed the local citizens get their nick name. It was always hard to get parked there and there was invariably a long queue and an even longer wait, but you were rewarded in the end by what could only be described as 'exceedingly good pies!' As for a drink, well we tried a few pubs around Central Park over the years including 'The Park', with its large framed pictures of famous Wigan games and personalities, but we never found Orwell's famous pub, 'The Moon Under Water' which is hardly surprising as it never actually existed either, (Well it didn't until Wetherspoons named their new establishment in the Town centre after it in the late 90's). So I guess what I do know is that when it comes to a history lesson centered on Lancashire, you could say Wigan is famous for several things, most of which never existed.

'Stuffing' the Pies and the advent of the 'Wigan walk'

Wednesday 12ᵗʰ January 1989   *Hull 35 – Wigan 20*

Central Park was a grand sight back in those days, and 'doing what it said on the tin', was smack in the middle of Wigan. It had massive terracing on three sides and a lower seated stand that had a roof painted in red and white stripes, down the other. If a great sight during the day, under floodlights it was nothing short of magnificent and a great example of a traditional Rugby League stadium. As we stood on the 'Spion Kop' there were around 12,000 braving the elements that night and they created a great atmosphere. In fact the roar that greeted the Wigan team as they ran out led by Andy Gregory, struck fear into the hearts of the 500 or so Hull fans, that had made the long trip over the Pennines. We had every right to be fearful too because Wigan were on a run of six straight wins, the last of which had been a victory the previous week in the John Player Trophy Final and the team that ran on to parade the Cup before the game read like a 'who's who' of Rugby League. Although we had actually won our last five games, it seemed like we faced an almost impossible task as Andy Gregory rolled his sleeves up to his shoulders, took a divot out with his heal, and placed the ball on the centre spot to kick off.

The first half turned out to be a tight affair with both sides defending well. Wigan looked the stronger, so it was quite ironic that it was Hull that took the lead with Garry Pearce landing a great penalty goal after Iro had upended Moon 30 yards from the line. To return the compliment, Wilby then tripped Bell as he ran past him and a Gregory penalty tied the scores. A sweeping move down the left hand side saw Ellery Hanley dance between Price and O'Hara to set Wigan's winger Preston flying down the touchline. When Hanley broke through like that he was a wonderful sight to see, providing you weren't playing against him. Preston then passed back inside and there was Bell to scoop up the ball and fly in 10 yards from the corner flag. Gregory missed the goal but at 6-2, things looked to be turning against us.

Straight from the restart, as the rain came down; Moon broke away down the centre, outstripped the defence and touched down near the corner flag, too wide out for Pearce to convert. However, back came Wigan through a Preston try two minutes later, when he seemed to juggle with the ball for ages before touching down, and with a Pearce penalty for a trip by Betts on Wilby just before half time, we went in just two points down, which was seen as a 'moral victory' as far as the travelling fans were concerned!

If the first half had been tense and nervy, then the second was a revelation and will be remembered forever by anyone who made the trip that night. Craig Colman, (a masterstroke of a signing by 'Smithy') started the second period in fine style as he proceeded to give Great Britain number 7, Andy Gregory, the run around. The game however took a truly dramatic turn after Pearce had kicked a superbly angled penalty from the 40 yard line to level the scores. 'Porky' then took the ball on the third tackle and without a player near him, struck a massive drop goal from 38 yards out, to edge us ahead. What followed however can, only in truth be described as 20 minutes of some of the most remarkable Rugby League I have ever seen.

On 53 minutes Wigan's Shelford knocked on and from the ensuing scrum Pearce broke magnificently, stepping first to the right then to the left, leaving Hanley and Edwards 'for dead'. Colman shot through behind him, took his inside pass and floated a fantastic looping ball to Divorty out on the right. As the defence 'funneled' back and caught him, Gary stood in the tackle and popped a pass out to Colman to score under the posts. Pearce converted and it was 10-17.

The home side were visibly shaken as they dropped the ball again almost straight after the kick off. Pearce shot through the line and this time using a fantastic dummy which left the cover grabbing at thin air, passed onto Colman again. Craig handed on to Price who went in untouched to score. A further conversion saw us 23-10 in front and while a hush spread through the ranks of the 'Cherry and White' supporters, we were dancing on the terraces to the chants of 'Brian Smith's Black and White Army'.

Next it was Colman again, this time drawing Byrne and Shelford before, to a great "Ooooh" from the crowd he slipped out a wonderful pass behind his back to Divorty who hung the ball in the air long enough for Paul Fletcher to romp over to the right of the posts for his first try of the season. It was champagne stuff. A Pearce goal meant that with 19 minutes to go we were 10-29 up and scoring at a point a minute. We were coasting, but coasting for Hull FC has always been a problem! We missed several tackles and Hanley, who was always a danger, strode in to restore some of the home sides pride as the locals sensed a possible comeback.

However any hope they had was short lived because nine minutes later it was Craig Colman who again roared away from the defence. This time he fed Tim Wilby who timed his run perfectly and careered down the field. As the defence scrambled back he flicked the ball out of Gildard's tackle and as it went to ground, Pearce 'fly hacked' it forward and Jon Sharp touched down to end the rout. A late Bett's try and Gregory goal added some respectability to the score line, but Wigan were well beaten and we witnessed an early example of the 'Wigan Walk', as the rain came down and the stands emptied well before the end. However on the hooter, as a couple of hundred Hull fans danced a conga on the terraces, the aging corrugated iron roof over the 'Kop' echoed to the strains of 'Old Faithful', while Brian Smith, as usual, came out onto the pitch after the game to applaud the crowd and we all sang and danced until the stewards moved us on towards the exits.

The wizardry of Coleman and Pearce swept us into 4th place that cold night at Central Park, and after two years in the doldrums, Brian Smith and the Hull lads had posted the 'FC are Back' signs across the Rugby League world. What a night, what a performance and what a memory. Wigan 'Star' Shaun Edwards was interviewed afterwards and, talking about Hull, came up with the classic quote... "I knew they were good, but I didn't know they were that good". That night the depression that had descended on my life since the demise of Arthur Bunting packed its bags and moved out and it is without doubt a moment in time that I will cherish forever.

One in the eye for a Wrestling fan and an umbrella up the backside for Fit Finlay!

Things at the City Hall were still going well and Wrestling was still surviving despite falling attendances. I mention it again not because I like the 'sport' but simply because it was always a source of stories both serious and comical. In 1989 Wrestling still featured the same old heroes and villains that had been around for years. That January it was the turn of perennial bad guy 'Fit' Finlay to be the star of the show and he won his bout quite easily in the end. As he sat in the corner before leaving the ring, he was harangued by the usual irate females, one of whom stuck the pointed end of her umbrella firmly up his back side actually drawing blood. Finlay reacted as anyone would and flailed behind him with his arm, catching the now animated fan smack on the cheekbone.

With a scream she ran off to find Tony the Hall Manager, closely followed by an entourage of shrieking women in shell suits and trainers. The lady who had been caught in the face was quickly developing a black eye and Tony immediately summoned the promoter. In the mean time the women was shouting to everyone, "Finlay hit me and I'm going to sue him for a million pounds". Soon Anne the promoter arrived and settled the woman down by saying that Finlay was "Sorry for what he had done, but it was just a reflex reaction to the umbrella incident" To this the woman screeched, "I'm suing him for a million quid, so there" to which Anne replied, "Well 'Fit' has sent you a signed photograph and here are two free tickets for the next show" She looked at them and screeched "Are they Ringside", Anne nodded, and the irrate fan just said, "Fine" and nothing was heard about it again.

Back in the Shed Again!

Sunday 5th February 1989   *Hull 18 – Salford 6*

That February I again made the trek over the Pennines to Salford. Hull had been on a great run of 8 league games without defeat but had suffered a disappointing reversal in the Challenge Cup against Castleford, in a low scoring game at the Boulevard the previous week. I made a rare regression to coach travel that week with a group from 'The Tiger' pub in Cottingham and watched a great victory when once again all the Hull fans took over the famous Shed Stand.

It was not all good news that day though because when we returned to our Coach elated but hoarse, we found that some 'well wisher' had slashed both the front tyres. We sat in the cold for 3 hours that evening before a local coach company arrived to take us home back over the Pennines to Cottingham and a few pints in the Tiger Inn.

On 'Look North' the following night we watched a recording of David Watkins presenting Jon Sharp with the Man of the Match Trophy and a post match interview with Brian Smith proved him to be at his 'outspoken' best. When asked if Hull FC were good enough to win the Championship. Smithy just said, "No", there was a long pause and then the broadcast switched back to the studio!! At times, Smithy was a man of few words who usually preferred his actions to do the talking.

Brickman, the Play-offs and a silver salver for 'Smithy'!

Wednesday 5ᵗʰ April 1989   *Hull 23 – Widnes 16*

The newly formed Vice Presidents Association held a dinner at Willerby Manor that April and I went along with a table of supporters representing several of the pubs in Cottingham. Over 400 attended and the 'new found confidence' that was growing since 'Smithy' had arrived was everywhere. We were now fifth in the League and heading for the Premiership play-offs with just two games to go; a massive clash with Widnes the following evening and a home game to round off the season, against Salford. That night, despite him only having been our Coach for a few months, Brian Smith was presented with a salver and gave an impassioned speech which ended, "If we're all in this together, we will succeed" which certainly sent us all home fired up for the game the following evening. It was a sad occasion too, because it was that night that I heard of the death of Roy Francis, the Coach who invented the

'Panzer Pack' all those years ago in the 50's who had passed away that afternoon in a Leeds Hospital.

We beat the League leaders 23-16 the next night, in a game that saw our number 6 Gary Pearce totally outplaying the visitor's 'Welsh wizard' Jonathan Davies in what was a typical all round team effort. Everyone worked for each other as Hull swept aside the class barrier in devastating fashion and a 12-6 win against Salford the following week confirmed our place in the play-offs!

That last weekend of the season, over at the other side of the City, Hull KR were playing their last game at the old Craven Park ground on Holderness Road after occupying the East Hull Greyhound Stadium for 67 years. That Sunday, 9th April and just a week after we had beaten them, they entertained Widnes who were victors 13-16.

At work the going was hard and the hours long, but there was still plenty of lighter interludes to keep our spirits up, particularly at Committee meetings, which were for me becoming an almost constant source of amusement. The latest idea that was causing a stare was a hair brained plan to get more tourists into the City by commissioning the Public Artist Anthony Gormley to construct a massive 80 meter high 'Brick Man'. This edifice, the Tourism sub-committee planned, would gaze out across the Humber from Sammy's Point at the convolution of the River Hull and the Humber. A debate on this topic raged on the letters page of the Hull Daily Mail for weeks which at one point saw the 'sexist' lobby demanding a Brick Women as well! However it was all brought to an abrupt end when Gormley had one session with a Council Committee and decided that he didn't want to build it anyway, saving the City a few hundred thousand pounds in the process. Who knows Hull could have been as famous for its Brick Man, as Blackpool is for its Tower.......but I doubt it!

"Give us the ball mate". Kevin Dick appeals to the Halifax scrum-half as a scrum forms in the Challenge Cup semi-final replay at Headingley on 30th March 1988. Hull went on to lose 3-4 after a freak Halifax try won the game.

Two pictures which show the heartbreak of losing the Premiership Final at Old Trafford in 1989

Above, Paul Fletcher is inconsolable and leaves the pitch, while below Andy Dannett leads the lads to the disappointed Hull crowd at the Stretford end.

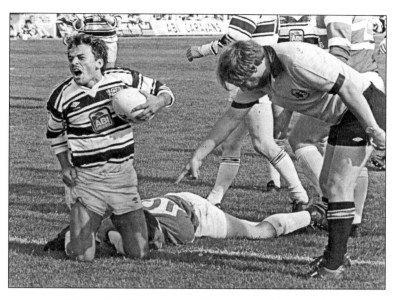

No mistake about that one then ref!
Phil Windley and the official agree "It's a try", against Salford at the Boulevard in 1988/89.

A typical study of Gary Divorty on the rampage against Leeds, the team he was eventually to join.

A piece of history is destroyed, as the iconic and world famous
Threepenny Stand is demolished in 1990.
(Courtesy of Hull Daily Mail)

Scrum-half Greg Mackey,
Coach Brian Smith and
the Australian High
Commissioner Douglas
McClelland prepare to dig
the foundations of the
New Threepenny Stand in
July 1990.

Good Friday 29th March 1991: Ian Marlow takes on the Hull KR
defence as Hull are victorious 28-16.

Victory in the Premiership Final at Old Trafford 12th May 1991.
Hull 14-Widnes 4.

Raising the Cup, the picture that says it all! Greg Mackey and Lee
Jackson at Old Trafford, 12th May 1991.
(Courtesy of Stephen Kirkwood)

The Lord Mayor of Kingston-upon-Hull, Councillor Dennis Woods
and his Lady Mayoress Gill Woods, launch the Boulevard Kids in
the bar in the New Threepenny Stand.
(Courtesy of Hull Daily Mail)

A close encounter at New Craven Park on 17th March 1992 saw Hull win 12-8 to secure First Division survival. In a torrid and brutal encounter Steve McNamara and Lee Jackson tear into the Rovers forwards. *(Courtesy of Hull Daily Mail)*

Supporters Club official Bill Girvin and a throng of young fans hand in a petition to the Board of Hull FC after a poor season in 1992/93 *(Courtesy of Hull Daily Mail)*

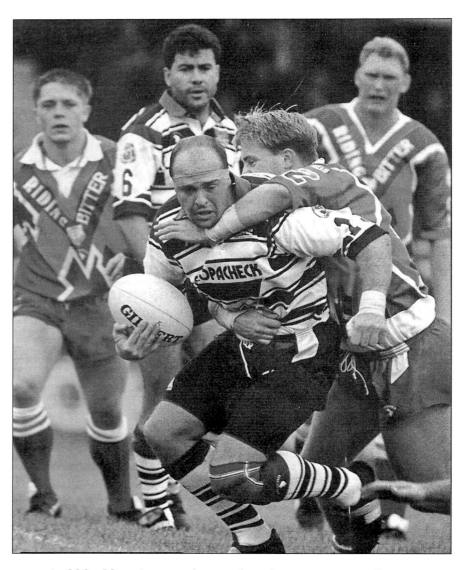

A typical blockbusting run from John Sharp against Hull KR at the Boulevard at a time when the opposition were going through one of their 'fancy dress' fazes!

From bottom of the League in September to the play-offs in April, Brian Smith was a hero!

Sunday 23rd April 1989   *Hull 32 – Castleford 6*

So the season finished with Hull FC in the play-offs and as we took on Castleford at home in the first round our Coach announced in his abrupt and inimitable fashion, "Stop Joyner and you stop Castleford". We did both and easily progressed to the semi-final. I remember that day, young forward sensation Dean Sampson (who the Castleford fans had knick-named 'Diesel'), had a shocking game in the wake of relentless haranguing by the Threepenny Stand, who, because of his long flowing blonde hair, 'christened' him 'Marilyn'. Smith cranked up the excitement in the week following that win by announcing that he has signed Steve Folkes for the next campaign and that "at least 12 other Australians of high repute" had contacted him about coming over to join Hull.

We had finished 4th that year which only guaranteed one home draw, but results in the first weekend of the play offs went for us and we were at home again in the semi finals. The other surprise package that year was our next opponents, Featherstone Rovers, who had finished 7th in the League and were actually a bit of a bogey team for us that season. Under Peter Fox they had made great strides forward and were the only Club to have completed the double over Hull FC that year.

Another brilliant team performance in front of 11,169 fans saw us win again, this time by the emphatic score line of 23-0 and amazingly after starting the season so badly, we were in the Premiership Final a week later at Old Trafford. My over riding memory of that Featherstone game is of Brian Smith coming onto the pitch after the hooter and running towards the crowd in 'The Threepennies' displaying with his finger that there was just one game left before we became Premiership winners. I remember saying to Gary and Billy as we stood applauding on the terracing at the Airlie Street end, that 'Smithy' appeared to be every bit 'as excited as we were'. Whilst all this was going on, the newly refurbished tannoy system was blasting out, "Keeping the Dream Alive" by Freiheit and every time I hear it (usually at Christmas these days) I immediately remember that moment! It was priceless!

Craig Colman the player that Brian had brought from Australia earlier in the year, had returned home early because of playing commitments with his Club over there, but as soon as the news was out across the world that we were in the Final, he asked to come back and play at Old Trafford. We all admired Craig, but in typical belligerent fashion Brian Smith declined the offer and kept faith with his replacement Phil Windley who had stepped up so well since Colman left.

As usual, sleep was impossible in the week before the Final, something that never changes, however old I get! As a distraction however I was asked to judge the Final of the Tower's 'Battle of the Bands' contest 'Soundtrack' on the Wednesday night prior to the big game and a Hessle band called 'Looking for Adam' were the winners. It was a good evening with free beer for the judges and served to occupy me for what would otherwise have been another restless evening in the build up to that Final.

Final disappointment...... but "We'll be back"

Sunday 14th May 1989   *Hull 10 – Widnes 18*

So we were at Old Trafford for a game in which no one gave us a hope. However this was a new Hull FC, this was Brian Smith's team full of battlers and passion and anyone wrote us off at their peril. We looked hungry that season, the work ethic was fabulous and the fans knew that even if we didn't win, we would give it our absolute all. Once again that Wednesday we queued down Airlie Street to get our tickets and the atmosphere, despite the drizzle that was falling, was simply amazing. Widnes had a side packed with stars, whose success had gained them the 'tabloid' title of 'The Cup Kings' and we were the under dogs, which suited us down to the ground. Thousands packed the M62 on the way to the game and at Saddleworth Moor the whole Motorway ground to a halt as a convoy of traffic crawled the rest of the way to the Stadium. It was a great atmosphere even in the traffic jam, as cars behind us hooted their horns on seeing my new "Don't follow me, follow Hull FC" sticker.

We parked in an Industrial Estate, which was to become my regular parking spot for future visits to Old Trafford and once inside, the atmosphere was nerve tingling. Although the Widnes fans only had a short journey down the 'East Lancs Road', as always, in a crowd of 40,000, we outnumbered their fans at least, three to one. In the end it was a game that was decided by three defining incidents either side of half time, these in effect dictated the outcome and the fate of the two teams that contested the Final.

From the kick off it was apparent that if we were to compete, our forwards led by Dannett, Steve Crooks and Paul Welham, had to get on top. So, in the early stages it was pleasing to see them pushing the Widnes six back at every opportunity, whilst in possession, Lee Jackson was masterful at acting half back 'scooting' first this side, then that, to consistently wrong foot the opposition. Of course as often happens after such endeavour, Widnes scored first. Hull had kept 'Danger man', Emosi Koloto, quiet for 20 minutes until he broke a Windley tackle and started off down-field. As Fletcher came across to affect the tackle, he passed to centre Darren Wright who dissected our retreating defence to score. Next we received a real blow as, having been sandwiched in a tackle between McKenzie and Joe Grima, Hull scrum half Phil Windley was knocked out cold. He was carried off, but in his absence and for the rest of the first period, Gary Pearce stood in brilliantly at scrum half.

Back Hull came as Gary Divorty stepped out of a Hulme tackle and sped towards the line where he almost scored himself before slipping out a short pass for Welham to crash over. Pearce goaled and we were level. By this time 'Porky' Pearce was really controlling things, as he almost got first Eastwood and then Sharp in for tries. In the end though a penalty on the Widnes 'twenty five' saw him grab two more points to give us the lead for the first time. At this point we were threatening to snatch the initiative away from our more illustrious opponents but then came the first of those three defining incidents, deep in the Widnes half.

In the last minute of the first half Pearce was contemplating a drop goal attempt when Jackson instead went blind at the play the ball and fed centre Price. The youngster sent a bullet like grubber towards the corner flag for O'Hara to chase, but somehow Andy Currier got his hands on it, knocked it in the air caught it and was away. Brilliantly, Price somehow recovered and moved in to tackle the Widnes man only for Tony Myler to step between the two players and obstruct him. The referee completely ignored this infringement, which left Price on his backside and Currier haring away down the left wing to score so at half time we trailed 10-8. The battalions of FC fans were certainly not happy and as they gave referee John Holdsworth a deal of abuse as he left the field with chants of 'Cheat, cheat', we went off in search of a beer.

The second half had hardly started when Widnes scored again. Paul Fletcher who sparkled all afternoon at Full Back for Hull pounced on a loose ball and ran off, only to be called back by the referee, who had already indicated a knock on and a scrum with the 'feed' to Hull FC. "What happened to the bloody advantage rule?" yelled Billy, but to no avail.

Amazingly we only lost one scrum with 'The put in' all afternoon and of course it had to be this one. Again, as the ball was passed across the Widnes' line, Price was pulled down and obstructed, this time by Currier, and once Alan Tait had given Martin Offiah his only decent pass of the game, what happened then was a foregone conclusion, as he scorched down the wing as only he could. Another Davies' conversion meant that suddenly we were 16-8 down and in need of a quick score. We looked to have got one three minutes later, as the third and final critical incidents began to unfold.

Paul Welham was pulled down inches short of the line and from the play the ball Lee Jackson dummied before shifting play the other way for O'Hara to cross the line and clearly put the ball down. He was immediately carried out of play by both Pyke and Wright but as we all celebrated and the Widnes players' heads went down, amazingly the touch judge ruled no try and the referee pointed to a '25 yard re start'. By this time we were all fuming, frustrated and struggling to come to terms with what we were witnessing.

There was still plenty of time left, Pearce landed a good angled penalty on 58 minutes and Blacker, Nolan and Fletcher all went close, but in the last quarter of the game we couldn't add to our score, although we never stopped trying to the very end. As the hooter sounded we had lost 18-10 in heartbreaking and disappointing circumstances. At that stage I felt numb, rather like when you stub your toe and there's that awful hiatus between the impact and the pain setting in. However there is little doubt that after cheering and applauding the FC players who had given so much, we all made our way home believing that we had been robbed; a feeling that over the years we had grown to get used to. I remember being proud of my team and disgusted with the officials and after getting stuck in what seemed like a interminable traffic jam I channelled all that anger and frustration into driving fiercely in whatever direction other cars didn't seem to be travelling in and we soon got lost in Manchester.

Next day suffering with a hangover I took a day off work 'with cold' and having studied the local newspaper headlines that declared, "The Try that Never Was", I consoled myself with the words of the now 'God Like' Brian Smith, when he said in the post match press conference, "We'll be back and next time we'll show you we can be winners" Brian Smith that man of few words had once again said just the right thing. Three weeks later, as the pain of that defeat started to subside and from back home in Australia, our Coach announced that he had secured the signature of the biggest, roughest and hardest player there was in the game at that time. "Noel Cleal will be here by October" was an announcement which immediately made a difference to season ticket sales, as the thought of 'Crusher' in a Hull shirt inspired hundreds of Hull fans to re-subscribe to the dream.

Divorty wants more money!

That summer, after having been back in the City Hall flat for a second spell, this time for 4 years, I decided it was time for another change simply because you can only take so much of being on call 24 hours a day every day of the year. I bought a house in North Hull in Wensley

Avenue just off Cottingham Road and spent that summer sorting it out. The closed season was the usual drag and there was some concern when Gary Divorty, one of the great young successes of the first Brian Smith season, was put on the transfer list at £180,000 because he couldn't agree personal terms with the Club. Jon Sharp was also in dispute but 'Razor' finally agreed to stay, however it was to be the end of Divorty, at least for now.

The 2nd August was a significant date as it was then that the Club announced another signing, this time it was 'power house' prop forward Karl Harrison who came in from Featherstone. However the two Clubs couldn't agree a fee and so the recompense was eventually left to a Rugby League Tribunal. At work the City Hall was swathed in scaffolding both inside and out as the venue went through a £1.3m refurbishment, which included new seats, carpets, lighting, a rebuilt stage and a new sound system.

"Pathetic Hull in Poor Start"

Sunday 3rd September 1989   Hull 12 – Bradford Northern 30

Despite all the high hopes a new season brings, on this occasion once again we were disappointed. We played Bradford at Odsal and despite young Steve McNamara scoring on his debut, we lost badly, causing the rash headline above to be plastered across the local paper. Then Widnes beat us at home and we sunk to the bottom of the League with a further string of disappointing results. Brian Smith threatened "Big Changes" if things didn't improve but they didn't and I remember travelling back from Castleford, after another defeat by 18-10, contemplating the fact that perhaps we hadn't learned that much, because what we were experiencing was almost a mirror image of the start of the previous campaign.

There was a lot happening off the field too as the dispute between Gary Divorty and the Club came to a head and Gary finally signed for Leeds in another 'disputed' deal reported to eventually be worth

£80,000, which again a tribunal had to settle. More problems followed when that game at Castleford left Gary Pearce with a serious knee injury which saw the Club citing the West Yorkshire team's hard man 'Rambo' Gibbs for an "illegal late tackle".

While Brian Smith's latest money raising scheme the 'Go for Gold Lottery' was raising £35,000 in just three months, 'Crusher' Cleal was on his way from Australia and boy did we need him! Whilst all this was going on at the Boulevard, it was hectic at work as the newly refurbished City Hall was literally bursting with concerts, dances and conferences. The new stage and new lighting 'Flying' facilities in the roof of the Main Hall meant that bigger and better quality concerts were coming to Hull. That autumn, the charismatic David Essex, Gary Newman and the rather inebriated 'glam' rockers 'Dogs D'Amour' headlined the opening month of concerts. Hull Fair was the usual 'nightmare' with a baby being born behind the Dodgems on the first night (prompting someone to say of the mother, that it was usual just to come home from the Fair with a coconut and a bag of candy floss) and a man breaking his leg on the Bobsleigh ride as he tried to get off whilst it was still moving. For me personally there is little doubt that those weeks in Walton Street every October were the most stressful in my career at the Council.

The biggest Hull player I'd ever seen!

Sunday 15th October 1989   *Hull 44 – Salford 8*

In over 50 years of watching Rugby League I have seen some characters and some pretty intimidating and awesome players. It's always been a sport where the little guy would often go after the 'big fella' with varying degrees of success, however once or twice in a life time you come across a player that opponents actually physically fear. Mal Menninga was maybe one such player but they are certainly few and far between.

At that time 'Smithy' was doing everything he could to improve the team and had introduced Glenn Liddiard and Steve Folkes from Australia, but he was still looking for some real power as well as someone who would inspire and capture the imagination of the fans. Our new arrival however ticked those boxes and, reputed to spend his 'time off' wrestling wild boar in the 'Outback', he looked like the 'Wild Man of Boneo'. Noel Cleal was a real phenomenon and a player that had for years terrorised everyone he played against from Club games to International matches. In 1985/86 he had come to England and played for Widnes scoring 12 tries in 16 games and Hull KR had almost signed him, before he was declared bankrupt and therefore unable to leave the sub-continent.

The first game in which Noel made a real impact was against Salford at the Boulevard on 15th October 1989. That Sunday afternoon around 7000 fans witnessed a display of such power and aggression it had the whole City talking about 'Crusher'. The National Press said that 'Crusher' Cleal had the Salford defence "Quaking in their boots as Hull went on the rampage", and that wasn't far off the mark. There is a nice tale about the day that Cleal arrived in Hull and arranged to meet the Club representatives in 'Darley's Arms' on Boothferry Road. Noel walked in and as he stood at the bar, his head touching the glasses on the rack above him, the Barmaid said to her colleague, "You serve those two guys in the Lounge and I'll serve Mr Cleal". Noel parted his tousled hair looked up and said quietly, "How do you know my name" to which the barmaid replied, "You're in a 'Rugby City' now 'Crusher', so you'd better get used to it because you can't hide, here everybody knows your name!"

If Hull Fair had just finished in Walton Street, the Circus was just beginning at the Boulevard. After the trials and tribulations of early season this was to be the day when the 'jigsaw' was to start to fit together again, with Cleal cutting an unusual figure in the centre as opposed to his more accustomed role in the pack.

The game kicked off with Brian Smith stood up high in the top of the Best Stand in his newly erected 'Crows nest'. Salford took the lead in the 8th minute when Jones beat Eastwood and Liddiard and put Hadley over but within two minutes we were level. At last Cleal got the ball in a flowing move when slick passing between Windley, Liddiard and

'Crusher' saw Eastwood head for the corner and brush Full Back Steve Gibson aside to score a try that Eastwood converted. Anthony 'Chico' Jackson made his debut that day on the wing, where he was a surprise inclusion in place of Dane O'Hara.

After an Eastwood penalty, 'Chico' actually got on the score sheet himself, as Folkes brilliantly switched play to the blind side and Steve Crooks sent out a precision pass to Jackson, who putting his head down, ploughed in at the corner. The experiment of using Richard Gay at Stand Off and Nolan at Full Back was working well and after a further Eastwood penalty by half time Hull were well on top when a massive 'ball and all' tackle, on the hooter by Cleal, saw his opposite number Bragger needing attention long after the players had left the field.

Just six minutes into the second half a quick play the ball saw Lee Jackson pass straight to Cleal, who set off towards the Salford line. Brown, Worrell and Evans all fell off him as he scattered the 'would be' tacklers like skittles and as two other Salford players showed unbelievable hesitation with regard to confronting him, Crusher crashed on, to cross the 'whitewash' for his first try for his new Club. It was a fabulous sight that even had the fans in the 'Best Seats' on their feet and cheering long after referee Asquith had awarded the try.

Cleal, clearly 'blowing' a bit, was substituted and Doherty came on and took over in the centre where he immediately dropped a ball that Evans gleefully pounced on to score the visitor's second try. Then it was the turn of debutant Chico Jackson again. A shrewd inside ball by Dannett out of a tackle found Windley who threaded a great grubber kick through towards the corner flag for 'Chico' to scoop the ball up from round his boots and slide over the line for his second try.

Back onto the field came 'Crusher' to take over from the limping Liddiard and soon the giant was back in the action again. Salford had visibly lost the appetite to tackle a player that simply seemed impossible to put to ground. In fact the referee was having difficulty calling held because Cleal kept moving forward, even with five players on his back and round his legs. The big man was now rampant and as Windley put him through again he drew an ambivalent Burgess before this time passing to Eastwood who roared over in the corner and it was starting to look like a rout. Substitute Paul Welham scored another five minutes later before the game finished with the move of the afternoon. Cleal hit Jones (so hard he just crumbled in a heap) before passing to Sharp who ran across the half way line and looking to open up a gap he passed to Gay who found Welham. The second rower then switched the ball back inside for Doherty to gallop in to end a glorious move under the posts where Eastwood's 8th goal from 9 attempts made it a final score of 44-8.

We all stood and applauded the players while Brian Smith came out onto the pitch to join the adulation for a good win in which we had seen an amazing performance from a man who had caused mayhem and confusion and was more like a bulldozer than a rugby player.

Always on the lookout for talent, in late October, Brian Smith signed the little known Australian scrum half Greg Mackey from Warrington. The diminutive player had featured for Canterbury and Illawarra before joining the Lancashire Club a few months earlier. Warrington saw him just as a stop gap signing but he was an unexpected success, leading them to victory in the Lancashire Cup Final. He was reported to have just agreed a new two year deal at Wildespool when Brain Smith swooped and signed him for Hull FC. The Warrington Board accused Hull of an illegal approach but later settled for a small compensation payment and 'Bluey' Mackey was ours. We had to sadly release the injured David Liddiard to make way for him on the quota but what a great signing Mackey would turn out to be, as despite missing his second game at the Club, Mackey went on to play 94 consecutive matches for Hull FC before returning to Warrington in 1992.

Garry Glitter gets a leg up!

Concerts continued at the City Hall unabated, however a particular memorable night was the visit of 'The Garry Glitter Gang Show' on 27th November. This was a massive production with over 500 lights suspended from the ceiling, pneumatic lifts and even a hydraulic drawbridge in the centre of the stage. As the 'punters' queued around the Hall before the doors opened it was more like a football crowd than one for a Rock Concert. At the top of their voices they, chanted "I'm the Leader, I'm the Leader" and wore 'Glitter masks' and wigs, much to the amazement of the good citizens of Hull who walked past as they made their way home from work. These big productions needed big stages, often much bigger than the one that was in the City Hall and so a stage extension was added to the front of the permanent platform to increase the size.

These were usually provided locally by a registered supplier but on this occasion the promoters needed to keep their costs down and assured us that they were 'touring' an extension which would suffice. Of course, once erected, it did anything but 'suffice' and I remember ex Hull FC players Shaun O'Brian and Alan Wardell who were security in the front of stage pit that night commenting on the 'flimsy' nature of the structure even before the concert had started. As the crowd poured in, the atmosphere was amazing with everyone in the 'full house' that attended 'hell bent' on partying. As the lights went down and the sumptuous velvet curtains opened, the stage was in darkness. A Bass Drum started to pound and the chants of "Leader", "Leader" and the stamping of hundreds of feet rocked the very foundations of the old building. At the back of the Stage a spotlight picked out a massive juke box at the top of a steep flight of stairs and as the front opened, Glitter appeared to thunderous applause, he danced a while and then whipped off a mask to reveal that it wasn't him at all, but just one of his six piece dance group. This was repeated until all six had whipped off their masks and the seventh and final one to appear was Glitter himself.

As each dancer was revealed, they stomped down the steps and lined up at the front of the stage on the 'extension', stamping their feet in time to the thunderous pounding of the audience who had now been whipped into a frenzy. Under this pounding the flimsy structure of the stage extension swayed back and forth and was in danger of collapsing onto the crowd. At times like that it is almost impossible to stop the show and it's easy to see just how real problems occur. I was certainly as scared as I had been at any event I'd promoted and some speedy action was needed.

Suddenly, quite voluntarily about a dozen security staff and stage crew crawled under the stage extension and laid on their backs to support the underside of the stage with their feet. Looking under the structure it was an amazing sight with all these guys acting as human shock absorbers as the dancers on top bounced up and down on the plywood staging. Somehow we got through the night and no one in the crowd knew, or could see what was happening under the stage. As for Glitter himself, well I never liked Paul Gadd and even before he was to become so infamous all those years later, he came across as being arrogant bigot who was pretty easy to dislike, still everyone in the audience at 'The Gang Show' had a memorable evening including Brian Smith and his family, who sat up in the Balcony.

'Crusher' switches on the Christmas Lights while the Reverend wins the booze!

By December Hull FC had moved into the mid table positions in the League and music fans across the nation were getting excited about a press report that the remaining three Beatles were contemplating getting back together again. However in just one 'sound bite' George Harrison scotched all the talk of a reunion, when he said, "There will never be a Beatles reunion whilst John Lennon is still dead", and that was that!

Back in Hull Noel Cleal had settled in a house in Cottingham and had been invited to switch on the village's Christmas Lights that year. As Steve Massam of Radio Humberside conducted the 'Count-down' and 'Crusher' pushed the button, the village was illuminated to thunderous applause, only for the system to fuse seconds later, as the whole of the main street was plunged back into darkness. Club Chaplin the Reverend Allen Bagshawe was having better luck however, when at a Vice Presidents' Dinner at the Willerby Manor Hotel that I attended, he scooped the first prize in the 'sit down, stand up' 'Irish' Bingo, winning 12 Bottles of wine and a bottle of Whiskey. I bet the Bagshawe household had a good Christmas that year! Meanwhile at the Boulevard Hull FC had an 'injury crisis' and 'Smithy' moved swiftly to sign up winger Neil Turner from Doncaster sending both Wayne Proctor and Neil Puckering, who were now surplus to requirements, in the opposite direction.

The Fabulous Baker Boys open the Odeon, whilst Juliet 'Gets them out'

That spring, Hull FC's gradual improvement continued as 'Smithy' slowly worked his magic and Cleal just got stronger and stronger. January brought big wins over Halifax and Barrow whilst a brilliant performance saw us get the better of Wigan at the Boulevard 30-20, but we were still struggling to win away from home and most of our journey's over to West Yorkshire and Lancashire saw us returning 'empty handed'. However that improved home form spurred us on to winning eleven of our last thirteen games to get into the end of season play-offs for a second year.

That April I was invited to the Gala Opening of the new Odeon Cinema complex built on reclaimed dockland adjacent to the Ice Arena in Kingston Street. My first experience of a brand new 'Multi-Plex' Cinema was certainly an eye opener and as I watched the 'Fabulous Baker Boys' with the Lord Mayor, the Leader of the Council and all the other worthies from the Guildhall, I glanced around the sumptuous surroundings and pondered that whilst the refurbished City Hall was an adequate venue for live music, it was easy to see where the future leisure time of the people of the region was destined to be spent.

Two days later I went (again as a guest, I might add) to the Hull Truck Theatre in Spring Street to see local hero Roland Gift, starring in a very 'avant garde' interpretation of Romeo and Juliet. It was a strange adaptation which proved that perhaps the classics are best left as just that; classical. The sight of Mercutio and Benvolio rolling drunk and relieving themselves against a wall, then appearing next day in sunglasses and taking copious amounts of Aspirin, was bizarre indeed; still I tried to enter into it. Much of it went over my head, while no doubt along with many other males in the audience, I occupied myself with observing that Juliet, played by Daphne Nayer, was certainly a 'fine women' and pondered on the possibility that perhaps bra's had not been such an essential in 16th Century Verona.

I was certainly not prepared for what came next! As she started the balcony speech with "Romeo Romeo wherefore art though Romeo...." slowly but surely she started to peel off her T shirt!! Stood there naked towering over us all on a raised balcony, it's fair to say that the males in the audience, (who had up to this time been shuffling around and wondering what time the bar stayed open till), didn't hear much of the rest of her speech, as with eyes focussed on the 'proceedings' we all wondered 'where to look next'. It's also fair to say that all the ladies in the audience tried to give the impression of knowing what it was all about, while us lot just sat there transfixed in one of those communal 'I mustn't look, but I cannot avert my eyes' moments. You could have heard a pin drop as no one dare change their facial expressions, with a smirk or a titter (excuse the pun) certainly out of the question! It's funny the moments of high culture you remember!!

I loved the old Hull Truck Theatre in Spring Street and saw some great plays there, including the brilliant John Godber tribute to his Rugby League roots in Featherstone, 'Up and Under'. There were also some great concerts to cherish and I remember with great affection watching the late Kirsty McColl, Ian Matthews, Prelude and Bronx Cheer at various times, at the Theatre. The place spawned so many great stories particularly in the early days when John Godber and Barry Nettleton and Hull Truck were just starting out.

On one occasion Barry secured some sponsorship from BAE systems at Brough to build a new bar. In tribute to their benefactors they had it constructed in the shape of an aircraft's wing. It was perfectly formed and looked brilliant, but it had one glaring design fault. As it was aerodynamically moulded just like a real wing if you put your pint down on it, the glass would slide toward you and spill your drink down your clothes. It was the only bar I had ever drunk in that had a sign saying "Please do not put your glasses down on the Bar"

Those awfully nice 'Macc Lads' come to Town

Living at 1 Wensley Avenue I was managing to get by and as we had by now entered 'The Decade of the Frozen Lasagne' I was even eating more healthily. However it was still all work and rugby although the breadth and diversity of popular culture was growing all the time. On 5th April that year the City Hall played host to probably the worst band I have ever seen, and believe me I have seen a few bad ones! Hailing from Macclesfield, 'The Macc Lads' were renowned for their outlandish songs, lude lyrics and constant genitalia flashing on stage. The crowd of almost 1000 was made up of aging punks, young skin heads and old rockers, who from the moment the group appeared spat and threw missiles at the stage. It is the only time I have seen a roadcrew erect a net in front of the stage to protect the band from the missiles thrown by their own fans.

Still undaunted and covered in spittle they hammered out their repertoire included gems like 'Al O'Peesha', 'All day drinking', 'The Appentice Dentist', 'No sheep till Buxton' and 'Julie the Schoolie'. Their final song was their only hit (number 87 in the charts for one week) a little ditty entitled 'Sweaty Betty'. This features the most poetic of lyrics, which include "Sweaty Betty, she eats a lot of pies, Sweaty Betty, she's got enormous thighs, Sweaty Betty, have you smelt her breath, Sweaty Betty, she'll crush a man to death". Needless to say they didn't come back again and luckily the 'City Fathers' didn't get wind of what had gone on either.

At the other end of the musical spectrum it was around then I met Mark Knopfler, when he took some time off from playing with Dire Straits to appear at the City Hall on 30th March with his new 'Project' The Notting Hillbillies. He was a really nice guy who sat and talked to us in the bar (in bare feet) before the doors opened to the public. However, if Mark was approachable, his drummer on the tour was a fabulous guy. Ed Bicknell was an ordinary chap who had met Mark at Leeds University and then become Dire Straits Manager because, he said, "They already had a drummer". I asked him what it was like managing probably the biggest band in the world at that time and he just smiled took a gulp of his pint and said, "I guess if I'm honest it's rather like being in a bank with a shovel"

Away with the 'A' Team

Friday 6th April 1990   Hull 'A' 33 – Bradford Northern 'A' 10

In all my time of supporting Hull FC, I think it's fair to say that with the exception of the odd sojourn across the City to Craven Park, I haven't been to many away games with the Club's Second Team. However on a breezy Friday in April I was joined by another 1500 Hull fans in a crowd of 3450 at Odsal Stadium in the first stage of an attempt to win the two major Trophies in the 1989/90 National Reserve League. That night Billy the Wizz and I travelled to the West Riding to watch our second string take on a big and physical Northern 'A' and we played them off the park. The antiquated Stadium echoed to the sound of 'Old Faithful' long before the end, as the team led by Player/Coach Steve Crooks, scored six tries which included a hat trick by veteran winger Dane O'Hara. Crooks himself dropped a goal and the side which included players like Chico Jackson, Mark Cass, Lee Hanlan, Mike Dixon and Paul Welham, stuck to a game plan that featured brilliant counter attacking and kicking early in the tackle count. Tactics that ensured the bulk of the game was played in the Northern half.

We all ran on the field and mobbed the team at the end before we chaired 'Crooksey' around the field, as he proudly held the Cup aloft. Two weeks later we won the League Championship title too and that double was attributed to the dedication of Steve Crooks and of course his mentor Brian Smith. It was a team made up of some old hands and some brilliant youngsters, some of whom would form the nucleus of our team in years to come and after just two seasons all the hard work that the Club had put into selecting good young local players and bringing them through 'the ranks' was starting to come to fruition.

The first team met Widnes in the play-offs and the team that beat us the previous year in the Final beat us again at Naughton Park 18-

8. However what I remember most about the game was the appalling refereeing which afterwards prompted Brian Smith to report the match official John Holdsworth to the Rugby League; of course that didn't do any good at all and Brian Smith and the Club heard nothing else about it.

A farewell to Dane

Sunday 27ᵗʰ May 1990   *Hull 38 – Hull KR 20*

At the end of the season it was good to see the old enemy across the river coming over to the Boulevard to show that they had finally got over the Black and Whites signing Dane O'Hara from 'under their noses' all those years earlier. The game was the now veteran Kiwi winger's Testimonial Match and over 6000 of us went along to thank a player who had begun his career with a punctured lung and finished it being the first ever overseas player to receive a Testimonial in this Country. He played 276 games for the 'Airlie Birds' and went on to sign for Doncaster, where injury restricted his appearances before he retired from the game completely in 1992.

That day at the Boulevard however, despite us all waiting and clapping him after the game, Dane strangely didn't do a lap of honour, which we all found pretty bemusing. Afterwards he explained, "As I received the Trophy, I felt my legs go and my eyes filled up with tears. I intended to do a lap of honour but I was just too emotional, I love this Club and those wonderful fans and I always will". That was explanation enough for all of us.

So, amidst the chaos and anarchy of the Poll tax riots that raged in many Cities against the new levy launched by Margaret Thatcher's Tory Government, the Rugby League season ended at the Boulevard on a sad note, with Widnes the team of the moment fast becoming our arch nemesis, but our day was to come in the following campaign and in the most spectacular fashion.

Chapter 6

The death of a 'National Monument' and the end of our spiritual home!

The 1990/91 season was one when I did precious little else besides go to the pub, work and look forward to the weekend. With Brian Smith 'driving' the Club both on and off the pitch, we were moving forward apace. However none of us were ready for the shock announcement that the Club, desperate to upgrade the facilities at the Boulevard, were planning to demolish the Threepenny Stand for it to be replaced with a new £300,000 structure that would seat 880 fans, have 14 hospitality boxes, a television gantry and standing room for 450 spectators.

The artist's impressions certainly depicted a futuristic structure but few of us were prepared to say goodbye to the most feared and intimidating viewing gallery in the game and I think, looking back, we probably greeted the plans with a certain amount of sadness. I went down to have a look at the old place on the same day the announcement was made and, I guess, to sort of conduct my own silent vigil in memory of a lifetime of wonderful memories. To my horror I found that the demolition was well advanced as a lone demolition man stood at the top of the last vestige of that famous terracing, wielding a lump hammer and removing the corrugated iron roof.

The Club purposely didn't announce that work had started and for many people in West Hull it was a case of the Threepenny's being 'here today, gone that afternoon'. However, I wasn't on my own that day as several other resourceful folks found out about the imminent demolition and went straight there to see what could be salvaged. I got three long metal nails and a length of roofing felt, whilst my pal Steve Roberts, got a small piece of wood he cut from the terracing. He had his 'little piece of history' mounted on a small plinth and to this day Steve needs no excuse whatsoever to produce this iconic artefact, and were it the Elgin Marbles it wouldn't hold more of a historical significance for him. So that world famous monument to our game that held 6000 fans, was made from Red Russian Pine and that had withstood the bombs of the Third Reich and the corrosive effects of the urine of countless generations of Hull FC supporters, was no more.

I felt a real sense of loss as if it was the family home that had been demolished and rather like the pilgrimages I made when I was 16 to that little house in Aylesford Street where I was brought up, I went back to the Boulevard a few times in the next few weeks and just looked at the space where 'The Threepenny Stand' had stood.

Then, as if even the fates regretted the demise of the old place, immediately after it had been demolished and every trace of it removed, the whole scheme ran into financial turmoil as the Rugby League reneged on their promise to providing £150,000 towards the replacement structure. Eventually the game's administrators found £50,000, and two months later the scheme was rescued by a brewery and 'The Tetley's New Threepenny Stand' finally started to take shape.

They're rioting, in Goroka, Papua New Guinea, and Victoria Square in Hull

That summer Lee Jackson and Paul Eastwood were rewarded for a great season at Hull by being selected for the British Lions Tour of Papua New Guinea and New Zealand and while in Hull City Centre the youth of the City were showing their disapproval at England's exit from the football World Cup in Italy, by showering the Humberside Constabulary with bottles, there was even bigger trouble for the Rugby League Touring team in Papua New Guinea. Writing in the Hull Daily Mail Hull FC's

Paul Eastwood painted a picture of mayhem, danger and the majority of the players "Wanting to come home". The tour had started well with a couple of wins over regional teams, but it was the happenings at the first Test Match in Goroka, (a regional capital that is home to around 19,000 people), that made the 'sporting world' take notice.

In a poorly disguised appeal to the Rugby League, Eastwood wrote an open letter to the paper and under the title of, "Get Us Out of Here". He said, "We are living in appalling conditions and since our win in the First Test the Hotel has been under siege from irrate fans brandishing sticks and even knives". He continued, "The Test Match was a disaster, the ground held 2000 but there were 5000 in there and many stood on or over the touch line. Stones and sticks were thrown on the pitch and by the end our eyes were streaming from the effects of tear gas which was used continuously by the Police throughout the second half. There was also another 4000 locked outside waiting for get at us and it was a very scary situation indeed. The Hotel has Cockroaches and the food is shocking, please get us out of here".

Meanwhile at the Boulevard we were all looking forward to big things in the upcoming season as in came Patrick Entat, a nippy scrum half from French Club Avignon, Brad Webb an 'Aborigine' back and Ian Marlow a new recruit from local Rugby Union Club Beverley. Ian had actually been to one of Smithy's open trials in the past and had decided to try his hand at League, knowing of course that it would be the end of his Union career. Sadly however, fans' hero Steve Folkes did not return from Australia to complete his contract after being diagnosed with calcification of his leg muscles, which led to his retirement. Still, with record season ticket sales and several new faces, we all felt good about our prospects, but how good they were actually to be, was probably beyond our wildest dreams.

The last rites of the old Hull Show

The Autumn Craft Fair took place again that year at the City Hall but it was starting to lose its attraction and the only outstanding feature was probably the fact that in the Victoria Bar where the Bees and Honey competitive section was taking place they had a large 'contained' Hive with 'real live' bee's on show. The event was opened by the Lord Mayor but the Honey Show soon closed when the bees got out and took up residence as a swarm in the domed roof above the bar. Sadly that was to be the last Craft Fair to take place and so the last vestiges of the old Hull Show, where I had started work back in 1966, disappeared forever.

It is only on rare occasions that you know that something big is happening at your Club. You often hope it is, but rarely do you actually know it is. However we all had a really good feeling about the squad that year. Brian Smith had successfully developed some great young players like Steve McNamara, Richard Gay, Paul Eastwood, Jon Sharp, Russ Walker, Rob Nolan, Lee Jackson and Dean Busby and when blended with imports like Damien McGarry, 'Crusher' Cleal, Brett Webb, Patrick Entat and Greg 'Bluey' Mackey they formed a really cohesive unit. After two seasons of starting badly we began that year with five wins, including a 20-14 victory at home against Saints and a pulsating 24-22 win away at Leeds. We were flying, Brian Smith was idolised by the fans and the crowds were flocking back to the Boulevard.

Battering Wigan while the 'spies' look on

Sunday 7ᵗʰ October 1990   *Hull 24 – Wigan 4*

That October, once again it was time for Hull Fair and the one day I got off from the incessant grind of injured kids, moaning parents, drunken fracas and grumbling Showmen was the Sunday, and thankfully, that year, we were at home to Wigan. The visitors had a team of stars but had started the season slowly, having won just two of their first five games. The invigorated and confident Hull FC on the other hand, hadn't lost and were top of the League.

The Boulevard had certainly been upgraded that summer and the influence of Brian Smith off the field was manifest in the newly refurbished 'League's Club' at the Airlie Street end of the Ground and of course that new Tetley's Threepenny Stand. However some things, like the catering, didn't change and the only two choices of confectionary you had were still Mars Bars and the ubiquitous marshmallow biscuits known as Wagon Wheels, the latter along with 'gangrenous' burgers being the staple diet at most, if not all RL grounds back then.

We all got there early that day to secure the 'Lucky Step' on the Airlie Street end terracing where the catering was still dispensed from an ancient caravan adjacent to the Division Road gate. It was a sunny afternoon and at least for once I wouldn't have to take shelter in the Gents under the new Stand during half time. I remember being amazed that despite the newness of the Stand and this almost palatial sanitary provision, these toilets managed to perpetuate the same acrid aroma that the back of the old stand used to embrace. Who knows, perhaps it was the 'lingering spirits' of thousands of phantom 'urinators' still relieving themselves in the ghostly portals of that famous old Stand?

That afternoon we welcomed, with the usual trepidation, the reigning title holders, and the team that had dominated domestic rugby for the last five years. The game had been 'hyped up' in the media all week but the over-riding memory for me that day, came as we were joined on the terraces by two nuns wearing habits and wimples, who nodded and smiled to us before leaning on an adjacent crush barrier to watch the game. That was, for me, in a life time of watching Rugby League, a really surreal moment. I have seen plenty of men dressed as nuns at games, but these two were definitely the real thing. The animosity on the field began before the game had even kicked off when the Hull team came out to warm up behind the try line at the Airlie Street end. You could see that our players were certainly focused on the task ahead but minutes later, out came Wigan to do their warm up and they purposely ran to the same end.

This was obviously seen as a way of intimidating the Hull players, and, as both sides refused to move, the warm up session descended into chaos as players from both sides collided with each other. As the Hull team started back to the changing rooms and much to the amusement of the fans, a couple of our players (John Sharp and Noel Cleal) could clearly be seen to walk straight into two Wigan players, knocking them both sideways. It was great fun for the spectators and as I stood eating a Wagon Wheel, on my 'Lucky Step' with my pals all around me, there was nowhere in the world I would rather have been.

As referee Kevin Allett blew the whistle and we kicked off, Wigan came under an unyielding battery of crushing tackles and high speed collisions from a Hull pack that had obviously used the pre-match happenings as motivation. On attack too, we were 'all aggression' and within minutes both Karl Harrison and Andy Dannett had flattened Lucas and Dermott in blistering line breaking runs. The crowd of 10,900 was captivated as they roared every tackle and applauded every break.

After just 4 minutes Paul Eastwood converted a penalty when Myers tripped Rob Nolan, and then within minutes of the re-start Lee Jackson broke from acting half and found Patrick Entat on his shoulder. The little Frenchman scooted through the defence to face the Wigan full back Joe Lydon who felled the scrum half with a high tackle straight across his head. In piled Dannett and Harrison to shouts of 'OFF, OFF, OFF' from the 'New' Threepennies, and in the melee that followed Lydon was shown the Red Card. He tramped off, still protesting, to chants of 'tatty bye, tatty bye, tatty bye' and on reaching the tunnel the crowd struck up an impromptu rendition of the French National Anthem, as Entat staggered around in a daze. "You're a F*cking disgrace Lydon" shouted a guy behind me, prompting everyone to turn as one to look at the nuns. They were both fine and heartily laughing at this outburst, as if it were the good natured banter that's heard at the pantomime when the crowd boo and hiss the villain.

Andy Gregory was trying his best to get Wigan moving but a crunching tackle by Ian Marlow saw him limp from the field with a leg injury, to be replaced by Phil Clarke. In the 22nd minute Eastwood converted his third penalty and the atmosphere rose as we pressed and pressed the Wigan line. On 28 minutes the Lancastrian's defence finally cracked, when Ian Marlow scored his debut try for the Club. 10 minutes later Eastwood converted another penalty awarded for obstruction and then with just a minute left to half time we went in for the kill.

With just 2 minutes to go, a half completely dominated by the Airlie Birds ended with another great try. Wigan's Shaun Edwards took his eye off a pass from Betts and dropped the ball. Nolan snapped it up and ran at the defence before placing a measured kick towards the corner. Eastwood and the Wigan centre Dean Bell hared down field, shoulder to shoulder but both, in their desperation to get there first, over ran the ball, and Greg Mackey following up, touched it down. Eastwood converted from the touchline to make the half time score a quite unbelievable 18-0.

As the nuns devoured the remains of their burgers Wigan restarted the game and were certainly fired up, as four forwards immediately laid out Russ Walker in a gang tackle. The 'Pies' hearts must have sank though when who should come trotting from the bench to take his place but Noel Cleal. 'Crusher's' first tackle laid Kevin 'The Beast" Iro out cold, and the game had to be stopped whilst he was resuscitated with smelling salts. Eastwood then slotted over another penalty as Wigan got more and more frustrated. Next to suffer in the Wigan ranks was Dean Bell, who ran straight at one of his own players and was carried off unconscious. Back on came substitute Phil Clarke to last just 10 minutes before another Cleal special saw him helped from the field with a shoulder injury. During all this action Eastwood stroked over another penalty, and then there followed one of the best tries I had ever seen at the Boulevard.

The move started with a break in our own twenty by Nolan who passed onto young Steve McNamara who wriggled between two would be tacklers. Somehow Steve managed to pass onto Richard Gay, who had ghosted up on his outside and he spun out of no less than 4 tackles, before Cleal took the ball, stopping only to swat off the 'would be' tackle of a chasing Lucas, before 'feeding' the onrushing Neil Turner who scored in the corner. It was breath-taking stuff, which saw the remaining Wigan players collapse to their knees behind the posts. The game had been won by power and determination and although Wigan did get a consolation when Skerrett rolled over for a late try, as the hooter went the scoreboard at the Airlie Street end showed Hull 24 Wigan 4.

Brian Smith had the players wound up into a state of near frenzy that day and Wigan were never really allowed to get into the game. What we didn't know at the time was that as Brian and the boys celebrated with us on the pitch afterwards, spies from Australia Club St George were in The Threepenny Stand, laying their plans to meet up with 'Smithy' afterwards to try and entice him back to his home land. Perhaps it was best that we the fans didn't know really, because they'd have got lynched!!

Morons, skinheads and Greg Mackey's sexual preference for donkeys; it had to be Wildespool

Saturday 13th October 1991   *Hull 3 – Warrington 2*

I don't mind a good punch up on the field, few rugby fans do, but I don't condone bad behavior in the crowd in any shape or form. Although I have experienced some crude and disgusting behavior at rugby over the years I have never seen anything to equal the reception Greg Mackey received on his return to Warrington. Wildespool was known to most people in Rugby League back then as 'The Zoo'. The Board at the Lancashire Club perpetuated this title because they believed it referred to their big, rough, 'animal' like forwards, but most visiting supporters believed it was actually aimed at a section of their fans. It was an evil place at the best of times and I didn't like it at all, probably because it was there, in the Gents toilets at the Railway End, that I was punched in the face and lost a tooth back in the early 80's.

In those days the 'Wire' fans, (augmented it has to be said by Manchester United and Liverpool hooligans, looking for a bit of Sunday afternoon 'sport'), were renowned for their abuse and at times thuggish behaviour which was the last thing that most of us wanted as we arrived at the ground sedated by copious amounts of Greenall Whitney's Bitter. On occasions we had joined the home fans in the 'Royal Oak Branch' public house but that afternoon, with menace in the air, we went straight to the ground. The day Greg Mackey returned to the Club he had left in such acrimonious circumstances he got abuse from the moment he ran onto the pitch. 'Bluey' actually went back to Warrington after his spell at Hull FC, but some Warrington fans never forgave him for leaving in the first place.

As we arrived at Wildespool the home fans were waiting for us and we were threatened on the way through the turnstiles by a huge, feral skin head with hardly any teeth. Covered in tattoo's he wore cropped trousers and Doc Martin boots and looked like a throwback to the seventies. The game itself matched the atmosphere and was a tense affair, with both defences to the fore and only a penalty a piece to show on the score board after 78 minutes had been played. Our rear guard action was truly magnificent that cold Sunday afternoon and despite a constant tirade of "you're going home in a f*ckin' ambulance" from the hooligans to our left and the best efforts of the Warrington players on the pitch, Hull FC held firm.

We got few attacking chances and made 270 tackles that afternoon, with Lee Jackson making a total of 39. This, plus his support of the forwards, got him the Man of the Match Award. The 'Players', player of the game' was another youngster, Full Back Richard Gay, who on three occasions stopped the rampaging home forwards with crunching, ball and all, 'last ditch' tackles. Twice he stopped Paul Cullen inches short and then he held Gary Mercer up over the line, as the opposition's star player battled to get the ball down.

Up to the last 2 minutes wave after wave of Warrington attacks peppered our line. Then suddenly they were 'caught' off side at a scrum and a strong touch finding penalty from Mackey saw us at last get into their half. This immediately drew another round of chant about how Greg had 'a sexual preference for Donkey's' from the morons on our left and this was still ringing round the ground as Mackey got the ball 25 yards out on the third tackle. Cool as you like, and as if in response to the taunting, he stepped to the left, looked up and dropped the perfect goal, which triggered a state of hysteria amongst the 3000 Hull FC fans. We were still celebrating as several missiles flew into our Stand and a wave of Warrington fans, veins sticking out of their necks, charged across the terraces towards us through the ranks of cowering home supporters. A guy near me got a bottle on the shoulder which hit the ground and shattered, sending glass cascading over the crowd. However credit to the Lancashire Constabulary because they were soon escorting a dozen of these morons out of the ground, with their arms forced up their backs.

After all the abuse he had received it was a fantastic response from the little Australian. He refused to be intimidated and said afterwards, "If they had hoped to put me off, then they certainly didn't, the more they chanted the more I wanted to inspire Hull to victory". The final hooter went in what was by then a half empty stadium and we were pursued by more idiots who 'chased' us through the adjacent back street to our cars, but I guess our chanting of "There's only one Greg Mackey" as we drove away, didn't help much either. One coach we drove past, was having its side panels systematically kicked in by about 40 'Skinheads', as its frightened occupants peered out through the windows. I particularly remember one towering individual, the ring leader, because not only did he sport cropped trousers a string vest and about size 15 Doc Martin boots painted gold, he also, most bizarrely, wore a Bishops Mitre on his head. Crazy Days!

Shortly after that great victory we were as a team and a group of supporters, brought back down to earth with a bump when the 'Aussie' Tourists visited Hull and left us licking our wounds after a big defeat, but we ploughed on towards Christmas when the bombshell that we all feared, but dare not even contemplate, was dropped by the Club. Brian Smith, 'The Great White Hope' of the terraces, was on his way back home to Australia to take over at St George. The 'Spies' had got their man and West Hull was in mourning!

Dancing with tears in our eyes

Sunday 6th January 1991   *Hull 34 – Leeds 14*

When his final game arrived, once again, as I have said on many occasions already, if you were there that day you'll simply never forget it! The team played their hearts out for Brian and in the end easily beat a Leeds team who came to the Boulevard standing 3rd in the table. The 7500 fans who had come along to wish 'Smithy' well, were spellbound and at times left breathless by a sizzling game that had everything. Sky TV were there to broadcast a match that kicked off in the early evening and saw our forwards tear into the Leeds six with an awesome display of power and aggression that had the opposition, led by unpopular villain Garry Schofield, reeling.

After just 11 minutes Damien McGarry scored on his debut following a great pass by Webb, but then Simon Irvine got one back for Leeds before Nolan darted in at the corner and Webb finished off a flowing move. By half-time we were 16-8 in the lead before early in the second half Leeds forward Paul Dixon was sent off for a high tackle on Mackey and the party began. First Harrison blasted through the visitor's line to put Gay clear and he found Walker superbly supporting the play to score wide out on the left. Then Leeds Full Back Gallagher dropped a high kick and Rob Nolan nipped in to make it 28-8. Following a short spell of Leeds dominance when Phil Ford scored a brilliant 75 yard try, Harrison returned from the Sin Bin, immediately broke the line and passed onto Sharp, who wriggled and writhed his way over the line to complete our scoring. What a party we had as the scoreboard showed 34-14 and the final hooter sounded.

Coming as it did just a few days after a heartbreaking defeat at Craven Park against Hull KR, the result gave Brian Smith a 'fairy tale' send-off. The man who had transformed Hull FC from struggling relegation candidates to Championship contenders in just two and a half years was ceremoniously chaired round the ground by the players. I was standing in the Threepenny Stand where everyone was dancing and cheering as the entourage came past us, and as often happened for us fanatics in those times of joy, the tears flowed.

As Smithy went by signalling with one finger that we were the top supporters in the land, I was just overcome by it all. The 'hero of the masses' said afterwards, "I never want to forget tonight, this was something else, I thought I'd seen it all from this Club, but tonight has left me stunned and speechless". Most of the fans there that night would agree with those sentiments completely, it was the end of a short but glorious era and we were heartbroken.

Players can rarely alter our lives and affect our very being but each time you get a new coach you can dream dreams, and hold hopes higher and better than the ones before. When a coach like say Len Casey leaves then it's a blessing, but when someone of the calibre of 'Smithy', who had done so much to give us fans our pride back, departs, it's as sombre an occasion for a true fan, as the passing of a Monarch for a royalist.

Life of course had to go on with Cleal in charge and he certainly got the support of the Board who were at that time led admirably by Chairman David Kirkwood. David was a great character who always had a story. One such revelation concerned the weekly Board meetings that were held on Tuesdays, in the Boardroom, in the offices on the front of the Boulevard. Little had changed in Airlie Street since the days I was brought up down there, as David's story was to prove. On this particular evening, just as the meeting started, there was a pounding at the door but when David answered there was no one there. This happened a couple more times until he decided to stand by the door and wait for the knock. When the knock came again he flung open the door to find a young lad of about 7 grinning at him from outside. David said, "If you do that again I'll clip your lug", to which the lad replied, "You'll have to f*ckin catch me first you fat bastard" as he ran off across the car park. All David could do was laugh and relate the story till the day he died.

Sunday 13th was certainly unlucky for me, with a wasted journey and a car full of grit!

Sunday 13th January 1991   *Hull 0 – Widnes 0*
                                              (match postponed)

After that great victory over Leeds we were back at the top of the League Table and looking forward to the long trip over the Pennines to Widnes. Andy and Billy 'the Wizz' still travelled to away games with me in the now aging Opel Manta, which had seen better days. It was still a great car and could really motor, but at times it was prone to the engine 'cutting out' for no reason at all. This annoying occurrence was easily alleviated by opening the bonnet and letting the engine cool off. Then, after about ten minutes, it would amazingly start again and be as good as new.

That Sunday we set off early and as it was my turn to drive, as we motored out of Hull in glorious winter sunshine, the frosty verges glistened in the cold winter air. Alan another of our pals from the pub joined us, and Billy as always kept us amused on the journey this time with a small ventriloquist's dummy he produced from his coat. He called it 'Smithy' but we all agreed that despite his best efforts, Billy's lips were moving a lot more than Smithy's appeared to be. Still we had a laugh, as we got up onto the slopes of the Pennines the weather took a turn for the worse and it started to sleet. We stopped at a service area and telephoned back to Hull to hear that, according to Radio Humberside, the game was still on and so we started out again.

Of course just as we got to the highest part of the M62 at Saddleworth Moor, the car started to splutter and then expired altogether as I pulled onto the hard shoulder. It was freezing cold but I knew if I just left the engine a while to cool down everything would be alright. Whilst Billy (and 'Smithy') looked on from the back window, I got out of the driver's side and Alan did likewise from the seat behind me and between us, against a bitter wind, we opened the bonnet. At the moment we both opened the doors to climb back into the car a Gritting Lorry went past and filled the car with flying salt and grit. Boy, it hurt when it hit our faces, and I was still finding lumps of salt in the car the following summer. However after we had left it for the mandatory ten minutes the car started and after a four hour journey we finally arrived in Widnes at 2-00pm. We parked up in the housing estate next to the ground and joined the throng of Hull FC fans making their way towards the Stadium.

What happened next was most unexpected, suddenly we met other Hull fans coming in the other direction and as we approached them they shouted "It's Bloody off". We couldn't believe it, but we continued on to the ground not accepting what we had heard. However it was soon confirmed by the hundreds of Widnes and Hull fans who were trudging towards us and away from Laughton Park. By the time we got to the front of the Stadium, there was a mini riot developing, with Hull's new Coach Noel Cleal surrounded by protesting fans, some of whom were obviously agitated. Of course the condition of the ground was nothing to do with Cleal, although in the end he had refused to let our players out onto what was a frozen pitch, because he deemed it to be too dangerous.

Despite the ground being solid and declared unfit by a referee that morning, such a big pay day was guaranteed when Hull FC came to town, that the Directors of Widnes had thought that they would wait as long as possible before making a decision. This of course was totally unfair on all those Hull fans that had made the trip over the Pennines in good faith. So embarrassed was Doug Laughton the Widnes Coach, that he agreed to play the game, but Cleal was having none of that and fearing for the health of his players he called them out of the changing rooms and back onto the bus.

It was an absolute farce, still at least we got back to Hull without any more break downs and the game was re arranged for two days later, although the majority of Hull fans threatened to boycott it. Their protest was inconsequential in the end because Widnes was still in the middle of a mini 'Ice Age' a week later and we eventually went back to Cheshire to watch the re-arranged game on 27th February, when we were heavily defeated.

At the City Hall it was January and that usually meant a visit from Chubby Brown (the comedian, not the trumpeter) and although I had got used to fielding any flack there was from the public about his vulgarity, this time it was an extra worry because the very day he came to Hull, 17th January, coincided with the start of 'Operation Desert Storm' and the allies attempts to remove the troops of Saddam Hussein from Kuwait. Of course plenty of local people had loved ones out in the desert and I knew that Chubby would not be able to resist a dig at the expense of this military action. In the end it wasn't too bad really and all he said was, "You don't need to worry about that Saddam Hussein invading Hull, his tanks will never find their way around your f*cking one way system".

I got on well with Chubby, who never swore much off stage at all. He was certainly no trouble and usually sat in the Dressing Room with a pair of headphones on listening to his own shows so he could remember the jokes.

The Play-offs, and its Leeds.... again!

Sunday 5th *May 1991*   *Hull 10 – Leeds 7*

Smith's recommendation that 'Crusher' Cleal should take over from him as Head Coach certainly paid dividends as he soon had us marching towards the Premiership play-offs for the third year running. We beat Saints at home in a great game in the first round, and then met Leeds at the Boulevard in the semi final. What a game that was. Try as we may we could not get over the Leeds line, as they tackled everything that moved and hung on desperately to a 7-4 advantage. Then deep in the second half Greg Mackey hoisted a massive up and under, Gallagher the 'Loiners' full back, dropped it over the line and young Gary Nolan, who had only signed a few weeks earlier from amateur Rugby League, pounced to touch it down. We had got to the final and the scenes of jubilation on the terraces were amazing! Despite being in my early 40's I was so caught up in it all and over the fences and onto the pitch before I knew what I was doing. Mackey and Nolan were the heroes that night, as once again Old Trafford and Widnes were beckoning.

It's all the heartache that makes victory so sweet. The only thing that was missing was 'Smithy'

Sunday 12th *May 1991*   *Hull 14 – Widnes 4*

That year we had finished third in the league primarily because of 'Smithy's' influence and the fact that we won those first seven games, whilst the Cheshire team, who finished one place and six points in front of us, were hailed by the pundits as one of the greatest teams ever. Widnes had of course beaten us in the same game 2 years earlier and twice before that in the 80's, and were therefore on a great run and aiming for a win in their fourth successive Premiership Final. It was a surprise to everyone that we had even managed to get to the Final and at William Hills across the north of England very long odds were being offered on a Hull win. It was our second Premiership Final in three years and the players and fans alike had decided that this one "Was for Smithy!" That week I had done my bit to ensure a victory, wearing my lucky socks every day and sleeping in my Hull shirt every night! When I awoke it was a perfect morning, it was game day, the sun was shining, the birds were singing and the lawnmower was broken. We drove down to the game in my new Rover which was my first ever new car. To ensure my new mode of transport was safe we found a spot that was well away from the ground, in the area surrounding the Manchester Ship Canal.

Over 25,000 made the trip over the Pennines from Hull in a gate of just over 42,000. I remember before the game we were all heartened by speculation about the morale in the Widnes' camp as it was rumoured that their coach, Doug Laughton was leaving for Leeds and that their star player Martin Offiah was moving on. Both these rumours were eventually to be proved true. The 'Chemics' however had coasted to wins over Bradford and Featherstone in their previous two play-off games and were hot favourites to win the Final.

That day I stood with thousands of FC fans on the Stretford End where we sang ourselves hoarse. There were rumours abounding back in Hull that Noel Cleal had spent hours poring over videos of Widnes before the game, something that although common place now, was still rare in those days! It is said that Brain Smith rang the dressing rooms and spoke to the players and Noel beforehand, as the stage was set for a classic encounter. At last the Final kicked off. Karl Harrison and Andy Dannatt really got stuck into the Widnes' front row from the off and when we got the ball in the early plays, Patrick Entat and Greg Mackey completely outplayed the Widnes' half back pairing of Hulme and Dowd. This was exactly how we expected the game would unfold, as the general consensus was that Widnes would hold out and with their superior backs, take us apart in the last quarter of the game, however when the first try came for Hull and it was a classic. Nothing 'was on' as Richard Gay cut through the Cheshire Club's defence to touch down, and after Paul Eastwood had stepped inside to beat about 4 would be tacklers and put Russ Walker over, we were 8-0 up at half time and all I wanted to do was go outside, walk around the Manchester streets and pretend the score would stay like that until the end. Instead, I remember, I had a flat pint in a floppy plastic glass and hypothesised about how we could have been even further in front had we been a bit steadier in the goal kicking department.

As the second half started we all feared a Widnes' backlash and it came with a fantastic 75 yard move following a Soronson break, which ended with Offiah flying in at the corner. Then as a growing sense of the inevitable enveloped the whole Stadium, they threw everything at us and in the space of two minutes both Offiah and Davies were tackled into touch near the corner flag! Widnes's best chance came as their massive forward Emiso Koloto broke through. With Wright open to his left he switched play to Devereux at the other side and we scrabbled back to just grab him short of the line. Then Tait and Hulme were both held up inches short and it seemed just a matter of time before we cracked. It was however then time for some real 'fairytale' stuff, as Gary Nolan, the hero from the previous week scored the winner and it all unfolded right in front of us. Gary had come on for the injured Damien McGarry and we looked lost for ideas as we struggled to penetrate a resolute and uncompromising Widnes' defence. Then Greg Mackey slung out a sharp short pass to Nolan who was immediately enveloped by four Widnes forwards just five yards out. He writhed around in mid air and as they held him at 45 degrees, there, right in front of us, as we watched in amazement, somehow he pushed the tacklers forward. As we held our breath and as if in slow motion an arm came out of the ruck of players and plumped the ball over the line. The place went ballistic!

Eastwood converted from near the touchline and as 'Old Faithful' rang around that great Stadium; we held out for the last ten minutes and lifted the Trophy! In his six-week career at the Club Gary Nolan had come on as sub 3 times, and scored on each occasion! The scenes were fantastic as they always are in these situations, and as the team came over to us with the Trophy and Chesney Hawkes' hit, "I Am the One and Only" blasted through the speakers, it was the second tearful moment for me that season. One thing I remember so well was the way that all the Club's Directors ran onto the pitch to receive the adulation of the crowd, all that was, except one. Ironically, Mike Stanley, the guy who had brought Brian Smith (the Coach who had made all this possible) over from Australia, was content to stand out of the lime-light on the touchline, as showing great humility, he applaud the players with the rest of the fans.

It was a great victory and as we headed back to the car singing all the way, it was the end to a perfect day. Sometimes, just occasionally in sport something magical happens and that game is seared onto your brain forever. Those of us who were there at Old Trafford that day will never forget it. It was simply more than just a game.

Next morning when I woke up in an alcoholic haze, I looked out of the bedroom window at my new car down in the street and I looked again because I couldn't believe it. Whilst we had been parked in Manchester someone had jumped all over it and because it couldn't be beaten out, the cost for a replacement roof was £800! However even that couldn't dampen the fantastic feeling I had of winning that trophy. The 12th of May 1991 is still a very special day and one that will live with me forever, particularly when I polish the car roof!

A summer of discontent!

On 18th May we all went along to the Guildhall with another 8000 Hull FC fans and holding our cans of Lager aloft, we celebrated with the team up on the balcony as one by one they lifted the Premiership Trophy before retiring to the Banqueting Hall for a Civic Reception hosted by the Lord Mayor, Councillor Les Taylor. Sadly that was to be it, the pinnacle of our achievement for now at least, as tight budgets, underachieving attendances and over stretched resources in that great season, started to hit home on the balance sheet.

There were just too many twists and turns to outline here, but as fans at least we did our bit for the forthcoming season, as the Club reported record sales of season tickets, with £100,000 worth being sold by the end of May. The Directors had to decide whether to offer Caretaker Coach Noel Cleal a contract, something that took them almost a month to resolve. Poor old 'Crusher' probably didn't realise what was about to happen, otherwise he would have returned to Australia and been back 'wrestling Wild Boar in the Outback' like a shot.

We managed to get Mackey signed up for another year and at the end of the month he was joined by Coach Cleal also on a one year deal. Meanwhile a new Club, The Scarborough Pirates, had been formed and as they attempted to assemble a competitive team, their coach the ubiquitous Len Casey, signed the aging Gary Pearce for £15,000. Then the fans received a 'hammer blow' as the Club sold ace forward and mainstay of our pack Karl Harrison to Halifax for £100,000, citing desperate financial problems as the reason behind this shock move. So as the Green Sports Mail turned 'pink' and Hull FC opened their first town centre retail outlet in Princes Quay, the Club and the fans were in turmoil. In fairness we did sign Wayne Portlock and David Ronson from Manley. Then as two of our young stars Chico Jackson and Steve McNamara returned from a summer playing in Australia, we were also linked with Brian Smith's younger brother, half back Tony Smith, but nothing came of it.

The 'Charity Shield' and a 'sing-song' on York Station

Sunday 25th August 1991   *Hull 8 – Wigan 22*

First up that new season in an attempt to mimic the Football League, the winners of the League Wigan and Hull FC the victorious Premiership title holders met in a Charity Shield game at Gateshead Athletics Stadium. Ian, Billy and I went by train to the game although our performance was a shambles, and it was with some disappointment and foreboding that we returned to Hull that night, wondering if 'our journey had been really necessary'.

One point of note from that game surrounds Steve McNamara who made a piece of Rugby League history that day when, following the Rugby League's introduction of a Blood Bin, he was the first in this country to occupy it in a competitive game. On the journey back we got stranded for almost two hours between trains at York and so, with around another 50 Hull FC stalwarts, we resolved to partake of a few beers which soon turned into quite a party in the Station Buffet. Before long that grand old Victorian building was resonating to endless choruses of 'Old Faithful', much to the amusement of a handful of itinerant Sunday evening travellers.

However bad we were, (and we were pretty awful) we could usually beat Leeds

Sunday 15th September 1991   *Hull 16 – Leeds 11*

So it was that 8,255 attended the Boulevard for the visit of Leeds. It was a good turnout too, particularly when you consider that we hadn't won a Division One game by mid September and were bottom of the table. This was however a chance of revenge over a Leeds side that had the week before thrashed us at Headingley, as we clashed again, this time in the first round of the Webster's Yorkshire Cup. Thankfully Greg Mackey chose this game to regain his imperious form of the previous campaign, Wayne Portlock played his first game at stand-off and Jon Sharp and Richard Gay both returned from injury.

Leeds came to town with the tabloids 'nick naming' them 'The Millionaires of Rugby' because they had spent a fortune on building a team that included Darren Goulding, John Bentley and David Herron, as well as ex FC heroes, Garry Schofield and Gary Divorty. Also included that day was new acquisition Ellery Hanley who Leeds had signed the previous week, for a transfer fee in excess of a £225,000.

The game started with Hull's Steve Durham felling Leeds' Maskill with a real 'haymaker' of a tackle, after which he received attention before converting the penalty. Then Chico Jackson broke a tackle by

Heugh and scrambled thirty yards down field handing off Leeds tacklers as he went before he was hit late on the ground by O'Neill and from that penalty Eastwood levelled the scores. Portlock who had only had one training session since arriving was showing up well, particularly in defence, where he constantly blotted out the threat that Schofield posed at 6.

O'Neill, who was doing what he could to intimidate Greg Mackey, then swung a punch at our Scrum Half as he sidestepped past him and Eastwood converted the penalty again for us to lead 4-2. As half time approached you had to wonder how the two sets of forwards could keep up the high speed collisions that seemed to mark every tackle, but after a good set of drives from Leeds, Bobby Goulding stood back in the line and dropped a goal to send the sides in at the interval with Hull leading 4-3.

The Airlie Birds came out fighting and at last we scored a try. Mackey hoisted a stunning 'Bomb' which Steve McNamara caught before he fed Russ Walker and our second rower crashed in for Eastwood to convert. However as so often happened back then, it was to be 'Judas' Schofield who broke our hearts with a try in the 53rd minute. Portlock was starting to work well with Mackey and Sharp and on several occasions his flat 'Aussie' style passes put players into space, however he tried it once too often and of course in came Schofield to intercept and run 60 yards to score under the crossbar. With Hull's lead cut to 10-9 we started to panic and when Busby was caught off-side, Referee Morris awarded a penalty. Maskill, the visitor's kicker, steered it in from wide out on the right, and we were trailing by one point, which left us wondering if the floodgates were about to open.

That last twenty minutes was played out in a white hot atmosphere as the Hull forwards struggled to stop the marauding Leeds' backs running away with the game. Durham and Walker were immense, pushing Leeds back time and again and in so doing laid a platform for our backs to 'relieve' the line on several occasions.

Then in the 68th minute Mackey shot out of 'acting half' and drawing Hanley he passed to Sharp, who found Lee Jackson careering through a gap in the Leeds' line. With the 'alarm bells' ringing in the visitors defence three players tracked back to grab our hooker on the 20 meter line, but as he went to ground he slipped a pass to Greg Mackey, who had started the move, recovered and chased after the play. 'Bluey' caught the ball and accelerated away from the Loiner's defence to score. And as Eastwood converted the try, we led again 16-11. Amazingly that was it. Leeds threw everything at us in that last 11 minutes but some strong tackling and passion saw us home. Hanley, Schofield and Goulding all went close, but Hull's defence was simply superb and as the final hooter went, 'Crusher' Cleal ran onto the field to congratulate his players and we all gave them a standing ovation as the chants of "Spent a fortune won F*ck all.....Leeds......Leeds" and "Judas, Judas what's the score" echoed around the ground!

Derek Fox 'drops' us out of the Yorkshire Cup

Sunday 1ˢᵗ October 1991   *Hull 18 – Featherstone 21*

Around that time the Club announced that in the 1990/91 season we had lost over £107,000 against a profit the previous year of £87,000. This turn around, despite it being a season when we won our first trophy for years, fired a rebellion in the Board Room which saw Chairman David Kirkwood ousted to be replaced by Steve Watson, (although in fairness the Club was to fair little better under his control). Afterward Kirkwood, who was a sincere guy, said he was "Stunned and Heartbroken" with the actions of his colleagues on the Board and quite frankly, so were most of the fans, who handed a petition reflecting their unhappiness to the Board, the following week. David offered to resign completely and as the rest of the Board agreed, he left his beloved Hull FC; but he would return. It was a real shock for most of the fans because Kirkwood had always appeared to be a calming figurehead at our Club. I remember thinking that I might just 'pick my games' from then onwards but that was only a fleeting consideration, because I can't do that. Over the years I know that I have always envied those people who can treat their Club as they would a restaurant, and withdraw their patronage when the fare on offer goes off a bit, but as true fans you can't do that. Ironically of course that's the reason clubs keep going, because there are so many mugs like me who know we can't live with them and yet can't survive without them.

However someone who was proving to be a big success at the time was our new Commercial Manager John Fillingham who had opened the new store in Princes Quay and developed several money making schemes in the hope of refinancing a Club that was literally haemorrhaging money. In the three months up to Christmas, Hull FC sold 3,500 replica shirts, which was more than any other club in the British game. Not bad really, after several supporters had written to the papers earlier in the year saying that it was "The worst shirt the Club has ever produced". However on the field we continued to struggle as a deepening injury crisis once again hit us hard.

We suffered our worst defeat for two years at Wigan by 30-4 before redeeming ourselves at Belle Vue Wakefield with a good win, in which prop forward Durham broke his leg in two places. Then around 1000 Hull FC fans made the trip to Post Office Road Featherstone for a keenly contested Yorkshire Cup Semi Final when, because of all our injuries, winger Chico Jackson played at Prop and Lee Jackson and Greg Mackey shone. In the end we were desperately unlucky to lose, but finally went down as Derek Fox, their wily and talented scrum half, dropped two goals to see us narrowly defeated in pouring rain. After all the rejoicing and celebrations at Old Trafford just 5 months earlier, the season was starting to turn out to be a nightmare.

Welcome to the 'Zombie Zoo'

One of my best pals throughout the 90's was local Radio presenter Steve Massam who went to most home games with me. Around that time Steve started running the Friday Night Disco at the Dorchester Hotel on Beverley Road. The Hotel was owned by the Mays, who appeared earlier as owners of the Tower and those Friday nights soon became really popular, although the clientele was certainly 'different'. The joke was always that the more you had to drink, the better looking the ladies became and we soon branded those wonderful nights of people watching as 'The Zombie Zoo'. One lasting memory that I have of those 'Discos', watching a packed dance floor gyrating to 'Simply the Best', was the fact that you had to drink your beer really quickly and I mean really quickly. If you put your pint down to go to the toilet, when you returned it was empty and what was even more of a concern was that the only clue as to who had drunk it, was the fact that the glass usually had lipstick round the rim!

Kingston upon Hull pioneers 'Drive in' Fish and Chips

Hull Fair came and went with the only thing of note being the inclusion for the first time in many years of a Wall of Death. This was a cylindrical attraction where the public climbed stairs to watch from the top while inside motor cyclists raced round and round up the walls. There were only 7 surviving exponents of this dying art still riding and although they were all over 70, they were all in attendance at Hull Fair that year. It seemed a good idea, I thought, to have one site at the event dedicated to an 'old time' ride, however when the operator told me how old it was (100 years) I wished I hadn't bothered. Otherwise it was business as usual really. Local schools set no homework that week, retailers wrung their hands and talked of bankruptcy, banks were full of queuing locals withdrawing their savings and the Showmen left town taking with them hundreds of thousands of pounds from the local economy.

At the same time the region was gaining more national notoriety as 'Pioneering' when at Willerby in the West of the City the Hudson Bay Clipper Company planned to build the first 'Drive In' fish and chip shop in the Country. Being the historical centre of the national fishing fleet, Hull had always had a strong affinity to Fish and Chips so it was certainly an appropriate location for the Country's first 'convenience' Fish Shop. In those days it was still an affordable banquet and a real local favourite combining as it did all the essential food groups of Carbohydrate, Protein, Fat and Grease.

Of course the local newspaper, masters of the understated headline, didn't let this one go by and after an unsuccessful attempt to whip up a storm of dissent from the traditional fish and chip shops of the area, they lead with the headline, "Chippies take 'Drive In' with a pinch of Salt".

By the end of October Hull FC had won just 5 games in 13 but after Noel Cleal had survived a 'Vote of Confidence' from the new Board we had a more successful period when we won 5 of the next 7. At the City Hall business was booming and a sell out concert saw the crowds queued round the venue to gain admittance to a concert by leaders of the aptly named 'Madchester Movement', James. The story went back then that the group who had hits with 'Come Home' and 'Sit Down' actually made more money from T-shirt sales than they did from selling records. Whatever the truth was, James had been at the forefront of the Manchester explosion of the early 90's with the innovative yet beautifully simple J-A-M-E-S and daisy design T-shirts which everyone in the audience seemed to be wearing that night.

It was a great concert and as I went to collect the merchandising fee afterwards, the tour's Commercial Manager told me that he would be disappointed if he didn't sell at least £6000 worth of shirts a night. I've still got mine and although I don't often go out wearing a shirt with a flower on it, that yellow T shirt is still one of my prized possessions.

It was around that time too, I remember, when that once great bastion of the trawling community The Vauxhall Tavern hit the headlines for all the wrong reasons. With all the compulsory purchase and demolition that had gone on along Hessle Road there were few residents left and the surviving hostelries had to do whatever they could to keep going. 'The Vauxhall' opted to go for the 'Pink pound' and had gained a reputation as a 'Gay' pub. That October the Landlord was in Court in Hull charged with 'serving drink after hours'. According to the Hull Daily Mail he had be caught when two "Under cover" Policemen "Gained his confidence" and were offered drink after 11-00pm.

If the thought of two 'under cover policemen' in a gay pub is starting to fire your imagination, then consider the fact that the Landlord said in his defence that those partaking of drink were mostly the "Camp followers of the The Dragettes", the band performing that night. The report in the local paper concluded with the statement "The two Policemen left when the clientele started to spike their drinks". It's a story worthy of inclusion I think, simply because you couldn't make it up!

Andy Dannett, the High Court injunction and Ellery Handley's jaw!

Saturday 23ʳᵈ November 1991   *Hull 4 – Leeds 12*

At the end of November we suffered a heartbreaking defeat to Leeds at the Boulevard in a close game that could, right up to the last ten minutes, have gone either way. The main talking point was the fact that the Leeds' Captain, Ellery Handley, had his jaw broken in four places in a tackle by Hull Prop Andy Dannett, although at the time the referee took no action except to wave 'play on'. A week later after the full extent of Hanley's injury was known the Leeds' Board complained to the Rugby League. The Governing Body then took the unprecedented action of calling Dannett to a disciplinary hearing in retrospect, when convention was that the referee either sent someone off or decided on the day what action should be taken.

Hull FC then took an unprecedented step themselves and sought a High Court Injunction to prevent Dannett being summoned to the Rugby League for the deferred hearing. A Club taking this action against their Governing Body was almost unheard of in British Sport but at the Old Bailey the Club's objections were over ruled and Andy Dannett was subsequently banned by the RL for 8 matches. There was a great sense of injustice about the final outcome and the action taken by the Board of Hull FC saw them gain a deal of kudos with the fans at a time when they were about to need some.

What are we getting for Christmas? Well, certainly not Martin Offiah!

Sunday 15th December 1991   *Hull 12 – Wigan 24*

Again I travelled over the Pennines to Wigan in heavy sleet showers and then a deal of mist and murk to witness a disappointing reversal in a game where we played very well and Greg Mackey and new signing Ian Stephens, the ex Welsh Rugby Union scrum half, starred. Next day, expecting to read the report on the game, I was amazed as the front page of the local paper announced "Hull make bid for Offiah". "What's this", I thought, "April Fools' Day". I knew that the best player in the world was reported to be unsettled at Widnes and wanted a move, but I also knew that the fee demanded by the Cheshire team was £700,000.

However, Widnes' Chairman Jim Mills indicated that Hull FC had made an enquiry and were "Going away to consider making us an offer" and the Hull fans were sent into a frenzy of eager anticipation. As everyone eagerly awaited developments, rumours were everywhere and included the fact that Offiah had been seen in Woolworths, a betting shop, a fish shop on Hessle Road and even in a taxi outside Hull Royal Infirmary. John Fillingham said that the Club was putting together the necessary finance and sponsorship to secure the star and eventually just before Christmas we made a firm offer of £350,000. The Hull Board, in announcing the bid, said that it was a "Take it or Leave it" situation, but by now of course both Leeds and Wigan (where he ended up) were in the bidding and so in the end Widnes decided to "leave it". Still at least for most FC fans the situation had offered a modicum of distraction from the usual Christmas shopping. However the festive season was a disaster with defeats to Castleford, Wigan and Hull KR, but with the new Hull FC shop in the City Centre taking over £100,000 in three months; it wasn't all bad news for everyone!

A First-hand experience of a tickling stick

The following March for the first time since I had been involved with the venue, we promoted Ken Dodd at the City Hall. We had sold around 1400 tickets, about 200 short of a sell out, but this didn't seem to satisfy Ken who has a reputation for being a bit 'Careful with his Money'. Norman his Tour Manager told me he was unhappy that there was only one of his posters in the advertisement boards at the front of the Hall and so I was summoned to his dressing room. As I tapped on the door with the star on it, he shouted "Come in" in his best 'Dickie Mint' accent.

Once he had found out who I was, I got a real 'ear bending' about the lack of posters and the venue "not fulfilling their contractual obligations" however I can't honestly remember anything else about what was said because this tirade was administered by one of the world's top comedians wearing a Dress Suit Jacket, a 'dickie bow' tie and...... his underpants.

What underpants they were too!! They were utilitarian 'off white' heavy cotton trunks, with a gaping fly which displayed the 'Last Turkey in the shop' hanging there in full view. The thing was that Ken didn't seem to care at all and just continued shouting about his posters and yet I couldn't avoid it, it was there right in front of me. I guess it was a moment not unlike that 'topless Juliet' moment at the Hull Truck Theatre years earlier because although I shouldn't look, I just couldn't avert my eyes!! Of course you can guess which experience of the two I preferred, but I have never been able to take Ken Dodd seriously since that night. Still that is I guess the expected end-product of his act anyway, but until now few people who have watched him with me have been aware of what's making me laugh.

Mr Patel's quick weight loss diet; never have a pie in Rochdale!

Sunday 2nd February 1992   *Hull 34 – Rochdale Hornets 28*

I remember being really buoyed by some of our performances that spring and despite being drawn away in three consecutive rounds we got all the way to the Semi Finals of the Challenge Cup before going out in a close game to Castleford. The fact that we were drawn away in every round was really bad luck, but we won at Rochdale, Sheffield and Workington to get to Headingley where a polished Castleford side just saw us off 8-4. After that defeat although we beat Leeds (as usual) at the Boulevard we lost the next three games on the trot and sadly 'Crusher' Cleal was shown the door. However, before that happened that Rochdale game in the Cup was an exciting affair which we watched from the shed like Stand behind the posts with another 1,500 Hull fans.

The journey over the Pennines was a long one that day as there were several sets of road works which hampered the progress of an armada of cars and buses, so when we got there I was 'famished' and set off to find something to eat.

Spotland, being a football ground, accommodated the away fans in a segregated area and the only refreshment facility available was a small battered caravan with a large pink sign that announced "Patel's Pies; The Tradtional Taste of Lancashire" and perhaps I should have been a bit suspicious when I observed that they appeared to have had two goes at spelling 'Traditional'. This mobile dispenser of crusty comestibles was certainly popular, something that was confirmed by the queue of hungry 'Airlie Bird' fans that stretched round the side of the Stand. By the time I reached the front they were out of 'Beef and Gravy' Pies and all that was left was a rather dubious looking tray of 'Spicey Chicken Balti Pies'. "What's that all about then", I asked the guy in a turban, who I suspected was probably Mr Patel himself, but he just gave a sort of salute and grinned as I struggled to decide exactly how to eat the lukewarm spicy offering.

A guy in an obviously home-knitted Hull FC jumper and 'bobble hat' who seemed to have the whole situation worked out, saw the perplexed look on my face and advised me to bite the corner off the pie and drink the contents before consuming the crust bits that were left. I followed the instructions, the contents ran down my throat like soup and it appeared everything was going well, until they hit my stomach. The term 'gut wrenching' was the best description, but it 'filled a hole' and in a close game we eventually came out winners 32-28 and progressed to the next round.

In the middle of the night I discovered once again that it's not just your mouth that Curry burns and by Monday lunchtime, I was leaving my office at Ferensway and heading home with excruciating stomach ache. I had awoken that morning with a sort of shivering trembling feeling all over my body but put that down to the fact that the previous evening I had stayed in and not had a drink!

By Monday night I was experiencing violent convulsions (from both ends) and found myself in a condition that I would best describe as 'The Perfect Storm'. By Tuesday morning I had to call the Doctor, I was in so much pain. I honestly had no idea what had caused it until the Doctor announced that I had Salmonella poisoning, which he told me was caused by the consumption of poultry that is not properly cooked. "It was Mr Patel's, bloody Pie" I shouted, as right on cue my stomach contracted violently again. Of course I got better eventually and the loss of a stone in weight didn't go down too badly in the end either. However I have never eaten a pie at an away ground again and to this day, whenever I think of Rochdale, I don't reflect on the home of the Rochdale Pioneers, Gracie Fields or Lisa Stansfield; I just think of pies, and the night I had to keep the toilet role in the fridge.

Steve Crooks saves the day

Friday 17ᵗʰ April 1992   *Hull 12 – Hull KR 8*

Like Len Casey before him, Cleal's tough upbringing had made him a straight talker and that didn't suit everyone, he was unfairly compared to the affable and eloquent Brian Smith and that and some disappointing results were in the end his downfall. After Cleal had departed the Hull Directors asked long serving member of the backroom staff Steve Crooks, to become temporary caretaker Coach and after a bad couple of weeks Hull desperately needed a win to ensure they stayed in the First Division. However we faced a daunting task at Craven Park against a

Hull KR side who had lost their last three games and were desperate themselves. It was certainly a drab afternoon across the river and the pitch was heavy and devoid of grass. Crooks' team selection that day included a young Andrew Mighty playing on the left wing and Peter Spring returning from injury to play at blind side prop.

From the Kick-Off our forwards took control and keeping the ball tight set about winning the battle down the middle of the pitch. Although he had been at Hull around 7 years, Crooks was an ex Rovers Player, an East Hull lad and still lived at that side of the City, so sitting there on the trainer's bench trying to mastermind a win against Rovers must have seemed strange to him. On 15 minutes Gay ran from deep and sliced through the Rovers defence, Greg Mackey hoisted a kick that seemed to hang in the air indefinitely and David Ronson sped in to catch it and score.

The same player then completed a deft interception 60 yards out and again ran back down field to touch down. Eastwood goaled both tries and we had a 12-0 lead. Up front the Hull pack revelled in the heavy going while Rovers did us a favour by opting to get drawn into that game rather than utilising their faster and more mobile back division and Ronson's tries certainly silenced the Hull KR fans packed into the East Stand.

If the home team needed some inspiration then they got it just before half time when Barkworth, after fine work by Des Harrison and Hallas, scored wide out and with Mick Fletcher converting at half time we led by just 6 points. In the second half it was obvious that Hull KR Coach George Fairburn had changed the tactics as the home side utilised some booming downfield kicks by Wayne Parker to drive us back. It was now a real war of attrition as Rovers continued to persist down the middle of the field and Hull's forwards led brilliantly by Jon Sharp had to work really hard to contain them.

Hull substitute Dean Busby saved a certain try when he pulled off an amazing one armed tackle on the advancing Parker before Hull KR's flyer Sodje thought he had scored in the corner after a flowing movement between Harrison and Hallas, but referee Connelly had spotted a forward pass. The Rovers' fans goaded us as they celebrated 'a try' before the Hull fans retorted with the 'Red, Red Robin song' with the '"Shoot the Bastard" finale, as they realised it had been chalked off.

For the rest of the second half Hull tackled like demons although in fairness the Robins had few ideas and in the end it was only a good tackle by Bright Sodje that stopped Hull winger Paul Eastwood scooting in at the corner. As the light faded and the poor Craven Park floodlights came on, the referee blew his whistle and we had won. We had lost a lot of possession in our own half and certainly gifted Rovers the ball on several occasions although that day our tenacity and strength in the tackle got us through. Steve Crooks our new Caretaker Coach must have been one of the only folks smiling in East Hull that night because that victory kept us in the First Division for another season at least.

At the end, I remember, with a nod to the popular Manchester 'Music Scene' the ever inventive Hull fans struck up with their own version of the current Inspiral Carpets hit as they sang to the Hull KR supporters, as they tramped out of the East Stand, "This is how it feels to be lonely, this is how it feels to be small, this is how it feels when your teams' worth nothing at all"; brilliantly inventive! That year Hull KR had dispensed with a match day programme and instead produced a newspaper for each game. Ironically, as I left the ground at the end to go and see if I still had any wing mirrors left on the car, I noticed a copy of the 'paper' blowing around by the gates. The headline highlighting George Fairburn's first year as the Club's Coach said, "He's Loving Every Minute of it!" I laughed to myself and thought, "I bet he wasn't this afternoon".

Crooksy's reign as Hull Coach was to be short lived as following the final game of the year, a defeat at home to Castleford by 30-14, the Club announced that they had secured the services of an Australian Coach, Royce Simmons who had completed an accomplished career at Australian Second Grade Champions St Mary's. As fans the appointment came out of the blue but with thoughts of how successful 'Smithy' had been arriving in similar circumstances, we were all excited again. What surprised us even more was how the Club had managed to keep their move for the Australian quiet, but we weren't as surprised as Steve McNamara who, whilst sunning himself on a beach in Greece got a call from the Rugby League, and because of injuries, had to re-pack his bags to join the Great Britain Tour of Australia.

Simmons starts to build and Scott Gale 'breezes' back into town

The first thing Simmons did after he had arrived at the Club was to make a signing. The Hull Daily Mail carried a picture of our latest recruit Scott Gale wearing the new and controversial, Black, White and Purple shirt that Commercial Director John Fillingham had introduced. Scott, you'll remember, had been at the Boulevard four years earlier, before a bad shoulder injury caused him to return 'Down Under' after just two games.

However if it was to be a good summer for the fans of Hull FC, it was certainly not one for ex Viking Radio DJ Tim Finlay who branded the citizens of Hull, "A laughing stock in the music industry" after his proposed 'Party in The Park' pop music festival at the Boulevard, hit the buffers. In the end he lost around £24,000 on the deal, but after his comments about them, few Hull people had much sympathy. However many had empathy with Beautiful South's Paul Heaton and the Public Gallery of the Hull Magistrate's Court was packed when he appeared there having refused, as a matter of principle, to pay his Poll Tax. In the end he capitulated but he was certainly a hero in many quarters and the court had to be cleared when about seventy people stood to applaud him during the hearing.

Hull FC were, it seemed, planning for the future and the Boulevard Kids' young supporters group were doing really well and attracting over 140 youngsters to their meetings in the bar under the New Threepenny Stand. The Ex Players' Association were helping out too, sponsoring the Club's Academy as all the while Coach Royce Simmons continued with his team building. After the loss of Greg Mackey, who returned to Warrington, he signed Australian scrum half Ivan Hejeck from St George, James Grant from Balmain and Brendan Carlyle, from the now defunct Scarborough Pirates.

More pies more problems as 'Pearly' upsets Linda McCartney

At that time I still saw a lot of Billy (the Wizz) and was also going to home games with Steve a pal from Cottingham, but I had also become friendly with a guy called Stewart Spencer who everyone knew as 'Pearly'.

He was one of those blokes in whose company you never mentioned any bands or pop artists you liked because he had an almost encyclopaedic knowledge of all things musical and would drone on for hours about them. He made lists as well and had his top ten Country Songs with dogs in the title, top ten songs that had been made into rugby chants etc. etc. He would also make you 'tapes for your car' which usually contained a series of songs he liked, which you had to listen to and learn because you knew that he would be 'asking questions' about them the next time you met.

'Pearly' was around 60, an average sized bloke with a long unkept beard, and long hair that he tied in a pony tail with either a dirty bandana or an elastic band. 'Pearly' lived on his own with his records in a 'garret' flat in the Avenues area where he used to open the roof light and lay on his bed to sunbathe in summer. Above all though Pearly had an absolute love for all things Americana, so much so that on a couple of occasions Billy and I had to stop him setting off to away games in a Cowboy hat and spurs.

'Pearly' worked at a local Frozen food company, who were famous for supplying a wide range of food including County Pies for Linda McCartney, who championed 'tasty' food for vegetarians. That autumn after one home game he grabbed everyone's attention in the 'Eagle', when he told us how someone had accidentally filled 700 of these pies with Steak and Kidney filling. Apparently these got right through to the shops and Mrs McCartney received dozens of complaints and broke the story in the national papers, with the declaration that "It could be a mistake or even something more sinister" I commented to Pearly that if those vegetarians thought that they had problems with 'Steak and Kidney' it's a good job that they hadn't received one of Mr Patel's creations.

Another season and another mixed bag of emotions!

Sunday 4ᵗʰ October 1992   *Hull 26 – Halifax 8*

The 1992/93 season saw Hull FC and Royce Simmons start well. We were all enjoying our rugby again, while music wise we were listening to the Cure and Del Amitri, the latter after I had let Billy and Pearly into a concert by the Scottish rockers at the City Hall, which was an amazing evening. Of course, the next night both Billy and I were gifted a tape for the car of everything that the group had ever recorded.

The Rugby Season started with a 14-10 win at New Craven Park in the John Lydiat Testimonial match and then we won our next three games including an amazing 14-13 win at Wigan. That was followed by a victory at home against Halifax in front of a good gate of over 6000 fans where the guest of honour was Flo Holmes, who at 93 was our 'oldest regular attendee'.

Prince Edward wears his FC shirt with pride

That October Prince Edward made a flying visit to the City to tour Princes Quay and the Ferens Art Gallery and as City Entertainments Officer I was asked to make the arrangements and liaise between the Council, the Palace and the Police. I arranged for the speeches in Princes Quay to be outside the Hull FC shop, to hopefully get the Club some much needed publicity. The scheme worked better than I could ever have hoped because after the Prince had been welcomed by Centre Manager Mike Killoran, John Fillingham of Hull FC presented him with one of those new black, white and purple shirts. In response Prince Edward proclaimed that he would wear it the following week at Windsor, when he watched Prince Charles playing Polo, whether he did or not of course we'll never know.

Beating the Aussies is always great!

Sunday 6ᵗʰ December 1992

Hull Academy 24 – Illawarra Academy 12

In many ways 1992/93 was I guess a reasonably successful season, we reached the semi finals of both the Yorkshire Cup and the Regal Trophy, but the second half of the campaign was a disaster, as we won just one game between 2ⁿᵈ January and 9ᵗʰ April. One fixture I do remember however was a game between the Hull Academy and their Illawarra counterparts, before the Hull FC v Halifax game at the Boulevard in the Regal Trophy.

The touring youngsters were on a great winning run against the top sides in this Country and had already beaten England under 21's. I went with Pearly and Billy and joined around 3000 other FC fans that had arrived early for the 'Curtain Raiser'. In the end the Hull youngsters won 21-12, as everyone in the team raised their game. Hewitt lead us around the field and marshalled the team, whilst Jez Cassidy got the Man of the Match award. The game was won in the forwards where Paul Scott and Sam Murphy tamed the Aussie hard men and laid a platform for a great performance.

However looking back I suppose the rest of the season was a disaster and I have to admit right now that I didn't attend more than six away games in total that year. Was I losing interest, could the fixation at last be wearing thin? Of course not, you just go through a couple of those spells in a life time of supporting the team you love, and it would all come right again soon!

The passing of 'The Spider with the Platinum Hair'

On 29ᵗʰ April 1993 the lead guitarist of The Rats in the 1960's, the Spider from Mars in the 70's and most of all that thoroughly great bloke I met on Bilton Grange in 1968, Mick Ronson, died of Liver Cancer at his home in Hasker Street, in Knightsbridge, London. If you read the first part of this story you will know the significance of this 'ordinary Northern guy' in my simple story, and at the age of 47 the world was robbed of one of the greatest exponents of the electric guitar there had ever been. Close family and friends gathered for a Memorial Service at the Church of Jesus Christ of the Latter-day Saints in London on May 6th and next day Mick's body was buried in "A Hull Cemetery" with again, just the close family present.

Maggie, Mick's sister, who I got to know in the next couple of years, once told me that it was a still, cloudy day but as the Blessing was being said over the grave, a sudden gust of wind blew a shower of pink Cherry blossom from a nearby tree. Those in attendance all noted how the blossom fell only into the open grave and onto Mick's coffin. I had only really known Mick for around 6 months back in 1968, but he left a lasting impression on me. Even when I went to see him with David Bowie at 'The Spa' on 28th June 1973, he remained the same 'ordinary guy' and he impressed me all over again. Was it because he was such a talented musician? Was it because he became famous and I knew him? Was it because he came from Hull? Well not really, it was simply because of all the people you meet in a lifetime he was one of that really rare breed who ooze humility, honesty and plain Northern good nature. 29th April 1993 was a sad day for music, the City of Hull and me!

Chapter 7

Royce has a plan and the Chippendales have a ball

Times were hard at Hull FC which was hardly surprising with the average gate still well under 6000. However this didn't seem to put our Coach off at all and on the same day that our ex Chairman, Roy Waudby was elected President of the Rugby League, Royce Simmons announced that he had all but captured the signature of a so far un-named Australian International. Royce said, "We don't have enough cash to sign him, but this player is exactly what we need and therefore I am running 5 marathons in a week to raise the money. The player wanted an answer straight away, but when I put my proposed fund raising effort to him, he was prepared to wait". Billy, Pearly and I, it has to be said, doubted our Coach's sanity!

That month of July the City Hall started another venture that got me into 'hot water' when the American male burlesque troop 'The Chippendales', hit town for three nights. All the shows had sold out in a few days the previous March and the outcome was quite a personal 'Epiphany' as I had never seen so many women, getting into such a state, in one place at one time. This was even more surreal when I knew that several of this troop of American 'Strippers' spent most of their time backstage trying to proposition my 'all male' stage crew.

Keep on Running Royce; 5 marathons in 7 days!

On Friday 2nd July 1993 Royce Simmons started his marathons, and the City Hall staff and I left a Hull Choral Union Concert to cheer him on, as he passed the City Hall at around 7-00pm accompanied by local boxer Steve Pollard. We went over the road and put some money in the buckets his followers were carrying, and Royce thanked us and commented that his feet were swollen and his toes had cramp, he conclude, "I have got to keep going though because our Kirk (his son of 10 years) did the first 13 miles with me today".

A few days later on Thursday 8th July 1993, we were all in the Banks Harbour public house on Beverley Road as Royce finished his 5th and final Marathon. As 'Pray' by new 'Boy Band', Take That, blasted out from the juke box, Billy and I stood on chairs to see what was happening as to tumultuous applause, a rather dishevelled Royce entered a packed pub 'Tired but happy'. When he'd got his breath back and had a drink, he said that he'd raised enough money to sign his target, who he announced was ace play-maker Des Hasler the Australian International Half-Back. The place erupted and when a chorus of 'Old Faithful' finally subsided Royce, every optimistic went on to say, "That said we still need another player, so I'll do another Marathon tomorrow if someone will put £20,000 in the pot!" Thankfully, for Royce at least, no one came forward.

It was estimated, but never confirmed, that he raised £30,000 in sponsorship in those seven days, and despite the achievements of legends like Roy Francis, Arthur Bunting, David Doyle Davidson and Brian Smith, if ever there was a bigger effort made by a Hull FC Coach, or a better example of someone 'Going the extra mile' (or 130) for his Club, I have not, to this day, heard about it!

With great expectations and players on strike, another season begins

Sunday 5ᵗʰ September 1993   *Hull 18 – Halifax 18*

Trophy success apart, there has never ever been a better time for a sport's fan than the start of a new season. In 1993 we had a Coach who had proved his commitment to the Club, a good set of players, Des Hasler, and now the Directors had 'stumped up' for the second Aussie Royce needed, centre Jeff Doyle, who had joined from the North Sydney Bears. However there were still major financial problems off the field and lack of cash saw the Club closing their Princes Quay store and removing the whole of their merchandising operation back to the dilapidated shop next to the ground, on the corner of Carrington Street and Airlie Street. Several players were still arguing with the Club about contracts and Simmons decided that none of them could play for the team, until they signed. Even Andy Dannett, in his own Testimonial game, only featured from the bench as Marlow, Lee Jackson, Sharp and McNamara were all left out.

In fact, at a game against Halifax that we drew 18-18, Lee Jackson stood with us all on the Airlie Street terracing. Soon Marlow left for Wakefield and Simmons brought in Paul Sterling a young winger from Bradford and Bingley Rugby Union. We all eagerly awaited the arrival of Hasler and Doyle from Australia and after drawing two and winning one of our first six games, with the two Aussies settling in, we started to turn things round. Steve McNamara settled his differences, while Lee Jackson couldn't and left for Sheffield Eagles.

Needlers lose their needles!!!

That autumn, at the Council, I was desperately trying to find a sponsor for the 'Civic' Christmas Tree that we erected every year in Victoria Square. Needlers the local sweet manufacturers were a possibility, as they had recently been 'taken over' and wanted to reposition their image in the City. At a meeting with them I suggested that they might like to consider paying for the tree which we bought every year from

Wykeham Forest in North Yorkshire. They wanted to go one better and inspired by the Greater London Council who obtained their tree from Norway, Needlers said that they would contact their sister company in Kristiansand, on the south west coast of Norway, and get a tree shipped in from there.

This captured the publics' imagination and the Hull Daily Mail dispatched a reporter and photographer who witnessed the giant Sitka Spruce being felled and loaded onto a cargo boat for shipping across the North Sea to King George Dock. With the tree lashed to the deck it was a rough crossing with heavy sleet and gale force winds pummelling the little Coaster, but the City's 'Christmas centrepiece' finally arrived safely in Victoria Square. On Monday 15th the Council staff erected what was certainly a fine specimen, but by the big 'switch on' the following Thursday the tree looked awful. It was completely denuded of any greenery and the pavement around the tree was ankle deep in spruce needles. Apparently, the Parks Department told us, this was due to the effects of the salt spray pounding the Christmas Tree on the deck during the voyage.

It was really embarrassing and an appearance of the 'petrified tree' on the national TV news had Needlers racing to buy another one, which inevitably in the end came from Wykeham Forest! The Lord Mayor rang me at the City Hall and said, "Is it true the Christmas Tree has no needles?", I replied, "No it's not true" to which he retorted, "Thank goodness for that, BBC News at Ten have been chasing me about it!". The phone then abruptly went dead after I responded that there were, "Plenty of needles Lord Mayor, the problem is none of them are attached to the tree".

The Cold wind will blow and we shall have hyperthermia!

Sunday December 12th 1993   *Hull 10 – Widnes 6*

Over the 60 years that I have been involved in Hull FC, I have certainly attended a lot of matches when it's been cold, in fact I've attended one or two when it has been positively freezing but there was one game that was played at the Boulevard back in 1993 that will always go down in the annals of our great Club, as the coldest afternoon that we ever experienced at that great old Stadium. Back in December that year our form had certainly improved and we were all hoping for a good run in the Regal Trophy when, to our dismay, we were drawn against Widnes at the Boulevard. They were the 'Cup Kings' and although we had won 4 of our previous 5 games, including a narrow victory over St Helens at the Boulevard the previous week, it was going to be tough.

As 'Pearly', Billy and I walked down the Boulevard towards the ground it was cold; it was that sort of cold that grips your face and chills you to the bone. In addition, as the wind howled round the terraces and houses, it was just starting to hailstone. With it being a Cup game we knew there was bound to be some available space, so we decided to sit in the New Threepenny Stand, hoping that it would at least offer some shelter from what were Arctic conditions. As I made my way into the seats wishing I had worn a warmer coat, I was greeted by a succession of groans as I pushed my way past a line of middle aged fans with blankets over their legs and their soup flasks twinkling in the floodlights. I finally slumped down next to a heavily pregnant woman in her mid thirties to whom I said, "Hello, how are you doing". She scowled, took another drag on her cigarette and said, "Two weeks over".

When the teams came out, vigorously swinging their arms like demented windmills it was obvious that however fast and furious the action, for some it was going to be difficult keeping warm. Before he kicked off, Jeff Doyle was blowing on his hands and it was clearly going to be an 'interesting afternoon' for our Aussie imports.

Widnes were a great team, however we started strongly as Tim Street continually pushed their strong pack backwards. Then after around ten minutes, a full scale brawl broke out when Tim slapped Esene Faimalo in a tackle. The referee Mr. Ollerton waited for the melee to die down before giving both players a stiff talking too and awarding Widnes a penalty. Shortly after that it was certainly no surprise when the visitors took the lead as Goulding broke through a tackle by Sharp and put hooker McCurrie in under the sticks.

Goulding converted just as the leaden skies started to produce torrential freezing rain which came down like 'stair rods' driven on by a north-easterly wind blowing across the field and into our faces in the Stand. Already the cold was taking its toll as twice James Grant sank to his knees between plays shaking his head and vigorously rubbing his hands. Still on we battled, refusing to be intimidated by Widnes's reputation despite our current hero Australian Des Hasler being decidedly subdued and obviously struggling with the conditions.

Then we scored. Gary Nolan, who was in a rich vein of form and keeping his brother Rob out of the starting line up, took a pass from Chico Jackson and hurtled down the wing to score in the corner despite the attentions of three Widnes defenders. As we all stood to applaud a fine try Gary failed to get up, having in the act of scoring displaced his AC joint. He was stretchered from the field to be replaced by his brother Rob as Paul Eastwood missed the conversion but then scored with a penalty from wide out on the left. As Widnes started to get on top again, the hooter went and at half time as the wind howled and the sleet cascaded down in the floodlights it was 6-6.

I remember my knees locking completely as I tried to stand up and to another round of 'tutting' from the 'flask brigade', 'Pearly', with ice bristling in his beard, went off to get us three 'Bovril's'. Billy and I stamped our feet in unison with another 3,400 hardy souls who made up the meagre, but stoic attendance that day. Despite having played the first half with the snow, sleet and rain at their backs, the Hull Dressing Room at the interval was in turmoil.

The Club Doctor at the time, (I think it was Mike Dunham) was summoned by the tannoy to the Home Dressing Room and soon declared that 5 Hull players were suffering from the early stages of hyperthermia. He immediately approached the Referee and requested the game be called off for medical reasons, but when this suggestion was put to the Widnes officials they felt that they were on top and would win and so turned it down.

The half time interval was extended and as the announcers records ran out and we were treated to a second airing of a scratchy rendition of 'Uptown Girl', out on the terraces we all wondered just what was happening. Apparently Mike Dixon and Des Hasler were so cold that, in an effort to get their circulation going, Pete Standidge, one of the assistants that day, had to run to the Club House kitchen and get all the baking foil he could find to wrap the pair up. Finally after a break of around twenty two minutes the teams ran out into the sleet and the rain. Both sides changed their shirts, but Hull FC were for reasons unknown, still wearing the dirty wet shorts that they had worn in the first half.

We started well as big Tim Street and second rower Daniel Divet smashed into the opponent's formidable front row of McCurrie, Ireland and How. Then Moriarty broke through to be felled by a brilliant last ditch effort by Hull's Richard Gay that dislodged the ball and a certain score was averted. Hull needed a boost and they got it on 50 minutes. Tim Street went on one of those famous rampaging 'breakout' runs down the left to link with the pacey James Grant running at his side. The Aussie burst forward and slipped a perfect reverse pass to Rob Nolan who kicked ahead and chased the ball himself. Despite three blatant attempts to obstruct his path, Rob touched down just to the left of the posts and for a few seconds, we all forgot about the cold and danced in our seats, as Eastwood stroked over the conversion.

As my pregnant 'friend' lit up another cigarette, Hull FC might easily have increased their lead. Des Hasler was held on his back and Rob Danby went close while Paul Eastwood, down in front of us on the wing, amused himself by 'conducting' the crowd through several renditions of 'Old Faithful' which, when a string of four penalties went against us, morphed into, "Who's Ya Father, who's Ya Father, who's Ya Father referee, you haven't got one you're a Bas*ard, You're a Bas*ard referee!!!". Outside the ground it must have sounded like a crowd of 10,000 as Hull FC held their ground and the lead, until the hooter sounded and a famous victory was ours.

Several of the players ran straight off the field at the end and who can blame them, but Chico Jackson, Paul Eastwood and Jon Sharp (whose car broke down before the game, so he only arrived 15 minutes before kick-off) celebrated with us all before they ran off to be again swathed in tin-foil and we scurried off to the warmth of the pub.

Afterwards Richard Gay said, "I thought I was going to die I couldn't stop shaking, it was the most frightening experience of my life". While Des Hasler added, "For the first time in my life, I couldn't feel my fingers or toes at all! It was the coldest I have ever been or ever want to be". After that Des and a couple of other players wore skin tight wet suits under their kit, and if he doesn't remember anything else from his time at the Boulevard, I bet he still remembers that night in December 1993!

Simmons survives the curse of Swinton

By mid February we had made progress in the Challenge Cup with a narrow win at Third Division Swinton in what was a real 'banana skin' for Coach Royce Simmons. I say that because history dictated that it was a big hurdle for any Hull Coach to get over. By that point in the season we were making steady if unspectacular progress and the squad led by Des Hasler were starting to develop into a strong unit.

Rumours however abounded that the Board were again finding it tough financially and perhaps becoming impatient for success. On average around 5000 attended home games, but the commercial and sales side of things were in decline. The game away at Swinton saw the chance of a good Cup run and we had to win. In the end we did, but in a tight game a score line of 18-12 was hardly acceptable and despite the amazing statistic that previously Coaches Arthur Bunting, Len Casey and Noel Cleal had all left the Club after games at Swinton, Simmons survived.

Shaun Edwards breaks our hearts

Sunday 13th February 1994   *Hull 21 – Wigan 22*

When the draw was made for the next round, Hull got the pairing that no one wanted against Wigan the 'Cup Kings', a team that had won their last 32 Challenge Cup matches. They were a team full of recognised stars and the tie certainly captured the imaginations of the people in West Hull. As Billy, Pearly and I arrived at our lucky step about 30 minutes before kick off a load of folks we had never seen before were standing all over it. "At least", I thought, "That gives me an excuse if we lose!" I remember that I had a really bad cold that day but that was inconsequential really because I have battled to the Boulevard over the years with most ailments that don't require a toilet....and some that do.

The game saw the best first half performance by Hull since the Brian Smith days. We certainly meant business from the off and after a foul by Wigan's Kelvin Skerrett on Paul Sterling, Tim Street punched Skerrett and both players ended up in the sin bin. After a scare when Wigan's Connolly stepped in touch before crossing in the corner, Hull took the lead when Hewitt chipped ahead and the mercurial Hasler touched down. Frenchman Daniel Divet ran through the Wigan defence and scored with ease and then the 10,200 crowd rejoiced as Steve McNamara stroked over a penalty and a drop goal and at 15-2 we had the 'Cup Kings' on the rack.

On 35 minutes Wigan brought on International half back Shaun Edwards although at first it seemed to make little difference as Paul Sterling intercepted a wayward Wigan pass on his own 20 meter line and went tearing down the front of the Threepenny Stand with the desperate Wigan cover tracking across. They caught him 10 yards out but from the play-the-ball McNamara crashed in and although Barry-Jon Mathers scored a late try for the visitors, at half time Wigan were trailing Hull FC 21-6 and I just wanted the game to be over.

Predictably the second half was a different story as Wigan came roaring back and tries from Panapa, Farrell and another from Barry-Jon Mather saw us trailing 21-22 with just five minutes to go. It was an amazing performance by Edwards who mesmerised the Hull defence and was well supported by Lydon, Offiah and Andy Farrell.

Still we could have won it, when with two minutes to go Sterling broke away and in desperation, Edwards hit him with a high tackle and Eastwood prepared to take a match winning penalty kick just 30 yards out from the goal posts. Of course, as is the luck of Hull FC on these occasions, Paul watched, as we all did, as the kick dipped and veered past the right hand side of the posts. The game was lost and the media hailed the Wigan performance and the game itself, as one of the greatest comebacks in the history of the Challenge Cup, but that was absolutely no consolation to us lot at all, we had lost and whether it was by 1 point or 50 it was pretty inconsequential. I was inconsolable that night, I declining a drink with the lads in the Eagle after the game and went straight home.

I was gutted and even now it's a game that I find it hard to write about. Neutrals love the glorious theatre that are games like that, but I just want to go home grieve on my own and somehow start the process of getting up for the game the following week. When you're a fanatic there is simply no substitute for winning and when you lose in those circumstances, however long you have been in love with your team, its soul destroying!

Lest the People of Hull ever forget Mick Ronson

That Autumn I was sitting in my office in Ferensway when the phone rang and a female introduced herself as Maggie Ronson, Mick's sister. Maggie asked if she could meet me about financing a tribute to Mick in the City Centre and a date and time two weeks hence was agreed. That day we had a bite to eat at the Guildhall, I talked old times and she told me of her plan to stage a Memorial Concert for Mick at the Hammersmith Odeon the following spring. She wanted to raise some funds to thank the Macmillan nurses who had looked after her brother and to commission a statue of Mick to stand on Queens Gardens where he had once worked as a gardener.

It was an exciting idea, particularly when she told me of the many artists that had already said that they would get involved. At the time I was doing a lot of work with the young musicians in the newly formed Hull Musical Collective and suggested that rather than a statue, perhaps something that would help them, like a stage, would be a good idea. Before we got to the jam roly-poly we had hatched a plan and if Maggie could raise the cash, the Council would do the design work, donate the land and generally help with things in Hull. The seeds of an idea began to germinate, but more of that later.

'It's an ill wind' at Odsal

Sunday 4th April 1994   *Hull 32-Bradford Northern 30*

Hull FC were poor away from home that year although travelling out of a sense of duty rather than anything else, I had managed to see most of our away games. That April just 4,641 attended the ageing, crumbling, relic that was Odsal Stadium, of which around 1000 were from Hull. However, as the usual poor atmosphere was reduced to no atmosphere at all it was like playing in a Cathedral, and a pretty draughty one at that.

It was one of those times when I felt that trips away every week were becoming a little onerous, but you know how it is, just as you are about to decide to give a game a miss that feeling of duty, much as some must feel about church on Sundays, comes over you and off you go again. I had moved on from those boozy bus trips (probably because of a nagging worry that the pace would inevitably start to get to my liver), and so Pearly and I drove over to Bradford for a game we certainly did not expect to win. Our 'away day blues' was a worry and a draw at Leeds and wins at Swinton and Salford were all we had to show from 12 away games, while Bradford had only lost twice at home all season and sat proudly on top of the League.

That day as we stood as a beleaguered group of 'FC pilgrims' on the North End Terracing, a storm force 'South Westerly' blew round the bowl in a clockwise direction and straight into our faces. With the ferocity of the wind it was always going to be 'a game of two halves' and having won the toss Bradford decided to play into the wind in the first half. Almost immediately a brilliant one on one tackle by Hull prop Mark Jones was mysteriously penalised, and as Bradford quickly tapped the ball Greenwood put Cordle in at the Corner. When eventually we got into the Bradford half our first attacking move of the game saw Dixon and Busby exchanging passes and Rob Wilson crashing over near the posts. However, Bradford's Deryck Fox then slotted a perfect grubber kick through our right side which held up well in the wind and Cordle again beat the retreating Eastwood to the touchdown. Fox failed again with the conversion but against the wind the home team held an impressive 8-6 lead after just 18 minutes.

From that point onwards however the first half was all FC. Paul Sterling snapped up a sloppy David Heron pass to completely out pace the cover and score a brilliant try which Eastwood converted, and then Divet popped out a pass to Richard Gay who plucked it out of the air and shot in wide out.

Then Northern's Paul Grayshon knocked on and as the Bradford players set themselves to form a scrum, referee Mr Connolly waved play on, Divet picked up the loose ball, ran wide, drew centre Karl Hall and then found Sterling who flew in again at the corner for Eastwood to again convert and then a sweeping move between Divet, Doyle and Hewitt left the Northern defence mesmerised, before substitute Nolan took a pass to score in the corner. Eastwood missed the conversion but in blustery conditions we led 28-8 at the half way point.

Of course, as has always been the case with Hull FC you're never 'home and dry' until the final whistle and as if scripted, just when we needed to keep our line intact at the start of the second half Bradford's Cordle scored again. Luckily Fox was still having trouble mastering the wind and he missed the conversion, something he was thankfully to repeat throughout the rest of the afternoon. We needed a response and we got one when Hewitt hung a kick in the wind, which completely confused Summers, allowing James Grant to gather it and score. Eastwood again converted the try.

For the rest of the half Hull were under constant pressure. Newlove again got free and put the stretching Trevor Clarke in, despite a brilliant attempt at a tackle from the retreating Grant. To the cheers of an increasingly agitated FC contingent huddled on the terraces, Fox missed the kick again but with just five minutes to go another precision grubber kick from Fox saw Eastwood slip as he turned and Cordle pounced for his fourth try, only for Fox to miss again, but it was 20-32. A minute later Hall scored for Northern and Fox missed again! As the wind howled around us we all knew there was more to come and in the fourth minute of injury time Fox kicked through again, the ball bounced, shot up in the air and straight over Full Back Gay's head, for Hall to score. Thankfully the hooter went as Hall celebrated, and with just 4 points separating the teams, with the final kick of the match, Fox got his first conversion of the afternoon, and we'd won....just...32-30.

That day we got in the wrong lane at a roundabout on the way home and ended up driving towards Leeds on the A647 when we saw a great sign on some gates that had us laughing for years afterwards. We would often take a detour that way, just to show 'newcomers' a board that read 'Singh and Sons Builders, You've tried the Cowboys now try the Indians'.

Heaven and Hull

On April 29th 1994 a year to the day after Mick Ronson's death I travelled down to London with Councillor Fred Beedle to attend the Mick Ronson Memorial Concert at the Hammersmith Odeon. It was a fantastic evening with stars and personalities of the music business too numerous to mention giving their time to honour the life of a great guitar hero. The ones I remember include Roger Daltrey of the Who, Roger Taylor of Queen, Rolf Harris, Captain Sensible, Steve Harley, Bill Nelson, Dana Gillespie, Bob Harris, Joe Elliot, Garry Brooker and Ian Hunter. Towards the end of the second half Maggie came up to our seats in the centre block of the balcony and invited us to the after show party.

Held at the Embargo Club this was real 'showbiz stuff' and as a great David Bowie tribute band entertained the crowd of celebrities present, Garry Brooker fiddled around with a piano in the corner and gave an impromptu performance of 'A Whiter Shade of Pale', I had a chat with Bill Nelson about the Be Bop Deluxe days 20 years previously at the 'Duke of Cumberland' in Ferriby and Fred and I got 'wasted' in some excellent company. Well it was 'Rock and Roll' and despite the sadness there was around, everyone agreed it was the sort of informal gathering Mick would have loved.

At that party Maggie announced to tremendous applause the release of Mick's last album which was to be named 'Heaven and Hull'. Mick had 'Come Home' but was sadly not around to enjoy it. There was a lot of hard work and fund raising ahead before the Memorial to a local hero came to fruition and it was to be the Summer of 1997 before the Mick Ronson Stage and 600 Japanese kids came together on Queens Gardens, but more of that later. The rest of the rugby season was a mix of some good performances and a shocking 52-10 loss at St. Helens, before we won our last three games against Sheffield, Featherstone and Leigh. This saw us eventually finish in a credible 9th position in the League Table.

Roy Waudby to the rescue and 'all boys together' in bed with Royce Simmons

Sunday 24th April 1993   *Hull 70 – Leigh 16*

That Spring, with gates floundering and finances again a worry we were once more saved by Roy Waudby who put another £100,000 into the Club. He offered another £50,000 if someone came forward to match his proposed investment of £150,000. As usual they didn't but the Waudby family had doubled their stake in Hull FC, to help save the day. As Hull KR were relegated, at our last home game an amazing 70-16 victory over Leigh, there was a treat for the kids when they were all given a free meal voucher to use at the new McDonald's restaurant in the town centre. We obviously liked to encourage healthy eating back then!

Under difficult circumstances Royce Simmons had done a fabulous job at the Club and we all hoped that he would be our Coach for a long time to come, but trouble at his ailing restaurant business in Penrith meant that he had to return to Australia, and with Tony Gordon immediately announced as Simmons' successor, things were already moving on. That season end was a significant one as both Simmons and Geoff Doyle returning home (the latter to play for the new Perth Club, Western Reds) while it also heralded the end of the Daniel Divet who left for Featherstone and Club joker James Grant who went out with a bang. After that last game everyone was celebrating in the Dressing Rooms when Grant, who had scored 5 tries that afternoon, secretly lit a jumping cracker and threw it into the crowd of players. So intense was the noise that some players turned visibly white with shock, while Tim Street jumped up so high, he cut his head open on a girder in the roof.

Tim had only been signed a few months, but he was already a big fans' favourite. Rough tough and always looking for confrontation he had been a big hit that season, but like most of us, he liked a few beers. There is a great story about Tim being invited to Royce Simmons' house with a lot of the squad for a few goodbye drinks after the Vice Presidents' 'Farewell Royce' dinner that May. The story goes that the players had several large 'night caps' in our Coach's front room as they talked into the night! Once everyone had left, Royce locked up and went to bed and without bothering to take off his dinner jacket etc. he climbed in and was asleep in seconds. During the night he awoke, to find a loving arm wrapped around him. He rubbed his eyes and to his amazement there next to him cuddled up to keep warm and also dressed in his full dress suit and even patent leather shoes was Tim Street. Apparently the last thing that Street could remember was curling up for a nap behind Royce's settee, before he got cold in the night and decided to go up to bed.

Tony (The Tank); Good at fundraising not so hot at weather forecasting!

Once our new Coach Tony Gordon had arrived from the London Crusaders he decided that he wanted to make import Maea David his first big signing. For some reason and to this day I don't understand why, it was to cost £10,000 to get David here and of course we simply didn't have the money. Gordon certainly didn't have the stature to replicate the 'Marathon' efforts of his predecessor, so instead he devised a game called 'Tony Gordon's Parachute Gold Rush' (only at Hull FC!). That August he sold 'squares' on a giant grid on the Boulevard pitch for £100, with a prize of £1000 for the winner.

The idea was that once the grid was laid out and all the squares sold, a sky diver would parachute down and by landing on the grid, selects the winning square. 'Pearly' and I went down there on the Club's Open Evening and although it was raining we left the Club House to watch the fun. Typical of Tony Gordon's short but exceedingly eventful stay at the Club the whole thing went 'mammary's skyward' when the low cloud deemed it impossible for the Skydiver to leave the plane and so, in the end, the winning square was drawn from a hat. Happily the winner was Wally Simpson who had actually bought ten squares, so at least he got his stake back.

Mergers, Money and Super League; Rugby League goes mad!

That August 1994 saw the culmination of British Rugby League's attempts to keep pace with the burgeoning game in Australia when the RFL published its 'Framing the Future' document which called for a 'soccer style' Premier League and controversially club mergers. Information of which clubs were involved and how the whole new system would work was rather vague, but all would become much clearer very quickly. Meanwhile things were already going downhill for Tony Gordon. He was certainly a meticulous planner and drew up a comprehensive play book which he expected every player to digest and learn. The problem was that although supposedly 'Top Secret', soon copies were circulating the City and everyone seemed to have one and be reading it in the pub! As I remember there were a lot of 'Turn ball back inside', in the one I saw, something that the players were to get monotonously right as the season unfolded!

The 'Tank' grinds to a halt!!!

Sunday 11ᵗʰ September 1994   *Hull 12 – Halifax 46*

At the Punch we were all looking forward to continuing the progress we had made over two seasons under Royce Simmons, we signed Steve Craven from Ryedale-York, Lee Richardson on loan from Hull KR and young winger Leroy McKenzie. Gordon was backed by the Board to bring in talent from 'Down Under' and Hull welcomed three players from Canterbury in New Zealand. Mae David, Tevita Vaikona and Shaun Endecott arrived in October by which time we were rooted to the bottom of the League Table in the midst of a run of defeats.

The worrying thing for all the fans was the fact that we were simply not performing. I went to Halifax on an East Yorkshire Motor Services excursion with 'Pearly' and Billy where we witnessed one of the worst and most inept performances I have seen in over 50 years of watching Hull FC. Gordon was doing his best but he was losing the players' faith as quickly as he was losing the Club's tenure in the top Division. In fact after a loss at Sheffield in early October I remember he said, "We have hit rock bottom, it's hard to see where our first win will come from"; as you can imagine we were all really inspired. However they say that every cloud has a silver lining and although we all searched desperately to find one, at least out of the adversity came the introduction of the Black and Whites Association who were to become a great partner to the Club through some really hard times.

Our second win after scraping past a poor Wakefield side, didn't materialise until 13th November with victory over a struggling Salford team. Mark Hewitt was the star at scrum half, with Paul Sterling, Vaikona and Tim Street not far behind. At one point in that game things descended into farce as in a stoppage in the game, Stan Pickering ran on the field with a mobile phone and motioned to Shaun Endecott that it was 'for him!!' The call was actually from Tony Gordon (ringing from up in the 'Crow's Nest' high over the Best Stand where he had decided to watch, hoping no doubt that some of 'Smithy's' luck would rub off on him).

Apparently so broad was his accent that Pickering couldn't understand Gordon at all and so in the middle of the pitch he handed his mobile phone to Endecott for whom the instructions were intended, and left him to figure it out! It was farcical and something had to give! Meanwhile over at Craven Park in the East of the City, Hull KR were following the example set by our Directors back in 1971, as Speedway was re-introduced to the City to raise some much needed cash.

Sport in Hull at a low ebb as 'Tony the Tank' rumbles out of town!!

Sunday 4th December 1994   *Hull 26 – Barrow 16*

In 1994 sport in the City of Kingston upon Hull was suffering across all three professional teams. Phil Lowe stood down as Chairman of Hull KR to be replaced by Barry Lilley and at Hull City the Board was still trying to stave off the Official Receivers. Even the Ice Hockey team, the Council owned Humberside Hawks, was struggling and after a massive 12-4 defeat to the Fife Flyers the Chairman of Humberside County Council Terry Geraghty adopted a new motivational technique by sending every player a 'Written Warning' as to their future conduct! Terry was however prove quite the visionary, as during a Council debate about the demise of Sport in the region he suggested that a "Super Stadium" be built to accommodate all three Hull Clubs, to help them survive and kick start some regeneration in the City. However it seems that at least his warning letter seemed to work, as in their next home encounter at the Humberside Ice Arena the Hawks beat Basingstoke 19-3 and thus managed to stave off any Council disciplinary hearings.

However following an unconvincing win at home over lowly Barrow which attracted just 2,300 fans and after a total of just three wins and a draw in 14 competitive games, Hull FC announced on Friday 9th December that they had "Parted company" with Tony Gordon. As 'Perfect Day' hit number one in the music charts, it was apparent that Tony hadn't had many of those and the man who when interviewed on local TV always looked like he had soiled his trousers and hadn't yet decided whether that was a good or bad thing, was gone. At the Boulevard we were down to the loyal few supporters as I counted just 42 other hardy souls standing on the Airlie Street terracing at that Barrow game, with even less on the banking at the Gordon Street end opposite me.

Tony Gordon had done his best despite more financial turmoil and the ensueing disputes it brings with players over wages, so amidst rumours of player unrest and dissatisfaction in the dressing rooms, his departure was in the end pretty inevitable. Bringing in a recognised Coach was simply not a viable proposition either so the job was given (until the end of the season) to current staff members Russ Walker and Phil Windley.

A song for Hull and a run for some money!

One of the crazier ideas we came up with at the Council back then was to invite local musicians to write 'A Song for Hull'. This was a surreal experience to say the least and in the end the prize of £250 sponsored by Tetleys the Brewers was bestowed on local singer/songwriter Terry Rymer with a ditty entitled, "Take me Back". It was a good choice, although some of the others as you can imagine, were pretty unbelievable. I had put my telephone number forward in the media to give advice to potential 'composers' and one morning as I was sitting in my office opening the post the phone rang. As I picked it up I heard someone clearing their throat and then in a faint, warbly voice, an obviously aged female sang, "Hull is such a pleasant Place, Cobbled Streets and Shopping, the City Hall and Holy Trinity....and then I can't think of anything to rhyme!" There was then a pause before this budding Carole King put the phone down, never to be heard of again. It was certainly a strange life at times at the City Council.

Twelve months previously the sudden demise of a colleague of mine, who was the Hall Manager at a famous West Riding venue, had frightened me. We were the same age and he enjoyed the same 'beer, pies, curry and fatty foods' sort of life style as me. Jim had tragically collapsed and experienced a sudden heart attack on the way back to his establishment from a quick 'mid performance' trip to the pub and that was just a bit too 'close to home' for me! So, I started attending the gym at the Trust House Forte Hotel on Hull Marina and inspired by Royce Simmons I slowly started to build up my running with the intention of getting fit. This I hoped would do something about the 15 stone of flab and beer belly that I had managed to acquire without much effort and was described by 'Pearly' as my "Holding back the Years phase".

Jokingly I think, my pals encouraged me to enter a Marathon and so I applied for London, knowing I was likely to be unsuccessful in one of the world's most over-subscribed races. However no one was more surprised than me to be accepted for the 1995 race. When I started running I could barely manage a hundred yards, but I had stuck at it and despite keeping up a fair intake of beer, I shed around two stone. By November 1994 I could huff and puff for around 12 miles, much to the amusement of any pals I saw whilst out pounding the streets in my old 1983 'Wembley Bound Third Time Around' T shirt.

At the first game under the new coaching team against Halifax, a better crowd of over 4,800 watched a narrow defeat and an improved performance. In general however the fare was poor and I'd again started to choose my 'away trips' a little more carefully.

As the New Year dawned and the prisoners at Everthorpe welcomed it in with a festive riot, it was Challenge Cup time and the big news in the area surrounded the exploits of the Beverley Amateur Rugby League team. They had beaten Runcorn Highfield away in the fourth Round, which saw them lauded as the only amateur team to beat a professional outfit in 86 years of the competition and now they had been drawn at home to Second Division Batley. The game was staged at the Boulevard and as we had all decided against a January trip all the way to Workington with Hull FC, we instead went along to the Boulevard with another 3,275 folks, to watch a thrilling encounter which the gallant East Riding team eventually lost through two late tries.

Beverley had trailed 14-0 before unbelievably leading 20-18, with just 10 minutes to go. In the end they lost 30-20 but it was a close thing. No one who was there will ever forget Scott Sullivan starting that revival, when he took an inside pass near his own line and streaked downfield to score a brilliant 80 yard try with the whole of the Batley defence trailing in his wake. Coached by Len Casey and Martin Dunn, it must have been a strange afternoon for Casey the former FC supremo and then licensee of the Wassand Arms, as he returned to the Boulevard after his acrimonious departure 8 years earlier. He still got a few boo's as he left the field, although his charges received a standing ovation from a crowd that remained until the very end of a rip-roaring encounter. As for Hull FC, well they lost 30-12 in the same competition up in Cumbria and as the Club's supporters Coach caught fire on the way back, our decision not to travel all that way and instead watch Beverley, was certainly justified.

A narrow victory that's simply too little too late

Sunday 19ᵗʰ March 1995   *Hull 11 – Wakefield Trinity 10*

We were still struggling as the New Year progressed and that situation wasn't helped by Mark Jones our Welsh Prop Forward asking for a transfer and Dean Busby 'going on strike' over his contract. We only won one game in a run of 12 and 'Bunkers Hill' was certainly thinly populated that afternoon as 3,460 turned up to watch us try and rescue something from the season. We played Wakefield who had been on the wrong end of our only away success that year, when we beat them 29-22 at Belle Vue back in October. Sitting at the very bottom of the League, and without a win since 6ᵗʰ January at Featherstone, it was clear by the size of the gate that few expected us to get anything but another drubbing!

This game however holds two really strong memories for me, another fine performance by Tim Street, and the 'Golden' boot of Steve McNamara. Street was an uncompromising player with massive strength and determination. He also possessed a short temper and as Pearly observed "The face of a pit bull terrier chewing a wasp" but, as I stated earlier, he was also a big hero of the fans and quite a comedian on and off the field. When we travelled to Oldham in February to watch another defeat (this time by 19-14) Street was dispatched to the sin bin for a swipe at Oldham's Redfearne. The Oldham fans booed and jeered him as he left the field while Tim, to the delight of us Hull fans, blew kisses in their direction.

By this point, in a disastrous season with relegation looming we'd all had enough and as Johan Windley lined up the ball to kick off against

Wakefield, it blew over twice, which just added to the total sense of anti climax. The second time this happened a general groan went around the sparsely populated terraces as the referee summoned our mascot 'Manda the Panda' onto the field, with a bucket containing sand to support the ball.

After twenty minutes, the 'same old dross' had us all reading our programmes and stamping our feet to ward off the effects of a cold, damp afternoon, when Hull finally came to life and suddenly and inexplicably cut loose to play some of the best rugby we had seen for ages. We completely stifled the Wakefield attack gaining our first defensive half time clean sheet of the season, but with the number of chances we created in that spell, we should have been well in front by half time. Firstly, Tevita Vaikona turned back inside when it would have been easier to score in the corner, then Leroy McKenzie also looked to have scored before he was brought back by the referee for an obstruction in the attacking line.

Finally however Windley dropped his shoulders and went round Daio Powell to release Mike Dixon who careered through a gap and just as he was tackled Gary Nolan took the ball to score besides the posts. McNamara added the conversion and then a penalty and with a well taken drop goal by Windley, the score moved onto an unexpected 9-0 at the break.

Predictably Hull FC started the second half sluggishly and looked nothing like the team that had cut loose in that first half. As usual Tim Street continued to use every opportunity to bash his way up field, but conceded two penalties in quick time which Nigel Wright dispatched between the posts, the second of these saw Street's usual visit to the sin bin for arguing with the referee. It looked like it was going to be the same old story, when ex FC favourite Ian Marlow slipped out a ball to Wakefield's Nigel Wright who sent in Lee Childs at the corner. A towering conversion by Wright put Wakefield Trinity into the lead 10-9, as the now traditional air of despondency descended over the crowd. Street though was having none of it and once back on the field he was waving his arms frantically at the players as he demanded some action.

Twice Kevin Gray at Full Back stopped certain tries while Richard Gay, who played at 6 that day, managed to somehow get a hand on Steve McGowan as he reached out to put the ball down and to a sarcastic cheer from the crowd, it spun loose.

Wakefield were streaming forward sensing a win, but to our credit we showed great determination and even managing to go close through McKenzie and Maea David. The introduction of Chico Jackson from the bench certainly livened up the forwards in which Street continued to shine, before a head high tackle left Chico sprawling on the forty yard line as referee Holdsworth immediately indicated the penalty. This was the moment when Steve McNamara's hours of kicking practise on the training field came to the fore, and with a face caked in mud and just 11 minutes to go, he slotted the kick over and we were back in the lead 11-10. Strangely Wakefield showed little in those remaining minutes, although Kevin Gray had to scramble back as he spilled a towering up and under from Gary Spencer, but we battled on and as the hooter went we all broke into 'Old Faithful' as for the time being at least, our fight against the drop was given a little bit of credibility. In the Rugby Leaguer next day Steve McNamara said, "I have never been so glad in my life when the ball went over, I was really nervous, my legs were shaking and I even slipped in the run up, but it went over and that's all that counts" And it certainly was!

From then on as the season drew to its conclusion we did a little better as we recorded fine wins over Widnes, Featherstone and Doncaster but it was not enough to save us. A 66-12 defeat at Wigan heralded our departure from the top flight, although our fate had been sealed weeks earlier with a defeat at home to Widnes watched by just 2,540 people. Still at least in my private life things were looking up. After numerous attempts at relationships featuring females who had gone from finding my devotion to Hull FC rather 'charming and cute' to it being (as one told me), "obsessive, corrosive, selfish, childish and immature", I had settled down with the future and final Mrs. Allen, who took me for what I was.... poor woman!

It was a far, far better thing I did that Day!!! Sore feet, aching bones and mini Mars Bars!

So, with over £1500 of sponsorship pledged from friends and colleagues I had to succeed, and running in aid of The Lord Mayor's Charity Appeal, I went down to London to run the Marathon. The date was 5th April 1995 and no one was more apprehensive or terrified than I was that day as I stood in a park in South London. The whole race was an unforgettable experience, but I have to say here and now that since then I have majored on the philosophy that if you run one marathon you're a hero, if you run anymore your an idiot, because in the end, quite simply, it's a bloody long way. I had trained and got myself up to 20 miles, but that last 6 seemed to go on forever. However, having walked the first mile because of the crush, I waded through thousands of discarded mini mars bar wrappers, experienced temperatures in the low 70's, poured Isotonic drink from a drinks station over my head and watched as a 76 year old lady, keeled over and died on the Thames embankment in front of me, I at last finished in a time of 4 hours 17 minutes.

That really wasn't bad at all and I became a bit of a hero with all my beer swilling mates, who couldn't believe I'd actually started, never mind finished. Pearly even suggested that I had got someone to assume my name and run for me, but I've kept the running up over the years and although I can't now do anything like that sort of distance, I still run every few days, as a sort of 'counter balance' to the excesses, that even at 62 my life continues to embrace.

Protests, Mergers and the long shadow of Rupert Murdoch

Although at the Boulevard, Hull were having a torrid time, as I hinted earlier there was a lot going on nationally back in 1995. As Rugby approached the Easter programme, after months of 'behind closed doors' discussions between the Clubs, 'Super League' was announced. And there it was again, Rugby League's dirtiest word – Mergers. To the horror of every right minded Rugby fan in the Country on 8 April the

British Clubs voted unanimously to accept a deal from Sky TV worth an unbelievable £77 million over five years. The plan included up to 15 clubs merging, summer rugby and a 14 team Premier Division made up of these 'cloned' Clubs. The storm that greeted these proposals was perhaps unprecedented in British sport.

Of course Hull and Rovers were prime candidates for one of these proposed unholy alliances but it was never going to happen as fans across the City threatened to 'cut their own heads off' rather than have to support a Club in red and white irregular hoops. Down the M62 Castleford were told that they would have to amalgamate with Wakefield and open warfare broke out as the good folks of both proud West Riding strongholds of the game, pulled up the 'Draw Bridges' and prepared for war. The new Super League would include two French teams, Paris and Toulouse, Saints, Halifax, Wigan, Bradford, London and Leeds plus 6 merged teams. This last assumption was where the problem lay as far as the fans were concerned. The proposed new team of Hull FC and Hull KR was to be known as Humberside, Warrington and Widnes were to become Cheshire, Castleford, Wakefield and Featherstone – Calder, Salford and Oldham – Manchester, Whitehaven, Workington, Barrow and Carlisle- Cumbria and Sheffield and Doncaster – South Yorkshire.

To say that these suggestions proved controversial was an understatement and the announcement was met with supporters' protests in town centres, at Rugby League Headquarters and even on the pitch during games. The story at the time was that a lot of clubs were dubious about the whole thing but that the game couldn't survive without the money. At the Boulevard supporters invaded the pitch and a couple of fans scaled the rugby posts to unfurl a 'No to the merger' banner which was to re-appear a few years later, in even more dire circumstances. Across the game, over the next few days, the deal began to unravel.

One by one the clubs that had 'backed' mergers began to back away from them. However the 'troops' on the terraces were mobilised and never more strongly than in Hull where Hull FC were destined for the Second Division while Hull KR would sink eventually to the Third. On

30 April 1995, almost 100 years since the birth of the game, and under tremendous pressure and outrage from the fans, the merger proposals collapsed. The Rugby League withdrew them and although that wasn't the last time the idea was raised, at least for now common sense prevailed and we returned to three Divisions. To sweeten the deal and calm things down Rupert Murdoch's BSkyB agreed to a 12 team Super League, instead of the originally proposed 14 team set up, and threw in an extra £10 million to placate the Clubs that missed out.

Looking back I guess it was all ill conceived and no one on the terraces at either side of the City of Hull would have countenanced it for one minute. However one or two of these alliances might have worked. A strong Cumbrian team, (none of the 4 teams in that region were particularly strong at that point) with a guaranteed Super League spot and a bigger pool of players, offered something. Whereas Workington entered Super League, and were relegated in 1996, while ironically Carlisle and Barrow merged anyway in 1997.

In the end however the outcome was a distinct victory for common sense and 'Supporter Power'. I guess now, looking at some of the teams that survived and their plight in the modern game, a few Clubs' administrations might wish they had dug their heels in a little more and stuck a little longer with the idea.

Stephen Ball rides into town to 'rebuild the Boulevard'

Summer rugby was still to go ahead because that's what Sky TV wanted, but fans of the game in the City of Hull had a problem because as the 1994/95 season ended with us in a relegation position, it was apparent that the new Super League would not contain a Club from the famous Rugby League stronghold. However, in the short term there was still a few months to go until the new 'Super League' started the following February. Clubs could not sustain such a long period of inactivity and lack of income, and there were serious concerns that the fans would drift away from the game. It was therefore agreed that a truncated season running from August to December would fill the breach and so Hull FC's newly appointed Coach Phil Windley set about rebuilding our team to meet that challenge.

Over at Batley the Club Chairman Stephen Ball had certainly made a name for himself in the past two years. He had raised the little West Yorkshire Club from near bankruptcy to being solvent and built a new ground for them in the process. It was therefore a real surprise when Hull FC's Chairman David Latham announced that Ball had joined Hull to become our Chief Executive, with a mandate to do the same at the Boulevard. Within weeks he obtained planning permission for a new East Stand to replace the 'Best Stand' the only problem being the ability to raise the £2m needed to complete the scheme. In fact the whole overhaul of the famous old ground was to cost £6m but sadly it was to mean the demolishing of the last remaining quarter of the old Threepenny Stand, which was in any case no longer legal under the Safety at Sports Ground Act. However, there was another short stay of execution for the old structure as a grant application for the £200,000 needed to replace it was considered by the Sports Ground Trust.

In the City of Hull in general, ambition and grandiose schemes were everywhere as the newly formed 'City Centre Action Group' announced plans for a Super Tram system, Gondola's on the River Hull and a Convention Centre on Ferensway. However their problems were little different to those of the City's three professional sports Clubs in that, grand though they were, there was simply no money to deliver these schemes, and so one by one, they floundered on the 'rocks' of a lack of finance.

The lure of Super League proves too much for some

Sunday 24ᵗʰ September 1995   *Hull 56 – Wakefield Trinity 6*

Of course the introduction of the new Super League meant that the players' agents were all sensing a bit of cash for their protégés and Hull FC, being now in the 'lower' Division, were soon struggling to get players to sign new contracts. Mark Jones left for Warrington for a fee of £50,000, whilst Phil Windley, despite bringing in Olympic athletics coach Brad McStravick and taking the team to Aldershot for some 'Army' training, was struggling to prepare his depleted forces for the season starting that August. St Helens lured Busby to the new League, Jon Sharp went to Featherstone and Paul Eastwood who could not agree terms, was released from his contract. It appeared to all us fans that although great for the 'Big Boys' the newly introduced format, was seeing all the hard work that we had done over the years, come to nought! However we did at least sign Andy Fisher from Dewsbury and Gary Divorty returned to the Club from Halifax for a fee of £58,000. But we all wondered where the new 'Super League' was going to leave the Club we loved.

The most memorable game for me in that strange curtailed and largely forgettable season was one against Wakefield when as usual, out of adversity we produced a brilliant performance that showcased the skills of several FC players, and Phil Windley's (soon to be questioned) ability as a Coach. I remember Dick Tingle's headline in the Hull Daily Mail next day stated, "Trinity Cut to Ribbons" and that just about summed it up. Having rattled up 46 points away at Dewsbury in mid week, in a game I couldn't get to, Hull took their 'points for' tally, beyond 100 in a week, in a game that they totally dominated. Andy Fisher was the star but Gary Divorty and Richard Gay were not far behind as we scored 9 tries and everyone there left the game believing that we were contenders for the new Centenary First Division title.

Music in Hull still prospers even if Rugby doesn't!

At work there was a lot going on at the City Hall during that strange 'rugby' autumn of 1995 and live music in the City in general was experiencing a revival. In early October following a massive concert featuring Boyzone, 'Smokie' appeared at the venue as part of their National Tour. Previously a tragic accident on the German Autobahn had seen the Tour Bus skid into a Crash Barrier causing the death of singer Alan Barton. I mention this because his replacement at short notice for that tour was Hull born singer Mike Craft. That Concert on 10th October had a very special atmosphere, but the following night there was further indication of just how strong patronage for good music in Hull was, when Squeeze played at the Hall to a full house while at the Tower a return for one night to pop concerts saw Cast entertain 1000 people and new chart entrants, 'The Lighthouse Family' played another sell out gig at the Blue Lamp Club in Norfolk Street.

That night I went to the City Hall to ensure that everything was going well before going to 'Blue Lamp' to see what all the fuss was about this new Tyne-side duo who had just entered the national music charts at thirty-four, with their first single 'Ocean Drive'. I went with Pearly who had, he said, 'blagged' the tickets from a pal, which meant I got in for free but had to listen to him listing all the newcomers potential influences whilst everyone else went wild.

A final farewell to the 'Threepenny's' and the advent of the mysterious 'Mr Brown'

Wednesday 14th November 1995   *Hull 42 – Batley 8*

That Wednesday another little bit of history was to unfold at the Boulevard. We all met in 'The Eagle' on Anlaby Road and had a few drinks before clutching our special entry tickets, we abandoned our regular spot on our 'Lucky Step' on the Airlie Street terracing to go back in time. That night we watched our last ever game from the most famous viewing area in the game of Rugby League. Pearly had come equipped with a Lighthouse family tape for each of us and a pretty naff 'Salute to the Threepenny's' home made T shirt that we all managed to ignore! Steven Ball had at last secured the £200,000 needed to demolish what had been our spiritual home for so many years and replace it with an extension to the current structure that ran along the rest of the west side of the Stadium. Ironically in the end the old Stand was not as full as people had expected, as the special entrance tickets appeared to have put some people off, in fact in the end just 2,628 people attended the game which was in essence a wake for the remains of that great old wooden edifice.

Little did anyone know but huddled in a big sheep skin coat in the Best Stand that night, was a certain mysterious Mr. Brown, but more of him later.

The game itself was another easy win for Hull FC, with the one real standout moment for me a brilliant try by Tevita Vaikona. We had made a blistering start and were leading 16-4 when Full Back Richard Gay caught a ball over our try line and ran it out for ten yards before finding Tevita with an inch perfect pass. The Tongan burst down the touchline closely followed by winger Paul Sterling and as the cover came in they interchanged passes in devastating style before Vaikona finished off a 100 yard move with a brilliantly taken try. I also remember that teenage Half Back Chris Kitchen showed some quality finishing with two excellant tries.

This good performance was delivered despite the City being alive with rumours about the tenure of Hull FC Coach Phil Windley, who was doing pretty well in difficult circumstances. There were stories about certain Board members (led it was claimed by Steven Ball) wanting a new 'high profile' Coach to make one last effort to get us back into the 'Big Time' before the cash ran out altogether. Names that were circulating include Des Hasler and even the return of Garry Kemble but what we didn't know was that a little unknown Australian Coach Phil Sigsworth had travelled to this country at his own expense and was staying in the Royal Hotel under the pseudonym of 'Mr. Brown'. He had watched the team play that game against Batley and as Phil found out what was happening, he resigned as Coach on 17th November citing that, "I have known for two weeks that the Club has been talking to Australian Coaches behind my back". It was a time of change again at the Club, as Phil Sigsworth was destined to bring some short but much needed success back to the remaining 'Faithful few' at the Boulevard.

Chapter 8

The gloom of Whitehaven, the advent of 'Tingly Dick' and the origin of Manda the Panda!

Sunday 14th January 1996   *Hull 32 – Widnes 24*

So Phil Sigsworth was our new Coach and after he had returned home to sort out his domestic arrangements we were all inquisitive as to what difference he would make to a team that was already playing reasonably well. In his first game in charge we beat Widnes and I remember standing in the Well of the Best Stand that day looking across the pitch to admire the final part of the New Threepenny Stand as it neared completion. I was soon also rejoicing in the fantastic play of Tevita Vaikona and Gary Divorty in a 32-24 defeat of the much fancied Cheshire outfit.

It was a time of local government reorganisation and pretty tough for the Council financially as Humberside County Council was to disappear from 31st March 1996 and the City had to take over most of the services it provided. For a time even the City Hall was under threat of closure but as the Cultural Services Committee wrestled with the problem, a 'public outcry' helped ensure the venue stayed open.

It was always the practise at the end of each campaign for Billy, Pearly and I to attend the last game, wherever it was played. That year this meant travelling all the way to Whitehaven for the finale of that strange shortened Centenary Division One season. After a five hour drive to Cumbria the team performed terribly and the only lasting memory was the aweful condition of the floodlights at the Recreation Ground and 'Pearly' incessantly grumbling in the back seat all the way home. We had witnessed a dreary 22-14 defeat where the only bright spot was a brilliant performance from Chico Jackson, in a match that was almost indiscernible after half-time because the pitch was lit with an eerie half light, as the rickety pylons displayed more broken light bulbs than illuminated ones. As the small gathering of 50 or so Hull fans huddled together at the 'Kells End' sang, "Put a-n-o-t-h-e-r shilling in the meter" to the tune of "Is this the way to Amarillo", we took the wrath of a handful of the most inhospitable fans in British Rugby League. Over to our right the new Main Stand that had just been opened boasted 500 gleaming new seats, most of which were empty as both teams finished the season with a whimper rather than a roar and Phil Sigsworth must have wondered just what he had signed up for.

I remember a couple of days later bumping into the Hull FC writer from the Hull Daily Mail Dick Tingle, (who was fast being known by all the Hull FC fans as 'Tingly' Dick) and after lamenting a shocking display in the twilight of Cumbria, for some reason the conversation got round to what was behind the introduction of our laughable mascot 'Manda the Panda' who like Albert Walker on the tannoy and Graham Holmes our pitch announcer, had become something of an institution at the Boulevard. Our first real 'mascot' was an amazing sight as 'she' ran out onto the pitch to bring the sand for kicks or to 'get the crowd going' before games. Looking more like a reject from a fancy dress shop than an actual Panda, she was adored by the kids and ridiculed by everyone else. Dick said that as for the 'the origin of the species' the original idea of using a Panda was all down to Chief Executive Steven Ball who had a thing about Pandas and Bears when he was young, (It's hard to believe I know, but 'bear' with me). He apparently had a favourite Panda named Manda that he took everywhere with him, except when 'Bad' step-brother, and now esteemed players agent, David Howes threw her downstairs, much to young Steven's distress!

With the season finishing early, we were certainly all a bit disorientated. The players trained on, getting no break at all, because the new Summer Rugby extravaganza was just two months away and as the prospect of inflated full time contracts unsettled the aspiring players in the lower divisions, the new 'Super League teams' were snapping them up. Sky TV and our poor form had seen Hull FC excluded from the top tier of the game and so as fans we stood like school boys with our faces pressed against the sweet shop window of Super League, while the 'Big Boys' inside pinched all the jelly babies! Paris San Germain captained by ex Hull FC hero Patrick Entat, had been 'manufactured' as the token French team and featured in the first televised game that year. In the spirit of the revolution, all the lads came round to Wensley Avenue on 29th March 1996 to watch the first ever game of Super League rugby courtesy of my newly acquired satellite TV set up. The match took place at a very well attended Charlety Stadium in Paris where Paris St Germain beat the Sheffield Eagles 30-24. In the weeks that followed it became apparent that the majority of that crowd had received free tickets and gates in the French Capital soon fell to well below 10,000.

As ordinary fans who felt aggrieved by our Club's exclusion from the new 'Elite' competition, most of that first Super League season passed us by, although we did watch at least one game every weekend on TV. I guess, with Manda in mind, my lasting memory has to be the mascots. Who could ever forget Ronnie the Rhino standing for Parliament and getting 47 votes, and of course the sight of a man dressed in the guise of a meat pie on legs as Wigan's 'Pie Man'. He made our Panda seem almost 'life like'.

After 6 years loyal service our captain Steve McNamara left for Bradford in search of 'fame and fortune' and flying winger Paul Sterling followed him out of the door for Leeds after complaining about the problems he had travelling from his home in the West Riding. Still Sigsworth signed Aussie forward Dave Moffit, half back Dave Webber and unknown Papua New Guinea centre Marcus Bai who was to go on to have an illustrious career, (not the least at Leeds where years later in Cardiff he was to gift Richard Whiting with what was to be a fundamentally important try in our Club's history).

For our first game in National League One, we completely demolished Wakefield 52-2 at the Boulevard, on a day that the new extension to the Threepenny Stand was opened and we all stood in there to mark the occasion. A healthy crowd of 3,800 was in attendance and it was Vaikona and Kevin Gray who starred for Hull FC, with the former scoring two 'scorching' 80 yard tries.

The Winter Olympics come to East Yorkshire

As I alluded to before on 31st March Humberside County Council disappeared forever as two new unitary authorities, Kingston upon Hull City and the East Riding of Yorkshire Council's were created. For us at the City Hall is was an easy transition but one that was filled with intrigue after our Chief Executive the well liked Darryl Stephenson left his role in the Guildhall to take up a similar position at the new East Riding Council. Still, in Hull we all had the last laugh as on his first day in charge he was the victim of a massive hoax which had the whole region laughing.

An 'official' Press Release was issued from County Hall in Beverley that announced that the new Authority had made an audacious bid to host the 2006 Winter Olympics. The 'authentic' looking document contained quotes from Darryl Stephenson and the boast that if successful the Games would create 10,000 jobs, ironically just as the demise of Humberside had created 100 redundancies. Mr Stephenson said in the Release that Hornsea Mere would be ideal for speed skating, the Wolds for Ski Slalom and so it went on. One early edition of a local paper got caught out and carried a story entitled "Big Jobs boost for the Region" before the next hastily change it to 'Red Faced Councillors caught out by April Fool's Day Prank".

Hull FC merge with Rovers; but only for a meeting!

Every rugby fan in the City had only one word on their lips at that time and it was once again "Mergers". The new 'Super League' was doing quite well as the coverage on Sky TV saw satellite dishes springing up

In 1995 the Rugby League first raised the prospect of mergers as the way forward for the game. At the last game that season at the Boulevard against Doncaster, the fans make their feeling very clear.
(Courtesy of Hull Daily Mail)

On the same day 'more bed sheets go missing', as two young fans reflect the thoughts of all of us, as they ran out onto the pitch chased by the stewards. *(Courtesy of Hull Daily Mail)*

On 15th November 1995 after it had been condemned under the
Safety at Sports Grounds legislation, the remaining part of the old
Threepenny Stand was finally closed, after a game against Batley,
which Hull won 42-8. This photograph shows the grand old Stand
that night.

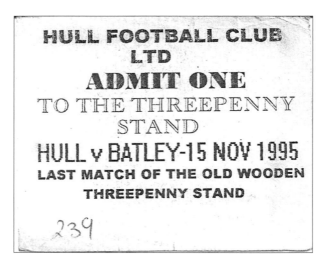

**HULL FOOTBALL CLUB
LTD
ADMIT ONE**
TO THE THREEPENNY
STAND
HULL v BATLEY-15 NOV 1995
**LAST MATCH OF THE OLD WOODEN
THREEPENNY STAND**

239

We stood on the old Stand that night, where admittance was by
ticket only. Sadly not everyone saw it as such a significant occasion
and the place was only half full.

The launch of the Memorial Concert in Hull in front of the Mick Ronson Stage in Queens Gardens. Present that day were Councillor Brian Petch, Maggie Ronson (Mick's Sister) and Kevin Cann.

The 'father' of the KC Stadium, Leader of the Hull City Council Councillor Pat Doyle and an unidentified Local Government Officer, launch the Hull 700 Festivities.

We've had some strange mascots and here are two of the senior
players in 1997 rather sheepishly pose with 'Sharky'.

Saturday 5th July 1997 and back in Super League with a win against
The Huddersfield Giants. Here the players celebrate at the end of a
game which Hull won 31-18. *(Courtesy of Hull Daily Mail)*

"I believe that's game set and match then Mr Lloyd!" Our owner walks out of the Hull FC shareholders meeting at the Ramada Jarvis Hotel in March 1998.

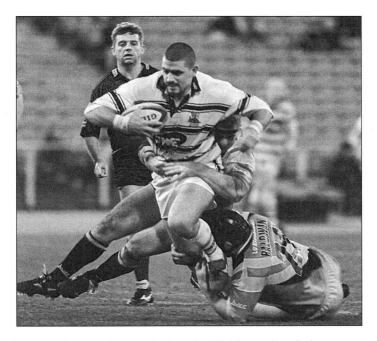

Steve Craven bursts through the Sheffield Eagles defence in a game at the Boulevard on 5th April 1999, which we lost 21-23.

A posse of Hull players swarm all over a young Andy Farrell in the
Challenge Cup Quarter Final against Wigan at the Boulevard on
Saturday 11th March 2000.

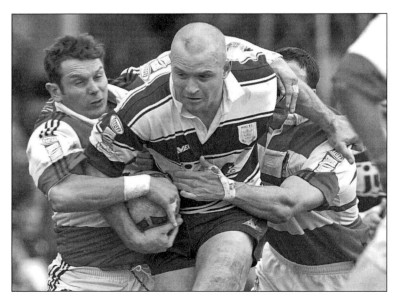

Wigan's Tony Smith desperately clings onto David Maiden in the
same game.

The aftermath of the defeat at the Mc Alpine Stadium in the Cup
Final against Leeds on 26th March 2000 when in front of an
international TV audience once again the idiots brought our Club
and the goal posts, down.

An utter disgrace!
(Courtesy of Hull Daily Mail)

Even after the merger, facilities were poor and the players still relied on the Gym in the Gordon Street School for some of their weight and conditioning work. *(Courtesy of Chris Turner)*

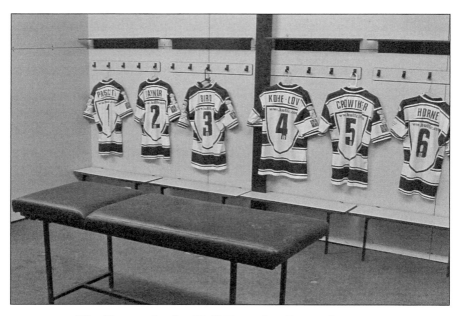

The line up in the Hull Dressing Room in 2002.
(Courtesy of Chris Turner)

on houses everywhere, but with only 12 teams taking part, there was already a deal of unrest from some Clubs about the lack of income that just 11 home games a season provided. Attendances for teams like Oldham, Sheffield and Workington were really poor and despite a good 'Hand out' from the proceeds of the Sky TV deal, several clubs were already starting to struggle to pay their players.

Rumours were rife that there were secret talks going on about co-opting more teams into Super League and about merging some Clubs to produce 'Hi-brid' outfits to geographically suit the requirements of the top Division. The Hull Kingston Rovers' fans who were that year watching their team play in the third tier or National League Two, were particularly upset about this rumoured development and even staged a sit in after a game against Swinton in June. Before that, in a move unprecedented in the City, the Rovers' supporters group invited the Hull fans to join them in a meeting to decide on a joint strategy to stop any such moves.

The gathering took place in the Hull KR Supporters Club on Wednesday 5th June and although none of my pals would join me, it was the one and only time that I have been in there. In fact about 50 Hull FC fans joined me to brave uncharted territory to attend, and we heard some passionate stuff from fans of both Clubs. I remember Syd Hynes the Chairman of the Rovers 'Supporters' Group addressing the meeting and stating "Make no mistake about it, this merger talk is the work of just three people, Roy Waudby at Hull FC, Phil Lowe at Hull KR, and the Rugby League".

As a spontaneous burst of applause broke out I found myself cheering along with the rest. We were told (and whether it was true or not it didn't seem to be of any consequence once folks 'got going') that the Rugby League had offered the two Boards of Directors in Hull £1m to amalgamate and would guarantee that the new team would be fast tracked into the Super league for 1997.

How much of all this was true of course was open to conjecture and we will probably never know, but it seemed to us that the Rugby League had missed the point because few Rovers or Hull FC supporters would be the slightest bit interested in watching an amalgamated team, choosing instead to probably drift away from the game altogether.

However while all this was going on, at the Boulevard, under the stewardship of Phil Sigsworth, we were experiencing a decent season with gates up 20% on the previous year. Chief Executive Steven Ball was doing well too and seemed to be able to raise money from various Charitable and Government sources as we found ourselves, for the first time for years, in a pretty healthy situation both on and off the field. This development was probably instrumental in the Hull Board eventually coming out and publically discounting the 'proposed' merger and so the 'No to the Merger' banners were put away, our beloved Club had its autonomy intact and we were safe....for now.

Back to Featherstone, where 'Irish eyes were smiling'

Sunday 9ᵗʰ June 1996　　　　　　*Hull 22 – Featherstone 20*

In a month when Pearly and I went to the Odeon to see the premier of 'Independence Day to marvel at the way that Bill Murray beat the aliens on his own, Hull FC were again concerned about the condition of the playing surface at the Boulevard. The dry summer had baked it hard and it was badly worn in the centre area. Ever resourceful, Steven Ball raised the finance to install a state of the art irrigation system which included a futuristic looking water tank at the Gordon Street end of the Stadium. This construction, 'Pearly' concluded, looked from a distance like one of the alien space craft from the film had actually landed on the South Terracing!

So it was back to Featherstone again as we travelled early to sample the excellent hospitality of the Supporters' Club and although the age old practise of covering the Pool table and having a performance from a couple of strippers, had now passed into the mists of time, we had a great afternoon with the home fans who always made us really welcome.

I enjoyed the first half of the game from the open terrace at the South end of the ground, with the usual array of locals watching from their bedroom windows or from the tops of their loft extensions on the row of terraced houses behind me. Featherstone was one place behind us in the table at 5th but we had won our last five games and had annihilated Batley the previous week at the Boulevard 68-12, so we were hopeful of an upset. Featherstone ran out, bizarrely, to soccer anthem 'Three Lions' the current Number One in the charts, and they were certainly fired up. They drew first blood after just 10 minutes when Darren Hughes sent Steve Molloy over and this effort fired the home fans into some chanting although at least half of the meagre 1800 crowd had made the journey from Hull. With Molloy and Derek Fox running the game for the 'Colliers', only some resolute defence from Chico Jackson and Andy Fisher kept the home team at bay.

Then a sweeping move down the field saw Chico Jackson pass to Tevita Vaikona who brilliantly beat Owen Simpson to motor into the open and ex Featherstone favourite Fisher took his perfectly weighted pass to steam over the line for our opening score. Under 21 International scrum-half Mark Hewitt at hooker tagged on the points and we were level.

Just 4 minutes later after Dave Webber had been tackled 20 yards out, it was Chico Jackson who ran into acting half back and brushing would be tacklers Gibson, Pearson and Summers aside, to score in spectacular fashion. Hewitt then landed a difficult penalty from wide out on the left and despite Pearson reducing the deficit with another penalty for the home side, we went in at the break leading 14-8.

At half time most of the Hull fans changed ends to stand in front of the score board and as was expected Featherstone came out all guns blazing. Hull were struggling to hold the big Featherstone front row of Malloy, Roebuck and Tuffs and it took a last ditch high tackle from our full back Peter Fitzgerald, to stop Eddie Rombo going in at the corner. Pearson converted a penalty and after a great downfield move by the Featherstone backs, Fox touched down so after 60 minutes we trailed again, 16-14.

Hewitt levelled with a penalty when referee Mr Taberne decided that Fox had strayed off side in the defensive line, but then disaster struck as the official Mr Taberne sent Hewitt to the sin bin after he held Summers down in a tackle near our line. While he was off the field Featherstone capitalised on their extra man advantage and Molloy stormed in after a long spell of pressure to make it 20-16. At that point our forwards were performing heroics in defence and in one five minute spell 'Irish' Dave Moffat (who held an Irish passport) pulled off nine tackles which was pretty amazing for a second rower.

Tackling everything that moved, he and Jon Aston kept us in the game in that torrid spell, but then as Hewitt returned with 9 minutes to go we managed to wrestle our way back into the game. Chico Jackson almost got over and Marcus Bai was forced into touch inches from the line. It was a bit of magic from Gary Divorty that eventually found the home defence tired and flat footed. He stepped outside two players and found Moffat with a smart pass back inside which left the big forward a clear 10 yard run to the line. With a Hewitt goal we took a 22-20 lead which we clung on to, until the hooter went.

It was a victory that registered Featherstone's first home defeat of the season and brought Moffat his third consecutive 'Players' Player of the Match' award, although Chico Jackson must have pushed him close that day. Mark Hewitt did well that afternoon too and didn't miss a single kick at goal.

98 points at Spotland and not a pie in sight

Sunday 4th August 1996   *Hull 58 – Rochdale 40*

As a good season continued, there was certainly no problem with us scoring points and at Spotland we beat Rochdale in a 98 point thriller in which, if I remember correctly, Glen Liddiard, who was on a short 5 match contract, scored 4 tries. Rochdale, stalwarts of the Rugby League were struggling financially, gates were on the slide and that day the Hull supporters outnumbered the home fans around 3 to one. I went to the game with Billy although after my past exploits with the pies, we both stayed well clear of having anything to eat or drink while in the ground.

That said there was no sign of Mr Patel's Pies and it did cross my mind that the great reduction in the number of home fans over the past couple of years could well have been down to him.

Why we all owe a lot to the Keighley Cougars

Sunday 1ˢᵗ September 1996   *Hull 28 – Keithley 41*

In the end we finished fourth that season and as was tradition we went to the last game, a hard fought play-off match at Keighley. The little West Riding Club, whose stadium nestles in the foothills of the Pennines and overlooks Ilkley Moor, were in crisis, although a year earlier they had been on the brink of Super League. Then, as the infamous 'Cougar Mania' swept the town, the little club had harboured big ambitions. They invested in good players, played an expansive exciting style of rugby and their crowds had increased from an abysmal 350 in 1989, to an average of over 4,000 in 1995, which was not bad for a town with a population of only 67,000.

The Cougars had developed their stadium in Lawkholme Lane, built a new club-house and appointed a new coach, ex Great Britain supremo Phil Larder. They even changed the name of the Ground to Cougar Park as the team went full-time in 1994. All this effort led to Keighley winning the Second Division Championship in 1995 and therefore presumably promotion, however, when Super League was created for the following 1996 'summer' season, Keighley were not included. The disappointment of being denied promotion cost the Club both fans and sponsors. They took out an injunction to try to stop the new competition kicking off and only withdrew their legal threat when Super League released more money for all the lower division clubs. That was money without which many would have gone to the wall so, despite their personal disappointment, in the end all those in the lower divisions that survive to this day, owe a lot to the stand that the Cougars made in 1996.

We lost that game in the play-offs 41-28, despite a big fight back by Hull in the second-half, however what I remember most was a safety barrier collapsing in front of us which saw us all fall forward with some fans spilling onto the pitch. It followed Keithley scoring from a blatant double movement, just after they had been awarded another try after what appeared to all of us to be a 'dodgy' forward pass. In anger at the decision the Hull crowd surged forward and the wooden advertising hoardings gave way, resulting in a broken leg, a few arrests and a brief pause in proceedings while order was restored. I think also at that point, an amateur photographer who was taking pictures of the Hull fans on the field, was chased by one FC supporter who caught him in the 'in goal' area, grabbed his camera and stamped on it just under the posts. He was the only Hull fan that was arrested that day, although a few were pretty dazed and confused. It was a serious incident which was investigated by the West Yorkshire Police and their findings led to the already struggling Cougars having to find another £30,000 to replace barriers right around the perimeter of the Stadium.

So the season ended with Phil Sigsworth heading back home 'Down Under' for a break before bringing the team back for training in November, in preparation for what was destined to be an exciting and rewarding season. Tevita Vaikona who was becoming a much coveted player was our top try scorer that year with 15 and Mark Hewitt was top points scorer with 152, thanks mainly to an 82% success rate with 'the boot'.

Over at Boothferry Park it seemed the 'Fan power' that both the Hull Rugby League Clubs had used with such success to avert the dreaded merger was catching on as on 5th October after an embarrassing 2-0 defeat by local rivals Scunthorpe, a mass sit in was staged by fans demanding the resignation of Chairman Martin Fish and Coach Terry Dolan.

Sigsworth does his homework

Sunday 9th February 1997   *Hull 16 – Huddersfield 16*

In the Eagle at the corner of Coltman Street, which had now become our regular 'watering hole' before games, we were all Phil Sigsworth fans and our Coach had left nothing to chance as far as our bid to get up into Super League was concerned. It was of course too early to tell whether we would be successful, but there was little doubt that the new Premier Division needed us if only because we were a rare commodity in those days; a team that could regularly take in excess of 2000 fans to away games. Super League was certainly meeting the requirements of Sky TV, but the change to summer hadn't suited all the fans and many clubs struggled to get comparable attendances and there was already stories circulating about teams being in dire financial straits, mainly because of the pressures of sustaining a full time squad of players.

At our regular 'meetings' in the Eagle we all felt that the signings Phil had made prior to that next season were good. We now had a full 'quota' of 6 overseas players made up of Tevita Vaikona plus new imports Liddiard, Boyd, Lester, Wheeler and Holmes. However there were certainly mixed feelings amongst the fans when the Board of Directors announced that the Club, in an effort to be fully prepared for Super League, would change their name to the Hull Sharks. Luckily, at least for that season, all the Club strips and leisure wear (in traditional hoops), had been on sale for a while so it was a just a change in name; the 'fancy dress' shirts and 'cringeworthy' mascots, were yet to follow.

The season started with an easy Challenge Cup victory over Castleford amateurs Lock Lane and then we were drawn in a difficult looking game at Huddersfield. I travelled by train that day and after a few beers at the George Hotel I enjoyed a hard fought Cup-tie in which it looked like we would be defeated before just on the hooter, a late try by new stand-off Gary Lester saw us secure a draw. We won the replay and then travelled to St Helens for an almighty drubbing by the Super League Club, 54-8. Almost 3000 of us made the trek to Lancashire and although we were well beaten no one could question the team spirit that Phil Sigsworth had engendered, particularly when it became apparent that to ensure they were properly prepared the whole squad stayed overnight in Manchester, the night before the game, at their own expense.

We opened our League campaign with a home win over Swinton in front of 3,300 fans, Chico Jackson shone that day and scored two great tries, whilst Tevita Vaikona who was now a real hero, had another superb game, something that prompted our Board to issue a 'Hands Off' warning to Leeds, who were believed to be interested in obtaining his services. We beat Keighley in our next game which saw Hull already sitting at the top of the League. I also remember that around that time Sigsworth's wife Julie was providing 'Friday pasta nights' in the Club offices as the players watched videos of that weekend's opposition. Although prospects were good at the Boulevard, in general sport was poorly attended in the City with the total combined average attendance at Hull FC, Hull KR and City fewer than 10,000.

A Philanthropist appears......and that's the start of the trouble!

Saturday 16ᵗʰ March 1997   *Hull 54 – Widnes 6*

Next we absolutely annihilated Widnes at the Boulevard but all the talk in the Eagle and on the terraces that day was not so much about the game, but more about an article that had appeared in the Hull Daily Mail the previous day. Rumours had been circulating for a couple of weeks concerning a 'secret' benefactor being about to offer to finance the Club. There were always rumours of course, this was Hull, but this time the Hull Daily Mail announced that it believed the person involved was Tim Wilby the ex FC player, who was reported to now be a businessman of some repute in London. The reality was that he was actually a caretaker of a block of flats in Lewisham but unfortunately that information was not to become apparent for at least another year.

The article indicated that Wilby was to put £300,000 into the Club and to become senior shareholder and Chairman. The man himself was even reported to have watched the Widnes game in the midst of the Hull fans in the Threepenny Stand, but whether that is true or not we will probably never know. By Tuesday that week the appointment of Wilby and the injection of his money into the Club was confirmed and everyone including the players, the current Board and Phil Sigsworth hailed it as 'The last piece of the jigsaw' as far as promotion to Super League was concerned. All we now had to do was win our matches. It wasn't exciting times everywhere however, as at Hull KR they were struggling in the hands of the Official Receiver and at Boothferry Park, Hull City was facing a winding up order in the High Court. Hull FC was however going from strength to strength at the hands of a potential 'Messiah', although history was to prove that I should use those words reservedly!

"Boxing Show Ends in Punch Up".........Hull Daily Mail

So read the headline in the Hull Daily Mail after a night of mayhem at Grange Park Hotel in Willerby. That Thursday I had dug out my dinner jacket and patent leather shoes to attend an amateur boxing evening as guest of a local engineering firm. From our ring side table we certainly had a great view of an event that featured boxers from the Kingston Amateur Boxing Club and as the beer was free on our table that night, I certainly had a few, as did Billy who I had taken along as my guest. As the fights unfolded there was some great boxing on view, one in particular was a really 'brutal' affair, after which a lad was led from the ring blood streaming from his nose. Billy, I remember, commented, "It's a lot safer sat out here with a pint and a steak, rather than in there being pummelled!" but how wrong he was about to be proved!

I noticed that at the back of the room family, friends and supporters of the boxers had been allowed to attend in an area separate from the diners. On the next table were a few representatives from Hull City who sponsored the event and the senior officials of the Kingston Club. All was going well until just after the 8th bout when all hell broke loose.

Billy and I had just started on a 6th round of drinks when the trouble began quite innocently. A guy on the Hull City table who had obviously had even more to drink than we had, offered a teenager (who had wondered down from the 'public' area at the back), £5 to pull down the shorts of the young lady who was carrying the 'Round Boards' around the ring. To howls of laughter he obliged, but when he demanded his £5 the guy who had made the bet refused to hand it over. A heated argument ensued between the two, which saw Geoff, the Secretary of Kingston Boxing Club, move in quickly and ask the youth to leave.

Then, from nowhere, a man ran from the back of the room and punched Geoff on the jaw, in waded Reg Lewis the President of North-Eastern Counties Amateur Boxing to try and stop the melee, as another five or six men ran from the back of the room to join in. As shouts for the Police to be called rang out and Billy and I sank onto the floor and under the table to drink our beer in safety, bottles flew across the room and glasses crashed on the table above us. Around us it was like the final scene from 'Blazing Saddles' as dinner jacketed guests rolled around the floor, wrestling with guys in jeans. The Tournament was abandoned, four men and a youth of 15 were arrested and Reg was admitted to hospital with a broken nose. Geoff followed him in the next ambulance, suffering from a dislocated jaw and as we left, the place resembled a 'Wild West' bar-room with broken furniture everywhere and shattered glass crunching under our feet. It was, looking back, an experience not to be forgotten and a night when you were probably safer in the Boxing Ring, than you were in the audience.

The first sign of trouble, but we're blinded by success

Friday 28th March 1997   *Hull 18 – Hull KR 14*

As March progressed our new Chairman started to exert his authority and we were all impressed when Wilby brought in Andy Ireland and Jason Donaghue from Super League Club Bradford Bulls, action that was followed by the appointment of Peter Walsh as Team Manager, something that Sigsworth certainly welcomed at the time. Phil said, "I know Peter well and I certainly need some help and he has an impressive track record". It transpired in the end that few people actually knew Walsh or indeed Wilby very well at all.

I suppose we should have wondered a bit really when as Hull City faced a £240,000 winding up order from the Inland Revenue, Wilby commented that he might be able to 'Bail them out' in exchange for them agreeing to play in a new Super Stadium he had planned for both Clubs. It was a strange comment for someone so new to the City but as fans we just glossed over it as we continued on through the season with a draw at Whitehaven and a good win against Hull KR in the first Derby of the year at the Boulevard.

That game on Good Friday was watched by a superb gate of over 12,000 and the kick-off had to be delayed whilst everyone got into the ground. It was so busy that I only managed to get in thanks to Club Director, Brian Tindall who had been pressed into action as a temporary turnstile operator. The game itself was a strange affair really as Hull completely out-played the Rovers to shoot into a 18-0 half time lead. However in the second half Hull KR wrestled their way back into the game and in the end we were pleased to come out 18-14 winners as we held on to get the two points. As we left the Boulevard that day, some 'Robins' fans had daubed Graffiti all over the wall of the Supporters Club and the legend of 'FC are Shight' said a lot, we all thought, for educational standards over in East Hull.

The first signs that perhaps the Walsh/Sigsworth alliance was not working too well became apparent in early April, when despite us still being unbeaten, Wilby announced a 'Vote of Confidence' in our Coach saying his position was safe, but that it would be reviewed at the end of the season. There were rumours of a rift in the Boardroom, as Peter Tonks came in as Chief Executive to replace the departed Steven Ball, and of a secret financial backer supplying Wilby with the wherewithal to run the Club. Still as I said earlier, success on the field covers a multitude of intrigue off it, and as fans we were just enjoying a great season where we appeared to be sweeping all before us.

Graham Hallas arrived at the Club from Halifax while Peter Walsh was now being talked about as Coaching Co-ordinator. Still, it appeared that an increase in gates of over 1000 on the previous year was impacting on sales in the Club shop. Frank Killeen ex local Ice Hockey player and now Commercial Manager reported that we had sold over 4000 shirts that year, as opposed to the previous season's 500 and this success and Mr Killeen's friendship with Princes Quay Manager Mike Killoran, prompted the Club to re-open a City Centre retail unit in that shopping centre. At that time promotion looked a distinct possibility and business was booming.

A monument to 'Ronno'

After several delays the City Council started work on the Mick Ronson Stage on Queens Gardens with a low key ceremony as Maggie, the guitarist's sister, ceremoniously cut the first piece of turf. She had worked tirelessly for 3 years to ensure that the memory of her beloved brother would never fade and we all agreed that a stage would be a more appropriate solution when compared to a statue. In hindsight the way that the Council has let it fall into disuse since then, dictates that perhaps a statue might have at least survived. The idea was to provide a stage in Mick's memory augmented with some changing rooms and a small Cafe to the rear. The total cost of the structure was around £30,000 which had been raised at the Concert at Hammersmith, from the proceeds of a live album of that event and a big donation from the Japanese group who Mick had produced, Yellow Monkey.

Hurrah for 'Hullywood'!!

It was also around then that I came across a young Film Producer called Mark Thomas. He was based in London but I met him when he asked the Council if we could provide an office and telephone facility from which he could facilitate the fund raising and location setting for a new film he was hoping to make based on John Godber's play 'Up and Under'. I saw this as a great opportunity to bring a lot of exposure, jobs and hopefully cash into the City and so we readily agreed and gave him a small office in 79 Ferensway. He was a nice guy who was very 'Showbiz', spoke about Thompson and Brannah as "Em' and Ken" and who seemed to have an endless procession of guests for meetings in his office.

We even got a visit from actor Tony Slattery, as the casting began in earnest. In the end of course with the exception of the first few scenes being filmed on the Humber Bridge and Hessle Foreshore the rest of the movie was shot in South Wales. This was disappointing but caused by the unavailability of the necessary film processing facilities needed for the Director to see the previous day's work (or the 'rushes') before filming continued next day. Still, the fact that it was by John Godber and based loosely in Hull did the City no harm and at least I got an invite to the Premier in Hull which drew to a close a brief but interesting adventure in Hullywood!

Tevita hypnotises the Robins!

Sunday 8th June 1997   *Hull Sharks 32 – Hull KR 25*

That season had many highlights, none probably more significant than the 40 tries Tevita Vaikona scored in 32 games! This statistic meant that the centre was second highest try scorer for the Club to Jack Harrison who had scored 52 tries some 82 years earlier. In fact in one seven match period Tevita scored 16 touch downs. It was a tremendous record and one that was to get him the title of Division One Player of the Year.

As the season continued Hull had a difficult looking game at New Craven Park against Rovers in early June where the home side were in disarray and their desperate financial position was fuelling more rumours of a merger. Of course on the terraces we were all making our feelings on the subject very clear and anyway we were going well, and undefeated in 15 games, with only a draw tainting an unblemished record. We didn't need a merger! There already appeared to only be two teams (Hull and Huddersfield) in line for the title but Hull KR always proved hard opposition in Derby games. With a normal attendance of around 1000 for home games, the little ground was rocking with almost 6000 people packing the place as the Hull fans completely took over the East Stand. It was to be a memorable match and well before the end the chants of "'O Aah Vaikona, I said O Aah Vaikona" were ringing round the ground and could probably be heard in Withernsea!

Rovers opened up in whirlwind style and were unrecognisable from what Dick Tingle described next day in the newspaper as the "Rag bag outfit of the previous week". They shot into a 7-2 lead and had us on the back foot before over confidence and a couple of silly penalties saw the Sharks storm back. In the 17th minute Hull KR's Stanley Gene was in two minds whether to end a set with a deep kick or a short grubber and in the end he managed neither as a sloppy punt was easily picked up by our full back Steve Holmes. He made ground down field to our 30 yard line, before releasing Tevita who ran a full 70 yards crashing straight through a tackle by Rovers full back Bob Everitt as if he wasn't there. Holmes converted but Rovers charged back from the kick off and within 6 minutes they carved out a golden opportunity. Ex Hull player Rob Wilson hurtled towards our line and looked to be over but the forward was stopped in his tracks by an amazing last ditch tackle by Vaikona and the chance was lost.

Within a minute the Sharks were back as Fisher dummied twice to beat the cover and put Garry Lester in under the posts and four minutes later we were on the scoreboard again this time Fisher swung out a great pass to Vaikona who crashed over the line again, wide out on the right. Then just as we grabbed the initiative the Sharks dropped a couple of balls and Rovers hit back through Wilson. As the second half started another lucky effort when the home side seemed to lose the ball over the line brought Hull KR right back into the game. In the 59th minute it got worse as a mix up in our defence released Bob Everitt who shot in under the posts and after he converted his own try and a drop goal was scored, the scores were reversed with the Rovers leading 21-20.

However Holmes completely out foxed the Rovers' cover with a short kick which he collected to score a simple try on 68 minutes and the conversion put us back in front 26-21. Then in the 77th minute, Stanley Gene seemed to have won the game for the Robins. He set off on a 70 yard run which saw him round Holmes and beat the oncoming cover by arcing out towards the touchline to score. Just one point behind and with the conversion to come we all held our breath as Everitt's kick just slid to the left of the post, but we need not have worried, for it was the Sharks who were to have the last word.

Deep into injury time, with Hull KR desperately trying to get the ball back Peter Wheeler made a great break out from our own half. He ran downfield with all the Rovers cover chasing him before passing onto Holmes who produced a sweet inside pass which Vaikona gleefully took as he strode in for the clinching try. The Rovers' fans protested that Wheeler had been tackled and that the last pass had been forward, but to no avail.

Like all good teams we'd taken our chances when it mattered and we remained in the East Stand singing and dancing long after the Rovers fans had gone home. They had been outplayed on the field and out sung off it. The Hull fans had been amazing that day and goaded the Robins, who had recently won the Rugby League Plate Trophy at Wembley, in cartoon fashion by waving paper plates at them all afternoon.

Shortly afterwards Jim Leatham signed from Leeds and we also signed local 16 year old, Paul Cooke on a two year deal. Mark Hewitt was, I remember, making a big name for himself as one of the games' most accurate goal kickers and probably prompted by these claims Wally Simpson promoted the Simpsons Seafood's Goal Kicking Challenge at half time in the game against Dewsbury Rams on Friday 13th June at the Boulevard. In this former FC favourite and now Bradford Bull star Steve McNamara, top Aussie kicker Ryan Girdler from Penrith and top amateur marksman Dave Roe from West Hull joined Mark in the contest.

Each player had three kicks from the touchline in front of the Threepenny Stand and the only one to kick all three was Hewitt who was crowned the winner and received a cheque for £100. However it was disputable whether it was Mark, or the baiting of the other kickers by the lads on the Threepenny Stand that won the day. McNamara in particular got a real lambasting from the fans which led to him slicing one attempt yards wide. Girdler, on the other hand, simply looked bemused by all the abuse he was getting.

Wilby owns the 'Tiger Sharks' and reveals his mystery backer

Meanwhile Tim Wilby was being hailed everywhere as the saviour of Hull FC and becoming quite a visionary as in an article entitled "Wilby's vision for the City of Hull" printed in the Hull Daily Mail the Editor said,

> *"This time the long term impact will be massive and dramatic as property speculator Wilby is here for the duration and hell bent on making Hull FC great again. Impressive? You bet; Wilby's here to stay. The man has employed in Hull the same attitude that has helped him build up a business empire in Chelsea, where he has 1200 properties".*

Had the 'has' in the last sentence been replaced with 'cleans' it would have certainly been more accurate as it transpired in the months to come that his property business was little more than a 'janitor's room' in a block of flats where he was the caretaker. Still like the Mail, we the fans were all taken in and should have perhaps taken more notice of folks like my pal Kathy. She observed at the time, while he was pontificating in the Bar beneath the New Threepenny Stand after one game, that both Wilby's 'plastic' shoes were split along the seams. Not exactly the hallmark of a millionaire property speculator!

However no sooner had he started talking about building a 'Super Stadium' to house City and Hull FC than he threw the soccer club a life line and 'bought' the ailing Tigers. This prompted another outrageous Hull Daily Mail headline stating "Tiger/Sharks Born as Wilby buys City"

Wilby certainly had us all (besides Kathy) taken in, and even the Leader of the City Council who was a man of great integrity and strong religious beliefs said in the same article, "I am pleased that someone has come in to rescue us in Hull, like John the Baptist, Tim Wilby has come out of the wilderness to help us". Tim was on the outside a suave and sophisticated businessman who was always immaculately dressed in a quality suit. However you can't keep anything secret in Hull and soon the bar at the Punch Hotel was resonating to stories about his claims of a close friendship with George Michael, his rumoured financial backer and him having to be rescued from the Three Tons on an occasion or two when he was allegedly 'mixing it' with rival supporters before Hull City matches. Roy Waudby he wasn't but a lot of folks chose to overlook the rumours, although they were to be in for a pretty rude awakening.

It was then that Wilby announced that his financial backer wasn't George Michael but in fact David Lloyd the ex-Tennis Player, Gym owner and Captain of the British Davies Cup Team. Still who cared where the money was coming from as long as it was coming? In another development we all went down to Brantingham Park the home of Hull Ionians because there, as part of a deal that our Board had done with the Rugby Union Club to loan them our players in the off season, we played our first Academy game against Halifax who we beat 22-4.

The best laid plans............

Saturday 28ᵗʰ June 1997   *Hull Sharks 4 – Featherstone 18*

So as a brilliant undefeated season came to its climax, we just had to beat Featherstone at the Boulevard to gain access to Super League and be 'back up there where we belonged'. We were four points clear of our nearest rivals Huddersfield and the game was seen as a formality for many, although all through the week leading up to it I was, as always, fretting, worrying and fearing the worst. Sky TV billed it as the 'Division One Decider' and the trophy was there ready to be presented to us at the end of the game. Many fans even wore 'We are the Champions' T Shirts bought from traders outside the ground before the game, that fact alone should have told us what was about to happen.

It was to be one of those games when everything went wrong, not just for the Club but also for the fans and Phil Sigsworth. The field had to be painted ready for Sky TV and although we had that all done by the Wednesday, heavy overnight rain rendered it useless and it had to be re-painted with logos etc on the Friday Morning. Then Hull's top try scorer Tevita Vaikona pulled a hamstring in training and was ruled out and as a fabulous gate of 7,100 watched on, it all unravelled on the field too. Steve Craven and Matt Schultz were our best players that day but Featherstone completely out played us and scoring four tries to our one, the trophy was put back in its box, the champagne left on ice and the celebrations put on hold until the next week, when we faced a daunting looking task at our nearest rivals Huddersfield.

Back up where we belong!

Saturday 5ᵗʰ July 1997 Hull   *Sharks 31 – Huddersfield 18*

So we come to the game that for the second week running the media christened 'The Season decider'. Just three years old the McAlpine Stadium was a great sight to see as a crowd of 6,200 made for a reasonable atmosphere in what were cavernous surroundings. The Sharks' fans certainly made themselves heard as the Hull team ran out, led by Captain Andy Fisher and as they emerged from the tunnel each player was patted on the back by our charismatic coach Phil Sigsworth, who was still loved by the players if not by the administration. Phil knew he wouldn't be there the following year but it was credit to him that he stuck at the task knowing that a single win would get us into Super League. I bet the whole of Rugby League held its breath that day as all of the teams in the top Division willed Hull FC, with their massive travelling support, to do well.

I think myself looking back, that Phil had a thing or two to prove that afternoon. However the home team's player/coach, one time Hull FC hero and now the fans favourite 'Judas', Garry Schofield, had claimed in the press all week that they would beat us that day and it looked like his predictions were to come true. After just 3 minutes Huddersfield forward Jon Neill popped out a 'basket ball' pass for Matt Sturm to crash in and then straight from the re start Garry Schofield, (who was getting his usual 'roasting' from us FC fans), shot out a long pass to put Craig Weston through a gap. Weston returned the pass inside as Schofield scored with ease and as he put the ball down he 'gestured' sarcastically to the Hull fans. This really riled us all, although we were at that point starting to wonder if all the hard work over the previous games was in danger of being undone on that sunny afternoon.

The conversion was good and after just 10 minutes we trailed 12-0 and looked to be facing a drubbing. However, we were an honest hard working team galvanised by a strong resolve and Sigsworth's excellent tactics and thankfully the next 70 minutes were a different story altogether. It was the man that iconic radio commentator David Doyle-Davidson christened 'The Mighty Atom', Mike Dixon who started the comeback. Mike got the ball in his own half and exploded in "sensational" style with a darting run into the heart of the defence. He stepped through a gap in the home team's line and found Matt Schultz who charged through a two man tackle and slipped out the perfect pass to Andy Fisher, for our Captain to glide in under the posts to score.

A Mark Hewitt conversion cut the Huddersfield lead to six points and 4 minutes later he was on target again to level the match. This time, from nowhere, Rob Nolan suddenly made a midfield break, the hard working Boyd and Fisher, who were to punish Huddersfield all afternoon, handled quickly to open the gap further and Fisher found Graham Hallas on his inside as the centre ran away from the defence to touch down.

After a rocky start The Sharks' fans were in full song and although a penalty on the 27th minute restored a two point lead for the Giants, the introduction of new signing Brad Hepi from the bench saw our intensity increase. Hepi looked a great buy that day, full of aggression, bite and direction. He took the ball from acting half back, dummied both ways and shot forward before passing onto Hewitt. Mark feigned to go outside, but instead kicked forward with the outside of his boot, the ball came back across the front of the Huddersfield post and as the home defence stood and watched in amazement there was little Mike Dixon to catch it over his head and score on the stroke of half time. Hewitt's conversion made it 18-14 at the break, and we all sighed with relief that having trailed twice, we were now in the lead.

We needed to score first after half time and we did just that. As Gary Lester produced a stunning midfield break, substitute Rob Danby, appeared on his shoulder to take a pass and he in turn produced a deft inside ball for winger Kevin Gray who cut back inside and wrong footed the home team's defence to touch down under the posts. Gray had a try disallowed for a forward pass and it could have been a critical error because shortly afterwards the Giants hit back with a Paul Dixon try from a Schofield pass to reduce our lead to just 6 points. However Hull surged forward and after Hewitt had dropped a goal to stretch the lead to 7 points, we produced probably the simplest try of the afternoon, but the one that to this day, I remember most.

Hepi went on a typical side stepping run after getting the ball twenty yards out from the home team's try line. He wrestled and twisted himself to within five yards of the line, and then got up quickly to play the ball. Lester shot into acting half, feigned to pass one way and then stepped the other, before twisting his way over the line for the winning try. Immediately a 'conger' of Hull fans started to make its way around the empty wings of the seated stand that was allocated to the away fans, as the 2000 Sharks' fans in attendance went wild. Hewitt rattled over the 'extras', I shed a tear and the celebrations began. As the final whistle went coach Phil Sigsworth appeared from the tunnel with a bottle of Champagne and we all enjoyed one of those rarest of occasions in any fan's life; the moment 'you win the big one'.

After the game and as the chants of 'Judas, Judas' rang around the Stadium, Schofield shot off the field without even shaking any of the Sharks' players' hands. I was determined not to miss a moment of that great celebration and stayed until we only had the stewards for company.

It's all starting to look a bit dodgy!!

Sunday 20ᵗʰ July 1997   Hull Sharks 66 – Workington Town 0

"It's all starting to look like a bit of a mess" were the words of one rather astute senior City Councillor, as changes to sport in Hull came thick and fast. Tim Wilby was still very much the front man of the David Lloyd operation and soon appointed Mark Hateley as the new Player-Manager at Hull City. The Sharks faced their last League game already crowned Champions and it was to see an easy win over an already relegated Workington Town, who were in dire financial straits. The highlight was a hat trick by Gary Lester, but otherwise Hull won at a canter. There was a real carnival atmosphere that day with Steve Massam of Radio Humberside taking the microphone on the field and bouncy castles and face painters entertaining the crowd before kick-off. As the game finished Wilby and all the players paraded the trophy round the field and we all looked forward to a 'contrived' eleven game Premiership Competition that was designed to keep the season going until September.

Then came the first 'bombshell' of many, as Wilby and Lloyd announced that Hull City were to leave their Boothferry Park Ground and move into the Boulevard, where new changing facilities, car parking arrangements, segregation, crush barriers and seating was to be installed to bring capacity up to 12,000 and the Stadium in line with Football League requirements. This was to be an interim arrangement until the new 'Super Stadium was complete. The quality of the playing surface at the Boulevard was the main concern and after a hair brained scheme to move the turf from Boothferry Park to the Boulevard was dismissed as "Ridiculous" by Hull City's Groundsman John Cooper, it was decided that he and his staff would work on the Boulevard pitch while our Premiership games were moved to Boothferry Park. Of course Cooper and the rest of the Ground Staff realised that the Boulevard would never be suitable or meet the criteria of the Football League, but things were moving fast.

Siggy signs off as Peter Walsh gleefully takes over

In the week before the Premiership competition started Phil Sigsworth was called in for a meeting to "Discuss his future", the outcome of which saw him resign his position at the Club on 24th July. It was generally thought that Walsh had gradually worked Phil out and Dick Tingle reported in the Hull Daily Mail that actually after that loss against Featherstone a few weeks previously, Sigsworth had taken a back seat.

Steve Crooks, ex player and hero of the late 80's and early 90's returned from Coaching Hull KR to be Walsh's assistant and that was it as Phil left for Australia and we all wondered just what would happen next.

While this was going on Tevita Vaikona who was shortly to smash Garry Schofield's record of scoring 38 tries in a season was honoured by being awarded an Honorary Degree from the University of Lincolnshire and Humberside. Next to leave the Club was ex Chairman Alan Mason who departed after once again falling out with Tim Wilby. Mason complaining at strong arm tactics being used to force things through in the Boardroom while up at Boothferry Park, 'Saviour' David Lloyd was making a starring appearance on the field before a game against Notts County. However it was apparent that Lloyd had arrived to protect his investment and subsequently cuts were being made everywhere.

That Premiership competition was a convoluted affair really but we won our way through to the Final which was a 'Curtain Raiser' game for the Super League Grand Final at Old Trafford. We were easily beaten by Huddersfield on one of those rare occasions when the Club I love were an embarrassment. We lacked any zip or commitment and all our players looked ridiculous, having all shaved their heads for the occasion. At the Boulevard and Boothferry Park things were changing fast as our benefactor was wielding the axe and within days of the season ending, Wilby, Tunks and City Chief Executive Ian McMahon resigned, as Lloyd brought his own men in.

9th/10th August 1997: 600 Japanese tourists, a hotel full of pop stars and 'All the Young Dudes' on Queens Gardens

That summer at work the weekend we had all been waiting for arrived as the City Council's Entertainment Staff and the authority's Tourism team worked tirelessly to ensure the City was ready for the 'Mick Ronson Festival'. The 600 Fans who had travelled from Japan to Hull to support Yellow Monkey (a band Mick had produced and who had championed Mick's music in the Far East), invaded the City and there were young Japanese people everywhere. Every hotel room in the City was full and banners across the streets announced 'Welcome to Hull home of Mick Ronson' in both English and Japanese, whilst guided 'Ronno Tours' were organised and shops throughout the City Centre dressed their windows to celebrate the life of a local hero. I remember wondering just what my old mate from those days at Alderman Kneeshaw Playing Fields some thirty years earlier, would have made of all this fuss; not a lot I'd wager.

The evening before the concert at the Ice Arena I went down to the Trust House Forte Hotel on Hull Marina to meet Maggie to make the final arrangements for that Sunday's Queens Gardens event, that would mark the official opening of the Memorial Stage. I walked across from my office in the Guildhall, entered the Hotel, called her room and settled down on a sofa in the Reception Area to wait for her. Looking round, the place was like a 'who's who' of Classic Rock. Glen Matlock ex of the Sex Pistols and Ian Hunter of Mott the Hoople were stood talking in the Reception, where Steve Harley (of Cockney Rebel fame) was perusing the photographs on the wall, whilst in the nearby bar, I could see Mick Jones and Big Audio Dynamite standing around 'sucking' on a few bottles of lager. In fact by the time that Joe Elliott of Def Leppard had arrived by Taxi, I thought to myself, "This can't be Hull can it?"

That Saturday afternoon several of the same 'stars' could be spotted mooching around Hull, Mick Jones, Glen Matlock and Joe Elliott attended the Bowie/Ronson/Mott themed Record and Collectors Fair in the City Hall where they all bought some keepsakes, while Steve Harley attended a wedding in Doncaster. Meanwhile everywhere in the City Centre from Queens Gardens to the Station Hotel was adorned with dozens of female Japanese tourists holding hands, wearing 'Yellow Monkey' T shirts, chattering in high pitched tones and clicking their cameras.

The concert that night was a memorable event. Although the Ice Arena opened at 7-00pm, more than an hour before that, a queue 'snaked' its way around the building and the first 600 were all Japanese. It was an amazing sight, with one British and four Japanese TV crews outside in the queues capturing the excitement. The only disappointment that night was that the 'Wildhearts' who were scheduled to appear had to pull out. Still Steve Harley came from the wedding still dressed in his tuxedo and played an acoustic rendition of 'Make me Smile' and there were performances by Ian Hunter, Big Audio Dynamite, The Spiders From Mars (featuring Joe Elliot on vocals), The Yellow Monkey, The Rats, Michael Chapman and Glen Matlock to name but a few. It was a great evening.

Afterwards there was a party back at the Hotel and I, as always, had a few beers as the Ronson Family celebrated Lisa Ronson's 20th Birthday, one or two of the younger musicians got drunk, whilst most of the older ones went to bed! None the less everyone arrived at Queens Gardens the next day ready to rock. A covered stage was rigged and sound checked in the morning and as the sun shone down from azure blue skies around 8000 people danced and sang along to most of the artists that had played the night before, plus Eddie and the Hot Rods who had come down especially to play the gig. Most of the artists had either played with Mick or been produced by him and were just there to pay homage.

The highlight was the finale of the afternoon when Joe Elliot fronted the Spiders from Mars and ripped through a set made up of the early 70's David Bowie repertoire including, Ziggy Stardust, 'The Jean Genie', 'Don't Look Down', 'Moonage Daydream' and 'Suffragette City'. The sun got hotter as the whole of Queens Gardens was rocking and the stewards at the front of the stage threw water on the crowd to cool them down.

Then just as we all thought things couldn't get 'much higher' onto the stage strode 'super Cool' Ian Hunter to perform a brilliant version of 'All the Young Dudes' which of course includes that iconic guitar introduction penned by 'Ronno'. Then that was it, the end to a perfect weekend and a fitting celebration of the life of a wonderful bloke. It's a pity that afterwards the City Council let that stage and its surroundings fall into such disrepair and over the years that statue to Mick has been muted, but never come to fruition. After all that hard work by Maggie Ronson and all those musicians to raise the finance for the project, you would have at least thought that the City Council in Hull would have done more to preserve Mick's memory! Some of us will however never forget Mick Ronson.

I have spent some time describing what was for me an almost life defining weekend and one I hope you will forgive me for covering in so much detail. I had struck up a friendship with Mick all those years earlier when we were all gardeners and now I was there helping to manage his Memorial Concert and the dedication of a lasting tribute to a real local hero. In their book about Mick, 'The Spider with the Platinum Hair' the authors 'Weird and Gilly' gave me probably my only real claim to fame. They said, "The Idea of building a permanent stage in memoriam to Mick was that of Pete Allen, Assistant Director of Leisure Services. Pete had known Mick when he worked with him at the Council in the Parks Department all those years ago".

"In the future, everyone will be famous for 15 minutes" said Andy Warhol and I guess that mention is probably my quarter of an hour!

Roy Waudby is back..... and gone again, before we'd had time to be relieved

As the Number One record "The Men in Black" blasted out from everyone's radios (to probably optimise the situation at both West Hull's professional Clubs). We were all relieved and heartened to see Roy Waudby, the 'voice of reason', returning to the Club as Chairman. At the same time a new Chief Executive Michael Appleton was appointed by Lloyd, but Roy only survived 29 days before resigning again, citing the fact that he and Appleton couldn't get on.

Following his appointment Appleton sent a letter to all staff and players warning them that redundancies were possible as the Club could go into liquidation. The letter was marked PRIVATE AND CONFIDENTIAL but that made little difference in Hull and the contents were being announced in the media within hours. The sports scene in the City was in turmoil. Even Hull KR, (who was now in the hands of the Administrators) had two potential buyers, John Stabler and Russell Greenfield, who wanted to disband the Club and move it to York.

"Vaikona goes or I shut the Sharks"

However at the Boulevard at least we had Super League to look forward to, but the fans were dealt another body blow on 25th October when Lloyd announced the sale of our prized possession and fans favourite Tevita Vaikona to Bradford Bulls for a fee of £80,000. Tevita said, "I am gutted and just hope my leaving helps the Club, Hull is my second home after Tonga". Whilst Bradford Coach Matthew Elliott thought it all really funny and added sneeringly, "We can't believe our luck". The remaining (original) Directors at Hull FC, Allen Mason, Brian Tindall and John Adamson all stated that they had not been consulted about the deal and tried through the Rugby League to get the transfer annulled, but it was too late and in The Eagle and all the other pubs and clubs in West Hull we lamented the departure of the fans favourite player. David Lloyd's name was mud.

The Hull Daily Mail next morning found Lloyd in belligerent mood, as its headline read, "Vaikona Goes, or I Shut the Sharks" The three remaining Directors responded by locking Michael Appleton out of the Boulevard, while he retorted by threatening to call an Extra-ordinary General Meeting to throw them off the Board and so, frustrated and stripped of their authority, all three Directors resigned. As fans we watched helplessly and despaired.

We didn't have to wait long before another long diatribe from Lloyd indicated that he was to build his 'Super Stadium' and home for both Hull City and Hull Sharks, on Council land at Kingswood. Roy Waudby, mirroring the fans outrage, fronted the "No to Kingswood" campaign and we were off again! Two days later while I was having a pint in the Manchester Arms in Scale Lane, a petition against Lloyd and his confrontational style was passed around which everyone in the place signed.

This originated from several worried supporters including Jim Gardiner, Shaun Cassidy and Garry Bullock who were doing all they could to take Lloyd on; the excellent fanzine, 'In Any Kinda Weather' which was the only real 'mouth piece' the supporters had, was leading the calls for Lloyd to go. I remember going to a packed fans' forum at the

Charleston Club in Walliker Street where Roy Waudby announced that he would buy back the £195,000 of shares he had sold to David Lloyd as he continued his 'No to Kingswood' campaign. Of course our new owner was to decline the offer, but there were lots of passionate speeches that night, including one from an older member of the supporters who I remember likened Lloyd to an 'Evil Uncle' who had come to the reading of the will to claim everything.

The best....and the shortest firework display the City ever saw

Despite all this intrigue and manoeuvring at Hull F.C. it would be wrong for me to omit mentioning what was an amazing evening down on the Pier Head in Nelson Street, that Bonfire Night. I was responsible for promoting all Firework Displays that the Council staged and we had a good team in place to ensure spectacular and safe displays for the public. That 5th November, (as incidentally an epidemic of nits swept East Hull), there were around 20,000 spectators amassed around the Pier to watch the annual display. Roger, one of our Parks Management staff was trained to fire the pyrotechnics and he'd spent all afternoon setting things up. He had cordoned off the Pier Head and the idea was to ignite several banks of rockets, synchronised with mortar shells fired from twelve inch Cardboard tubes. A metal box was used to house the bulk of the shells which would be lit and dropped into the cardboard mortar tubes as the display progressed.

At 7.00pm prompt, Roger walked through the set pieces on the Pier igniting the fireworks with a lighted torch. Everything started well with a thunderous shower of rockets bursting over our heads, but then things started to go wrong. Someone had forgotten to close the lid of the tin box that contained the rest of the fireworks and a spark flew into it and within two minutes £15,000 worth of fireworks had gone off at once.

Flares shot out at all angles as Roger and the lads could clearly be seen running 'for their lives', back up the Pier. Mortar shells that should have been fired from tubes splashed into the river and squirmed around like demented snakes, Rockets came out at all angles and had several of the crowd ducking as they shot over the heads of those watching over at the other side of the lock pit. Within two minutes it was all over and the crowd applauded loudly, having seen the biggest most spectacular (and probably shortest) display the City had ever seen. Some said, "Is that it then" but most just enjoyed the spectacle, although few knew exactly what had happened. From that night onwards the Council used professional fireworks companies for all their future displays!

As the Deep Submarium finally opened to the public the City was certainly on the up and it seemed locally that the car suspension and exhaust business was the one to be in, as Hull received another national accolade, this time for being the City with the most and highest, speed bumps in the country.

Same old Wigan, always moaning!!!

Across the game of Rugby League, Clubs were struggling and in Super League it was not just the 'usual suspects' that were struggling financially. All the promise and hope that had come with Sky TV money and summer rugby was starting to look decidedly tarnished and as Richard Branson bought London Broncos, Wigan's Chief Executive David Bradshaw stated that they had lost around £1m because of the shift to summer rugby and the increased contract costs, and that the Lancashire Club was threatening to lead a return to playing in the winter. Then, after a poor season in Super League at the end of which they were relegated, Oldham Bears were the first Super League team to actually go to the wall, with many of their players leaving or being grabbed by other teams before it happened.

Lloyd tries to make amends

However on 11th November, after reading yet another 'open letter' from David Lloyd on the front of the Hull Daily Mail, I settled down to watch TV, when the phone rang and it was 'Pearly'. He excitedly asked if I had seen Tele-text (BBC's information service) and as I quickly flicked it on I read, "Hull FC are reported to have captured, International backs Steve Prescott and Alan Hunte and forward Simon Booth from St Helens for a fee in the region of £350,000". I couldn't believe what I was reading because these players were revered names in the game and the mainstays of the very successful Lancashire Club. I continued to flick over to the page all night, just to ensure I wasn't imagining it all, but I wasn't, and although it took a couple of weeks to agree terms with the three players, the deal was done and Lloyd had, at last, put his money where his mouth was.

The season starts with a 'life saving' Derby

Sunday 25th January 1998 *Hull Sharks 48 – Hull KR 6*

In East Hull, Hull KR was struggling to keep going, having been in Administration for months now. In an effort to help them out and to generate some income for Hull FC, the once traditional pre season Derby was re-instated as a Friendly at the Boulevard. The deal was that Hull KR got 25% of the gate receipts from the game plus two of our surplus players, Rob Danby and John McCracken. A good crowd attended and Hull fielded a strong team featuring 11 new signings including recent acquisitions Glen Tomlinson, Jason Temu and Alan Hunte. In a one-sided game Hull won 48-6, Hunte was Man of the Match and at half time on the pitch two youngsters, Craig Farrell and Richard Horne, signed their first contracts. As we all chanted "There's only one team in Hull" and with the Super League season still two months away, things looked better than perhaps they actually were. But wins in local Derbys do invariable make things seem a whole lot more acceptable; they always have done.

In another piece of good news it was announced (after the protestations of John Cooper and the other guys who had been given the task of trying to make the Boulevard a 'Football Stadium') that the idea of Hull City playing there was finally to be dropped, although the prefabricated complex on the front car park in Airlie Street would continue to accommodate the administrations of both Clubs.

Cinemas at war; as I attend a World Premier

After months of Council co-operation, John Godber's film adaptation of 'Up and Under' had at last been completed. John insisted that the Premier be in Hull and a vitriolic public argument then broke out between the Odeon and the UCI Cinemas as to who should stage the glittering event. After a deal of 'mud-slinging' in the local media the Odeon was finally chosen and I dug out my dinner suit and black tie to attend with two of the stars of the film, Adam Foggerty and Tony Slattery, a host of civic dignitaries and a plethora of 'worthies' from the local business community.

At 7-45 that evening John himself gave an impassioned speech, in which he paid tribute to Brian Glover who died after the film had been completed and to whose life 'Up and Under' had been dedicated. Brian was a celebrated, traditional northern actor and at one time a professional wrestler. He was of course the infamous school teacher in the film 'Kes' and I had the honour of meeting him, just once in 1992, in the boatshed on the Marina where he was rehearsing for an open air production of Richard III. During a gap in rehearsals, he was sitting on a pile of timber reading the 'Daily Mirror' and when he spotted me he said "Noo then young fella, arrrm parched, is there any tea?"

After the Premier there was a Civic Reception in the Eclipse Night Club in Anne Street, but I didn't stay long, it was all too 'stage managed' for me really. The film was well received and at the end of its first week's run it was third in the National Film charts behind 'Titanic' and Boogie Nights'. It was also pleasing that the opening credits retained some footage of the Humber Bridge and Skidby Mill, while in closing it thanked Hull City Council for its support.

That March I attended the Club's Annual General meeting at the Ramada Jarvis Hotel at which David Lloyd tried to complete a new share issue which would see our current share value reduced to just 5p and him buy them all up and issue 10 million more. Roy Waudby led the opposition and sent all us shareholders a letter beforehand which recommended that we vote against the move. At the meeting Roy stood up and said, "I am not as wealthy as you Mr Lloyd, but if you withdraw the share issue idea, I will make £250,000 available to the Club"

This brought a great cheer from the floor of the meeting and much throwing of papers in the air. In response Lloyd shouted, "I'm running out of cash fast, back me or I will walk away" before he stood up and stormed out of the meeting. Quote of the day had to go to Richard Marriott, who was sat just behind me. As our owner petulantly marched past him, Richard said, "I believe that's game set and match then Mr Lloyd?"

It was the City AGM that afternoon in the same venue and I believe he fared little better at that one either. On the same day, almost as an aside, we signed Auckland Warriors forward Hitro Okesene.

In the Hull Daily Mail next day, Lloyd again threatened to quit and said of the people of Hull, "You'll always be crap", an observation that went down well with everyone, not least on the letters pages of the same newspaper. So once again, instead of us all harbouring a sense of anticipation and excitement we faced another season with a mixture of fear and disbelief.

Back in Super League, in Sheffield and in trouble!

Sunday 5th April 1998   *Hull Sharks 34 – Sheffield Eagles 24*

It seemed that David Lloyd could do little right, as an announcement that he was talking to Don Robinson about the possibility of relocating Wimbledon, the now homeless Premier League team, to Hull to replace the Tigers, saw Hull City fans in open rebellion. Meanwhile we drove all the way to Whitehaven to watch Hull win in the Challenge Cup before, despite a brilliant performance from Jamie Smith at full back; we were dumped out of the competition 41-10 at Salford. The first game we ever played in Super League was away at Sheffield Eagles and I drove over to the Don Valley Stadium along with another 2000 FC fans on a warm and sunny afternoon.

As the Hull team ran out, led by Alan Hunte, we all wondered what sort of fare was about to be served up. However we didn't have to wait long for an answer, when after just 4 minutes Brad Hepi spotted a gap, went to it and as it closed, released Glen Tomlinson with an inside ball for the number 6 to coast over the line, Hallas converted and we led. We were the pundits firm favourites for relegation and it was not long before Waisle Sovatabua spotted a gap in our line and kicked ahead for the home Club's mercurial scrum half Mark Aston to collect. He ran forward drew our full back Steve Prescott and then released Darren Turner who scooted in for a converted try that levelled the scores. Matt Crowther the Sheffield right wing was a constant threat but on 18 minutes Lester and Tomlinson combined and inter-passed around him before a long speculative ball from Lester landed in the arms of a grateful Steve Prescott who stormed in untouched to grab back the lead.

Five minutes later Sheffield pair Watson and Taewa got in a terrible tangle and while neither seemed to want to pick the ball up, Hallas nipped in and ran on to score our third try. He added a penalty shortly afterwards but when Lester was 'sin-binned' for 'persistent laying on' Sheffield took their chance as Sovatabua scored and a conversion and further penalty for Aston, saw us go in at half time just leading 16-14.

It was certainly important that we scored first in the second half if Hull were to have any chance of regaining the initiative. We got what we wanted after just 3 minutes when a 20 yard 'cut out' pass from Tomlinson found Hunte and he scorched downfield to score a brilliant 55 yard touch-down. Hallas converted to give the Sharks an eight point lead.

Back came Sheffield and a great run by Matt Crowther got them a try, which Aston converted and a further penalty was added when Okesene held the Eagles' Dale Laughton back in the line. With the scores tied at 22-22 it was certainly tense stuff, but on what was to be a rare occasion that year, this was to be our day and when a Tomlinson kick rebounded off Aston, Hallas pounced. Snatching the ball from the turf he drew Sovatabua before presenting Steve Prescott with his second try and as Hallas converted we were six points in front with ten minutes to go.

Aston reduced the arrears with a penalty but the final action was to come from the Sharks.

Superb interplay by Hull which involved Lester (twice), Leatham, Hallas and Johnson, mesmerised the opposition and was finished off when substitute hooker Stephenson powered over and with Hallas again converting, the hooter went and we had won our first game back in Super League 34-24. We all celebrated as a group of lads next to me started singing 'There's only one David Lloyd', which is no doubt something they choose to forget and regret to this day. There certainly was to be 'Only one David Lloyd' and that good start was to last just one more week, when in pouring rain we scraped past London at the Boulevard with a last minute try by Mark Johnson. Steve Prescott was magnificent in defence that day and we stood top of the League after two rounds but it was a sad occasion, as before the game we observed a minutes silence to commemorate the tragic death of local girl Kirsty Carver whose body had been found at Spurn a few days earlier.

That was it really although at times that season we flattered to deceive it was a strange year for me and one where I honestly got closer to losing interest than I ever have in all my life. I can only truly love Hull FC if I honestly believe that the owners, Coaches, Directors and the Players love the Club as much as I do and in 1998 I certainly didn't believe that at all.

There we were running around in turquoise shirts, almost bankrupt, with an owner that changed his mind and his stance 'with the wind' and a load of import and journeymen players who appeared to be 'only here for the beer'. At times in the crowd it was like being in a national convention of pessimists, we had in Sharkey and Shark Boy probably the worst two mascots in the League, and even the most hardened supporter, who thought he had seen it all, was left downhearted and bemused. Of course we all struggled on and kept going, what else can you do when you're in love with your team? But I bloody hated David Lloyd.

Matthew Elliott breathes a sigh of Relief!

Sunday April 26th 1998   *Hull Sharks 24 – Bradford Bulls 26*

Amidst more rumours of a merger, one of our best early season displays was at home to Bradford Bulls where a narrow defeat caused the famed Bradford Coach Matthew Elliott to go into a long post match diatribe about "....how good Hull FC really are" as he genuinely seemed relieved to have left the Boulevard with two points. His fears had been heightened by a storming end to the game, when we almost snatched a point. I don't remember much about the game except that it was televised and that ex FC stalwart Steve McNamara produced the standout moment for me as he seemed to purposely direct a floating pass behind Tevita Vaikona so as to highlight to the TV cameras a home-made banner in the crowd proclaiming, "We're Black, We're White, We'll never Merge with sh*te".

As the tennis balls, in protest against Lloyd's action and suggestions of a merger, rained onto the field, that narrow loss was just one in a run of 8 straight defeats which saw us hit rock bottom. Our Coach Peter Walsh had few solutions and we only started getting the odd win after we had signed Craig Murdoch, a wily scrum half from Wigan, on loan. He made his debut at Halifax along with another signing from Wigan, Steve Barrow and although we all went hoping for a reversal of fortune, after a good start we lost again, this time by 30-16. I remember that Fili Seru and David Baildon scored good early tries but we fell away badly after that.

At work the Leader of the Council had asked me to head up the forthcoming celebrations to honour the 700 years anniversary of the City being granted a Royal Charter (and thus becoming 'Kings Town' upon Hull). I was soon working with Dickie Arbiter and the guys from the Palace again, on the likelihood of a Royal visit and approaching Desmond Tutu about the possibility of him coming to Hull to deliver the annual Wilberforce Lecture. Meanwhile the crazy world of entertainment in Hull continued to amuse us all, as an unholy row broke out when Al Jolson impersonator Clive Baldwin was slow handclapped on the New

Theatre stage because the patrons said he, "Wasn't authentic" because the Council had banned him from 'blacking up' to imitate his hero. It's never dull in Hull.

The 5 O'clock Sauna Club

I was still training three or four times a week at the Trust House Forte Hotel on Hull Marina and every Friday after work I would have a work out and then meet several colleagues in the sauna where we would discuss the week past and generally 'put the world to rights'. Most of the lads were not rugby fans so it was also a blessed escape from my everyday pre-occupation with mergers, David Lloyd and our abysmal season. Council comrades Paul 'Jacko' Jackson and Graham 'Francey' France were always there, as was John a local teacher and Accountant Dudley Moore. These 'regulars' were augmented by a whole host of other itinerant members of the 'Five O'clock Club' who would come and go from week to week. This little gathering gained a deal of notoriety back then and many at the City Council, both officers and elected members, believed that most of the suggestions and initiatives to come from the ranks of the salaried staff the following week, were conceived and developed in that sauna. In reality the conversation rarely touched on serious stuff and was more likely to range from who's hot and who's not (female wise) on the authority, to what we were all having for tea.

(Almost) The 'Great Donkey Derby Disaster'

I mention the '5 O'clock Club' because at that time the Lord Mayor of Hull was Councillor Brian Petch. His year in office was certainly a busy one for all us officers of the Council as he commissioned us to devise a wide and diverse programme of events for his charity appeal. One Friday, somewhere between Joke of the Week and who was 'at it' with who, I remember commenting to the 'sweaty' gathering that Brian wanted to promote a Donkey Derby event for kids at the Cricket Circle that July. It sounded fraught with problems and the staff certainly did their best to pour cold water on the whole idea, but Brian was having none of it.

The Lord Mayor knew someone who had some donkeys and did this sort of thing and so one sunny Sunday afternoon in July, we all gathered at the Cricket Circle to witness the occasion. There were about 500 people there that day and all the kids were invited to take their turn at being jockeys. The guy with the Donkeys who was called 'Cammy' had come up trumps and supplied ten different sets of 'junior' riding silks and a full programme of 10 races was arranged each with a title, while each donkey displayed its name on a badge worn round its neck (no doubt something that remained from its stint on the beach the previous day).

A straight course of about 200 yards was marked out with posts and rope and as the sun beat down the first ten kids, ranging in age from 4 to 10 years old, were supplied with helmets and strapped carefully into their stirrups, so that they couldn't get off, even if they wanted to! The starter dropped his flag and they were off. However the Donkeys didn't seem to get this at all, as two turned and trotted back towards the horsebox and the rest chomped on the grass and didn't move. 'Cammy' had however seen all this before and walking along the backs of each animal in the line, he slapped each in turn, hard on the buttocks. To a rousing cheer from the crowd congregated outside the bar, the frightened animals shot off down the track.

As they reached the finish-line there was a clear winner and another cheer went up from the increasingly inebriated parents and supporters. We had of course overlooked one thing and that was that no one told the Donkeys that it was the finish-line and they just kept going on and on...... and on! They crossed the Cricket ground and as we all stood open mouthed, headed for the old football field beyond. Furthermore what was even more worrying, as the kids looked round in anguish to see where their parents were, was that the Donkeys seemed to be enjoying their new found freedom, and bucked and pranced as the children, now being tossed around like rag dolls, screamed and hung on for dear life. Jacko and I raced off after them and I just caught one lad as he was about to fall sideways out of the saddle, and several others had miraculous escapes as panting parents some still with their pints in their hands arrived at the scene. After that we had a row of parents at the finish line to catch the donkeys as they arrived, but although it provided a real laugh for everyone in the sauna the following Friday, just for a moment, it could have been disastrous! 'Petchy' of course thought it was wonderful and we made a lot of money for his charity that afternoon, but the sight of those kids, disappearing into the distance looking like miniature Rodeo stars, will remain with me forever.

Lee Radford signs a new contract and leaves

There then followed another blow for the fans when the Club lost one of its best young players, local lad Lee Radford, who was being tipped to play International Rugby in the near future. Hull called a Press Conference to announce that the out of contract youngster had signed a new deal at the Boulevard and Radford seemed really happy about it. However a few days later it was announced by the Bradford Bulls that he had actually signed for them. Hull demanded a sight of Bradford's contract and found that it was signed before ours, so in effect Radford had signed for us in the knowledge that he was already a Bradford player, well that's how it was reported at the time anyway.

After they had 'grabbed' Vaikona some 10 months earlier, this incident certainly sent the Hull fans' hopes plummeting again. Operations Manager Bryan Callam said at the time, "We went through all the rigmarole of signing a contract and calling a Press Conference, only to find that Radford had already signed for Bradford". To this the player retorted, "That's all rubbish, I only signed for Bradford a couple of weeks ago and if Hull wanted me, then they should have offered as much as Bradford" The Rugby League were called in, but as usual it made little difference, and it was obvious that Lee had simply followed the money and who could blame him for Hull FC were in a mess.

I was certainly depressed with the state of my Rugby Team and had little appetite for the constant disappointment and turmoil that each day brought. Of course at times like that I want to be like those people I mentioned earlier who can treat their Club like their local take away, in that, when the quality of the fare they are served up becomes sub standard, they take their custom elsewhere, but of course I can't do that where else would I go? As Nick Hornby once said, "For us in the end, the consumption is all, the quality is immaterial".

While all this was happening at the Boulevard, up at Boothferrry Park things were much worse and before the new football season had even started, Lloyd put the Club up for sale. By October he was saying to potential suitors Don Robinson and Tom Belton that the Club was available for £1.5m and announcing that they must, "Buy it or I'll shut the Club, next Monday" and as if to ensure we weren't left out he added as an afterthought, "...... and the Sharks will be sold next!" The City fans went into melt down, as sport in Hull hit an all time low. Still as always there were still some good guys around. One was Chico Jackson, who had played for Hull FC for 12 years and who was to start a benefit year announced that he would give half of the money collected to his adopted Charity, 'The Dove House Hospice, so it was great to see that there was still some humanity about in Sport in the City.

Lloyd reaches for his cheque book and there's a bit of hope for the future

Finishing 9th in the table in our first season in Super League was I suppose something that we should have been celebrating had we all not been preoccupied at trying to best guess what our owner would do next, as David Lloyd sold Hull City to a consortium made up of West Yorkshire businessmen. As their new Chairman Tom Belton took over at Boothferry Park, Hull FC fans looked for some closed season activity in the transfer market. We didn't have to wait long before the Club signed Matt Calland, the ex England centre from the Bradford Bulls and Karl Harrison, hero of the 1991 Premiership Final victory, returned from a seven years spell at Halifax. These two were quickly followed by the capture of Rob 'Two Bobs' Roberts and Andrew Purcell. These were all good acquisitions and although we lost the services of scrum half Glenn Tomlinson to Wakefield, the further addition of Steven Holgate from Wigan gave our squad a much more balanced look and for a few weeks at least we had new heart and an appetite for the forthcoming season. Such is the lot of the fanatical fan, we are always optimistic between seasons, but as so often then happens, how ill founded our hopes were to be proved.

Chapter 9

Selling 700 shirts in two hours!

The fact that we had survived a season in the Super League and that Hull KR were continuing to struggle across the River made for a Happy Christmas that year. David Lloyd was keeping a low profile and Chief Executive Brian Callum and newly 'reinstated' Chairman, David Kirkwood, seemed to be able to secure the cash needed to make signings. The team looked a lot stronger than the one that had finished the 1998 campaign, conceding almost 180 points in the last 6 games and our faith in what was happening at the Boulevard was further consolidated when it was reported that we had turned down a £30,000 bid for winger David Baildon.

On Tuesday 15th December, I left the Guildhall at lunchtime to attend the Princes Quay Shopping Centre where Hull FC launched their new kit. It had been designed by a fan through a competition in the local newspaper. It was great to see about 1000 supporters crammed into the Central Atrium and I watched with Chris Davidson and Alan McGlone, two of the Club's heroes from the 60's and 70's. Everyone was delighted to welcome the return of a shirt that embraced the irregular hoops and sported the logo of JWE who had paid a record amount for the sponsorship. Vince Groak from our seminal fanzine 'In Any Kinda Weather' commented, "At last we look like Hull FC again" and he was right!

The players, wearing the new strip, descended the escalators to a resounding cheer that broke into a hearty chorus of 'Old Faithful' and within two hours the initial supply of 700 shirts had sold out. When you add to that, the fact that the Club were selling around £5000 worth of season tickets a day, it was easy to see how I and many fans thought we had at last turned the corner and perhaps better times were on the way.

Hull 700; Celebrating the Past, Pioneering the Future

Friday 5ᵗʰ March 1999   *Hull Sharks 6 – Wigan Warriors 56*

Throughout these ramblings I have tried to reflect my career at Hull City Council. This had started with my recruitment as an apprentice gardener and more by good luck than good management I was now in the heady position of Head of Entertainment, Events, Design and Marketing. Quite how I got there is anyone's guess, including mine. As the City prepared to Celebrate the 700ᵗʰ anniversary of the granting of the Royal Charter, I was tasked by the Leader of the Council, Pat Doyle, to head up the celebrations and provide events to complement the landmark year.

We put together a steering group that included the Bishop of Hull, various local industrialists, the Editor of the Hull Daily Mail, the President of the Chamber of Trade etc and despite a limited budget we promoted around 100 events throughout the year. With two Royal visits, open air lectures and historical re-enactments, it was certainly my biggest test so far and the fact that I was only able to employ one additional member of staff, Lou Howard, the Festival's Community Director, meant that I needed to inspire and motivate the rest of the local authority and the people of the City to do the rest. If ever my love of Hull FC was put on 'the back burner', this was that time and the pressure of delivering the festivities meant that I missed one home game and seven away fixtures that season which proved in the end, to be a blessed relief.

New Season and a new hope, (there's nothing new there then!)

Sunday 17th January 1999   Hull Sharks 20 – York Wasps 20

It was certainly a seminal year in my career however I make no excuse in the next few dozen pages, for relating in detail what was a historic and almost catastrophic year for Hull FC. It started so hopefully, with big signings and those record shirt and season ticket sales, only to end with my beloved Club peering over the abyss at extinction.

There was certainly no shortage of supporters attending the Boulevard on 17th January, when we faced York in our first pre season game. However despite a plethora of new names and a deal of hype around the place, we could only draw 20-20 with the team from the bottom division and that only after being rescued by a stunning performance in the snow, from Chico Jackson, who was now in fact a part-time player. I remember that day thinking that the players looked over-weight and under skilled, as they did a week later, when we were beaten at home on a frozen pitch by lowly Dewsbury, 14-10. It was pretty chaotic off the field as well and a pre season 'Bonding' trip to Majorca had to be cancelled when Peter Walsh couldn't get his passport back from Immigration. Already the hope and hype of pre-season was draining away and it was business as usual at the Boulevard.

As we signed Martin Hall, the Wigan hooker on a two year deal and Simon Cawkhill took over as our Commercial Manager, things were already falling apart and a third 'Friendly' saw another defeat, this time at Sheffield Eagles. However 28th March 1999 was a significant day for our Club which went by almost un-noticed, as at the Guildhall the first meeting of the Super Stadium Project Board took place to make the first tentative steps toward the City building its own Sports Stadium. The group included Ian Blakey as Chairman, Pat Doyle, former local Olympian Pam Piercy, Hull FC Chief Executive Brian Callum, City Chairman Tom Belton and John North, Head of Industrial Development at the Authority. It was certainly a weighty body that was some four years later, to deliver a dream.

Meanwhile the Sharks first League outing saw a real drubbing at Wigan when the home side scored 11 tries as after a bright first ten minutes, we fell apart. The patience of the loyal travelling supporters, who had made the trek to the JJB Stadium was severely tested and next day, following our protestations and booing at the end of the game, the Hull Daily Mail headline read "Hull Fans are Insane". This was a quote of what Hull Coach Peter Walsh had said at the post match press conference and it whipped up such a storm amongst the fans that he had to publicly apologise about it later in the week.

Still, Hull 700 was going well as we hosted 'Question Time' at the City Hall and welcomed The Duke of York to the City on Charter Day, 1st April. His was a flying visit and after attending a packed 'Charter Service' at Holy Trinity Church he spent time talking to the thousand or so residents that had gathered in the Market Place outside the Church to listen to a relay of the service.

"Down with your Trawlers". Is there any wonder 'We all hate Leeds!

Friday 16th April 1999   *Hull Sharks 18 – Leeds Rhinos 22*

At the start of that 1999 season Hull Sharks went 12 games in all competitions without a win. In fairness at times we did play some good rugby and several games were settled by narrow margins. We lost 8-3 to the Bradford Bulls at home, 12-10 to the London Broncos away and then 23-21 to the Sheffield Eagles at the Boulevard in a Rob Roberts inspired performance where we were really unlucky. There was an occurrence of note at half time in that London Bronco's game on Friday 2nd April 1999, when a couple of young players were signed to great ceremony on the pitch, one of them a 15 year old half back from Myton Warriors called Kirk Yeaman, was destined to become a real hero in future years. Next we went to Headingley on 16th April where Leeds narrowly defeated us in a great game that I watched from the South Stand and where I witnessed youngster Richard Horne making his debut at full back.

Aged 16, Richard, for whom Hull had just turned down a Wigan bid of £25,000, was the youngest ever player to make his debut for the Club.

Two other youngsters Craig Poucher and Richard Fletcher also made their debuts that day in a fine 'backs to the wall' defensive performance. It was a sizzling game, played in front of a thrillingly rowdy crowd, in a Stadium where the excitable, razzamatazz of the 'Sky' machine had been a recurring theme for several years.

However the over exuberant home fans certainly disgraced themselves when they started singing "Down with your Trawlers, you're going down with your trawlers" on what was the day after the latest report on the 'Gaul' tragedy was published. This action prompted comments in the national press next day and letters to the Hull Daily Mail. There was a deal of self control from us Sharks' fans that day and there is little doubt as to why over the years since then much animosity has prevailed between the two Clubs. However in the end we were still defeated, Leeds got the two points and Hull Sharks remained rooted to the foot of the Super League table.

Things get worse...........and the tennis balls are back!

Then David Lloyd, who had been quiet for a while, again became the centre of attention as rumours swept the City that he was about to put Hull FC into administration and/or sell it to South Yorkshire businessman David Caddick. When asked about this by Dick Tingle of the Hull Daily Mail, Lloyd was (as usual) not available for comment, but Chief Executive Bryan Callum said antagonistically, "I speak to David Lloyd every day and I know nothing about this at all. Who do you think is buying Hull FC, Alice in Wonderland?" They were certainly tough times for us committed fans as by that time things were getting 'curiouser and curiouser'.

The month ended with local Chris De Burgh impersonator Ian Moore winning the popular TV show 'Stars in Their Eyes', Hull FC bottom of Super League, the Tennis balls reining onto the pitch in protest everywhere we played and Coach Peter Walsh animating what everyone else was thinking by declaring "My job is on the line". Despite Hull 700 providing a massive year of celebration in the City of Kingston upon Hull, at the Boulevard Hull FC was in utter turmoil. Even the mascot 'Sharkey' was in dispute with the Club, being sacked and then mysteriously re-instated a week later and the only thing that was consistent at our beloved Club was the fact that we always lost!

Injuries didn't help either with Steven Holgate out for the season there was little hope of recent casualties Martin Hall or Matt Calland getting back for months either. We were all so despondent, so much so that even the hardiest of us fanatics, were 'picking our games' away from home. Still as always we were driven on by our unrequited love for our team, although that was something that seemed to have been lost completely on our owner. A predictable home defeat to Saints, which was marked by Paul Cooke's debut and a Man of the Match performance by Paul King followed and then amidst rumours that David Lloyd had said that, should we be defeated at fellow strugglers Wakefield, then Peter Walsh would go, The Sharks actually managed to get their first two points in the 1999 competition. We all travelled to the game expecting to see the back of our Coach and instead witnessed a scappy 29-22 victory of which I have few memories besides the incessant singing of the Hull contingent in the crowd. As it meant that our Coach kept his job I guess I have to admit to being disappointed to win that day, however it was a short rest bite because having gone 12 games without a win we were destined to struggle through another 10 before we saw another victory.

By mid May, after another defeat this time at Gateshead Thunder, Bryan Calum was appealing for the players to play for the Coach because, "His very existence at the Club depended on it". However despite the players coming out with a vote of confidence in Walsh, the following week we were defeated by Castleford at home in front of just 4,500 fans. Even Steve Roberts and the guys at our Fanzine 'In Any Kinda Weather', who had supported Peter Walsh, turned on him and declared that it was time for a change and headlines like "Shambolic Sharks" in the Daily Mirror, at last prompted Calum to suspend Walsh. Sadly just from the Club rather than the rafters of the Stand!

It transpired that amazingly our Coach had no written deal with the Club and was working under a verbal contract he had made with David Lloyd. As Sam Goldwyn's famous quote that, "A verbal contract is not worth the paper it isn't written on" came to mind, Walsh was sacked that Wednesday. We had a single victory to our name, gates dipped below 4000 and all hope of anything but relegation into the lower Division had long since disappeared. The names of several potential Coaches like Neil Kelly at Dewsbury and Lee Crooks (who publicly pleaded to be given a chance), were touted around by the fans, but possibly because of diminishing resources the Club swiftly installed second team Coach and ex Hull KR supremo Steve Crooks in a 'Caretaker' capacity. Although he faced a daunting task, it was to prove an inspired appointment. Bryan Calum had obviously had enough by this time and walked out of the Club, to be replaced as Chief Executive by Brian Johnson.

While all this was going on, David Lloyd who still owned Boothferry Park as well as the Boulevard refused, in a very public argument, to sell the football Ground to the new City owners Nick Buchanan and Stephen Hinchcliffe. Instead he insisted on only working with ex City Chairman Tom Belton who the two afore mentioned City Directors had just sacked. At the Council we knew that Lloyd was aiming to try and buy New Craven Park from a beleaguered Hull KR, sell all three grounds to firstly pay off his debts and to then try and build a new Super Stadium to house all three teams with what was left.

To cut costs Steve Crooks immediately released injured players Hall and Calland and in a game against Salford at the end of May he played two Hull youngsters Paul Cooke and Richard Horne together at half back for the first time. Meanwhile at the City Council the Stadium Project Board were appointing project consultants to look at potential sites for a Council owned Arena and on 3rd June Kingston Communications the City's own Telephone Company that was part owned by the Council, was floated on the stock exchange.

Probably one of the biggest days in the history of Kingston upon Hull

In a career at the City Council that spanned 37 years there is little doubt about the one day that I will always remember as being, I guess, the pinnacle of my career. 1999 was, as I said before, the year that I headed up the City's Hull 700 celebrations with no time for days off or holidays at all. The zenith of those celebrations was without doubt 4th June when the Queen and the Duke of Edinburgh visited the City. However in an attempt to get more impact in the national media we included on the same day, arguably one of the world's most influential civil rights campaigners, Archbishop Desmond Tutu.

Months earlier we had sent a speculative invitation requesting that he consider delivering the 5th Wilberforce Lecture in the birthplace of the slavery abolitionist and to do it outdoors on Queens Gardens. Back in 1998 when we suggested a combined event it seemed a good idea but as the day drew closer and I spent all my time with representatives of the Palace, Special Branch the bomb squad and the local constabulary, I wasn't so sure.

On a cloudy 4th June, the Queen arrived on the Royal Train at Paragon Station and made her way by car to Holy Trinity where a row of Civic dignitaries, (with me on the end), were presented to Her Majesty; I don't remember much about it really, except for the fact that this time I at least managed to bow without falling over. After the service, at which the Queen had presented Desmond Tutu with the Wilberforce Medal, there was a walkabout amongst the thousands that had gathered in the Market Place. Those crammed against the barriers to get a glimpse of the Royal Party were of course unaware of marksmen positioned out of site on the surrounding roof tops as I walked in front of the Royal Party with two representatives of MI5. We led them through the newly refurbished Indoor Market, (where the Monarch declined a gift of a cabbage), and back to their cars to head off for lunch at the Guildhall. That was a fine affair when we were all organised into groups in the Reception Room to meet the Royal Party. Afterwards the Duke went off to the Daily Mail and the Queen went up to Bransholme to inspect the new Garths

Development before they left together and we switched our attention to preparing for the Lecture on Queen's Gardens. The Wilberforce Lecture Series was the brainchild of Councillor Colin Inglis who appeared to be as nervous as I was about the whole thing and just about smoked himself to a standstill that afternoon. We started the evening's proceedings in warm sunshine with a set of songs from Labi Siffre, before Desmond Tutu, a man of great presence, humility and humour, took to the stage.

On a normal day Queen's Gardens was invariably a safe haven for those lucky folks who seem to be able to afford to sit on the grass all day, drinking Cider and shouting at passers-by and so the possibility of some ill informed heckling was always at the back of my mind. However despite almost 3000 attending, a stunning silence fell over the crowd as he spoke for around 30 minutes about the alleviation of World debt and his beloved South Africa. I sat with him before he went onto the stage and he joked about his hotel and the train journey from London before treating me to a parable about the difference between the grass on the Velt in South Africa and that in Hull on Queen's Gardens. I was much too preoccupied to really appreciate what he said then but afterwards I think he was intimating that the grass was like the people of the two countries, and although they are continents and cultures apart, they are in essence exactly the same. However it all went right over my head because by then my brain was totally addled.

It was career wise, a life changing day and I guess I apologise for the detail in which I have described it here. However I do look back with some pride on what we achieved that day and that year in general because lots of people came away with fond memories, while nationally we made a lot of people sit up and take notice of the City of Kingston upon Hull.

David Lloyd; 'the louder he talked of his honour the faster we counted the spoons!'

While all the headlines in the local press spoke of celebration and merriment, on the inside pages David Lloyd's very public dispute with just about everyone raged on unabated. He even made an official bid to

Receivers 'Price Waterhouse' for the purchase of New Craven Park and threatened to close all three local grounds if he was not allowed to build a Stadium. This challenge however thankfully came to nought as the East Hull ground was sold to the City Council and the Game Group who duly leased it back to Hull KR. Every week it seemed there was a change of direction from our owner as far as Hull FC was concerned. Talk of rescue packages was everywhere and a consortium of ex players led by Alan McGlone came up with a scheme by which 500 people were asked to come forward with £2000 each to buy out David Lloyd. This got off to a good start with ex players like Johnny Whiteley, Mally Walker, Tony Dean, Brian Hancock and Len Casey all pledging their support, but of course it was impossible to sustain that interest amongst the rank and file of the fans and with only 40 people coming forward, nothing more was heard of it.

We were as fans totally dejected and not surprisingly crowds continued to decline. Attendances at home games were now below the level of season ticket sales and a game against Huddersfield, where both Steve Prescott and Craig Murdock were stretchered off the field, attracted just 4,066 fans. Worse was to follow with an attractive televised game at home to Leeds (who were unbeaten for 11 games and which after we had led 18-10 at one point, we lost 26-18), drawing just 3,522 spectators. The terraces looked terrible on the TV, with most of us sitting down for the duration of the game while even the 'jocular' posturing of commentators Mike Stevenson and Eddie Hemmings couldn't mask a complete lack of atmosphere. With season ticket sales reported to be around 4,200, as we looked around the stadium that day, it was obvious that even people who had invested at the start of the season, were now staying away.

Still one of the only plus points for us long suffering fans was the amount of young players Steve Crooks was forced to promote to the first team and on 16th July, Richard Horne, one of our great hopes for the future, signed a professional contract at the Club amidst rumours of interest from Leeds, Bradford and Wigan.

Making the headlines again, as the players go on strike

Wednesday 4th August 1999

Hull Sharks – 12 Gateshead Thunder 40

Several of our players were on wages of £80,000 per year and by the end of July with falling gates, Lloyd was obviously running out of both patience and cash. In an unprecedented move he capped all the wages to £2,000 per month which in essence affected around 11 players, who were not amused at all. The playing staff then announced in the local newspaper that they were contemplating going on strike. They threatened this action for two games that week against Gateshead and Halifax, and with the national media 'camped' on the Boulevard Car Park, a meeting involving Maurice Lindsay of Super League, Abi Ekoku from the Players Union, Hull Sharks and the players themselves was convened. Lloyd and Calum didn't turn up but joined Brian Johnson in a three way telephone conversation and after two and a half hours the situation was resolved and the games went ahead. Just 3,200 turned up for the Gateshead Thunder match which was played in an eerie silence. I remember, as I left the game envying the mobility and strength of the newly created Gateshead team and thinking how good it would be if we ever had a group of players like that.

Mergers are back and this time the Rugby League means business

As the fans kept the faith as best they could and rallied behind the fanzine 'In Any Kinda Weather', Chief Executive Brian Johnson seemed to accept defeat and announced that "The drop out of Super League would not be a bad thing for the Club". While in a final desperate move the Ex-Players Association, the Black and White Association and the Vice Presidents got together to fund the purchase of Ian Pickervance from the Huddersfield Giants. He was a big rangy ex International second rower and although the move was a worthy effort by all concerned, to us lot on the terraces it was all too little, too late.

Then, in late July, just as we all thought things couldn't get any worse the shortage of money across the Super League in general saw a 'secret' behind 'closed doors' meeting of all the member Clubs and the Rugby League take place in Leeds. After this meeting some very worrying rumours were starting to emanate from Rugby League headquarters which implied that should Hull and Rovers combine, then over £1m would be made available for the new Club. In fact in reality, when all was revealed a few weeks later, the deal was that "Should any two Super League Clubs merge before 30th September 1999 then they would get £1.25m for the new Club, or towards paying off the debts of both the participating Clubs, but after that date, the deal would remain 'on the table' but the payment would drop to £1m". In addition the administrators had also introduced a new 'points' scheme to rate grounds, financial suitability and youth development which was, I guess a crude forerunner of the licensing scheme, introduced almost 10 years later. As the more artistically minded members of the 'FC Army' were pinching their mothers bed sheets to make "No to The Merger" banners in time for the upcoming Halifax game, you could almost hear David Lloyd salivating at the prospect of getting this unexpected handout. Of course as fans we were going to fight this proposal but how to do it was a question that no one seemed to be able to answer.

A 'Lazarus like' comeback makes Steve Crooks a hero!

Sunday 8th August 1999   Hull Sharks 24 – Halifax Blue Sox 21

On the field we had managed to scrape another two wins at the Boulevard against Salford and Wakefield but with just 3 wins in 27 games, the bookmakers had stopped taking bets on us being relegated, with only Wakefield and Huddersfield anywhere near us at the bottom of the Super League table. Steve Crooks had decided to rely on the enthusiasm of the young players at the Club and we certainly had some real prospects (Parker, King, Poucher, Cooke and Horne) who had certainly taken their chances to replace a few of the 'Roll over and Die' brigade I have always hated at my Club!

That Sunday, as we clambered to get our copies of the Fanzine which was fast becoming the clarion call for the 'revolution', a sort of picket of banner waving fans had formed across the car park. We were to face an in-form Halifax side, while still smarting from an embarrassing 74-16 humiliation at St Helens, which was the biggest defeat in the Club's long history.

I attended the game after carefully planning a week in Tenerife between fixtures and Hull 700 events. Coming home from holiday that same morning, I remember the aircraft descended through the thick Manchester clouds as a feeling of despondency and gloom gradually enveloped me too. After 7 days of sea, sun and sangria it was with a heavy heart, that I dumped my cases and made my way straight to the Boulevard.

That's the problem you see, in those situations you don't want to go, but you can't stay away; the greater the adversity the more you have to be there. There's always a chance of a win, but the banners and chanting outside before the game made me realise that in general, hope was running out fast. Just 3,400 other fanatics were there that day, as the crowd at the Airlie Street end, totally disillusioned, sat on the terracing and didn't even get up when the teams ran out.

It was one of those rare games when, because of other folks still being on holidays, the uncertainty of my arrival back and a lot of the casual crowd having already run out of patience, I found myself on my own, sat there in glorious isolation on Bunker's Hill as the drizzle started to fall. After about 20 minutes everything was 'going to plan' and we were 18-0 down. I had moved from my 'Lucky Step' at the Airlie Street end, to the Threepenny's, in part to shelter from the rain, but mostly to see if a new viewing point would bring a change of luck. Already the visitor's props Broadbent and Mercer were dominant, whilst as usual, exiled 'local lads' Hodgson and Pinkney had scored their annual 'Boulevard' touchdowns.

At half time I was so frustrated and angry, I left the Threepenny's, collected a burger from that awfully nice lady in the little caravan, who had the bouffant hairstyle and those unforgettable black fingernails, and went and stood on my own on the sparsely populated terracing at the Gordon Street end. There was only the Best Stand left now! I just wanted to grieve on my own, if we lost this one we were down, and that first half had been like sitting at the bed side of an old friend, watching helplessly as he slowly slipped away.

I remember at the start of the second half Halifax's Mercer barrelled in for another try, only to be pulled back by the referee for a 'double movement', but they converted a penalty, while amidst chants of "You're on the P*ss", from the Threepenny's Hull's Michael Smith dropped the ball twice, when it appeared easier to score and it was little different to the first half, as Halifax piled forward again. Then, after 60 minutes things started to change. Logan Campbell 'fed' young Richard Horne who went over in the corner and 'Two Bobs' Rob Roberts added the goal. Before we could even talk of this being a consolation try, Hallas stole the ball and sent Gary Lester flying away on a 60 yard run for Steve Craven to score our second. All of a sudden the tiny gathering of 'pilgrims' was sounding more like a 'proper' crowd and I hurried back to the 'New' Threepenny's to join in the fun. Our excitement was tempered when Halifax's Holroyd dropped a goal, but soon after that Michael Smith actually caught the ball before stumbling over the line on his knees and amazingly we were just three points behind!

Then, of course, as always happens when you're down and there's a glimmer of hope, the unbelievable and then the inevitable happens to extinguish it. Firstly, with just two minutes left, Richard Horne belied his years to brilliantly kick ahead, collect and score, we went barmy before of course, Referee Connolly disallowed the try. Why? Well to this day I'll never know, but that was it, or at least it should have been. With just seconds to go Horne took a ball from a scrum, kicked a desperate up and under and Graham Hallas somehow got underneath it, to cruise through a gap and over the Halifax line, 'Two Bobs' goaled and we were victorious 24-21. It was an amazing scene, we'd not won anything but 2 points and a game against the ridiculously named Blue Sox and we were not even safe from relegation, but women danced, children screamed and grown men wept!!

I remember years afterwards my pal Kathy said that by that time all her family had given up hope and so she, like me, attended by herself. At the end she was so overcome by the drama of it all, she searched desperately to find someone to dance with and hug. At half time the win seemed impossible! The question is of course was it all down to my constant moving around the ground or was that perhaps a lucky burger? Well I'll never know, but years later I asked Steve Crooks about that game and he told me that he can never ever remember shouting at a team like he did that day in the half time break, and that most of what he said was totally unrepeatable.

The next few games were 'business as usual' and as the banners were unfurled and the local shops sold out of tennis balls, we lost by a big margin to Castleford, Bradford, Wigan and London, luckily however Huddersfield who were now also marooned at the bottom of the table, couldn't win either, but as the last game approached they were still two points above us in the table. It all came down to a final round showdown that was to determine our survival in Super League and the very existence of Hull FC.

Happy days are here again...well almost!!!

Sunday 12th September 1999
Hull Sharks 33 – Sheffield Eagles 16

Throughout the week leading up to that history defining game I'd been tense and listless, unable to concentrate on work, with my head full of thoughts about that last, desperate, 80 minutes which would decide our destiny. All I wanted was a Club to support the following Monday morning. As far as closing the Club down was concerned David (the Fat Lady) Lloyd, (despite the offer of £1000 a man win bonus), had not exactly started to sing but he was certainly clearing his throat. The thought that perhaps the very existence of Hull FC depended on just one game of rugby haunted my waking hours, as did the Hull KR fans in the Guildhall, who came looking for me, verbally 'rubbing their hands' in anticipation of our demise.

In fact that week I probably dreamed about it too, because that's just the way I am at times like that. I certainly woke up in a cold sweat at 3-00 a.m. that Sunday morning, with the sheets round my neck and commenced to have a good worry about the day ahead. I knew from my contacts in the Council that Lloyd had said in several meetings that if we didn't stay up, then he would walk away and as I couldn't reveal this knowledge to anyone, having to bottle it up made it even more difficult to cope with.

We had a lot of injuries too. The previous week we had lost to London and witnessed a bizarre incident when Bronco' Dom Peters had run the width of the pitch, side-stepping referee Nick Oddy on the way, to smash Hull's Steve Craven on the jaw and depress his cheekbone. We had also lost Grahame Hallas who had missed the game in London because of a couple of "Dodgy meat pies" and was then expelled from the Club after allegedly having a slanging match with Steve Crooks at training.

In addition things were further complicated by the fact that the actual drama was left to the 'bitter end' with the game being staged on Sunday night, so as to run concurrently with a critical televised game over at the McAlpine Stadium. Earlier that week the Club had moved the kick off time when Sky announced that they were to broadcast the Huddersfield v Castleford game, which, had we played at our pre arranged 3-15pm kick-off, would have left our nearest rivals knowing exactly what they had to do to survive. There in West Yorkshire, whatever happened at the Boulevard, the other basement club only had to win or draw to survive. So the equation was quite simple really; we had to win and Huddersfield had to lose.

Throughout the day as the clock crept round and counted down to the match, I played those stupid games that had haunted me for years, like the one where I tell myself, "If the next car to come round that corner is a blue one, we'll avoid relegation, but if it's a green one we've had it" (I always choose green because there aren't that many green cars about, however it's surprising how many you encounter when you play that game). It was in these most frenetic of circumstances, that I partook of a pint or three of 'Dutch Courage' in the Eagle before the game. In the pub that Sunday tea time I remember that the crowd resembled a family gathered to have a quick beer, before they went off to the funeral of an old friend. Few could be found that offered any sort of odds on Hull winning, with even fewer backing a Huddersfield defeat to Castleford. We had lost so many games, accrued so many injuries and had our fill of David Lloyd's threats, mood swings and posturing. We were all numb and totally convinced that we would never ever see anything that resembled a bit of 'good luck' ever again.

So, it's safe to say everyone felt that we were doomed, but as at any funeral gathering, we were determined to do our bit to honour the occasion and if it were to be the last rights of the Hull Sharks then we would give our 'loved one' a good send off, full of passion, pride and fighting spirit.

The 'FC Army' were not to be found wanting that night. As I left the pub an urchin dressed in a Hull KR shirt shouted, "Good Luck" and as I smiled, he added, "You'll need it". Typical, I thought and wouldn't we say the same, were the circumstances reversed? As we took up our place on the now famous 'lucky step' at the Airlie Street end of the ground suddenly, as if someone had blown a whistle or dropped a chequered flag, the whole place was alive, it was just like the 'Glory Days' all over again, I couldn't remember the last time I had experienced an atmosphere like it. Garry watched the game with a radio tuned to Radio Leeds pressed to his ear, from which he would provide a constant running commentary of what was going on over in West Yorkshire. What a cauldron of emotion the 5,437 'Faithful' created that night. If it hadn't been in such dire circumstances, l would have loved it, but although I chanted and sang (and even booed as Sheffield came out), I knew that like me, no one was smiling and that we'd all experienced a torrid week and an endless Sunday which had now culminated in a final 80 minutes of destiny deciding rugby. It was, after all those years of fanatical support, my Club's 'High noon' and we just had to win.

Sheffield had already beaten us twice that year and as they kicked off I felt physically sick. In the first set of six, twice Michael Smith crashed into ball carriers Steve Molloy and then Simon Baldwin, leaving both the Eagles players laid out on the turf. Then after just two minutes Rob Nolan, playing his last game for Hull FC, took the ball, dummied to the left and released Lester on his right. As the crowd roared the diminutive number 7 brilliantly zipped inside, then back out again and evading the grasping arms of Mark Aston he flew in to score. The ground rocked as Garry reported "Still 0-0" and we watched as Steve Prescott converted from a narrow angle. At 6-0 a nervously subdued chorus of 'Old Faithful' radiated across the terraces and slightly after that score, Sheffield's Mick Slicker dropped what looked like an easy pass and as we regained possession from the scrum we saw a really memorable moment of action.

Paul King our young hooker, who was tackling everything and timing some great passes from acting half back, got the ball in the line and released rangy prop Pickervance. Ian roared onto the ball, before curving into a gap in the defence and going off on a 30 yard run to the line. His progress went into 'slow motion' as the chasers gained on him, but in the end he just got there for a wonderful touch-down.

Shortly afterwards, before Sheffield could get the ball back, Logan Campbell had scorched down the wing in front of the New Threepenny Stand to be stopped by a high tackle from the Sheffield full back Dave Watson. Stuart Cummings, the referee, immediately gave a penalty which Steve Prescott dispatched between the posts to further increase our lead. We cheered every pass and tackle until Garry said, "4-0 to Huddersfield" and my heart sank and as the news transmitted itself across the crowd like an unwanted infection, worried and fretting faces were everywhere.

Sheffield couldn't get their hands on the ball at all, but after Molyneux and Gareth Stevens had combined well to move play into the Hull 20, Paul King wrestled the ball from Johnny Lawless in the tackle and play went back up the field through a flowing move featuring David Baildon, Craig Poucher and Paul Parker. This set up a good position near the Sheffield line and after Hull were awarded another set of six tackles after a Sheffield player had got a hand to the ball in a tackle, Lester mesmerised the visitors defence again and Karl Harrison crashed in for a rare touchdown next to the posts. Prescott's conversion made the score 18-0 just as Garry announced, "8-4 to Cas." which brought a resounding cheer from everyone as the crowd came alive again.

Sheffield tried to play some rugby but the effort that they had put into stopping the rampaging Hull forwards meant they had little energy left and on 23 minutes Rob Roberts drove them back again with a brilliant 40-20. Straight from the restart Lester fed Campbell, he drew three tacklers before slipping the ball to Prescott, who passed on to Paul Parker to score wide out. Sheffield brought on young Chris Thorman, to replace hooker Chris Molyneux and just before half time Mick Slicker came on for Michael Jackson who was 'Blood binned' with a nasty looking cut across his forehead sustained in a Paul King tackle. A try by the Eagles Jeff Hardy after a great breakout by Matt Crowther proved a brief hiccup, but as Garry announced that Castleford were 20-4 up at the McAlpine, Lester and Nolan inter-passed down the middle for Campbell to brilliantly finish off and as we led 30-4, the party started.

We simply could not believe what we were seeing and as Vince Groak the Editor of the Hull FC Fanzine commented at the time, "It was almost worth all the heartache and previous defeats to experience that feeling" Of course this was Hull FC and it was always going to be hard to maintain that sort of pressure. We were certainly not helped by Referee Cummings who awarded a string of 'unfathomable' penalties to Sheffield in the second half which saw tries from Bright Sodje and Chris Thorman, but our lads, on this occasion at least, were not prepared to crumble.

Firstly Sodje tripped substitute Steve Barrow and Prescott stroked over the penalty (something that prompted the first real 'relaxed' comment of the night from my pal Steve, who said "That wasn't very Bright Sodje") and then 'Two Bobs' Rob Roberts dropped a goal and we were home.

"Survival is triumph enough"

As the final score from Hudderfield was announced just before our game finished (32-10 to Cas) the whole place erupted and although we all knew it should never have come to this, the final hooter saw old men, women and several stewards climbing over the perimeter fence and racing onto the field to celebrate with the players. It was utter and absolute heaven, as we sang and danced on the hallowed turf.

It was a wonderful moment and there were fine words afterwards from all concerned, including the ubiquitous David Lloyd. He said he didn't mind paying the £1000 bonus, (something that prompted Karl Harrison to comment "You bet he doesn't"), and that he would make sure we were "Never in this position again". Little did we know what he was to try and do, to ensure that was the case, or that our 'Evil Uncle' was in fact just happy that the win gave him a more saleable commodity to tout around the Rugby League. But that night who cared? We stood on the field till the stewards asked us to leave and then went back to the pub and got wrecked!!!!

Eleven Super League Clubs had tried to kill us off and failed. It was however now the turn of David Lloyd, Hull KR and the Northern Ford Clubs to do their damndest to finish the job.

A tip-off concerning Halifax

At this point I should reiterate that as we enter one of the most complicated and yet critical periods in the whole history of our Club I tell it as I remember it, like everything else in this book I might not have got it exactly right but I've had a go.

On 21st September I was sitting in my office up to my eyes in Hull 700 stuff when the phone rang and I was speaking to a pal from Bradford City Council who was a Bull's fan, but otherwise a really nice guy. He told me confidentially that Bradford Councillors were saying that Halifax were about to merge with Hull FC and were to do it before 30th September so as to be able to claim the maximum 'sweetener' of £1.25m from the Rugby League. Like everyone else of a Black and White persuasion in the City, I didn't trust Lloyd and yet I was in a quandary because I had been told this in absolute confidence. However this was my Club and although professionally I couldn't really say anything, I had to do something! It was the first time I had ever used professional information for my own end, but this was Hull FC, and we were in danger. I made a couple of phone calls, not to the boys at the fanzine, but to a couple of folks who knew them well. The main thing we had to do was get this out in the public domain so that as fans we could do something about it.

By lunch time the word was out across West Hull although thankfully no-one knew where it had come from, in fact to this day I don't know whether it was my intervention or that of another 'Whistleblower' that had got the word out. By this time there were so many rumours circulating it was hard to know what was founded and what was pure mischief making. That evening I remember, Vince Groak from our Fanzine was on Radio Humberside and next day it was all over the Mail. No one from the Club would comment of course, but there was little doubt that things were moving and moving fast.

Seven weeks of anxiety, grief and sleepless nights as we stared over the abyss – the battle to save the Sharks

Eventually a Club spokesman intimated that, "It was a no to Halifax, but if the right deal comes along then we will have to look at it". We were all digesting that statement when the moment we had all feared arrived, it was late on the evening of 30th September, the last day that the £1.25m was on offer from the Rugby League for mergers. That night Hull FC officially lodged an 'Intent to Merge' with the Gateshead Thunder Club. The Hull Daily Mail immediately took on its best crusading guise and on behalf of the fans, launched a 'No to the Merger' campaign, printing a poster for us all to put in our front windows. Vince Groak was the first to break the stunned silence when he said, "This is not a Merger we are simply selling our Super League place" and he was certainly right about that.

It was indeed ironic that the announcement should be made on that day because as the news appeared on the front page of the local paper on 1st October it was superseded by a headline that read "£36m Circle of Dreams" and a photograph of Ian Blakey the Stadium Project Board Chairman and Pat Doyle Leader of the City Council as the preferred site for the new Super Stadium was announced. For once even the Council didn't know what Lloyd was about to do and the Gateshead link came as a shock.

On 7th October, as placard waving Huddersfield and Sheffield fans besieged Rugby League Headquarters, the RL Council met to ratify the merger between those two clubs, but thankfully didn't have time to discuss the Hull/Gateshead alliance, so that was deferred to their next meeting on the 27th October. In just 6 days, 7000 people had signed the Hull Daily Mail's petition against the merger and it became apparent behind the closed doors of the Guildhall, that the deal would only go through if the City Council were prepared to buy the Boulevard to pay off Lloyd. The whole City was in turmoil and rumours abounded everywhere while Roy Waudby was in and out of the Guildhall trying to broker a deal that would save the Club he loved.

As time passed towards the fateful meeting, there were a few worrying developments. David Kirkwood, the beleaguered Club Chairman, said that having seen the perilous position of the Club's finances, a merger was, "Probably the only way to save my beloved Club". While in a surreal development Brain Johnson our Chief Executive announced that if a new Hull Club was formed in the lower division then Jon Monie the ex Wigan maestro and most successful Coach in the modern era, would take over, assisted by David Topliss in the position of Football Director.

The merger plan was for both Hull and Gateshead to get £1.25m, Hull to lose its Super League status and apply to start again debt free in the Northern Ford Premiership. However then already battered and down hearted, we were dealt the cruellest blow of all as on Wednesday 13th October 1999, the man who was battling to save the Club our Champion, Roy Waudby, passed away. It was for many the final blow, because it was believed that Roy was on the verge of completing a deal to buy out David Lloyd and return the Club to local owners. At a passionate meeting at the Charleston Club only a week previously, we were all told by Roy that he would put up £200,000 to buy the Club if anyone would match that sum. The day after his death, a meeting took place at the Boulevard where all the associates of the Club, the shareholders and several members of the press were briefed by Johnson on the Gateshead buy-out, but it was all so muddled that the meeting raised more questions than it ever answered.

The end of an enigma; Roy Waudby bows out

On Tuesday 19ᵗʰ October amidst all the turmoil and uncertainty there was surrounding the future of our beloved Rugby League Club and the excitement and anticipation at the Council that surrounded the embryonic advent of the new Stadium, everything paused. Time stood still as we all paid tribute to the passing of a father figure in the history of Rugby League in the City. It was in some style that I travelled down to St Matthew's Church on the Boulevard, where all those years earlier Dad had been a Church Warden and I had sung in the choir. Councillor Pat Doyle the Leader of the Council and I were invited to travel down with the Lord Mayor, Councillor Brian Wilkinson, in the Civic Car KH 1 and we arrived to find the area around the church thronged with dozens of fans who had turned up to stand and pay tribute. As the Cortege arrived everyone was dressed in black and white, and stood hats removed in silence as the family entered the Church. St Matthew's was packed and I joined the Civic party and other guests in the choir stalls whilst people stood in the side isles and the porch-ways. I am sure that I will do an injustice to someone here, but I can only list those I remember being there on that sad occasion.

In the front pews there was Tony Dean, Arthur Bunting, Dave Elliott, Dave Topliss, Gary Divorty, Charlie Birdsall, Trevor Skerrett, David Kirkwood and Brian Johnson. The Rugby League was represented by Neil Tunnicliffe and Rodney Walker and they were sitting with Maurice Lindsay and Chris Caisley from Super League. Colin Hutton and Barry Lilley represented Hull KR, whilst from more recent times Lee Jackson, Andy Dannett and Steve McNamara were sitting on the left. I am sure that there are many that I have missed out in what was a wonderful gathering of Rugby League luminaries, brought together to remember 'Mr Hull FC'. The rest of the church was packed with favour wearing FC fans. The service was conducted by Club Chaplain Allen Bagshawe assisted by the 'Robins' Chaplain John Leeman. There were certainly several poignant moments, none more so than when Maurice Lindsay described Roy by saying "He was a man who loved the game, in fact no one loved Rugby League more than Roy. Whenever you needed advice

Roy was always someone you could turn to because his word was his bond".

Then Roy's son Roger, flanked by his brothers spoke passionately about his Dad, his love of Hull FC and the way he fought right up to his death to save the Club. He described him as "A great man" and coming as it did as the Club was about to fold, it seemed to all of us there that day that the funeral was not just to honour Roy but, because he was so instrumental to our survival, perhaps it would also mark the passing of our Club. The last hope we had was gone, or so it seemed, because it was only those meetings at the Charleston Club with Roy that had kept us believing Hull FC would survive the wrath of David Lloyd, Roy was a patriarch and our champion and now he was no more. Still, rather like Clive Sullivan's all those years earlier, we didn't just give Roy a good send off, we gave him a Hull FC send off, it was, without doubt, the least we could do.

Why doesn't anybody like us?

Without Roy at the helm, things went from serious to critical. It transpired that the problem with the merger idea was that the Northern Ford Premiership Clubs were not that keen on us joining them. Super League had refused to admit the NFP's Grand Final winners, The Hunslet Hawks, that year and so the member Clubs were not that keen on conveniently admitting any remnants of a 'Super League' merger into their competition. There was certainly a whiff of mutiny in the air and it looked as if it was to be the Hull Sharks that were to 'walk the plank'. As the meeting at Rugby League headquarters approached, Brian Johnson dramatically warned the Super League Clubs that they must, "Back our merger or Hull Sharks go bust!"

On the day of the meeting I couldn't work, it was just impossible and I spent the whole day listening to Radio Humberside expecting a News Flash or something of that ilk that would confirm our demise. When it came it was a bit of an anti climax because, although the Rugby League Council confirmed the merger was to happen, they added that it would only be ratified if Hull were accepted into the Northern Ford Premiership. Thankfully it appeared that some of the other senior Clubs did not wish to see the end of Hull FC and, no doubt, their lucrative band of travelling supporters. Once everyone concerned had been consulted and the actual ramifications fully considered, the Rugby League were to make a final decision at their next meeting a fortnight hence.

Someone sticks the boot in!

There is little doubt that we were caught in a political battle between the Super League and the Northern Ford Clubs and some of the latter saw an opportunity to make an example of the Sharks by excluding us. Barry Lilley the Chairman of Hull KR made a curt statement about the situation in the Hull Daily Mail after the meeting and in the late edition on 27th October 1999, he said, "There is no way that they (Hull FC) will be allowed to take a place in the Premiership and Hull KR will be the only Club in Hull with their own identity". That went down really well in the West of the City and is something that many remember to this day.

As I was drowning my sorrows on a regular basis, others were better employed as unbeknown to most of us, Vince Groak, Steve Roberts, Pete O'Connor, Jimmy Gardiner and a few other fans had convened a 'secret' meeting with Gateshead's Chief Executive Shane Richardson in the Rugby Suite at the Boulevard. Vince said afterwards that 'Richo' stated at that meeting that, "If I was thinking with my heart instead of my head, then I would be moving down here and trying to turn this Club around". It was hoped by those present, that Richardson took from that meeting just how much Hull people love their rugby and how utterly dejected they were about the actions of the Rugby League and the Northern Ford Clubs. Perhaps the seeds of doubt had been sown, or the germ of an idea had been planted in Shane Richardson's head, although if perhaps it had, then it was going to take a couple of weeks to manifest itself.

Ironically on the same day, (with my radio secreted on my knee and headphones at the ready for any new news) I had to sit through a Council meeting that ratified the use of £38m of the KC shares windfall on building the new Stadium at the Circle on Anlaby Road. This in essence swept away the last hurdle to the 'Super Stadium' dream becoming a reality, although for us Hull FC fans what was happening to our Club was more akin to a nightmare.

Cometh the hour, cometh the heroes

A couple of days later there was a hastily convened meeting of the NFP Clubs after which it was stated the discussions about admitting Hull FC had ended as 'inconclusive', as some wanted us excluded, whilst others were dead against it. We were left to wonder which Clubs they were! It was generally believed that the Rugby League put a deal of pressure on some of the member Clubs to ensure that Hull FC lived on for at least another week. Our beloved Club was in limbo and owner David Lloyd was running out of patience. We had few players and even fewer Directors; we had merged with a Club but hadn't, wanted to start another club in a lower division but couldn't and were all but bankrupt. They were tough times for everyone in the Black and White family, but every cloud has a silver lining and it's likely that beer sales in West Hull were up in early November 1999.

As part of my ever burgeoning duties at the Council I was now responsible for the operation of the Press Office and every morning I would go down there and furtively search the statements and releases coming out of Pat Doyle's office for any news, but all was quiet as the Council made not a single statement about what was for me the most significant occurrence in the City since the war. Bugger Hull 700, this was serious! Of course behind the scenes a lot was happening about which, even this 'Senior Officer' who had his nose into most of the 'Intrigue' going on in the Guildhall, knew nothing.

On 5th November the City Council staged a massive Hull 700 Firework display on the Marina and despite the fact that I was, I guess, responsible for the safety of over 30,000 people that night, all I could think about was Hull FC, it had totally taken over my life. I couldn't eat properly, I felt sick and no doubt like hundreds of other 'faithful' Hull fans, every night I would lay awake tossing and turning and going over all the various scenarios in my head until dawn broke.

That day too, questions were asked in Parliament about the "shambles" that was the British game of Rugby League. The MP's present came to the conclusion that there was a need for "a sweeping review of the Rugby League's governing body". I think we could have told them that. I knew that the Leader of the Authority, Pat Doyle was a big Hull FC fan and that he wouldn't just let us go down without a fight, but try as I may to get a word with him, I couldn't because he was always in meetings, in fact, I got the distinct impression that he was avoiding me!

At the Club no one had been paid for over 5 weeks, sponsors JWE had withdrawn their last two monthly payments of £10,000 and wanted out and as pre season training commenced, only 7 players, Murdoch, King, Poucher, Ireland, Holgate, Schultz and Fletcher, turned up. The Hull Daily Mail headlines announced, "Monday is D Day for Sharks" and intimated on that day the now aligned Northern Ford Premiership Clubs were prepared to vote 'en bloc' against Hull's entry into their competition. We were on the very brink of extinction as every Hull Sharks' fan waited for that next critical meeting and held their breath.

After another sleepless night on Sunday, Monday really dragged. I couldn't work and just fretted away the morning waiting to hear from the meeting in the West Riding. As was my habit, around lunchtime I once again wandered into the Press Office and riffled through the Releases. To my amazement at last I found one, which had 'Embargoed until 12-00 midnight on Monday 15th November 1999' emblazoned in red ink across the top. The title of the release was 'Hull City Council welcomes the management of Gateshead Thunder to the City'. I had to read it three times before I realised what all the meetings that had been going on in Pat Doyle's office, had been about.

Vince, Steve and the Boys from 'In Any Kinda Weather', The Hull Daily Mail, Hull City Council, Shane Richardson, the Council Leader (and FC fan extraordinaire) Pat Doyle and the fans of Hull FC had between them somehow, combined to deliver a miracle.

'Super Tuesday'; back in business, back in the hoops and back as the FC

When the Americans talk about the big day in their primary elections as being 'Super Tuesday', they don't know the meaning of the word. When the news broke that famous morning, the whole City and indeed the whole of the sporting world was talking about it. The official statement from the Rugby League read:

> "Super League clubs yesterday gave their unanimous backing for a merger between Gateshead and Hull Sharks. The move brings to an end Super League rugby in Gateshead as the newly-formed club will play in Hull. The mergers acceptance means the new club will receive £1.25m over two years. These payments will satisfy the creditors of Hull and Gateshead. As a result of the merger, David Lloyd no longer has any involvement with or ownership of the company. The merged team will play Super League matches in Hull, initially at 'The Boulevard' and then at the planned new stadium in the West of the City. The existing playing squad and administrative staff from Gateshead will transfer operations to Hull and join forces with the remaining players and staff there".

The first comments from our new owners made it perfectly clear that the 'Sharks' were no more, the 'fancy dress' was gone forever and Hull FC were back, playing in Black and White hoops. All I did at work that day was field an endless stream of telephone calls from pals and visit other fans who were just as relieved as me. There was little productivity of note that day in many places of work across the City, but that's acceptable when you're faced with such a life changing event. At 49 years of age I was as elated as a kid on Christmas Day and after weeks of despair and worry, nothing could have prepared me for the wave of unmitigated joy that overtook me.

However old you are, when you're a fanatic you never learn do you, and so I went to seek out one or two Hull KR followers who had spent the past 6 weeks taunting and 'ragging me' about how they as a Club would soon be the only team in the City. That day, the look of disappointment on their faces was pretty sweet believe me. My case was assisted by the front page of the Hull Daily Mail that showed an old photograph of Stanley Gene, sitting on a bench on Hessle Foreshore eating fish and chips. The hero of New Craven Park who had left just two months earlier for the Thunder, was making a quick return to the City where he was idolised, but 'sadly' (for the Hull KR fans) for the wrong team! I remember pointing out to those same Hull KR fans that what had happened was little short of a miracle and how ironic it was that the Northern Ford Premiership Clubs who included Hull KR had, by refusing our admission, actually facilitated the whole process.

We might have seen The Queen, Desmond Tutu, the Duke of York, Civil War re-enactments, firework displays and rock concerts in a very special year in the City of Kingston upon Hull, but for this particular rugby fan there is little doubt what was the best thing to come out of Hull 700.

New Beginnings

Of course there were casualties in all this change and the fans of the Gateshead Club were certainly unhappy about the outcome, threats of legal action were made and even, allegedly, a brick thrown through Shane Richardson's garage window. They may have been few in number but a thousand or so Gateshead followers signed a petition to stop the merger going through but it was too late, the deal was done. The City Council had played a big part in the 'revolution' and the payment they would make to the new owners of the Club for the Boulevard Stadium, ensured that once they had received the £1.25m that the merger provided from the Rugby League, both Hull FC and Gateshead Thunder would be debt free.

Two nights later, on the Thursday, we all went back to the Charleston Club, this time not for a crisis meeting but rather to celebrate and meet two Directors of the Gateshead Club, who were now on the Board of Hull FC. The place was buzzing that night as we discussed the 15 strong

Australian contingent of players that had suddenly become our new 'heroes'. It was then that Vince Groak and Steve Roberts reiterated the idea of forming an Independent Supporters' Group and so HISA (Hull Independent Supporters Association) was born. We all signed up on what was a great evening particularly as Olga Waudby, Roy's widow, took pride of place at the front of the crowd. How proud and relieved Roy would have been that night and how sad it was that he couldn't be there to see it.

The following Monday season tickets went on sale for the forthcoming Super League campaign with over £50,000 worth being sold on the first day, a total that rose to £100,000 by the weekend. That first day of sales I joined a queue that snaked across the Boulevard car park and the 'buzz' as we all waited patiently to invest in our new dream, was akin to what we experienced years earlier, before those great Cup Finals. However it was not all plain sailing and as on the Stock Exchange KC shares started to lose value, in Hull Shane Richardson had to move quickly to quash rumours that the Club was being liquidated.

This was just another rumour borne out of the fact that the first instalment of the £1.25m from the Rugby League would not be forthcoming until 1st January so cash flow was a problem. The City Council came to the rescue with an advance on the sale of the Stadium and Willie Peters, our talented Australian Scrum Half, was sold to Wigan for an unlikely £100,000 which helped to balance the books.

There were benefits to the merger on both sides. The big plus for the ex Gateshead administration was the quality and depth of young players they had inherited and it was certainly no surprise when Richard Fletcher, Andy Last and Richard Horne were called up to play for the Great Britain Youth team against the touring Australian Secondary Schools at the Boulevard in mid December.

While the Club was busy securing accommodation for all the players and staff that had to move down from Tyneside, over at New Craven Park the enemy across the river were licking their wounds as the details of their own rescue became public. As Shane Richardson (the new hero of at least one side of the City) left to fly back home to Australia for

Christmas, the Council put in £450,000 and the Gain Group £200,000 to allow Hull KR to enter into a Creditors Voluntary Agreement which, although they were owed well over £1m, at least guaranteed that their creditors would get something.

The 'new' Hull FC Board get down to business

Sunday 23rd January 2000   Hull FC 27 – Halifax Blue Sox 12

As Christmas and the Millennium celebrations in Hull came and went, I was certainly relieved that Hull 700 was over and that the year of events had been such a success. It was estimated that the 12 months of celebrations generated an additional £40m for the local economy and there is little doubt that the people of the City enjoyed the festivities. What was even more important was that I still had a rugby team to follow and a group of people in charge who seemed to feel as passionate about them as I did. Shaun McRae our new Coach was sorting through the players that had been retained from the Sharks and although we were allowed to keep Gateshead's enhanced overseas player quota of 14, there was a deal of horse trading going on, both at the Club and outside it, to keep the squad within the salary cap.

At the turn of the year as half the team were training at the Boulevard and the rest at Gateshead, Rob Roberts, Craig Murdock and Steven Holgate were put on the transfer list. However by 4th January everyone had moved to Hull and preparations for the new season started in earnest. I couldn't wait, and it was great when the man who did so much to try and rescue the Club, the late Roy Waudby, was honoured by having the first pre season game against Halifax dedicated to him. His family later also sponsored the Threepenny Stand which from then onwards bore his name.

More good news saw David Kirkwood (the man who had fought Lloyd and made more comebacks in a 17 year career at the club than Frank Sinatra) become Honorary Club President. David was followed back by David Topliss who after he had retired and sold his engineering business, returned as Head of Youth Development. It seemed that Richardson and the rest of the Board were making all the right moves and 3,306 turned up for that Roy Waudby Memorial Trophy game against Halifax when Hull FC came out easy winners. Hull, back playing in the most famous strip in the game, played some great rugby although at times I found it difficult knowing who was who, but at least we all gave our old nemesis Stanley Gene a great welcome and he obliged by scoring two tries. He said after the game, "The fans gave me a great reception for which I thank them". Good old Stanley, always the diplomat.

The Season begins with disappointment at Halifax

Friday 3rd March 2000   *Hull FC 27 – Halifax Blue Sox 30*

Trish Goldsmith who had followed the Club down the A1 from Tyneside as Head of Marketing was being innovative in attracting sponsorship and despite having pulled out in the Lloyd era, JWE were lured back to the Club as shirt sponsors while player sponsors included organisations as diverse as The Yorkshire Bed Centre (David Maiden) and The All Electric Fisheries (Craig Poucher).

As was the practise back then, the Challenge Cup rounds started before the regular Super League season and two good home draws saw us matched firstly with Lancashire Lynx and then Rochdale Hornets. Both games were one sided affairs in which we scored over 160 points in total but then we were drawn at home in the quarter finals against the then Cup Kings the Wigan Warriors. Before that we had to travel over to the still unfinished Shay Stadium at Halifax for our first Super League game. The ground had an incomplete look about it as building work on a new Stand at the east side of the Stadium had been abandoned when the cash ran out and it stood empty with just 37 seats fitted in the centre block. In fact the score board that night was a piece of hardboard onto which the scores were chalked. Undeterred by a frosty, misty March night, 2000 of us travelled to the West Riding, where we were goaded by two coach loads of Gateshead fans who had gone to the game to protest about the merger and who seemed to find it difficult to decide whether they wanted to back their old heroes, or Halifax.

The game was a personal victory for winger Brian Carney who scored a brilliant hat trick and although we had trailed by 16 points at the start of the second half with just four minutes to go a brilliant drop goal from Craig Wilson saw us leading 27-26. However with almost the last move of the game Stanley Gene, who had found the step up from lower league rugby tough, fumbled a short kick from Moana right in front of the Hull fans, and Florimo crashed in to win the game.

The good old days return and the Boulevard is buzzing

Saturday 11th March 2000   *Hull FC 14 – Wigan Warriors 4*

The week leading up to that Cup quarter final was one that was fraught with injury problems that threatened to scupper any slim chances we had of winning a game that all the pundits and bookmakers had down as a 'banker' for the competition's favourites. In came youngster Paul King at prop and after Australian Adam Maher had been taken ill and withdrawn on the morning of the game, McRae had to call up an even younger Richard Fletcher onto the substitute's bench. In the presence of the BBC Grandstand cameras we all awaited our first really big game since the merger. Referee Russell Smith blew the whistle and Radlinski struck the ball deep into the Hull half, prompting a massive roar from the 7700 crowd. This seemed to be counter-productive and appeared to surprise the Hull players waiting to receive the ball as Broadbent fumbled it forward and Maiden retrieved it in front of him in an off side position. This left Farrell with the simplest of penalties, to give Wigan an early two point lead.

That really poor start didn't deter Hull, who immediately started to make inroads into the Wigan defence. The home team's enthusiasm was certainly apparent when Robinson kicked into the corner where Wigan's Dallas fielded the ball only to be swamped by five chasing Hull players. Youngster Richard Horne was certainly prompting and probing around the ruck and he almost got Jenkins in after 7 minutes as Hull pushed forward. Then an over-worked Wigan defence conceded a penalty for off-side and Sammut, from 30 yards out and to the left of the posts, hammered home the kick. Wilson sustained a head wound after a high shot by Dallas and went to the blood bin which saw youngster Fletcher come into the second row but then on 15 minutes, Hull took the lead.

Richard Horne again made a half break and fed Will Robinson. The scrum half immediately stepped inside and then superbly passed to Maiden, who crashed over near the posts and as Sammut had landed the conversion, to our amazement we led 8-2. We were standing on the Airlie Street terracing that day and the place went wild as Will Robinson shot in again after a brilliant move involving a defence splitting break by Collins, however on consulting the video referee it was decided that Will had lost control of the ball as he put it down and the try was disallowed. Still the crowd sang and cheered and at regular intervals 'Old Faithful' rang around the old place; it was just like the Brian Smith years all over again.

Next however Carney was sin binned for what was described by the referee afterwards as a 'deliberate offside', but as the half came to a close Wigan started to come back into the match. With an amazing 7 minutes of injury time being added, Hull FC had to cling on before Jason Robinson went close for Wigan, but his grubber kick was brilliantly tidied up by Matt Daylight. Then Renouf intercepted a wayward pass from Hull's Felsch and the Wigan centre looked certain to score. However Carney, straight back on from the sin bin ran directly across the width of the field to cut the Australian international centre off, 10 yards out, and as half-time arrived, we were all elated and physically drained.

The second half started with Maiden kneeing a loose ball forward and almost recollecting it, but in general Wigan were starting to exert the pressure again and although the crowd did their best, much of the dominance we had shown in the first half had disappeared. Despite all their pressure Wigan could not penetrate a resolute FC defence led by Fletcher and Broadbent and in the end had to settle for a penalty when Fletcher was accidentally caught off side. In what was developing into a titanic battle, twice we lost possession in our own half as several Hull players looked to be feeling the pressure. Felsch and Robinson went off, to be replaced by Stanley Gene and Wayne McDonald and Mick Cassidy and Dennis Betts both went close for Wigan. At the Airlie Street End we just stood stressfully on that lucky step and prayed.

Then with 10 minutes to go and Hull hanging on resolutely, the whole place suddenly erupted as the game took another dramatic twist. A couple of fortuitous penalties at last relieved the pressure and we found ourselves in possession in the Wigan half. Firstly, the returning Robinson managed to work a gap in the defence, but was injured again as he was tackled by Terry Newton and Willie Peters. Straight from the play the ball Stanley Gene sped away down field in a mad dash for the line. He fell to a good tackle but this set up a position some ten yards out and two tackles later Gene, operating at acting half back, brilliantly supplied a short pass to 6ft 7ins Wayne McDonald who somehow hurled his body over the line. Sammut added the conversion and as they stood behind their try line, gasping for air, it was obvious that Wigan were shattered.

As we all held our breath Wigan threw everything at us. To rather premature chants of "We're the famous Hull FC and were off to Wembley" we now had some 'steel' in our defence and as the game wore on the young players took their opportunities. Horne made a great break, only to be felled by Betts in an illegal tackle and then both King and Gene were held inches short of the line. Then a dropped ball saw Wigan sweep back down field and Renoulf sent Newton away to be stopped a foot from the Hull line by a mighty tackle by Deon Bird. However, Sammut had to be alert as Farrell kicked through, before the hooter went and on the terraces the celebrations began.

The scenes that followed were reminiscent of those great days in the early part of the previous decade when against all odds Brian Smith steered us to the Premiership Final. There was the same sort of high emotion everywhere and I remember having tears in my eyes, as all the tension and pressure of the Lloyd years ebbed away on a tide of rejoicing and euphoria. "HELLO, HELLO, FC are Back FC are Back" echoed round the ground and we all stood there and applauded the team as they completed a lap of honour. Although Wigan were to score over 120 points against us in our three other meetings that year, after all that had gone before, it was great to be watching Hull FC win such an epic encounter. It was certainly a famous victory for us all and one that will live in my memory forever.

The following Monday Hull FC were drawn to play the Leeds Rhinos in the Cup Semi Final at the Galpharm Stadium at the end of the month. No one knew what a disaster that was to turn out to be, for sport in general and my beloved Club in particular.

A great performance, a bitter dissapointment and a hoard of morons!

Sunday 26th March 2000   *Hull FC 22 – Leeds Rhinos 28*

Shortly after that wonderful victory and as Shaun McRae's renaissance continued, Craig Murdock left to join his old team mate Brad Hepi at Salford City Reds while Rob Roberts joined the Halifax Blue Sox. Although there was League games to consider, most of us FC fans could think of nothing else but that semi final because it seemed impossible that a club that was literally hours away from going out of business was now 80 minutes away from the Challenge Cup Final at Murrayfield. I remember wondering what those small minded Northern Ford Clubs that had refused us entry felt about it now, because had it not been for them turning our application down, all this would never have happened.

At last the day of the Semi Final arrived and I joined another 9000 Hull fans as we journeyed over to Huddersfield to face Leeds Rhinos for a place in the final. However from the moment I arrived in the town centre I sensed that all was not well. I travelled to the game with Linda and Vicky that day but on arrival in Huddersfield we were amazed to see dozens of drunken Hull fans cavorting on the road outside the pubs and shouting at the passing cars heading down to the Stadium. I saw one idiot roll over a car bonnet, whilst others 'mooned' at passing Leeds coaches and then as we walked past 'Ricky's' pub we had to scatter as a man covered in beer and completely naked (except for a hull scarf round his neck) was paraded out of the door and into the street, on the shoulders of one of his 'pals'.

What was even more worrying was the way that four policemen on horseback sat across the road watching and laughing as all this was happening. I just hoped that there would be plenty of police and stewards inside the Galpharm Stadium, because this lot had obviously been drinking for hours. We hurried along to the game but my heart sank as I got inside and saw that the stewards policing the perimeter of the pitch were at least 20 meters apart and there wasn't a policeman in sight.

As a gigantic silk FC flag was passed over the heads of the Hull fans the usual "We all hate Leeds" chants rang round the Stadium, but that day they had an even more vitriolic edge to them. Down the terracing in front of us, most fans were standing behind their seats, and many were stripped to the waist. A fight broke out between two Hull fans who seemed to be arguing about a youngster waving a flag in front of them and everyone seemed angry and wound up. It appeared to me that a small but vociferous minority of the Hull crowd were out of their heads with alcohol or 'whatever', and intent on making a nuisance of themselves.

It was therefore a relief when the game finally kicked off and we could concentrate on the rugby, rather than the antics of the idiots in front of us. In the first minute a Sammut penalty put Hull into the lead, before some sloppy defending out on our right hand flank allowed Richie Blackmore to score for the Rhinos. Back came Hull as Paul Cooke and Deon Bird linked brilliantly for Matt Daylight to scoot in at the corner but then a pass that was suspiciously forward freed Leeds' Francis Cummins and Ryan Sheridan stole in for a try. In that first 30 minutes we received a real battering from the Leeds forwards who led by Barrie McDermott were intent on 'softening up' the Hull pack. The atmosphere in the crowd was certainly 'white hot' and not for all the right reasons. However Daylight scored his second try as Will Robinson made the initial break, Paul Cooke brilliantly engineered some space for Tony Grimaldi as his inch perfect long pass found our winger unmarked and able to canter in at the corner. At 14-10 at half time, despite being on the back foot for a lot of the game, we were certainly still in it.

Youngster Paul Cooke was having a great game and it was he who was involved in getting the first try of the second half. Having just stopped Blackmore in full flight, Cooke hoisted a steepling up and under towards the corner flag and with a huge leap Matt Daylight beat Leroy Rivett to the ball to grab his hat trick try and level the scores at 14-14. Almost before we had finished celebrating a shrewd kick to the corner by Sheridan evaded Carney, and Cummins touched down to restore the Rhino's lead. Bird then had a try disallowed by the video referee, when Rivett had lost the ball over the line, before Harris and Sammut both kicked a penalty apiece.

The game was set for a tense finish but Anthony Farrell broke through the Hull defensive line to touch down and at 28-16 it seemed all over. Back came Hull in the last few minutes and after what looked, from where we were sitting, as a perfectly good try to David Maiden was disallowed for a forward pass, it was left for big Wayne McDonald to power over near the end. That score was too late and as the hooter went the Hull players sunk to their knees, whilst the Leeds outfit joined their fans in dancing for joy at the other end of the Stadium. It was I guess, looking back, all really a question of goal kicks. Iestyn Harris having landed all six of his goal attempts while Ben Sammut had much more difficult kicks and missed three, despite two of those hitting the posts. Of course, after what had been a really exciting game it was what happened next that everyone remembers!

"I will not let these yobs destroy this Club"

As we got to the end of our row of seats on our way out, the teams were just leaving the field. Then dozens of Hull FC fans climbed onto the pitch and started to antagonise the stewards who were trying to confine them to the terracing. We all just stood in disbelief, as fans poured onto the field and several attempted to scale the goal posts, which saw the cross bar at the Leeds end soon smashed in half. Another group of hooligans tried to rip the post out of the ground as others started 'running battles' with the police who had now arrived belatedly on the scenes, to confront well over 100 'fans' standing in front of the Leeds end. These hooligans were goading and threatening the children and families that had, a few minutes earlier, been celebrating the Cup holders return to the Final.

We simply couldn't believe our eyes and we all shouted "Get off the pitch" but of course we couldn't be heard and as the tannoy announcer mirrored our sentiments to little effect, it was obvious that the situation was well past any sort of reasonable resolution. Shane Richardson is said to have been in tears after the game, and said, "I will not allow these yobs destroy this Club". 17 fans were arrested that day and it was in disgrace and disbelief that we drove back to Hull in complete silence.

The story in all its graphic detail featured on the national TV news that night and next day the Sunday newspapers were full of all the wrong sort of publicity for the great game of Rugby League. Once again a small minority of the fans of the Club I loved had brought scorn, shame and loathing on all of us, just when we looked to be in the ascendancy and getting back to the standing we deserved in the game. Of course the Hull Daily Mail on Monday was full of it and the following week they mounted a 'Shaming our City' campaign to name and identify the culprits. I was so embarrassed and saddened by it all. You always love your Club but at times like that, just like in any relationship, that love is severely tested. There is little doubt that the entire population of Hull had been disgraced because outside the City we were all seen as thugs, hooligans, drunkards and bad losers. No one said that supporting Hull FC would ever be easy and at that time it certainly wasn't!

True fans, true colours!

Sunday 2nd April 2000   Hull FC 32 – Warrington Wolves 16

As the week wore on, my personal shame hadn't abated much and the thought of accompanying that rabble to, of all places, 'The Zoo' at

Warrington the following Saturday, was not a pleasant proposition. Of course there was little doubt about me attending because I felt I had to out of a sense of duty. That week the Club launched a Fans' Charter, which was designed to ensure that Hull FC were seen to be valuing the average, decent supporters whilst ostracising the hooligan element who had done so much damage at Huddersfield. I signed up on the Thursday and the Hull Daily Mail got 1000 fans registered in just 48 hours. Then we all went along to a Rally at the Boulevard that Saturday.

I was certainly surprised how many turned up that morning as around 1500 FC fans packed the Threepenny Stand. Some arrived pushing prams, others in wheelchairs but everyone wore their colours, although the mood was certainly a sombre one. I sat and listened to Shane Richardson, Shaun McRae and Steve Roberts of the Independent Supporters' Association as they talked of restoring the pride, outing the culprits and of the true fans "leading by example". We all listened sitting behind a massive banner that proclaimed, "From the True Supporters of Hull FC..... SORRY" and a final, sombre, chorus of 'Old Faithful' affirmed everyone's commitment to the cause.

I went home feeling a lot better but certainly concerned about what would happen that night, on TV, at the worst ground in the country for antagonistic fans and potential trouble. If ever the problem was to reoccur again it would be there. But as often happens in times of need all the old gang rallied round and Billy, Steve and Pearly all travelled with me to Wildespool as we talked briefly of the disaster at the McAlpine, but mainly of old times and happier away trips.

We arrived in Warrington early, but already the town and its inhabitants were prepared! As we walked towards the ageing Stadium we passed 'The Royal Oak Branch', a pub we had frequented so many times in the past, where the walls of the Public Bar were always heavily decorated with rugby memorabilia and reminders of the home town Club's past glories. Billy pointed in the direction of the front door and said "Look at that" as outside were hastily prepared signs announcing "No Away Supporters" as on the front door 'Bouncers' asked everyone "Are you from Hull" At the turnstiles we were frisked by the police for cans of beer and Pearly, who sported an 'Americana' waistcoat and baseball cap that day, was asked to empty his pockets. At over 60 years of age, he thought it was great and no doubt, knowing Pearly it was the highlight of his week!

We were strong now, the Lloyd stuff had made us strong! On the terraces in the 'shed' Stand at the Railway End there was a fabulous turnout of singing and chanting Hull supporters and right in the middle of them was the man himself, Shane Richardson, standing with us FC fans, singing and chanting. The 'Sorry' banner that had been displayed at the Boulevard earlier in the day was again spread out over the perimeter barrier no doubt for the benefit of the TV cameras and as the teams ran out few of us could ever remember when so many cameras had been pointing away from the pitch and at the fans. Later the behaviour of us Hull FC fans was described as "A rousing display of well behaved bravado" and I was proud to be part of the 'FC Army' that day. There was still a couple of rounds of "We all hate Leeds", and it was great to see Shane joining in as we chanted "Are you watching Hull KR" and gave ex Sharks 'star' Alan Hunte some stick. It wasn't the end of the disgrace, but perhaps that night, it was the beginning of the end.

Although it was almost academic in the bigger scheme of things, we beat a well fancied Warrington, in a rousing display that showed the team wanted to do their bit to rectify things too.

The massed ranks of Hull fans sang the lads home and despite some stylish play by Lee Briers we completely outclassed the 'Wolves' in a six try performance, that completely over shadowed the home team's big name signings, Allan Langer, Andrew Gee and Tawera Nikau. It was a fine way to end a terrible week and all the way down the motorway home fans tooted their horns and shouted out of car windows, as if we had just won the Cup!

The following week local fan Dave Dosdale was appointed Hull FC's Away Fans 'Liaison Officer' and the Fans' Charter ended up with around 7000 signatures. In spite of the fact that the semi final was held on a neutral ground, Hull were eventually fined £25,000 by the Rugby Football League for "Having inadequate security", and an additional

£10,000 two days later after 'a Club official' described the League's decision as "absolutely disgraceful" and threatened to withdraw Hull from the 2001 Challenge Cup. It was the end of a sad episode in the illustrious history of Hull FC and one that I have detailed here lest, as Rugby League fans and indeed sports fans in general, we ever forget what a few mindless idiots can do to an institution that is loved by thousands.

Chapter 10

Bringing it all back Home...a new Stadium becomes a reality

Most of what comes next will still be pretty fresh in the mind of the reader, so it seems only appropriate that I don't labour that much on the final five years of this yarn of an ordinary guy and his love of an extra ordinary Rugby League team. I think personally, that writing about everyday happenings from such recent times hold little in the way of revelations or entertainment but none the less in the first five years of the new Century there were certainly some significant developments and milestones. These came both on the rugby front and in my own life as my story finally winds down through the final years that lead up to that life defining and magically sunlit day in Cardiff!

At work the success of Hull 700 had left me in a strong position, and I was now operating under the rather grandiose title of 'Head of Image and Promotion' which saw me managing a team of over 70 people. The disciplines within that organisation ranged from the Civic Office which managed the Lord Mayor, through the Tourism, Entertainments and Sports Promotion Teams, the design staff and (probably because no one else wanted to manage it), the Covered Market in the City Centre. In addition to all that, I was also still overseeing the Council's Press Office and had to spend quite a bit of time facing the TV cameras and radio microphones, whenever 'the wheel came off'. Something that was, it has to be said, a pretty regular occurrence at Hull City Council. If the Authority weren't drumming the Head of Education out of the City, we were suspending Chief Executives or facing Member bullying charges, it was certainly never dull in Hull.

After 34 years of working in the Leisure Services Department, a reorganisation saw my team moved into the Economic Development Directorate, where we worked under Director, John North, who turned out to be a top bloke. John deserves a big mention here because although the concept of a Community Stadium was Pat Doyle's, John was the driving force behind this unique vision becoming a glorious reality. Along with his Stadium Project Manager John Topliss, he ploughed a lone furrow backwards and forwards to places like the Stadium of Light in Sunderland and the Emirates Stadium in London, gaining information and ideas and whenever there was a problem, or an obstacle, it was the two Johns and the Leader of the Council, that found a way through it. I actually believe that without John North, it's unlikely the KC Stadium would ever have existed. I think too that afterwards everyone realised that it was thanks to him (in the light of the well publicised Millennium Dome fiasco and the overspending and over running on the Wembley Stadium refurbishment) that the KC Stadium was delivered on time, on specification and slightly under budget.

The search for unexploded bombs and a home for the lizards

Much of the interesting stuff that year for us Hull FC fans was concerned with watching as the preparatory work on our new home began in earnest. The site was now agreed and so began the harrowing and at times frustrating business of getting through all the legislation that needed to be in place before a single piece of turf could be lifted. In May 2000 the first community consultation meetings began and I attended several in the nearby Newington Ward, where there was a surprising amount of goodwill to see the development become reality.

There were now some futuristic designs to show everyone and talk of a Community Sports Hall, Skateboard Park, a shared railway halt with the Infirmary and a remodelled West Park certainly captured the public's imagination. By September the Council had granted planning permission and although the whole scheme was then 'called in' by the Government, it was approved by the Secretary of State in December. So at last and despite a colony of Common Lizards (a protected species) being discovered on the allotments at the back of the site, we could all look forward to work starting on Hull FC's (and Hull City's) new home. The Lizards needing a protected habitat has, to this day, always offered an excuse for the undeveloped areas found at the South of the Stadium.

First up it was necessary to 'Search the site' which was a time consuming affair involving a lot of scanning and the digging of numerous holes to thoroughly examine the ground that the structure was to be built on. On an undeveloped site like the Cricket Circle they were looking for everything from the unlikely, such as Roman remains, to the more than likely (in Hull), unexploded bombs, but thankfully found neither. John North tells a great story about how, on that first morning of the search, he cancelled all his meetings and sat in his office watching the telephone, waiting for it to ring, as he feared yet another setback. With the site given the all clear, Birse Stadia in place *as* approved contractors, and all the community and legislative hurdles cleared, work at last started on site in October. I went down to a Ground Breaking Ceremony with the Council's Press Office team, where Trish Goldsmith said a few words, while children from 5 local schools buried time capsules in the foundations of what was to be the West Stand. At last, despite our sadness about leaving the Boulevard, the dream of a new home was becoming a reality.

The last incredible journey of Charlie Rowlin

In a year when the Labour party in Hull were doing so badly that The Lord Mayor, Brian Wilkinson, lost his seat to the Independent candidate John Considine, a rumour about some very unusual happenings concerning a party of Hull FC supporters, who had travelled to Murrayfield in Edinburgh for the Challenge Cup Final, was circulating the Guildhall.

We all thought it was just another urban myth, until the Hull Daily Mail featured a front page 'scoop' on the singular circumstances surrounding Charlie Rowlin's last trip to a game of Rugby League.

Charlie, who was 77 and suffering from cancer, was a real character who even had his own seat, 'Charlie's Corner', in the Yorkshireman Pub in Hull City Centre. He had travelled to Murrayfield with his pals and although he survived long enough to see his 51st Cup Final contested between Leeds and Bradford, that night in his Glasgow hotel room, he passed away. According to the newspaper Charlie's close friend John O'Laughlan, who was looking after him, didn't know what to do for the best having tried to rouse Charlie before discovering his pal's sad demise. After talking to a couple of pals it was decided that Charlie certainly wouldn't have wanted to be laid to rest in a strange mortuary in Scotland and so they proceeded to dress him in his best suit and with his trade mark flat cap pulled down over his eyes and a pal under each arm to support him, they 'walked' Charlie outside and onto the bus home. John seated Charlie next to him in the seat right behind the driver and only told the rest of the passengers what had happened after they had been driving for around an hour.

On the journey they telephoned home to break the news and the heartbroken family in turn contacted an undertaker, who agreed to drive north to meet the bus. However Charlie's pals refused this suggestion, preferring instead to deliver Charlie back to Hull because, "Charlie would have wanted it that way". The Police then rang and were given the same answer as (like some Viking longboat bearing home the body of a great warrior) the Coach carrying Charlie, sped onwards towards Hull and 'Old Faithful' rang out from the travellers. Eventually it was flagged down by two Police cars on the A1 just outside Boroughbridge. It was a monumental and pretty unbelievable chapter of events, which I think opitomised the camaraderie that has always existed amongst those in the fellowship of Hull FC.

In the end, whatever the ethics involved, the action of those lads that day was all about friendship and doing what their pal would have wanted. Charlie's daughter said afterwards that her Dad was loved by many people and added, "Causing a big fuss like that would have just put the lid on his life. He'd have loved it".

If his last journey home was momentous, Charlie's funeral was none the less sensational, as after the cortege had driven past his beloved Boulevard Ground, a New Orleans Jazz Band led a procession into the Northern Cemetery on Chanterlands Avenue, playing (as Charlie had requested) 'When the Saints go Marching in' and of course during the service, the chapel rocked to a rousing rendition of 'Old Faithful'. What a guy Charlie Rowlin was, and what a story.

We beat Leeds but injuries blight the season

Sunday 14th May 2000   *Hull FC 26 – Leeds Rhinos 22*

There was a particularly exciting game that May when we entertained Leeds, in a game that I remember particularly for the second half.

Over 8000 watched as Leeds charged into the lead, and we trailed 16-4 at half time. Afterwards, we were told that Shaun McRae's half time talk was "X rated", but it worked and by the 60 minute mark, we had reversed our fortunes to lead 20-16. At that point, led by big Wayne McDonald and half backs Richard Horne and Will Robinson, we looked to be turning the tide, before Karl Pratt crashed in at the corner to restore Leeds' lead.

That day I watched from the New Threepenny Stand and from where I was sitting I could see Shane Richardson doing an impression of a 'Jack in a Box', springing from his seat, punching his hand and constantly asking the PA announcer "How long to go". However three minutes from time as we trailed the Rhino's 20-22, Shane and the rest of us, were in raptures, jumping up and down and punching the air together.

We had all just witnessed the mercurial Will Robinson instigate a brilliant cross field move, which culminated with prop forward Andy Hick scoring next to the posts. A last minute Leeds break was thwarted by a great 'ball and all' tackle by Hick and before the Leeds player could get up, the hooter went and the crowd erupted as once again we had beaten Leeds and once again, we didn't want to go home.

I saw all but four away games in that 2000 season and it was certainly a better year, however the rest of the campaign seemed to pale a little into insignificance following the happenings and backlash from the Galpharm Stadium incident, although the Club, the Independent Supporters' Association and the fans themselves worked tirelessly to rebuild the tarnished reputation of a Club that, as far as the sporting world was concerned, was definitely on probation. That season perhaps didn't quite match the expectations of our new owners as far as the size of the crowd was concerned and attendances certainly declined towards the end of the year.

Still Hull FC finished 7th in the Super League table with 12 wins, which was a distinct improvement on what we were used to, but our efforts in an extended post season play off series were beset with injuries and we won just two games. In mid season Andy Hick retired with a knee injury, at a time when we had a total of 11 players side lined. Still at least that crisis saw a lot of good youngsters stepping up to the first team with Craig Poucher, Andy Last, Paul King, Richard Horne, Richard Fletcher and Paul Cooke all getting their chance to shine.

Rising from the Cricket Circle – the coming of the KC

For the 2001 season, because of the Rugby League's quota regulations, the Club had to take a serious look at their overseas contingent. An amazing 20 players of the squad that started the 2000 season left the Club as we looked to rebuild the team. Our big capture was Jason Smith, who arrived to be hailed as perhaps our most significant signing since Peter Sterling. The 'Smiths' didn't stop there either because we also brought half back Tony from Wigan and winger Chris from St Helens, while fans' favourites Lee Jackson and Steve Prescott returned to the Club. Other additions included youngsters Gareth Carvell and Gareth Raynor from Leeds and Matt Crowther and Paul Broadbent. I'll always remember when we re-signed Lee Jackson, that he was asked at his press conference where he was when he kicked his one and only career drop goal, to which he replied, "In front of the posts".

Things were going well at the Stadium site until the whole project was thrown into doubt by the impending demise of Hull City. It was 6.30am on a dark and dismal 6th February 2001 when two white vans from Multi Lock Ltd. arrived at Boothferry Park. Armed with padlocks and chains the drivers secured the gates, posted 'No Trespassing' notices and locked the players, staff and management out of the Stadium. By 9-00am the story was being covered by the national sporting media and a few days later the Administrators moved in.

With the future of the City's professional football team and the KC Stadium project in jeopardy, it was in a hotel at a windy, cold service area on the A1, that John North and Ian Blakey (the Chairman of the Stadium Project Board) were invited to a clandestine meeting. Into the foyer that afternoon walked the confident, distinctive and charismatic figure of Adam Pearson, with whom they were to discuss the Council's plans for the Stadium. Pearson was excited by what he heard and immediately revealed his intention to buy Hull City. At the Council we were privy to these negotiations but had to keep everything confidential for an anxious few weeks until, in early March, Adam was announced as the new owner of the Football Club and the Stadium project was back on track again.

Shortly afterwards as the sale of the Boulevard to the Council for £750,000 was finally completed, I attended a meeting in the Leader's Office at the Guildhall where in the presence of their legal teams, Adam Pearson and Shane Richardson signed up to leases which would enable their respective Clubs to play at the new Stadium for the next 25 years. Hull KR had been offered the chance to join the party and play there too, but they declined the offer citing, "Not wanting to move from their core support in East Hull, into a Stadium that would probably be too big for them anyway".

As the 'Red and White's' number one fan, Deputy Prime Minister John Prescott, hit the headlines for landing a right hook on the jaw of an egg throwing protester at the hustings, people in West Hull were more concerned about Hull FC hitting the ground running at the start of the 2001 season. The team spent a week at the La Santa Complex in

In this 2002 view from a Private Box in the Roy Waudby Stand at the Boulevard you can see the KC Stadium rising above the West Hull skyline. *(Courtesy of Chris Turner)*

The KC Stadium starts to take shape.

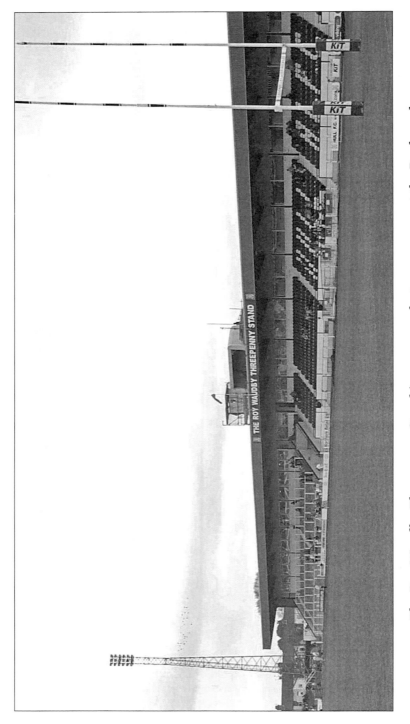

The Roy Waudby Threepenny Stand in 2002, our last ever season at the Boulevard.

The Challenge Cup Semi Final 30th July 2005. Motu Tony seals the victory and doesn't he enjoy it! *(Courtesy of Hull Daily Mail)*

We're going to Wembley! The triumphant Hull FC squad savour the moment after beating the Saints in the Cup semi-final 2005.
(Courtesy of Hull Daily Mail)

Some fans had an eventful journey to Cardiff and none more so than Ian Puckering whose car was hit by a Leeds Rhino's vehicle when the driver decided to do a U turn into the oncoming traffic.

Motu Tony kicks ahead to score; an iconic image from the Challenge Cup Final, 27th August 2005.

(Courtesy of Hull Daily Mail)

Cardiff 2005 and Richard Horne breaks the Leeds' line and looks for support.

At the Millennium Stadium, Airlie Bird gets to be the first Hull F.C. Club Mascot to ever raise the Challenge Cup.

Gareth Carvell, Jamie Thackerey and Ewan Dowes
enjoy the moment.

Stephen Kearney takes on the Leeds defence in the 2005 Cup Final
at the Millennium Stadium.

A day we'll never ever forget as Brough, Chester, Dowes and King
come over to the fans.

(Courtesy of Hull Daily Mail)

Fans in the Millennium Stadium couldn't believe what they had witnessed and didn't want to leave at the end.

(Picture: Sez it all)

The afternoon after the day before and the Hull players and staff celebrate on the balcony of the City Hall in Victoria Square.

(Courtesy of Hull Daily Mail)

Lanzarote, where Coach McRae set a target of a top five finish, before we began the season with four wins and a draw.

Throughout what was a memorable campaign a major factor in our success was our ability to beat sides in the lower reaches of the League. Halifax, Salford, Huddersfield and London were all beaten home and away and our only real stumbling block was a dour Castleford side who took three points off us. In mid season, injures hit us hard again and we brought in Australian Scott Logan, who, despite playing in the Premier Division of the Australian game benefitted from having a British Passport which meant he was able to arrive almost immediately.

That year Skipper Tony Grimaldi did a tremendous job in his last season at the Club, Luke Felsch was outstanding and Steve Prescott superb at times. A seven match winning run completed the League season in some style. In fact only a 3 point defeat by the Wigan Warriors and a 4 point reversal at St Helens in the Eliminator Semi Final saw us fail to get to Old Trafford and the Grand Final. The biggest disappointment however was the level of attendance at the Boulevard and an average of less than 7000 wasn't good enough to sustain our current level of investment. It's hard to entice fans back after years of disappointment, but we all joined Shane Richardson in hoping that the following year, our last in the Boulevard, would see a vast improvement.

As 2001 drew to a close I drove to West Park every Thursday afternoon to watch the new Super Stadium taking shape, while the Club moved quickly to secure more new signings as Toa Kohi Love arrived from Warrington, Craig Greenhill and Sean Ryan from Australia and Chris Chester from Wigan. However bad news was to follow as our charismatic Chief Executive Shane Richardson left in December to move back home to Australia, where he took up a similar position at the Penrith Panthers. It was a sad day when he left, and the Hull Daily Mail carried the front page quote from a fan, "Thanks Shane for Saving us" which, for every Hull FC fan, just about said it all!

The last year at our spiritual home begins and we're straight out of the Cup at Wigan!

Saturday 9ᵗʰ February 2002   Hull FC 10 – Wigan Warriors 34

That Christmas, a web cam was positioned on the top of Hull Royal Infirmary so that we could all follow the building of the new Stadium and we played a special Boxing Day Challenge game at New Craven Park against Hull KR. On a bumpy, bare playing surface that Shaun McRae described as "Unbelievable" and with 13 players still out of the Country or recovering from pre season operations, we fielded an inexperienced team that featured youngsters Kirk Yeaman, Graeme Horne, Matty McGuire, Dean O'Laughlin, Craig Cook and Ian Bell. Following the departure of 'Richo', Trish Goldsmith was appointed Managing Director and her flamboyant style saw the previous season ticket sales record of 2,400 surpassed in just 12 weeks. That March my old boss at the Leisure Services Department Colin Brown, who was now Chief Executive at the Deep, supervised the opening of the world's first 'Submarium', which attracted 50,000 visitors in the first 13 days. This development was to be shortly followed by the opening of the new Museum Quarter in High Street.

My 'Hull Tourism' team was really busy that summer and the City was buzzing as visitor numbers rocketed, but at the Council things were changing with a new senior management structure in place that was dictating a new direction for the Authority. The latter seemed to me to shift the emphasis away from delivering services to the people (which let's face it, is the reason for having local authorities in the first place), onto bureaucracy and paperwork. As the feedback, procurement procedures, monitoring and general form filling started to mount up, I was getting a little disenchanted with the whole thing and after 36 years working at Hull City Council, for the first time since I was terrorised by 'Mudball' in Eastern Cemetery back in 1969, I wasn't enjoying work at all.

On the rugby front we were all excited by the new season but our expectations were dashed when we drew Wigan at the JJB Stadium in the Kellogg's Nutrograin Challenge Cup Round 3 and I travelled over the Pennines for a game in which we were well beaten 34-10. However another new recruit Graham Mackey made a superb debut and although the powerful centre scored a storming try it wasn't enough to stop us exiting from the competition at the first hurdle. That disappointment was however followed by a wonderful home performance against London on the 1st April.

That day Hull FC weren't 'the fools', as almost 7000 fans watched an enthralling game, as young forward Gareth Carvell and experienced Aussie, Craig Greenhill terrorised the visitors with some awesome forward play. Carvell scored a hat-trick in a game that at one point saw Hull FC trailing 26-12, before three late tries snatched an unlikely 30-26 win. Then four days later, a long trip to Wigan in foggy conditions was all worthwhile as we ended a run of 12 consecutive defeats there by beating 'The Pies' 18-20 in another thrilling encounter. About 1000 of us sang Hull FC 'home' that night and the highlights of a fine performance were the tenacity of Greenhill and Co. in the pack, and an amazing match winning individual try by 19 year old Richard Horne, just 7 minutes from the end.

Lee Briers 'drops' us in it

Sunday 6th May 2002   *Hull FC 16 – Warrington Wolves 19*

Things were going well, so well that the visit of a struggling Warrington Wolves to the Boulevard in early May was seen by most as a formality. We were undefeated at home, sitting 2nd in the Super League and celebrating Shaun McRae's 200th game as a Coach in this country. Warrington on the other hand arrived in Hull after 7 defeats and were under extreme pressure from their fans (who were demanding 'the head' of their Coach, David Plange). The stage was set for a higher than average gate to witness a mauling, but Warrington scrum half Lee Briers had other ideas.

Three times during the game he used good field position, gifted to the visitors by some sloppy Hull play, to drop a goal. If it hadn't have been for the constant heckling from the Threepenny Stand that tally could have been a lot higher, as he missed with another 4 attempts. Chester scored a great try for Hull when he broke, fed Deon Bird and took the return pass to touch-down and reduce the Warrington lead to just 12-15, but two minutes later, hero became villain, as Chester dropped a speculative pass close to the Warrington line, which Briers swooped on to run 90 yards to score. It was, I remember, a really disappointing performance and despite Mackey crashing in from a short Paul Cooke pass with 4 minutes to go, it was all too little, too late and we went down to our first home defeat of the season.

It was a story of missed chances, as twice Crowther saw his attempts at goal hit the post and bounce agonisingly wide and Paul Cooke could have scored had he spotted the gap to his left. Paul King lost the ball near the line and after a great break by Gareth Raynor, a possible scoring move broke down as Mackey wasted the chance with a pass straight into touch. All three Warrington tries came from Hull mistakes, including an easy score for Rodwell, as the ball bounced out of Crowther's arms in our in-goal area and the Warrington captain gleefully pounced.

In the end it was a perfect example of how patience and tenacity often supercedes over confidence. That game was certainly a reality check for everyone and left us all coveting Lee Briers, a man who was to torment us time and again over the years.

Chesney should have known Better!

That July I had another stressful weekend when on a boiling hot Sunday afternoon East Park played host to one of the biggest pop music gatherings the City had seen. 25,000 kids turned up to watch Blue, Darius and Gareth Gates and the excitable crowd had to be regularly dowsed with water to keep them cool. As the promoters hadn't engaged enough security staff, keeping order away from the stage was difficult and several fights broke out as the lethal cocktail of sun and alcohol started to take effect. This volatile situation wasn't helped at all by probably the oldest person on the bill that afternoon Chesney Hawkes.

He decided to augment a rousing rendition of his only real hit 'I am the One and Only' by climbing up the lighting rig. As it swayed backwards and forwards under his weight and the security staff tried in vain to get him down, I concluded that, "I really don't need all this!"

In the world of Rugby, Castleford had latterly become our bogey team, but we laid that ghost in 2002 following two good wins, but July was a disappointing month after we came so close to beating both Bradford and St Helens at the Boulevard.

After leading 22-6 against London at Griffin Park we went down 46-32 and results in August and September trailed off again, culminating in a 52-10 defeat at Headingley and a 64-10 defeat to St Helens. Without doubt both performances were horror shows, I know I was there, and after the Saints' game Shaun McRae came desperately close to quitting, citing "A Cancer that is apparent within the team". We never really got to the bottom of what he was alluding to, but thankfully after a weekend of reflection our Coach changed his mind. However in three seasons we had finished 7th, 4th and 5th in Super League and for the fans that was certainly a lot better than the trials and tribulations that had gone before.

I guess that as seasons go the 2002 campaign, the last at the Boulevard, was a successful one, although Shaun McRae did take the opportunity early on to remind us of what he said back in 2000. Then, as we started to digest the implications of a merger he said it would take five years to get the Club winning trophies again and in that context, he was pleased with our progress. Shaun was of course to be proved blissfully right at the end of that '5 year plan' but our downfall in 2002 was without doubt our lack of consistency, both during games and over the season. On several occasions we established a commanding lead before becoming careless and letting the opposition back into the game. On the terraces we all agreed that our main failing was a lack of pace, when compared with what Leeds, Saints and Wigan had to offer.

As if to address our concerns and to improve our chances for the next campaign the Club brought in Aussie flyer Colin Best and iconic London Bronco's centre Richie Barnett, both of whom were really fast players.

A Life Changing Moment

I have spoken previously about the fact that at work, things were changing and as the Liberal Democrats ousted the Labour Party to take control of the City Council for the first time in living memory, more Management re-structuring was taking place and I wasn't too impressed. My position was fine and I seemed to be going from strength to strength, as I now added management of the City Centre to my 'portfolio' of responsibilities. However years of working 50 and 60 hours a week and being on call for Councillors, the media and other public agencies 24 hours a day, had worn me down. At last I was really settled at home, content with my lot outside work and living in a cottage in Beverley. Despite only being 52 I'd certainly had enough of the constant stress and as toughing it out wasn't really in my make-up, I just tried to put on 'a brave face' for the staff, when in actuality inside it had all just worn me down. The Doctor prescribed me some tablets to help me get through, but I had starting to feel permanently tired and pretty vulnerable.

The final straw came that October as once again the worry, anxiety and pressure of overseeing Hull Fair returned. That year the Fair was going reasonably well until the Tuesday night when there was a near disaster, after a 17 year old girl fell 30 feet from the 'The Bomber' ride and was rushed to Hull Royal Infirmary critically ill with head injuries. The ride was stopped with four other riders stuck at the opposite end of the rotating arm for almost an hour, and they were subsequently also admitted to hospital with hypothermia.

The incident caused an uneasy air around the Fairground that night, as some of the attractions closed early while rumours flew round the Showmen and staff like wildfire and I struggled to find out what had actually happened. As I worked with the Police and Fire Brigade, the Health and Safety Executive inspectors from Sheffield arrived and word spread quickly as I started to field what was to turn into an avalanche of enquiries from the local and national media. There is nothing a hack likes more than an accident at a Fairground! I couldn't find anything out about the condition of the girl, and it wasn't until after midnight that night that I arrived back home totally drained and rang the Chief

Executive of the Authority Jim Brookes to inform him of the incident. He was brilliant in his support that night, but next day there was a 'media frenzy' and I was in the middle of it. The team that had run the operational side of the fair so brilliantly for me for so many years were obviously in shock too, so it was down to me to face the music and take the heat from the media.

That day, as I stood with my legal representative and good pal, Jeff Turgoose, Sky News, BBC1's News at Ten, the local TV networks and Channel 4 all queued up to interview me in front of a Bingo stall on Walton Street. The outcome was predictable really and despite my best efforts to highlight the insurance and vigorous testing procedures each ride had to go through before it opens, it was in the end as far as they were concerned, the Council's fault. That was certainly a stressful and defining moment in a career that had over the years been littered with many such occurrences at the City Hall, Open Air Events and of course the Fair.

The injured lady thankfully made a good recovery and the Council were exonerated, but I knew the way I had been dragged through the media with little support from my superiors had left me deflated and uneasy and although I was still only 52, I was tired of it all. That cold wet night at Hull Fair was for me, the 'tipping point' and the time when I knew that if I were to have any life at all after work, I had to get out. That incident just highlighted for me where I was at as a person, and an influx of new managers, a more strategic and complex approach to delivering simple services and a change in the political focus of the organisation, (coupled with that stress) now made 'Escape' an imperative. I didn't know how I would do it but with the City Council needing to reduce its workforce and the saving grace of the 'Final Salary Pension Scheme' that I has subscribed to since I was 18, there was certainly scope to give it a go.

As the Doctor increased the dosage of the 'downers', and I looked for an escape plan, there was still one very significant game of rugby left to go and as we had been disappointedly knocked out in the First Round stage of the play-offs by Leeds, all the Hull FC lads got 10 days off before they faced the New Zealand Tourists in the last ever game to be played at our spiritual home.

A last hurrah for the Boulevard

Tuesday 22nd October 2002　　　　*Hull FC 11 – New Zealand 28*

As a mellow, yellowing 'Old Faithful' moon hung over the trees that flanked the most famous 'avenue' in Rugby League, I turned into the Boulevard, glancing briefly beyond the Anlaby Road Flyover to my right, at the outlines of the new Stadium looming out of the night. Like hundreds of others and not wishing to miss a thing, I arrived really early and before taking up my place for the last time on that now infamous 'Lucky Step' at the Airlie Street end, I had a last pint in the bar under the Threepenny Stand surrounded by the memories on the walls.

Those framed icons that had for so long been 'part of the wallpaper' included the receipt for the transfer of 'Knocker' Norton from Castleford in 1978, a picture of Dave Topliss lifting the Challenge Cup and Clive Sullivan's International shirt. The whole evening was a celebration of one of the most famous Rugby League Grounds in the World and 12,092 Hull FC fans past and present were desperate to be part of it.

Before the actual rugby started there was a parade around the perimeter of the playing area led by the City of Hull Pipe Band which included a procession of ex Hull FC players that had come from across the world to be there that night. True to the definition that bagpipes are the missing link between music and noise, as they passed us, the band played a rousing 'Gaelic' version of 'Old Faithful' and as I looked round many of the 'old hands' that had laughed, cried, fretted and rejoiced with us over the years, were in tears. It was certainly a moving experience as I stood there with my family, while to my left Billy Jenkinson (and his five sons), Garry, Billy the Wiz, Pearly and all the gang with whom, over the years, I had shared my life-long obsession, came together for one last time.

Before the current Hull FC Super League team took on the touring New Zealanders there was a game featuring Hull Ex Players who took on Great Britain Ex Players. The story goes that at 71 'Gentleman' Johnny Whiteley was asked to lead the teams out for this 'Curtain Raiser'. Apparently, (despite having two replacement hips), he simply replied, "Lead them out, no chance, I'm playing". Garry Kemble one of those famous Kiwi's who played for the Club back in the 80's was out there, as were many of the other favourites featured in this tome. It was a real spectacle, but with the formalities over we all awaited the teams for the last ever game at the Boulevard.

Lee Jackson, still smarting from being told that he would not be retained at the Club for the following history making season, was made captain for the night, and he put in a vintage performance. It was also ironic that after all the memorable tries that had been scored at the Boulevard the best score that night, was possibly the longest drop goal the place had ever seen. It was a fabulous 51 yard effort by Graham Mackey who was also playing his last game for the Club. While he was still stood in his own half Graham struck the ball sweetly and it soared downfield and between the posts. It was a magical moment on a magical night as ironically the only other drop goal Graham had scored in his career was in Australia 11 years earlier. His shiny bald head meant that he soon acquired the nickname of 'Uncle Fester' a title by which he was know thoughout his stay at the Club. That drop goal came on the stroke of half time and saw Hull go in leading the New Zealanders 7-6, our try having come from Richard Horne, who chased a short grubber kick to the line by Lee Jackson. One blemish on an otherwise excellent half was the loss of Steve Prescott in the early stages with a sprung shoulder.

The second half started with the visitors introducing hooker Richard Swain from the bench and within ten minutes they were in front through a smart try, as Hohaia kicked ahead twice to touch down. Then tries from Nigel Vagana and Fa'afili followed before the last try to be scored against the Airlie Birds at the Boulevard, went to Francis Meli, who intercepted a Paul Cooke pass and raced 90 yards unopposed to touch down.

However the drama extended to the very end as the last try to be scored there was right on the 'hooter' and by Hull FC's Paul Parker. It came just 10 seconds before the end from an unlikely kick by Prop Craig Greenhill. Parker latched onto the ball 20 yards out and rounded Vaekiki in classic wing style to touch down to the biggest cheer of the night. It was a fitting and atmospheric end to 107 years of triumph and disaster at what was our spiritual home.

Afterwards the crowd demanded the traditional New Zealand battle cry, by chanting "Haka Haka Haka" and the Tourists obliged at every side of the Ground. It reminded me of the time it was performed by Arthur Bunting and the boys in 1983, in front of the old Threepenny Stand when we won the Championship. As the fireworks that read Hull FC 1865-2002 crackled and spluttered at the other end, 'Old Faithful' rang out continuously around the ground and no one wanted to go home. As I finally reached the top of the steps at the back of the terracing, I took one last look back over my shoulder to see the ball boys out on the now deserted pitch playing with the match ball, just as I had done as a kid almost 50 years earlier. Leaving the Boulevard left me saddened, empty and with nowhere to run when the going got tough!

That was it then, the "Round up Days" were well and truly over and the place that was "White with Clover" was no more. I had moved about a lot in my life both relationship and accommodation wise and although for the first time I was really settled and happy, the uncertainty at work meant that leaving the Boulevard behind was a big blow. Since I had left that little house across the street in Aylesford Street 36 years earlier, that Ground had been my emotional anchor in the past and I suppose if I'm honest, a 'Comfort Blanket' of sorts. It was somewhere that I was compelled to revisit every other week if I wanted to watch the team I loved, and thus, by default, I was also constantly in touch with my spiritual home and the world in which I grew up.

The old Stadium may have changed over time but it had always been there. Coaches came, owners went, players left and 'must win' matches were lost, there were the highs of emotional elation and the depths of despair, but the Boulevard was constant, even if what happened there wasn't. It always offered me security, friendship and most of all hope. It was a very powerful, evocative place which had played a significant role in my life and was for me in the end nothing less than home. Looking back, I probably felt more at ease there than anywhere else on earth and for all of us who frequented it over the years The Boulevard was the place where we'd be able to shelter from whatever was going on in the rest of our lives and where we'd been able to dream. You were always amongst friends, it was a safe haven and the only place where, for 80 minutes at least, reality was suspended and the pressures of the world were shut out.

A couple of nights later I went with Steve Massam and a couple of other mates to a dinner, in a marquee, behind the New Threepenny Stand. At midnight with Martin Dunn our then head of Junior Rugby, we all walked out onto the centre spot and raised a glass to the old place. As we walked back towards the Threepenny Stand that was it, foreclosure, The Boulevard was no more as far as Hull FC was concerned and although in the coming years I would return from time to time to stand and remember, as far as everything else was concerned it was over.

The 'Wow factor' lives up to its billing

So the task of 'flitting' across Anlaby Road began. The fans were certainly up for it with £100,000 of passes being sold on the first day they were available. That was 8 times more than in the corresponding period the previous year and on that first morning I was there queuing at the Boulevard for mine, as usual. We had to pick our seats from a photograph of the new stadium and I chose to sit in the East Stand, where we remain as a family to this day. It was certainly a new dawn for the City of Hull as the skyline now included the Stadium and the Deep and there was a feeling around the place that the whole area was going places.

My next big project for the Council was to manage the opening of the KC Stadium. On Sunday 15th December, ironically whilst millions of pounds were dropping off the price of KC shares on the stock exchange, the doors of the Stadium that bore that organisations' name were flung open to the public. Thousands, dressed in their Hull City and Hull FC favors, queued in a light drizzle to get a first glimpse of their new home. Before they were admitted, the first fan to actually experience the place was blind lifelong Hull FC supporter Donald Marshall and as the crowds started to file into the Stadium, I sat with him in the West Stand with another Hull FC fan, Lord Mayor, Councillor Terry Geraghty. In the lead up to that opening much was made by the media of the 'Wow' factor but for many, as they walked out of the access tunnel and into the Stadium for the first time, 'Wow' was for once a bit of an understatement.

New beginnings, as 11 men see off Halifax

Sunday 9th February 2003   *Hull FC 24 – Halifax Blue Sox 16*

The Hull players experienced their first taste of the new Stadium at a training session on Thursday 6th February and then the waiting was over as we all made our way to the KC Stadium for our first game, a Challenge Cup tie against Halifax. It was amazingly (for someone so young) Richard Horne's 100th game for the Club and 15,310 attended that day to witness one of the most bizarre starts to a game I had ever seen. Within 28 seconds of the kick off skipper and loose forward Jason Smith had left the field, sent off by referee Steve Ganson. It was only the second tackle when, to a stunned silence all around the ground, Jason trooped off having been found guilty of a high tackle on Halifax's Chris Birchall.

Roared on by the crowd, the shorthanded home team took the game to Halifax and in the 7th minute everyone was out of their seats as Colin Best flew in at the corner, to become the first person to score a try at The KC Stadium. Crowther converted, but back roared the visitors as loanee Dane Dorahy scored near the posts and his conversion and a penalty, saw the scoreboard soon reading 8-6 to the visitors. When Scott Logan was felled by a high shot Crowther converted a penalty to level things up and a further exchange of penalties made it 10-10, heading for half-time. Then a superb stadium was graced with an equally superb try engineered by Paul King and Steve Prescott. They made ground down field and broke the line before a magical piece of touch-line running by new signing Richie Barnett completely fooled Halifax full-back Finnerty and Barnett touched down in the corner.

We led 16-10 at half time and just two minutes into the second half we scored again when Toa Kohe-Love crashed in after Richard Horne had made the break. Then Greenwood scored a try for the opposition before, eight minutes into the second half, Hull's Richard Fletcher was also sent off for a high tackle on Andy Hobson. Down to 11 men and just leading 20-16, Hull FC, roared on by a fanatical support, really had to dig deep to hold out wave after wave of Halifax attacks.

Dwayne West ruptured his ligaments in the next move; an injury that was to keep him out for the rest of the season, but undeterred our defence was simply awesome, as tired and battered bodies were continuously put on the line. A 61st minute penalty by Crowther calmed our nerves and as the visitors started to get frustrated, he landed another one just before the hooter to seal a memorable win. That victory was later likened to another fabulous performance years earlier in 1974 when after a proposed 'walk off' by the Hull players, we beat Leeds again with 11 men.

Shaun McRae stood at pitch side after the game and applauded every one of his player from the field, he said afterwards that he was, "The proudest man in the Stadium" but that was debatable, because we all felt proud that afternoon having witnessed a dramatic and fitting 'christening' for our new home.

The young 'guns' shoot down Wigan

Friday 4th April 2003   *Hull FC 20 – Wigan Warriors 4*

Another memorable game that year was when Wigan arrived at the new KC Stadium, on a night that 12,000 fans would roar our heroes home to a famous victory under the KC lights and in front of the Sky TV cameras.

We'd won all our League games so far that year having been victorious over Wakefield and Warrington away and Widnes at the KC, but now we faced our biggest test in the shape of the Wigan Warriors. The visitors were rocked just before kick off when their out of contract star Julian O'Neill walked out of their hotel, to sign for the Widnes Vikings. From the start of the game Wigan put us under some pressure and Richard Horne, playing that day at full back, twice relieved the pressure by fielding a couple of big kicks hoisted by Lam. However Chris Chester twice lost the ball in our half to give the visitors good field position from which they pressed forward.

A short kick towards the corner by Lam looked to be ideally placed for ex FC hero Brian Carney who was now playing for Wigan. He raced downfield to be thwarted by Prescott as he slid in to take the ball at Carney's feet. Then Wigan's Hock and Mark Smith stole the ball from Greenhill and from the ensuing penalty Prescott added the two points for Hull FC to take the lead. Our defence was holding up well but our attack lacked variation and it was unfortunate when our best chance so far went to ground as a Colin Best pass was intercepted. Another penalty by Prescott made it 4-0, before we scored our first try. A Jason Smith kick spiralled in the air allowing Best, under great pressure from Dallas, to rise above the defence and bring it down over the line to score. David Doyle-Davidson, commentating that day on local radio, declared that Best "Rose like a Salmon", but Referee Kirkpatrick referred the decision to the Video Referee, who eventually awarded the try and we went in at half time, 10-0 up.

Jason Smith who was left hobbling in the first half after a crash tackle on halfway, didn't re-appear in the second, but after just a few minutes Adam Maher, who was having a superb game, took a kick through by Chester and beat Carney in a chase to the corner, where he scored his first try of the season and Hull's second of the night. Leading 14-0 and looking reasonably comfortable, Hull then had to endure some Wigan pressure. The visitors attack charged forward, but a fierce tackle from Chester caused Carney to fumble the ball and then shortly afterwards, a big hit from Richie Barnett saw Brett Dallas pushed into touch, as, on their feet, the crowd broke into another round of 'Old Faithful'.

However, after a great move orchestrated by Richie Barnett and Fletcher, disaster struck. The latter made a blockbusting run and fed Logan who barrelled downfield trailing tacklers in his wake and was just inches short of the line when he eventually went down under two Wigan forwards. He stayed on the ground as the players waived for medical assistance and after a delay of around 8 minutes Scott Logan was stretchered from the field with a broken leg. Just three minutes later Kohe-Love looked to have sustained a serious arm injury in the tackle and he had to go off too. The visitor's pressure was starting to tell and on 64 minutes Wigan teenage sensation Gareth Hock stole in for a try after he had dummied the Hull defence at a play the ball and dived through. With injuries disrupting things and Wigan on a roll, we needed a try badly, and we got one.

The injuries meant that we now had several of our young players on the field, and they showed their worth straight away as Graeme Horne ran down the blind side, Paul Cooke took on the defence and Yeaman side stepped twice, before crashing in to score. Kirk had done well in the centre of late and as always his score was particularly popular with the Hull fans. Prescott missed with the kick but was successful with a penalty shortly afterwards when a Maher break led to Graeme Horne being tripped, when he would have scored. At 20-4 the Wigan side had obviously had enough and the dejected Cherry and Whites played out the final minutes in midfield before the hooter was greeted with a cheer you could probably have heard in Wigan!

We played the Bradford Bulls early in June in a game that pitted second against first in the table. The match was attended by 3000 Bradford fans and the interest the Hull Club were generating since their move to the KC saw the biggest gate in nearly 30 years of 19,539 in attendance at a game that we eventually lost 26-20. Once again we were reduced to 11 men, (again by referee Steve Ganson), when Treister was sin-binned and then Fletcher sent off. Some referees it seems do enjoy being in the centre of things don't they?

That summer on the City Council was another interesting one as Labour regained an overall majority in the local elections and immediately suspended Jim Brookes the Chief Executive.

That was another national TV and radio nightmare, which, as Head of Media, I was right in the middle of, and as the Authority appealed for volunteers to come forward to make up a total of 2000 people that needed to be made redundant to balance the books, I decided that it was time to launch my 'Escape plan'.

Getting out while the going was good!!!

At the Council even after 38 years service, the process of getting a release on 'early retirement' was a long and convoluted one, particularly if you were any good at your job. The Voluntary Severance Scheme was often used to free the Authority of staff that they wanted to see the back of and for me at first as many obstacles as possible were put in my way, as everyone told me, "We aren't letting you go". However following an appeal through the Trade Union and an interview with the new Leader, Colin Inglis, (who played a blinder) I obtained the necessary signatures and a leaving date of 6th August 2003 was decided upon. I was still taking the tablets and totally disillusioned with the culture in the Council and the fact that many of the new Managers that had been brought into my Senior Management Team, were not even from Hull and seemed to have little interest in it as a City.

They simply didn't seem to understand the issues, seeing their positions as career moves rather than a vocation, and that made my decision all the easier. What was really hard however was leaving the staff in the Image and Promotion team, because most of them were my pals and although sometimes I had to be 'The Boss', we all got on well as friends as well as colleagues.

So it was that at 1-00pm on 6th August a gathering of around 200 people formed in the Reception Room of the Guildhall, as Councillor Dave Gemmell presented me with some gifts from the staff and the proceeds of a quite voluminous collection. Then we all went across Alfred Gelder Street to 'The Three John Scotts' and there I stayed sustained by a constant flow of friends, colleagues and beer, until after 11-00pm. That day, it is said that I broke the 'Council Retirement (All

Comers) drinking record', as all those years of practising at away games and in the Half Way, The Mermaid and The Punch came to fruition. It is still said in the hallowed portals of the Guildhall that I celebrated by consuming well over 30 bottles of Budweiser in one session and still 'lived to tell the tale'. What a shame it is that you work all those years, you retire, and the only lasting memorial to you is based on the amount of ale you drank on your last day!

I needed to make a fresh start and to try and get the Council out of my system so before that presentation I asked my good friend Ian, with whom I had worked (and laughed) for a lot of years, to accompany me and help as I bought my own mobile phone. As an officer famed for the fact that I wrote all my E mails out long hand and gave them to my secretary to send, I had always resisted owning a mobile phone and instead, (when I had to) I used the instrument that had been forced on me several years earlier by the Council.

This done, in a sort of ritualistic cleansing of all things Hull City Council, I went down to the Pier and threw the remains of my latest course of 'happy' tablets and my Council phone into the River. Next day I continued this process by throwing out most of my work suits, shirts and ties, and as if to demonstrate a weight being lifted off my shoulders, I shaved off my moustache. I think the rationale behind the latter action was due mainly to the amount of alcohol I still had in my system, after that mammoth session the day before, however its removal was to prove a talking point for weeks. Often women from work would stop me in the street and say "I didn't recognise you without your moustache" to which I would laugh and reply, "I'd like to be able to say the same thing to you!" Most didn't get it at all, while others probably chose to ignore me.

While all this was going on in my life, at the KC, Adam Maher announced his retirement with a year of his contract left and because the 'Overseas Quota' rules were changing, Craig Greenhill and Sean Ryan were allowed to leave for Castleford. Toa Kohe-Love had also refused a new contract when it was offered in June, and he was replaced by Michael Eager the ex-International Centre from Castleford.

A bigger squad and the arrival of Richard Swain

Flush with the increased income from the ever increasing gates at the KC, the Club decided that to succeed they needed to increase the size of the squad from 22 to over 30. Richard Swain, Paul McNicholas, Shaun Briscoe, Richie Barnett Jnr. Ryan Benjafield, Peter Lupton, Ewan Dowes and Alex Wilkinson all signed up for the 2004 season. These additions were joined in early January by two youngsters from Featherstone, Richard Whiting and Andy Bailey, who completed a squad of 31. There was however a shock before the campaign even began, when following an ugly incident the previous season, the Club received a heavy fine from the Rugby League. We were cited for an incident after a League match when on Anlaby Road Flyover a Leeds supporters' coach was 'bricked' by youths. The fact that our mascot Airlie Bird wore a bandana that proclaimed 'We all 8 Leeds' that day didn't help our case much either, as the old prejudices between the two Clubs surfaced again.

The Players then flew to their pre-season training camp in Spain, but only after their flight had been delayed whilst Paul King was removed from the plane, suffering from a severe case of claustrophobia. Still there were some fine performances that year none more than a great win at Odsal against Bradford on 23rd April, when after failing to beat the West Yorkshire Club for 10 years, 4 tries from Shaun Briscoe produced a memorable victory.

Despite the increased size of the squad the injury jinx continued and by May, after we had beaten Salford 82-6 in a Super League game, we were playing Warrington with 7 of our starting 13 players out injured. We won the match 24-18 but tragedy struck when Richard Fletcher was carried off with a double fracture of the leg after just 11 minutes, in a game that was his 'comeback' after another serious injury. Paul King also broke his hand that night but played on with it bandaged up. Scott Logan, still struggling after that broken leg sustained the previous season, became so frustrated with his demise that in May he tore up his contract and headed home. Across the City Neil Hudgell took over as Chairman of a struggling Hull KR, Jason Smith at last returned from injury for Hull F.C. and with Richard Swain driving the team forward, things started to look up.

However the injury toll continued to mount and in an effort to bolster our front row Nick Scruton a young prop forward joined us on loan from Leeds as many of the youngsters got their chance and Rich Whiting and Kirk Yeaman really went well in the centres, which was quite surprising when you consider that 'Yeamo' had asked to play in the second row at the start of the year!

In June tragedy struck when Shaun McRae's Father Jack was taken seriously ill in Australia and 'Bomber' headed off to be by his side. In his absence John Kear took charge and we won 4 and drew one of our 6 games that month. When McRae returned on 2nd July he immediately announced that he was to leave Hull FC at the end of the season and join his old pal Shane Richardson as Coach at South Sydney Rabbitohs.

Three days later as torrential rain closed schools and roads across the region, Rich Horne denied that he was going with McRae, although that didn't stop the rumours circulating until in the end they were proved to be unfounded. We had all been impressed with what John Kear had done in Shaun's absence and so were the Club, who immediately announced that John Kear would take over as Head Coach for 2005.

On the same day that Hull City signed Nick Barmby and Steve Prescott returned to the Hull FC to coach the under 16's team, Kear said, "If we don't win a trophy in 5 years believe me, I'll have failed". The last month of the season saw Hull FC rise to second in the Super League, only to be shifted into third place by St Helens on the last weekend of the competition but injuries continued to blight the year and a shortage of goal kickers prompted McRae to say, "We have a new tactic now in that whoever scores the try, has to kick the goal".

This injury situation was in the end to prove too much and we failed miserably in the play-offs. In an exciting game at the KC on 24th September (where half the side were sat in suits in the Stand), a sprightly Wakefield outfit beat us 28-18 in a game I remember best for a storming kick-off return run by Korkidas from deep in the Wakefield 20 at the start of the second half. He must have run through four tackles and for around 50 yards to set the tone for the second half, and our exit from the play offs. The following week 12 players faced surgery and a season that had promised so much but was ruined by injuries, drew to a close.

On 27th September I went to Shaun McRae's farewell dinner when 400 attended The Willerby Manor to hear Mike Stevenson and Eddie Hemmings as guest speakers, but there was hardly a dry eye in the place at the end of Shaun's farewell speech. As he circulated the tables afterwards, we asked Shaun why his nick-name was 'Bomber' to which he replied, "Only four people know that and that's how it will stay" Having sold out that dinner in just three days, another event was staged the next evening for another 400 guests. Later that week John Kear announced his Assistant Coach would be Richard Agar a part time joiner from the West Riding, who was currently coaching the York City Knights.

Kear had some strong thoughts about having his own team and playing his own way and he started to gradually change the style of play we had grown used to, since we moved to the KC. In came New Zealand legend Stephen Kearney plus Motu Tony, Nathan Blacklock, Tommy Saxton and Danny Brough. While Paul King again missed the pre season training camp in Spain because of his continuing claustrophobia and trained alone in Hull as he recovered from a knee reconstruction. 17,000 of us packed into the KC for the first game against Leeds when we were narrowly beaten by the World Champions 16-12, in a game in which Richard Swain again starred.

That February at a fans forum John Kear told us all of his love of the Challenge Cup, which he had won in acclaimed circumstances when he Coached Sheffield Eagles back in the 1990's. He said that night that you need a bit of luck in the Cup draw and that it was probably the best chance Hull had, at that time, of winning a Trophy If it was luck we needed in the Cup draw, then we got little of it, and after 4 wins in 7 games in the Super League we were drawn away at Wakefield in a difficult looking first round tie. 4000 Hull fans travelled to the West Riding that day and we amazingly won 36-12 as Shaun Briscoe, playing at full back and scoring two tries, had a great game. April however brought more injuries and a dip in form as we battled to get an unconvincing 22-22 draw at Leigh in torrential rain. However towards the end of the month, with props Paul King and Gareth Carvell back in the side we were unlucky to be defeated 36-34 at Warrington in a game when we all thought we could have just snatched a rare victory in the last ten minutes.

Brilliant attack, superb defence, "Someone up there wants us to win the Cup!"

Saturday 7th May 2005   *Hull FC 26 – Bradford Bulls 24*

Then it was back to the Cup and a daunting tie at home to one of the favourites, the Bradford Bulls, at the KC. In front of 11,350 fans I have seldom heard anything like the reception that Hull FC got that day as they ran out onto the KC turf. If the first half was a sensational attacking performance then the second was as good a defensive display as any of us could remember. It was our best performance of the season against the heavily tipped pre-match favourites from Odsal. In fact it was 25 years since our last meeting in the Cup, when Hull won 3-0 away on our way to the final. By half time, this time around, we had shot into an unexpected 20-0 lead after some glorious attacking play that had the visiting fans scratching their heads in disbelief.

Stephen Kearney was superb in defence and constantly hit, hurt and sickened the Bulls 'Big name' players, Harris, Fielden, Peacock and Robbie Paul. Shayne McMenemy, I remember, resembled a runaway train as he battered the opposition and made yards every time he had the ball, and Jamie Thackerey and Ewan Dowes were not far behind him. Young Richard Whiting in the centre also had a big game and constantly stopped the attacking thrust of the Bulls through the centre channels. Four first half tries saw us well in control but a half time talk from Bradford Coach Brian Noble certainly changed things as the visitors re appeared after the break to immediately score through Peacock. Back Hull roared as Motu Tony slid in after good work from Man of the Match Paul Cooke, but then for the final 30 minutes it was all Bradford, as Vainikolo grabbed two tries and then two minutes from time Pryce scored in the corner. This reduced the arrears to just 2 points and set up a frantic and desperate finish but we just held out! As I left the Stadium amidst scenes of adulation, I bumped into my pal Allen Bagshawe the Club Chaplin and said, "Someone up there must want us to win the Cup", to which he just smiled and said, "Let's hope so".

In the draw for the quarter finals at last luck was on our side, as a home game against another Super League team, saw us playing 'basement' Club the Leigh Centurions. It was a match that we won easily 46-14 and so we were into the semi final and drawn to play the Cup favourites St Helens at the Galpharm Stadium on 30th July. Although we had climbed to the dizzy heights of 2nd in Super League with several good wins in June, no one gave us 'a hope in hell' of winning that one.

"White Hot Hull", probably the best displays I've ever seen

Saturday 30th July 2005   *Hull FC 34 – St Helens 8*

It was certainly a big task against Super League's most successful team, the Competition favourites and a Club that was undefeated in their last 10 League and Cup games. Amazingly in addition to that, Hull hadn't beaten St Helens in a Challenge Cup tie for 70 years and that was in Round One way back in 1936. Who was going to back us against those odds?

We arrived to totally different scenes to those that greeted us in Huddersfield five years earlier before that fateful Semi-final against Leeds, as the pubs and Clubs were thronging with Hull and Saints fans. Everyone had a great time as the opposition felt confident that the game was a foregone conclusion and the 'FC Faithful' were intent on having a good day out.

In the Stadium as the Hull fans raised the roof and the teams ran out into bright sunshine, the script may have been written but our players hadn't read it and immediately the Hull pack tore into the St. Helens forwards. The season had seen highs and lows, but all the while Kear had stressed the importance of peaking at the right time and this was it. Hull's defence was superb as they 'crawled all over' the favourites and Richard Whiting gave a brilliant display as he completely snuffed out the threat of Gardner, Talau and Wellens. However it was the kicking of Danny Brough, Richard Horne and Loose Forward Paul Cooke that won the day as the Airlie Birds pinned Saints back in their own half, forcing a total of five goal line drop outs.

On the rare occasions that their defensive wall was breached Hull re-grouped valiantly, no one more so than Richie Barnett (Jnr) who scrambled back to pull off a brilliant tackle on Gardner just before the break, when Hull held a slender 8-2 lead. It was in fact quite amazing that Saints rarely threatened our line and their only try came from a mix up between Gareth Raynor and Shaun Briscoe when Jamie Lyon latched onto a Sean Long kick to go on and touch-down for an easy try.

Hull had started the game brilliantly as Cooke carved out an opening for McMenemy to charge in before we exchanged penalties and went in at half time in the lead. However after a half time break when we fretted and worried about a St Helens' backlash, the crunch came on 54 minutes after Whiting had brilliantly chased a kick to force a fourth drop out. Horne provided quick service for acting half back Cooke, McMenemy worked a run-around that Dave Topliss would have appreciated and Cooke backed himself to stretch out and score. At 16-8 for the first time we were two scores ahead and 4 minutes later we were in again when McMenemy dropped on a loose ball that Richard Horne had dribbled through the favourites' defence.

Saints had often been dubbed the comeback kings and as 'Old Faithful' rang around the Stadium no-one could relax. With 6 minutes to go Whiting made a stunning break out of our own half and set up a position from where Motu Tony, who had come on for the injured Barnett, crashed in to score and as we stood in disbelief with tears in our eyes Stephen Kearney brilliantly opened up the tiring St Helens' defence to send in Richard Horne and a remarkable victory was complete. Richard Swain, Kearney, Cooke, Brough and Horne had masterminded a sensational win and as "We're the famous Hull FC and were off to Wembley" rang around the ground the players celebrated, John Kear ran around punching the air, and I sat and cried.

Leaving the ground we were met by one of the most unusual sights that I have ever seen in 50 years of watching the game of Rugby League as hundreds of Saints fans lined the pavements and even got off their buses to stand and applaud us! That was so unexpected and a lot less predictable than was the cavalcade of cars, with fans hanging out of the windows, that tooted their horns all the way back along the M62 to Hull. It was without doubt the most complete and cultured performance I have ever seen on a Rugby League pitch and believe me the one that follows was pretty good!

After years of heartache and disappointment; catharsis in Cardiff!

The week before the final all the old anxiety was back! I couldn't stop thinking about the game for a minute; it was in my mind when I woke up, when I went to bed and when I was asleep. It was no longer a case of thinking about it every few seconds because I was never, not thinking about it. Finally Friday came, although the journey to the Millennium Stadium is all a bit of a blur really, as five of us travelled down to South Wales crammed into a Ford Fiesta. We journeyed along with hundreds of Hull fans overtaking and being over taken by buses, coaches and on one occasion a furniture removal van all festooned in black and white. We were in good spirits as only a week earlier we had narrowly lost 24-28 to Wigan at the KC in a game that at one point we had trailed 26-8. In fact most of us believed we would have gone on to win had a Danny Brough conversion, ten minutes from the end not bounced up off the cross bar and fallen short.

Once we got south of Birmingham we encounter quite a few cars full of Leeds fans. Some waved, others gave us the thumbs down whilst many flicked V's and gave that 'masturbatory' sign with their hands. However, all in all, unlike that of some others, mine was an uneventful journey. My pal Ian was not so lucky and almost spent Saturday afternoon in hospital instead of at the game. He had stayed in the Forest of Dean on Friday and on the morning of the game offered to give two Leeds fans that were stopping at the same hotel, a lift to the match.

On the way there at Newport another Leeds fan in a Range Rover, who was having a dispute with his wife about the direction to the ground, ('Sat Nag' I think it's called) did a U turn and crashed into Ian's car. The four occupants had to be pulled from the wreckage and were consigned to hospital. The Leeds fans agreed to go, but Ian and his son fearing that they would miss the game, somehow 'dragged' themselves to the Stadium. When Ian got home he was found to have a broken sternum. He had survived the car crash unscathed, but after the final Hull try, his son hugged his dad so hard, he sustained the injury.

A chance meeting on the proudest day of my life!

Saturday August 27th 2005   *Hull FC 25 – Leeds Rhinos 24*

When we arrived outside the Stadium there were a few long Hull faces as word spread through the crowd that on the night before the game, Shaun Briscoe had been rushed to hospital with appendicitis. A victory that seemed unlikely suddenly looked impossible and when we heard that instead of bringing in Motu Tony as a straight replacement, winger Nathan Blacklock was to play at full back, there was some concern. Still everyone was there to party and many donned fancy dress and there seemed to be Skeletons, Big Baby's, Gladiators and Clowns everywhere as young and old made the most of that rarest of occasions.

When we got inside there was plenty of antagonism going on out on the terraces between the Hull supporters and the already gloatingly, confident Leeds fans. Tin foil replica Cups glinted in the sunshine, scarves were waved and flags sprung up everywhere. The atmosphere was certainly charged with emotions as Katherine Jenkins led the singing of 'Abide with Me' and one Hull fan, Kevin Short, became quite a national celebrity as he was caught by the BBC TV camera's crying through the moment, as he remembered his FC supporting Grandfather.

The baiting wasn't just reserved for the terraces either and in the tunnel there was an altercation between Stephen Kearney and Leeds captain Kevin Sinfield. The latter had joined other Leeds players in shouting "Here come the losers", as Hull left the changing rooms. Kearney certainly put them right in the tunnel, the fans put them right on the terraces and the players put them right on the pitch.

After the Hull team had been led out by 'Number One' fan and brave Cerebral Palsy sufferer Scott Walker, the game kicked off in a cauldron of emotion, as the Hull fans did what they do best and easily out sang a smug Leeds contingent. Sinfield soon tested Blacklock but then following a towering bomb, a mix-up ended with Gareth Raynor trying to prevent Mark Calderwood touching down by pulling him back by his shorts. The video referee awarded a penalty try and Sinfield converted to give his side a 6-0 lead.

Midway through the half a couple of Rhino's handling errors allowed Hull to apply some pressure as a speculative kick to the right wing by Shayne McMenemy was brilliantly flicked on to Tony by Richard Whiting. The winger chipped over Marcus Bai and despite being crash tackled over the line, he beat Ali Lauitiiti and Richie Mathers to touch down. Danny Brough added to the score with a fine touch line conversion and we were level. However, despite a number of near misses, that's how it stayed until half time.

During the interval, I didn't know what to do with myself and I was in a trance like state as the tension really got to me. I wandered around aimlessly, before being approached in a refreshment area by a guy I had never seen before in my life. Sporting a Hull scarf and speaking in a broad South African accent he asked me if the Rosenberg which was emblazoned across the back of my shirt, was my name. I replied that it was actually name of my first FC hero, Wilf Rosenberg, 'The Flying Dentist', who I had watched at the Boulevard back in 1962. He immediately shook my hand and introduced himself as Wilf's nephew, who had made the trip over from South Africa to watch the game. I lament to this day the fact that I didn't speak longer with him, but my condition dictated that I didn't want to speak to anyone, and yet afterwards one of my only regrets from that wonderful day, was that I didn't get a contact number. It did however bring a strange symmetry to this story as an echo from the very earliest parts of this sojourn came back out of the blue, right there under the East Stand of the Millennium Stadium, on such a significant day in the recent history of our Club.

The gamble by Leeds to play centre Keith Senior with a painkilling injection in his injured ankle, came to an abrupt end when he didn't re-appear for the second half and soon a couple of loose passes by the Rhinos again put Hull on the attack. This time we took full advantage as Motu Tony, intercepting a pass from Mathers, set up a good attacking position. Blacklock squeezed out a superb pass for Raynor who scored in the corner, for Brough to again add the conversion.

Leeds drew level again when Sinfield put Danny Ward over and then converted, but then the Leeds captain sent a kick on the fifth tackle straight into touch to give Hull another excellent attacking platform. Leeds seemed to have weathered the storm when Bai collected Horne's grubber behind his own line, but the wingman tried to pass to Mathers, the ball popped out and there was Whiting to score the simplest of tries. Brough converted and then added a drop goal to give Hull a 19-12 lead going into the final quarter.

Just when Leeds were starting to look ragged, handling errors by Hull threw them a lifeline. Sinfield fed Mark Calderwood from a scrum after a Hull knock on and when Blacklock missed him, the try was inevitable. Bai made up for his blunder when he out jumped Tony, to grab a kick from Mathers to touch down and Sinfield converted both to make it 24-19 to Leeds with 10 minutes remaining.

Hull looked to be down and out, but summoned one last effort after a grubber kick from McMenemy yielding another six tackles deep in the Leeds half. As we all stretched and strained as if we were playing, at a play the ball in front of the sticks Horne feigned to go right, half dummied to just wrong foot the defence, and released Cooke to his left. As we held our breath and the action went into 'slow motion' our number 6 gliding through a gap to cross the line. We all grimaced as he celebrated before he put the ball down behind the posts, but get it down he did, and the place erupted. When Brough stepped up to take what was a simple conversion, he admitted afterwards that thoughts of Don Fox's Final miss for Wakefield in 1968 went through his mind, but he kept his nerve and we were a point in front.

However as often happens just when you think you have it won, a fumble by Jamie Thackray from the kick-off gifted the ball and the last set of six tackles of the game, to Leeds. They charged downfield to set up a position for the drop goal that would tie the scores, but as Sinfield aimed to stroke the ball between the posts somehow 'Captain Fantastic' Richard Swain raced out of our line, jumped in front of him and charged down the kick and the Cup was on its way to Hull. Still the game went on and we were awarded a penalty which we still had to take after the hooter had gone. I imagined all sorts of scenarios but as McMenemy tapped the ball and toe prodded it into touch the hooter went again and the celebrations began.

Kear, who had masterminded one of the Challenge Cup's biggest upsets when Sheffield Eagles beat Wigan in 1998 and who rated this victory even better, ran onto the field and hugged his players, whilst for me it was simply amazing. I couldn't cheer, I couldn't dance I just sat there with my head in my hands and cried, and this time, for a change, I wasn't on my own! All the heartache, all the frustration and all the disappointment endured since our last Challenge Cup victory back in 1982 was forgotten in an instant as all around me grown men and women were reduced to tears. It would have been so cruel on our players had we been denied victory because their passion and determination deserved to be rewarded, in what was one of the most emotional Finals of all time. It had been a long, long journey since Elland Road in 1982, full of disappointment, disenchantment and at times anger but at that moment, it was all so eminently worthwhile.

It was a time of mixed emotions, most of which I can't even remember, but I do recall that feeling of wishing, just for a moment, that I could see the faces of those Rovers supporters that have ragged me for so long, those smug buggers who always have an answer, always wound me up. What were they doing then; at that very moment? Were they silenced or just pretending it had never happened, could they be throwing the radio at the wall or the television through the window? Who knows, but just for a second it was great to wonder! I wanted time to stand still!

The ceremonials were just what I expected and what I had seen played out by those arrogant sods in Wigan, Leeds, Saints or Widnes shirts on so many occasions. But this time it was US!! Broughy put the Cup on his head, John Kear fell over the advertisement boards and even our Chair Kath Etherington managed to wave regally to the crowd (before commenting that the win was worth over £300,000 to the Club). For me all this seemed so unreal, it was all happening there in front of me, and yet I wasn't there at all, it was all flying by, whizzing past too quickly, just when I wanted it to last forever.

Forty minutes after the game had finished and as the 'banging and clattering' of the scaffolders dismantling the dais that had seen Richard Swain hoist aloft the Challenge Cup, echoed around the empty stadium, no one wanted to go home. Hundreds just stood there, transfixed and zombie like, long after the last diminishing chord of 'Rockin' all Over the World', had faded into the ether and the last of the brave 'Gladiators' had retired from the pitch to open their champagne, or in Leeds case, cry into their Yorkshire Bitter.

Eventually we had to leave, the stewards were almost begging us to "Go Home" but I was just overawed by it all and never wanted to be anywhere else, ever again! They should bottle that feeling and sell it as you leave games like that one. Then, when you eventually prepare to 'depart this mortal coil' you can uncork it, take a long sniff of the sweet smell of success, and exit this world in the knowledge that you know exactly what it was like 'Being There'.

Outside in the streets around the Stadium everyone with the exception of the 'grieving' Leeds' fans was hailing the great Hull FC, who had just done what had seemed to be the impossible. Not since the days of Sheffield Eagles great victory over Wigan in the mid Nineties had the underdog so captured the imagination of the whole of the Rugby League world, they all wanted to be part of it, and it was great to be liked as a Club for once. In the end, after all the adulation, whether they all liked it or not, the fact was that the prize was ours. It was the property of us supporters who had trailed across the country to be so often dejected, disappointed and depressed. All those years of ridicule at Headingley, jibes at Wigan and baiting at Warrington were gone forever; well at least they were for now. We were the Challenge Cup holders, who had beaten the odds and no one, but no one, could take it away.

"So now I can die a happy man!"

For reasons I have perhaps explained throughout this 'Journey' of an 'average fanatic' we have never as a group of fans, liked Leeds. That disdain probably goes right back to the days when they snatched Lee Crooks and Garry Schofield from us and perhaps to that day when they baited us with their despicable and totally unacceptable chants about the fishing industry and our lost loved ones. How could you ever have any respect or, after that day, any pity for a set of fans who stooped to that sort of inappropriate and insulting 'banter'. Since then they have pretty much held sway over us in most encounters but just now and again we beat them and it still feels so good and they hate it! That evening in Cardiff, as I walked down the Stadium steps towards the crowds outside singing 'Old Faithful', I caught a glimpse of my old pal 'Pearly' across the concourse. He didn't have to do much, he just shook his fist in the air and true to his reputation of never being the master of the understatement, he shouted "Now I can die a happy man".

We drove back to Hull early next morning and enjoyed every minute of the celebrations back home in Queen Victoria Square that afternoon. We were there in the early afternoon and got near the front of the crowd milking every moment as the team arrived and John Kear and the lads, soaked up the adoration and passion of those happy, barmy, hung over supporters. I once again simply didn't want it to end. I knew as a fan that once we left that gathering and made our way home, it would be another day, another week and soon another season. When you're not used to winning trophies it's so sweet when you do. You just want everything to 'Freeze' there and then, because you know that all too quickly those heroics will be forgotten by all except us passionate Hull FC followers, who will revisit Cardiff 2005 in detail, till the day we die. I *was* there. I have the programme and the ticket stub. I can half shut my eyes and summon up every detail of the scene as the final hooter went and do it in 'glorious Technicolor'.

When it gets you like it gets me, you have to make the most of those moments because as my old pal Charlie said all those years ago at Wembley in 1983, "You never really know when it's going to be your last Final, do you?" And of course you don't!

Epilogue

So I suppose in the end after almost 900 pages of unadulterated obsession there you have it! Fifty-five years of heartache, fretting and occasional moments of utter elation culminating in Hull FC winning the Challenge Cup in the most sensational and unexpected of circumstances and producing as important a moment in my life as there has been, or is probably ever likely to be.

I make that rather outspoken comment simply because I know it's true. It's true because it was for me and Hull FC, the main prize, 'Nirvana' and the 'Holy Grail' all rolled into one. It was a moment of destiny for the famous Black and Whites who are and always will be my team, my passion and I suppose, looking back, my life. It's times like that wonderful day in Cardiff that make you reflect on just what it is all about!

What have I learned? What has that and a few other amazingly magical moments in a lifelong love affair with a Rugby League Club taught me? Well perhaps firstly I now know that to be a real fan requires you to 'eat, sleep and live Rugby League' or whatever sport you find yourself obsessed with; being 'interested' or an 'only here for the beer' supporter is simply not sufficient. In essence it mirrors life itself, you have your good days and your bad ones, but whatever else it is, it's never about being a mere spectator – you can't just 'take it or leave it'. Its total immersion, total participation and friends, relatives and loved ones have to be prepared for your team to be central to your very existence.

Actually a lot of fans can take it or leave it, but if like me you can't, then times like Cardiff 2005 are moments that define your life. They're the moments during which you come within touching distance of the impossible dream and when you know paradoxically that it's all the depression, futility, frustration and anger that has gone before, that actually make those times so significant and therefore all that hardship so gloriously worthwhile.

But what makes us like that? Well of course, attending matches both home and away is a big help but you also have a duty to engage emotionally in the life of the team and the players. Don't get too close though, you don't need to know what they have for their breakfast, or what they do on their night off, that'll just disillusion you and cheapen the whole thing. You see, I have always believed that there is a certain magic in sport, very like that in theatre or cinema. When if you see how the 'trick' is done or what the reality of the 'magic' really is, then all the mystery and intrigue disappears.

That said, if your Club is central to your belief system, then it does automatically gift you the ability to know exactly what Kingy, Yeamo, Kearney or Swainey were feeling as they raised that glittering prize to the fans, that sunny August afternoon in 2005. That win at Cardiff belonged to me and all the other fans, every bit as much as it belonged to the players, because we had worked as hard as they had for it! Over the years as supporters we had all cursed, fretted, sweated, strained, made sacrifices, lost friends, been elated, frustrated and deflated...... and taken all 'that crap' together.

At that glorious zenith of 'fandom', you know exactly what everyone around you is feeling because you feel it yourself. It is at that moment that players and fans, Directors, boot men, shareholders, tea ladies and owners are as one, and when it's so rewarding and so, so special. What is even more intriguing however, is the answer to the question, just who are all those people who I have kissed, hugged and cried with over the years? Some of them are friends, some nodding acquaintances but most are complete strangers. In the end whoever they are, I have a massive bond and a really extraordinary intimacy with them and yet I know nothing at all about most of them.

However the difference between all us 'committed fanatics' and the players we adore, is that we have put in more hours, more seasons and more years than they have. We don't get paid and can't walk away or sign for another Club, we're stuck with the one we've got. That's why for us lot 5-00pm on Saturday 27th August 2005 was a seminal and life defining moment that actually suspended reality itself.

Those of you who have read both volumes of this tome will I hope relate in part to what I have tried to explain about that journey and can have some empathy with all its twists, turns, disappointments and occasional moments of unrequited joy! I can only be deeply thankful for how lucky I have been, in fact how lucky we all are after taking that great voyage of discovery that is a life of supporting the Club you love.

You see, I love Hull FC, they are my team, they always have been and they always will be! Occasionally I wish they weren't, but they are and I can do precious little about it! A life time culminating in that one great day in Cardiff is in the end for me what all this has been about and if for the rest of my supporting life Hull FC and I arrive home empty handed, I'll still have that memory to cling to and to smile about. We'll all go on, 'Roamin the Range Together' still collecting those battle scars from depressing defeats, tough times and bitter disappointments and because we are never in it on our own, we'll always have the best of friendships with whom we'll share those occasional and wonderful moments. We're the obsessed, preoccupied and passionate fanatics, we are Hull FC........... and aren't we lucky!!!!

Come on You Hullllaaaarrrr!!!!!!!

(To be continued.....by someone else)